Kendo

The publisher gratefully acknowledges the generous support of the Asian Studies Endowment Fund of the University of California Press Foundation.

Kendo

CULTURE OF THE SWORD

Alexander C. Bennett

UNIVERSITY OF CALIFORNIA PRESS

University of California Press, one of the most distinguished university presses in the United States, enriches lives around the world by advancing scholarship in the humanities, social sciences, and natural sciences. Its activities are supported by the UC Press Foundation and by philanthropic contributions from individuals and institutions. For more information, visit www.ucpress.edu.

University of California Press
Oakland, California

Library of Congress Cataloging-in-Publication Data

Bennett, Alexander, author.
Kendo : culture of the sword / Alexander C. Bennett.
    pages   cm
Includes bibliographical references and index.
ISBN 978-0-520-28437-1 (cloth : alk. paper)—ISBN 978-0-520-95994-1 (ebook)
1. Kendo.   2. Swordplay—Japan.   I. Title.
GV1142.B47   2015
796.86—dc23   2015004621

Manufactured in the United States of America

24   23   22   21   20   19   18   17   16   15
10   9   8   7   6   5   4   3   2   1

In keeping with a commitment to support environmentally responsible and sustainable printing practices, UC Press has printed this book on Natures Natural, a fiber that contains 30% post-consumer waste and meets the minimum requirements of ANSI/NISO Z39.48–1992 (R 1997) (*Permanence of Paper*).

To my high school kendo mentor, Sano Katsura

CONTENTS

ILLUSTRATIONS

TABLES

ACKNOWLEDGMENTS

I have been involved in kendo and other budo disciplines as a practitioner and researcher for nearly three decades. The guidance I have received from many mentors and friends throughout my journey has been truly inspirational. I would like to especially thank the following people and organizations for their assistance and support over the years.

First, I cannot express enough thanks to Professor Kenneth Henshall at the University of Canterbury for patiently guiding me with crucial feedback and keeping my work on track. I offer my sincere appreciation to all of the staff members at the School of Languages, Cultures and Linguistics at the University of Canterbury for the learning opportunities I have enjoyed over the years. I am also indebted to Dr. Denis Gainty and Dr. Roy Starrs for their useful recommendations and honest critiques of my work. I would also like to pass on my particular thanks to the anonymous reviewers of this manuscript, as their comments were invaluable in straightening out many shortcomings in my knowledge. Likewise, I am eternally obliged to the fabulous staff at the University of California Press for believing in the merits of this book from the outset and so kindly escorting me down the road to publication.

Completion of this project could not have been possible without the ongoing willingness of the Nippon Budokan and the All Japan Kendo Federation to provide me with many of the documents quoted in this book. I have also benefited immeasurably from thought-provoking conversations with professors Uozumi Takashi at the Open University of Japan, Ōya Minoru at the International Budo University, Nakajima Takeshi at Kokushikan University, Nagao Susumu at Meiji University, Nakiri Fuminori at the Japanese Academy of Budo, Murata Naoki at the Kōdōkan, Ōboki Teruo at Saitama University, Sakai Toshinobu at the University of Tsukuba, Nakamura Tamio at Fukushima University, Honda Sōtarō at Fukuoka University of Education, and Sakudō Masao and Kanzaki Hiroshi at the Osaka University for Sport and Health Science. My two academic mentors in Japan, Yamaori Tetsuo, formerly at the International Research Center of Japanese Studies, and Sonoda Minoru at Kyoto University, opened my eyes to the religious and spiritual culture of Japan. Their teachings continue to have a profound effect on my outlook on life, as does the sage guidance of kendo master, the late Inoue Yoshihiko. In a similar vein, I am beholden to kendo teacher Hayashi Tatsuo, for his friendship inside and outside the dojo; Kimura Yasuko, *sōke* of Tendō-ryū; Watanabe Tokiji and Mori Akira of Kashima Shinden Jikishin Kage-ryū *kenjutsu*; and Yonemoto Masayuki, Yamaguchi Remi, Okuura Ayako, Takahashi Hideaki, Eto Yoshihisa, Sato Nariaki, Takahashi Toru, Shigematsu Kimiaki, Dr. Miyasaka Masayuki, and Miyazaki Masayoshi. I will always be grateful for the great kindness of Hashimoto Kumiko, Nagahama Fumiko, and Tamaki Katsuko of the International Naginata Federation.

My *Kendo World* and other expat budo friends have, through mutual spurring or goading, always been a source of stimulation, making life in Japan much more gratifying. In particular, I would like to thank Michael Ishimatsu-Prime, Tyler Rothmar, Trevor Jones, Bryan Peterson, Jeff Broderick, Shishikura "Kan" Masashi, Hamish Robison, Michael Komoto, Dr. Lachlan Jackson, Antony Cundy, Randy Channell, Dr. Sean O'Connell, Greg Robinson, Steven Harwood, Duncan Robert Mark, Dr. Stephen Nagy, Dr. Mark Meli, Dr. Kate Sylvester, Arpad Macksay, Brett Smith, Paul Budden, Geoff Salmon, Jeff Marsten, and Frenchman extraordinaire Baptiste Tavernier.

My high school kendo club friends are still very much like family to me. As I allude to in the prologue, had it not been for their patience in teaching me about kendo and Japan, this book would never have been conceived. Similarly, I owe much to Okushima Yoshio and to the members of the Kyoto University kendo club for their succor; to Kawakami Takashi and the Kansai University kendo club, where I teach now; and to the International Budo University. The members of the New Zealand Kendo Federation have been particularly encouraging of my activities over the years, especially Graham Sayer, Ken Wells, Alan Stephenson, Bruce Middleton, Sue Lytollis, and Dr. Daryl Tong.

Thanks are also due to my younger siblings, Dr. Blake Bennett and Imafuji Masahiro, for their enthusiasm and undying dedication to the promotion of kendo.

Likewise, I am eternally obliged to the fabulous staff at the University of California Press for believing in the merits of this book from the outset and so kindly escorting me down the road to publication. In particular, acquisitions editor Reed Malcolm, production editor Dore Brown, copyeditor Genevieve Thurston, and indexer Alexander Trotter were enormously patient and always supportive.

During the course of writing this book, I received much-appreciated assistance from the Japan Foundation, Tozando, OBSERAI, the *Kendo Nihon* and *Kendo Jidai* magazines, and, of course, my place of employment, Kansai University. Thank you as always to Mum, Dad, Rhondda, and Oscar. This is what I have been doing all of these years. Finally, I would be remiss if I did not acknowledge the innumerable sacrifices made by my wife, Yoko, especially as she is the one with the unenviable task of washing my sweaty, malodourous gi after training, and does so without so much as a complaint.

Alexander Bennett
Kyoto, September 13, 2014

CONVENTIONS

Japanese words and expressions have been divided into their most logical semantic components to assist reading and correct pronunciation. Japanese terms have been romanized according to the Hepburn system and italicized. Long Japanese vowel sounds have been approximated using macrons. Macrons are used in most Japanese terms, except for commonplace names and organizations that have official English titles without macrons. Terms found in *Webster's Collegiate Dictionary*, such as "kendo," "budo," and "bushido," are written without macrons or italics.

Although traditional Japanese swordsmanship is generally referred to as *kenjutsu*, other terms were also widely used. *Gekiken*, or *gekken*, was coined in the mid-Tokugawa period and mainly referred to fencing with *shinai* and protective armor. Depending on the context, *kenjutsu* also had that meaning, but it encompassed the kata methodology as well. The term *kendō*, although not unheard of in the Tokugawa period, did not come into common usage until the twentieth century. Thus, the documents quoted in this book jump from one appellation to another depending on the historical period in question.

Organizations such as the Nippon Budokan and the Dai-Nippon Butokukai are commonly referred to as "Budokan" and "Butokukai," and they are sometimes shortened as such in the text. Also, the Japanese Ministry of Education (MOE) changed its name to the Ministry of Education, Culture, Sports, Science and Technology (MEXT) in 2001. Both acronyms are used in the text.

All era dates, such as the Tokugawa period (1603–1868), are given in accordance with conventions used in the *Kodansha Encyclopedia of Japan*. Many of the historical figures mentioned in the text changed their names during their lives, but I have used the most familiar names. Furthermore, personal names are written in the order of surname followed by given name in accordance with Japanese convention. The birth and death dates for a number of historical figures are impossible to verify, but I have used the generally accepted dates, and ages, when given, are calculated according to the inclusive Japanese method known as *kazoedoshi*.

All of the translations of documents and quotations from Japanese were done by me, except where otherwise stated. The titles of Japanese literary works appear in the original form, with English translations offered in parentheses after the first mention in the text. The English terms "school" or "tradition" are sometimes used to refer to formal organizations known as *ryūha* or *ryū*, which taught martial art systems.

PROLOGUE: KENDO BASICS

I first came to Japan in 1987 as a teenage exchange student and spent a year at a municipal high school in Chiba City. From the day I arrived, it was assumed by my guardians that I would join an extracurricular club for the sake of enriching my sojourn in Japan culturally and socially. I was an avid soccer player and was excited about the prospect of testing my skills in Japan. That particular goal faded away when I was shown the soccer "field," which was nothing more than an abrasive sandpit. Having grown up in New Zealand, it seemed implausible that outdoor sports could be played on any surface other than grass—a truly rare commodity in Japanese schools.

My host mother then suggested that I try something "a little more Japanese." It made sense, and the martial arts seemed like a viable option. Being particularly inconspicuous physically speaking, I was motivated to see what was on offer and imagined the kudos I would get back home with a *shodan* (black belt) as a souvenir of my time in Japan.

With so many martial art movies circulating in the mid-1980s, the mysterious power and respect demanded by the almighty black belt made it a dream for many young boys and girls. Had there been a karate club at my school, I would have undoubtedly followed in the footsteps of Daniel-san looking for my own Mr. Miyagi. Instead, I had a choice of judo or kendo.

I visited the judo club first, but, with only three members on the team, my interest was not piqued. I was then escorted down a long, dark corridor toward a curious room emitting the pungent aroma of sweat and goodness knows what else. The rhythmic clacking of bamboo sticks and a cacophony of shrill battle cries greeted me as I slid open the door. I had seen a picture of kendo a few years before on a card included as a free gift in a breakfast cereal box, but the extent of my knowledge of the sport amounted to what was given in the short explanatory paragraph on the back.

The school dojo was much smaller than any gym found at a New Zealand school. It had a relatively low ceiling, foreboding bars on the windows, and a Shinto altar on the far wall. I removed my shoes and entered the room with nervous trepidation. Inside, hordes of spirited trainees outfitted with blue full-face helmets, body protection, and split skirts were feverishly smashing each other with bamboo sticks. To my untrained eye, it seemed like nothing more than senseless violence. It all fit perfectly with my preconceived stereotypes of the Japanese. The ferocity of the scene conjured up images in my mind of kamikaze, samurai, and "hara-kiri."

Looking past the frenetic one-on-one battles unfolding in every part of the dojo, I found my attention drawn to the far corner, where a physically larger, fiercer-looking combatant appeared to be dishing out a hiding to some unfortunate soul of much lesser proportions. I remember thinking, "This is like a scene out of *Star Wars,* and that must be Darth Vader." The fanatical Jedi trainee howled as he launched attack after attack with his light saber, but his strikes were nonchalantly deflected and mercilessly returned with interest.

After some minutes of relentless but ineffective attacking, the lesser opponent was permitted to land a succession of cracking wallops on Vader's head, wrists, and torso. But then Vader upped the ante, retaliating with vicious thrusts to the throat, body clashes that sent the attacker flying backward, and foot sweeps that reduced him to a sagging heap on the floor. Just when it looked as if submission were his only option, the young Jedi somehow sprang to life again, and the painful process started all over. Corporal punishment had just been outlawed back in New Zealand, and thoughts that somebody should be calling the police crossed my mind as I stared in disbelief at the savagery.

Suddenly, a loud shout rang out over the chaos. *"Yaameeeee!"* Everybody stopped what they were doing, and Vader sat down in front of the small shrine attached to the wall. He removed his mask and waited as his underlings lined up opposite him, trying to control their panting. Vader was the sensei of the club—a physical education teacher at the school with a fearsome, no-nonsense reputation. At his signal, the students sat down and took off their masks, revealing no visible emotion. It was freezing cold, but steam rose from their brows and sweat dripped from their chins, forming puddles on the frigid wooden floor. They knelt down in two straight lines as they watched their sensei intently, without daring to wipe the perspiration cascading off their faces. He gave a nod, and everybody erupted in unison into a chant, which was followed by silent meditation.

Then the sensei spoke, breaking the dreamlike quiet—the calm after the storm. I did not understand Japanese at the time, but his expression was contemptuous, and a tirade of what sounded like angry advice rolled off his tongue and lashed their ears, just as his bamboo sword had done to their bodies minutes before. The trainees replied simultaneously with an emphatic "*hai!*" to indicate acquiescence, and then the daily two-hour session was over.

The sensei's penetrating gaze then zoomed in on me. "I'm Sano. You must be the new exchange student. See you here tomorrow!" I felt as if I were being strong-armed into joining the club, and indeed that was the case. The aggressiveness of it all frightened me, but I was curious to try my hand at playing samurai. I had no way of knowing it at the time, but this was a fateful first encounter with one of the most influential people in my life and, without a doubt, the scariest. Whether I liked it or not, I was in for a penny, and in for a pounding.

The following day, I meandered tentatively through the dingy corridors for my induction to kendo. I arrived at 16:02, when training was already in full swing. "We start at 16:00!" I was scolded, which actually meant I should have been there at 15:30. First I was taught how to hold the bamboo sword (*shinai*) in what is a most unnatural stance: both hands in front of the body, left hand gripping the bottom of the *shinai* hilt, sword tip at throat height, right foot forward, left heel slightly raised, and body perfectly upright in the attention position. Then I was shown how to execute practice swings (*suburi*)—a monotonous exercise repeated thousands of times a week to facilitate coordination of the feet, hands, *shinai,* and spirit.

I remember being embarrassed about yelling "*men!*" at the completion of each downward swing. Questions abounded. "Why can't I hold the bamboo stick with my right hand at the bottom?" "Why is my right foot supposed to be in front?" "Why do I have to yell '*men*' anyway?" The standard reply was, "just do it," with no further explanation. It was a far cry from the athlete-friendly sports coaching I had received back home.

While the rest of the club members donned armor and were absorbed in full-contact combat, I was left on my own to practice *suburi*. After an hour or so, my arms felt like lead and my throat was dry. It was, I thought, high time for a much-deserved break. Ten seconds into my self-determined respite, Sano-sensei's voice boomed across the dojo. "Hey! Get back into it!" He came over every so often to correct my deteriorating, lethargic form and my less-than-obedient attitude.

At 18:00, the long-awaited order to cease and desist resounded through the dojo: *"Yaameeeee!"* I wasn't sure where to line up, so somebody grabbed my sleeve and inserted me somewhere between the girls and the boys. We knelt down in two straight lines facing the front of the room, and those around me took off their masks. Vapor rose from their drenched faces and cropped hair, and the stench of fresh perspiration mixed with countless hours' worth of stale sweat caked into the equipment permeated my nostrils. (Years of training render this peculiar odor into something wistfully therapeutic, for *kendōka,* that is.)

The persistent screeching and clattering of bamboo against body parts had stopped, and the dojo was serene. The tranquility was abruptly broken as everybody started chanting the words emblazoned on the scroll hanging on the wall: "It takes one thousand days of sweat to forge the spirit, and ten thousand days of sweat to polish it. But a bout is decided in less than a second." I was informed later that these were words adapted from Miyamoto Musashi's *Book of Five Rings,* although I had no idea what this was at the time. We recited this chant religiously every day after training and then assumed the *dhyani mudra* posture and meditated in silence for a minute or so with the command *"mokusō."*

The student captain's signals at the end of meditation to bow, bow, and bow again, each time with the directive of *"rei!,"* transported us back to the mundane world. Sano-sensei then started to deliver another rather solemn-sounding speech. Of course, I had no idea what he was saying, but he appeared to be angry. Kneeling in the painful formal *seiza* position for the first time, I was nearing the end of my tether. I had spent two hours swinging a bamboo stick and following strange rituals, only to be made to sit through a growling homily that I couldn't understand.

One more *"hai!"* and training was finally over. After Sano-sensei left the building, the boys and girls made an instant transformation from clockwork soldiers into typical puerile teenagers. This was a great relief to me. But even my uninitiated mind could sense that hierarchical boundaries based on year group (first, second, and third) dictated the extent to which fooling around was permitted and who was authorized to be a provoker vis-à-vis a submissive target. Everybody knew their place, and the power plays and tiered relationships in the dojo, although prescribed by age rather than skill at kendo, were generally convivial and harmonious.

When it came to Sano-sensei, however, absolute deference was imperative. Respect was maintained at all times through a potent combination of fear and dependence. No one dared question his methods, answer back to him, or misbehave. He was in essence a drill sergeant, military chaplain, and commander all rolled into one. I found this authoritarianism disturbing at first, but more on this shortly.

The boys in the second-year group were given the unenviable challenge of showing me the ropes—or, more accurately, controlling my wayward-foreigner tendencies and bringing me into line with the Japanese code of behavior. Any mistakes I made in terms of my comportment, in or outside of the dojo, were on their heads. Thus, for the rest of the year, they went out of their way to teach me kendo, which I discovered provided an illuminating window onto Japanese society and culture as a whole. The self-restraint, strict adherence to procedure, and etiquette in action and speech that were literally beaten into me served me well in all aspects of my life in Japan.

Following this first foray into the dojo, it was close to 21:00 by the time I got back to my host family's home. I was sore all over, with cramped muscles that I never knew existed, and the soles of my feet and palms of my hands were covered in oozing blisters. Still, the thought of obtaining a *shodan* before going back to New Zealand in a year's time smoldered away inside of me, although it had not yet clicked that nobody actually wore belts in kendo!

This training regime continued seven days a week for the entire year. When there was no school, we would train from 9:00 to 18:00, or we might have an overnight training camp, a tournament, or practice matches with other schools. It was essentially boot camp—designed not to be fun but to instill discipline and toughen us up mentally and physically. We had our fun in the times between training, where the mutual bonds forged through blood, sweat, and fear intensified the joy we felt in the moments of liberty, away from Sano-sensei's omnipotence. However, my high school kendo club was by no means exceptional. High school club activities in Japan are notoriously harsh, even outright violent sometimes, but kendo has an extra layer of inherent solemnity for reasons I will explain in this book.

During the first six months, I struggled to justify continuing. I did not like kendo per se, but I remained because of the friendships I had developed and the simple terror of what would happen if I tried to quit. Sano-sensei generally treated me like everybody else, but he knew I had my own cultural standards that were slightly at odds with Japanese mores, and he introduced me to the intricacies of the Japanese system judiciously. Although he could not speak a word of English, he liked to have fun pointing out that my English pronunciation was flawed, since it didn't sound "Japanese enough." "It's not *Alec,* it's *Arekku,*" he would tease in an attempt to illicit exasperated responses from me. I once went to him with painful blood blisters on my feet, hoping that I could sit out training. Without a word, he pulled a needle, thread, and a lighter from his desk, motioned for me to sit down, and proceeded to lance them all. His grin, and the glint in his eye when the surgical operation was finished, told me to toughen up and get back on the floor. Evidently he was a medic, too.

In the dojo, his word was indisputable fact. He taught me that crows were white if he said so, and if I wanted to get good at kendo, I had to trust him totally. Although he terrified me, he also had a playful side that offered brief glimpses into the compassion that lurked beneath his iron exterior and underpinned his Spartan pedagogy.

When I was finally allowed to wear armor, I found kendo to be even more perplexing. The mask offered me security and protection on one hand, but it also made me feel claustrophobic, as I was incarcerated literally and metaphorically behind bars. It was from this point that the intensity picked up. When the mask is put on, there is no going back, no submission until the final "*yame.*" Faced with an opponent intent on striking you on any one of four target areas, the tit-for-tat probing for openings, trying to unbalance adversaries physically and psychologically in order to capitalize on that instant of hesitation, fear, surprise or doubt, is what makes kendo a highly complex battle of wills.

Landing the perfect strike that merges spirit, technique, and body is as much a mental game as it is a physical one. Timing, distance, and controlling the opponent's centerline is of the essence, and he or she who takes charge of these facets of the bout will prevail. Kendo has little to do with raw physical strength or advantages of height. Successful strikes are made with a well-timed cut to an adversary who is overwhelmed by pressure or by countering an attack the opponent was subtly coaxed into making.

Ultimately, the mind trumps athletic dexterity, which is why people can still effectively engage in kendo into their eighties and nineties. Many *kendōka* acknowledge the pinnacle of their kendo ability as being in their late forties to late fifties, when their minds and bodies have reached a state of equilibrium. When going head to head with a middle-aged or elderly kendo practitioner of advanced rank, you become like the prey of a cobra: hypnotized into inaction and cut down before the mind can grasp and react to the situation at hand. Similarly, you may become paralyzed in an incorporeal net of *ki* emanating from his *shinai*. Overwhelmed, you may be forced to step out of striking range as he closes in, until the wall stops you and there is nowhere to hide. In threatening situations, human instinct triggers the fight-or-flight reaction as a matter of survival. In a kendo match, even if the "fight" is not working, there is no way out. Because the mere thought of flight is considered inconceivably craven, you find yourself coerced into striking, only to have your blow deflected and countered in a split second of refined, minimalistic movement and maximum finality.

Then, your mind flustered by the damned if you do, damned if you don't dilemma, panic sets in. Game over. You yield to superior force and commit body and soul to a session of arduous attack practice orchestrated by the sensei as his *shinai* transmutes into a conductor's baton. He directs your every move, allowing the good strikes to connect while disdainfully nullifying the insufficient ones so that you recognize the difference between good form and bad.

It is not a contest any more, but rather an exercise intended to bring you to the threshold of your physical, technical, and psychological limits, and beyond. The session stops only when you have demonstrated adequate verve and fighting spirit and appear to have grasped whatever lesson the sensei is trying to impart to help you reach the next level of proficiency or competitiveness. This exercise of nonstop attacking is typically frenzied and excruciating, but it ends with a cursory pat on the back in recognition of effort and observance of rituals signifying mutual respect.

It was in one such session that I became catechized into the way of kendo once and for all. In the unbearably humid month of August, I lined up to practice with Sano-sensei. For me, a session was usually over in a couple of minutes, and I had never experienced the full brunt of the sensei's sword. On this particular day, suffering from culture shock, the debilitating Japanese summer, and the accumulated frustrations of life in Japan, I was at my belligerent worst. I hurled myself at him with unbridled rage, not respect. I succeeded in knocking him back once, then twice. These were small victories that gave me immense satisfaction, but it was his duty as sensei to return the favor. One body clash sent me backpedalling meters, and the next had my back against the wall. He moved in for the coup de grâce, like a colossal wave about to break over me. Rather than take it front on and get crushed in the process, I unwisely chose the flight option. But Sano-sensei gave me no room for retreat. It was attack, or be demolished. So attack I did, on and on, only to be cut down and summarily punished for committing the heinous crime of sidestepping the brunt of his attack. Fear turned to utter fatigue, and it was all I could do to stay on my feet as I tried to keep attacking. I collapsed many times, seeing fleeting glimpses of what it must be like to die, vivid images that remain etched in my mind to this day.

Every time I felt like I was about to pass out, inexplicable surges of energy from somewhere deep within miraculously revitalized my body and mind, and I found my second wind, then my third. The pain and fatigue dissipated, and I entered a trancelike state in which I no longer feared the sensei, or even the thought—which actually seemed more like an inevitability—of expiring right there on the dojo floor.

The better part of an hour had passed when the bout finally ended. I had no sense of time during the ordeal, but I was overcome with emotion as the magnitude of what had happened dawned on me. Sano-sensei had taken me to hell and back. Although I had not been searching for anything in particular, I realized I had found it. What "it" was exactly is still a mystery to me, but I knew instinctively that it was profound. The never-say-die attitude that Sano-sensei forced me to embrace was a spiritual revelation of sorts. It amounted to a temporary high, permeated with a sense of purity and clarity that cannot be replicated easily. That high, once tasted, became addictive and empowering, and it is what has kept me in Japan, and practicing kendo, ever since.

Some readers may be repulsed that such apparent abuse could be sanctioned in schools. The truth is that overtly austere instruction in sports, although once commonplace in Japan, is falling out of favor. In the last decade or so, the media has called attention to incidents involving the injury, or even death, of pupils due to physical or psychological bullying in sports clubs, leading to a change in social attitudes. Overly zealous instructors who carelessly, or arrogantly, spurn the line between discipline and unadorned abuse are no longer tolerated, and rightly so.

Nevertheless, that martial arts are rooted in violence is a historical fact. This is something I will delve into in the following chapters, but I would like to stress at this point that, although martial arts like kendo are popular competitive sports in the modern era, their principal teachings are often extreme. The official concept of kendo according to the All Japan Kendo Federation, for example, is "to discipline the human character through the application of the principles of the sword." The sword is a lethal weapon, once used for killing. Of course, we do not kill people in kendo, but many of the terms and concepts allude to death in the allegorical sense—paradoxically though, as an affirmation of life. In other words, practitioners learn to cherish life through the process of mentally and physically "sacrificing" themselves in each attack. This demands discipline and the capacity to control or overcome the fear of defeat.

The extreme side of kendo—which Sano-sensei heedfully introduced me to—is accessible only when one is able to let go and shed the ego. This requires a degree of external assistance and prompting. A venerable kendo sensei has already been there, is acutely aware of the dangers of overkill, and shoulders the burden of responsibility to guide his or her charges along the path of self-perfection based on personal experience. This journey is not supposed to be a sadistic abuse of power, but rather an act of benevolence in which the teacher and students have reached accord. Trust is the glue that binds master and disciple and guides them when the boundaries separating appropriate and inappropriate practices become blurred.

It is an unfortunate fact of life, however, that this trust can easily be betrayed, and it does happen. That is why it is said in Japan, "It is better to spend three years finding the right teacher than to start three years sooner with the wrong one." This is problematic if you do not know what "right" is. In this sense, I feel that I was lucky, and I have a weighty debt to Sano-sensei for his insightful guidance into a world so foreign to my own.

I now hold the rank of *kyōshi* 7-dan, the same as Sano-sensei. The irony that the first of his students to attain this rank was a foreigner was not lost on him, and he said that the supreme form of homage for a teacher is to be surpassed by a student. I would not dare claim to have surpassed him yet, but I owe it to him to keep trying for as long as I can hold a *shinai*. I meet with him twice a year in Chiba, along with the rest of his kendo students, for a dinner party to catch up and reminisce. Although the majority of my former classmates do not practice kendo actively any more, we appreciate the hard lessons we learned under our sensei's strict tutelage. None of us would trade the experience for anything.

· · ·

The rules and methods of kendo are complex, and its technical and philosophical framework is often indefinable. Nevertheless, it is important to have a basic understanding of how kendo works to contextualize the forthcoming discourse on its cultural significance.

The kendo armor (*bōgu;* figure 1) consists of the mask (*men*), plastron (*dō*), lower-body protector (*tare*), and protective gauntlets (*kote*). The *dō* is crafted

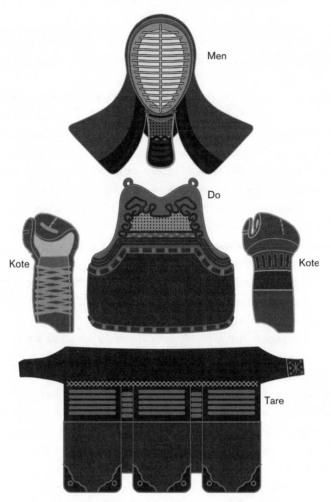

FIGURE I. Kendo armor.

from lacquered bamboo or fiberglass, and the grill on the mask (*men-gane*) is made from metal. The Hasegawa Chemical Industry Company also produces a type of *men* with a clear Perspex protective shield, although few people are seen using it. The rest of the equipment is made from thick padded cotton or analogous synthetic material, which is light and shock absorbent. The equipment weighs approximately ten kilograms and is attached by cords over a blue or white cotton top (*kendō-gi*) and a pleated traditional split skirt (*hakama*) made from cotton or synthetic material. The name and affiliation of the practitioner is attached to the central front panel of the *tare*. Apart from a few

FIGURE 2. The *shinai*.

improvements for safety, and the use of modern materials, the *kendōka*'s link with the swordsmen of yore is easily identifiable by the equipment used.

The weapon used is the *shinai,* written with the two kanji characters meaning "bamboo" and "katana" (figure 2). Original *shinai* of the Tokugawa era (1603–1868) consisted of finely split bamboo slats encased in a leather sheath. Today's *shinai*—90 percent of which are produced in China—are made from four slats of bamboo 120 cm or less in length, secured together with a leather tip, a leather fastening approximately a quarter of the way down from the tip, and the two-handed leather hilt.

A cord linking these leather pieces runs up the back of the *shinai* and represents the non-cutting edge of the blade. Even though the *shinai* is cylindrical, strikes made with the back or sides are not considered valid. The hand-guard (*tsuba*) is usually round and is fashioned from leather, pigskin, or plastic. In recent years, the Carbon Shinai made from composite materials by the Hasegawa Chemical Industry Company saw a phase of popularity among high school practitioners and non-Japanese *kendōka* for its durability and cost effectiveness. Sales have waned, however, as bamboo *shinai* have become much cheaper than before and are easily acquired via Internet kendo equipment vendors. In any case, almost all *kendōka* prefer the feel of bamboo, which is more ductile and mitigates the shock of impact.

The study of modern kendo consists of practicing prescribed forms, or kata with wooden swords (*bokutō*), and full-contact training with bamboo practice swords. The wooden swords are made in the same general shape and size as a katana. The Nippon Kendo Kata were developed in 1912 for the purpose of national dissemination in schools (described in chapter 4) and has ten forms. These kata include the five stances (*kamae*): overhead left and right (*jōdan*), blade at the side pointing back (*wakigamae*), blade held vertically at the side of the head (*hassō-no-kamae*), low stance (*gedan-no-kamae*), and middle stance (*chūdan-no-kamae;* figure 3). Apart from *chūdan,* however, these stances are rarely seen in kendo bouts fought with *shinai.*

The prescribed kata forms are practiced not so much for the purpose of acquiring kendo techniques, but rather as a reminder that the use of the cylindrical bamboo stick is predicated on the principles and theory of using

FIGURE 3. The middle stance
in kendo.

a real sword. The kata traditionally serve as a ceremonial beginning to tournaments and are performed by high-ranking instructors using steel swords with blunted blades. They are also an integral part of promotion examinations for *kendōka* of all levels, although most see kata as largely irrelevant in their quest for success in the competitive arena.

In *shinai* training, which constitutes the bulk of practice time, students usually face off in the standard middle-fighting stance, standing the equivalent of two sword lengths apart. Some practitioners prefer to fight from the overhead *jōdan* position, and a small but growing number of people use two swords (*nitō*), following in the tradition of famed seventeenth-century Japanese warrior Miyamoto Musashi. According to kendo rules, *jōdan* can only be used in competition from high school and above and *nitō* from university level. Thus, all beginners start their study of kendo by learning to fight from *chūdan*.

The valid targets are limited to strikes to the *men*, *dō,* and *kote* and thrusts to the throat (*tsuki*). Additionally, there are a number of complicated criteria that need to be met for the strike to be counted as valid (table 1). The practitioner hones his or her understanding of what constitutes a valid strike (*yūkō-datotsu*) through arduous and repetitive training. The typical training session consists of physically taxing repetitions of basic moves, applied techniques, and attack practice (*kakari-geiko* and *uchikomi-geiko*) so that the student learns to embody the techniques and is able to execute them the instant an opening appears.

For a point to be valid, the attacker must strike the target accurately and forcefully with the correct part of the *shinai*: about an eighth of the way down from the tip, with the blade edge. If the strike is too shallow, deep, or weak, or is made with the side of the blade, a point will not be awarded. The attack must also be made with upright posture and full spirit—which is indicated by bellowing out the name of the intended target. Spirit, sword, and body must be consolidated at the point of impact, and after the target is struck, the attacker must follow through and demonstrate continued physical and mental alertness (*zanshin*), proving him- or herself ready to thwart a possible counterattack. All of these actions must be executed in a smooth sequence, and then the cycle starts again (figure 4).

There are two categories of matches (*shiai*): individual and team. Team matches usually involve bouts between three, five, or seven fighters on each side, represented by the colors red and white. The bouts are conducted one at a time as teammates sit quietly and observe as they wait their turn. Match time

TABLE 1 Technical outline for a valid strike (*yūkō-datotsu*) to score a point (*ippon*) in kendo

Definition of *yūkō-datotsu:* "A *yūkō-datotsu* is defined as an accurate strike or thrust made onto designated targets (*datotsu-bui*) of the opponent's *kendo-gu*. The strike or thrust must be executed in high spirits with correct posture, using the striking section (*datotsu-bu*) of the *shinai* with the blade on the correct angle (*hasuji*), and followed by *zanshin*."[1]

Elements	Requirements
Shisei (posture)	*Datotsu-bui* (accurately striking the target)
Kiai (vocalization)	*Datotsu-bu* (with correct part of the *shinai*)
Maai (interval)	*Hasuji* (correct direction of the cutting edge)
Tai-sabaki (footwork)	*Kyōdo* (adequate strength of the cut)
Kikai (striking opportunities)	*Sae* (crispness of the cut)
Tenouchi (grip)	*Ki-ken-tai-itchi* (unity of sword, body, and spirit)
	Zanshin (continued physical and mental alertness)

Striking process

On-guard stance (*kamae*) → Mutual probing and applying pressure (*seme-ai*) → Detection of opening (see "Striking opportunities") and selection of appropriate technique → Execution of a valid technique (*waza*) with *ki-ken-tai-itchi* → Physical and psychological alertness after the attack (*zanshin*).

Striking opportunities	Technique selection (*men, kote, dō, tsuki*)	
	Shikake-waza (attacking techniques)	
When opponent is stationary or unbalanced	*Ippon-uchi-no-waza*	Single strikes to *men, kote,* and *dō,* and thrusts to the throat (*tsuki*)
↓	*Harai-waza*	Deflecting opponent's *shinai* and then striking
When opponent is on the verge of moving	*Ni/sandan-no-waza*	Combination techniques
↓		
Just as the opponent moves	*Hiki-waza*	Retreating techniques executed from close quarters (*tsubazeriai*) or after a body clash (*taiatari*)
↓		
As the opponent's technique takes form	*Katsugi-waza*	Shouldering the *shinai* before striking
	Maki-waza	Flicking opponent's *shinai* away with a circular motion
↓		
In the middle of the opponent's attack	*Katate-waza*	One-handed techniques
	Jōdan-waza	Techniques executed from the overhead stance
↓		
When the opponent's attack is nearing completion	**Ōji-waza (counter techniques)**	
	Debana-waza	Striking just as the opponent moves
↓	*Suriage-waza*	Parrying techniques
	Kaeshi-waza	Parrying and then striking the reverse side
After the opponent's attack is completed	*Uchiotoshi-waza*	Knocking the opponent's *shinai* down
	Nuki-waza	Dodging opponent's strike and then counterattacking

[1] Article 12, *The Regulations of Kendo Shiai and Shinpan*, International Kendo Federation, Revised 2015.

FIGURE 4. The sequence of a strike to the *men*.

depends on the tournament, but a typical bout lasts three to five minutes. Three referees (*shinpan*) holding red and white flags move around the court, judging the validity of the competitors' techniques and identifying any fouls, such as stepping out of bounds. Committing two fouls results in one point for the opponent. The first competitor to score two points within the designated time is the victor. If only one point has been scored when time runs out, victory is awarded to whoever has the point. If there is a tie of 0–0 or 1–1 in a team match, that bout ends in a draw, but in individual competitions, match time is extended and the bout continues until a winning point is scored.

In team matches, the aggregate number of wins decides the outcome. If both teams have the same number of wins, then the total number of points scored during the individual bouts (*hinkaku*), gravitas (*kigurai*), is calculated to determine the winning team. If that score is equal, a representative player from each team is selected to fight in a sudden-death bout.

Along with the sporting aspects of kendo, its spiritual and educational features are also a primary consideration. In the dojo, the modern kendo practitioner is taught traditional concepts and ideals that can be traced back to samurai culture. The student is encouraged to confront psychological weaknesses such as astonishment, fear, doubt, and hesitation, referred to as the "four illnesses of the heart" (*shikai*), and to maintain a "natural mind" (*heijōshin*), allowing him or her to confidently engage with any opponent with respect (*rei*), grace and dignity (*hinkaku*), gravitas (*kigurai*), total conviction (*sutemi*), and continued alertness (*zanshin*). After many years of training, the *kendōka* is expected to develop psychological strength, which facilitates good deportment and the capacity to resolve difficulties faced in the course of everyday life.

I was asked recently to describe what kendo means to me in five short sentences. Although wary of sounding too sanctimonious, I summed my thoughts up as follows:

1. To foster strength in body and mind in order to overcome challenges and adversity.
2. To develop confidence fortified with humility to identify and rectify failings.
3. To cultivate empathy, respect, and the capacity to assist others when needed.
4. To nurture a sense of gratitude and a zest for life.
5. To encourage *zanshin,* or continued awareness of one's surroundings and predicament.

I should stress that these are my ideals, and I do not presume to fully embody these virtues. Although kendo has given me direction in life, I dislike the perception that is frequently bandied about that studying it will automatically make you a better human being. However, I do believe in kendo's *potential* to enhance one's existence. In addition to the excitement of competition, the sport provides a set of mental and physical tools to deal with the vicissitudes of daily life, and its teachings serve as a barometer to gauge success and failure.

Kendo exposes one's shortcomings, and honest self-reflection and castigation are the only ways to remedy them. I can usually attribute failure in my daily pursuits to inadequate preparation in the basics, poor emotional control, half-hearted execution, or lack of vigilance after the fact. These are the same factors that could cause me to lose a kendo bout, and this is why I am compelled to train every day: to expunge myself of debilitating weaknesses and cultivate discipline.

Progress in kendo can be measured by promotion up the ranks. The first grade a beginner can be awarded is usually 5-kyū, and he or she will then typically advance to 1-kyū through periodic examinations. The time one must wait between examinations increases as the rank becomes higher. Six months after earning 1-kyū, the student will be allowed to attempt the *shodan* (1-dan) examination, followed by 2-dan one year after passing *shodan,* 3-dan two years after 2-dan, and so on. For reference, a strong university student would usually graduate at age twenty-two with the rank of 4-dan. The highest grade is 8-dan (it was 10-dan until the dan system was changed in 2000, but no one had been awarded the grade since 1974). To qualify for the 8-dan examination, the candidate must have held the rank of 7-dan for a minimum of ten years and be forty-six years of age or older. The pass rate is less than 1 percent.

Dan ranks are an indication of technical mastery, and additional teaching titles (*shōgō*) of *renshi, kyōshi,* and *hanshi* are awarded from 6-dan and above, subsequent to passing written exams and seminars testing the candidate's knowledge of kendo principles and the contributions he or she has made to promote the art. Thus, the highest possible rank in kendo now is *hanshi* 8-dan.

I should also make mention of the status of women in kendo. Although there are references to women practicing the sword arts as far back as early modern Japan, and there were some female *kendōka* in prewar Japan, their participation in the sport is largely a postwar development, becoming especially popular begining in the 1960s. Japanese schools traditionally taught naginata (the art of the halberd) or kyudo (archery) to girls instead of kendo.

Today boys and girls of elementary-school age compete against each other in largely coed competitions. Men and women of all ages train jointly but usually compete separately, although they may compete against each other in local tournaments and promotion examinations. There are also a number of kendo tournaments for women that are now well established and extremely competitive. The All Japan Women's Kendo Championship has been an annual event since 1962, but the women's division at the World Kendo Championships was introduced only in 2000, where it was held as a semiofficial event at the eleventh WKC, before becoming an official event at the twelfth.

Even though there are now hundreds of women kendo instructors teaching at all levels in Japan (and even a small number training in the elite police

TABLE 2 The registered population of dan holders in Japan, 2014

Rank	Male	Female
1-dan	550,130	263,960
2-dan	380,888	164,599
3-dan	181,703	61,831
4-dan	48,343	8,926
5-dan	44,972	3,813
6-dan	17,637	879
7-dan	16,134	246
8-dan	662	—
9-dan	4	—

riot squad teams, alongside their male counterparts), the presence of women in kendo education at a regional or national level is minimal. No woman has reached the highest grade of 8-dan, and the probability of it happening in the foreseeable future is very low. This is mainly due to the increasing disparity in physical power between men and women in their late forties onward, when practitioners become eligible for the examination. This means that, at least in Japan, female involvement in the top echelons of kendo governance is virtually nonexistent. Holding a high rank (usually 6-dan or above) is essential for maintaining credibility in the hierarchical, masculine world of kendo. The number of dan holders in Japan as of 2014 is shown in table 2.

I personally know a handful of Western and Japanese women practitioners who are conducting scholarly surveys on the issue of gender in kendo. To date, though, it is a largely untapped area of research. As fascinating as the topic is, I am by no means a specialist in gender studies, and analysis of this subject falls outside the purview of this book.

Finally, I should point out that most people who start kendo as adults, regardless of gender, will never be subjected to the harsh training doled out in Japanese high schools and universities. Still, the student will always be pushed to his or her limits, and this is an essential part of the sport. It is precisely this aspect of kendo that makes it so exhilarating, challenging, and satisfying, as well as frustrating.

The purpose of this book, however, is not to extol the virtues of kendo as a way of life, although this is the crux of my motivation to continue my own training. Rather, my intention is to fill a void in the way the culture of kendo is understood around the world. For many years, I have been sensitive to how little reliable information there is outside of Japan pertaining to the cultural evolution of kendo. Many enthusiasts I have met over the past three decades are oblivious to the political and social forces that molded kendo into the marvelous "spiritual sport" that it is today.

This knowledge gap is not limited to non-Japanese practitioners. Young Japanese university students, whom I teach now, tend to view winning competitions as the primary concern and have little time for tradition. As they mature, practitioners do often start to seek life lessons in kendo, but they generally possess only a rudimentary understanding of kendo's cultural and historical significance, and they often connect it with simplistic and historically questionable notions of bushido—the way of the samurai warrior (*bushi*).

Underlying humanistic discourses of personal and social betterment through both kendo and bushido is the belief that they represent uniquely Japanese virtues and epitomize the so-called Japanese spirit. This prevalent opinion often makes me seem like an enigma in the eyes of my Japanese colleagues. I explain to them that I study kendo not to be Japanese, but instead to be enriched by the intrinsic *universal* values and teachings that transcend the barriers of national identity.

Although this volume should not be thought of as a definitive representation of kendo, my desire is that it will contribute to a broader understanding of the sport's cultural legacy and facilitate a greater appreciation of where it has come from, where it is now, and where it could be heading. After all, the meaning behind the word used to denote training in kendo—*keiko*—literally means to "consider antiquity" in order to "shed light on the present."

Introduction

Kendo is a Japanese martial sport in which protagonists dressed in the traditional attire of *hakama* (split skirt) and *kendō-gi* (training top) use *shinai* (bamboo swords) as they compete to strike four specific areas on the opponent's *bōgu* (armor). The targets, each of which must be called out in a loud voice (*kiai*) as an accurate strike is made with a strong spirit, are *men* (head), *kote* (wrists), *dō* (torso), and *tsuki,* a thrust to the throat. Kendo is characterized by always showing respect to one's opponents, the honoring of protocol and culture, and the importance placed on enriching one's heart through training.[1]

WHAT IS JAPANESE BUDO?

The Japanese martial ways (budo) are multifaceted and enduring. Esteemed in Japan as the quintessence of traditional culture, they also have a reverent worldwide following. There are now tens of millions more non-Japanese enthusiasts practicing budo than Japanese.

To avoid confusion, a distinction needs to be made between premodern and modern Japanese martial arts. The various forms of budo that are popular as competitive sports today were developed during and after the Meiji period (1868–1912)—an epoch of frantic modernization and importation of Western ideas and technology. Martial arts in existence before this time are now referred to as *kobudō* (classical budo), *koryū* (old styles), or *bujutsu* (martial technique). Modern variants of these traditional martial arts trace their philosophical and technical roots to the classical styles, but their current forms, rules, etiquette, pedagogical methodologies, and societal objectives are very different.

There were hundreds of classical schools (*ryūha*) in premodern Japan, along with thousands of now-extinct one-hit wonders. They ranged from comprehensive combat systems to those that specialized exclusively in a particular skill such as grappling, spear usage, sword work, and even swimming. A smattering of these classical schools still remain today, sustained by small groups of dedicated adherents who take pride in being links in the long chain of their tradition. The Nihon Kobudo Association, one of the main umbrella societies overseeing classical traditions in Japan, currently has seventy-eight affiliated schools that trace their lineages back to antiquity.

Some modern budo exponents also study classical arts. I personally supplement my training in modern kendo by studying Kashima Shinden Jikishin Kage-ryū *kenjutsu,* Hōki-ryū *iaijutsu,* and Tendō-ryū *naginata-jutsu.* I have a keen interest in the esoteric teachings infused in the kata, and I find that *kobudō* is a window into the foundations of modern budo. Moreover, practical knowledge of *kobudō* has proved immensely beneficial to my academic research, as it helps me decipher the nebulous spiritual teachings recorded in Tokugawa-era martial art texts. My study of *kobudō* has also enhanced my comprehension of, and competitiveness in, modern kendo.

Alas, my enthusiasm for the classical martial arts is not shared by most of the kendo fraternity. When the Nihon Kobudo Association was established in 1979, there were nearly twice as many schools involved as there are today. The number of schools represented at various *kobudō* demonstration events is also dwindling, and the technical quality of many of the performances is questionable. A general lack of interest in taking up the classical arts in Japan will ensure the gradual loss of many of these martial legacies.

Another curious trend in the world of *kobudō* is the emergence of schools overseas. Some are authorized by the corresponding school in Japan and its current *sōke* (head of the tradition), but the lion's share are Frankensteins— totally fabricated and supported by bogus claims of historical legitimacy. Typically, the school's representative masquerades as a sanctioned professor of "such-and-such-ryu's ancient traditions," but in truth he or she has no association whatsoever with that ryu in Japan. (There have been numerous cases of counterfeit *kobudō* in Japan as well, extending back through to the country's distant past.) In addition, some of these small schools are plagued by incessant squabbling and infighting over matters of authentic sōkeship. The modern budo arts are a thousand-fold healthier in terms of the number of practitioners, although a degree of political factionalism exists in these federations as well.

The problem of how to effectively preserve and propagate the classical martial arts is certainly not limited to the twenty-first century. As we will see in the following chapters, when Japan modernized in the latter part of the nineteenth century, initiatives were made by educators and experts to safeguard and promote *bujutsu* as salient Japanese cultural heritage as well as a practicable form of homespun physical education. This movement culminated in the formation of highly influential private organizations, such as the Kōdōkan (Kanō Jigorō's school of judo) in 1882 and the Dai-Nippon Butokukai (Greater Japan Martial Virtue Society) in 1895. These societies succeeded in transforming traditional *bujutsu* into modern budo, making them more germane to modern societal needs, with a focus on education and competition. By the 1930s, however, the government had appropriated budo for political and militaristic machinations, which led to a blanket ban on martial arts by Occupation forces in the immediate postwar years.

Revived as "democratic sports" in the 1950s, budo rose to a high point when judo debuted at the 1964 Summer Olympics in Tokyo. The monolithic Nippon Budokan martial arts hall was constructed in the vicinity of the imperial palace in time for the event and became emblematic of the postwar budo renaissance.

Ironically, this hallowed venue, easily recognizable on the Tokyo skyline by the golden onion-shaped dome adorning the roof's apex, now hosts more high-profile rock concerts than budo events. Several nights a week, budo experts ascend the Kudanshita slope to the Budokan to test their skills in the great dojo located within; but on alternate nights small armies of dodgy scalpers line the same trail, illegally selling concert tickets to legions of eager groupies. Coexistence with the "way of the rocker" is, however, accepted as a necessary evil, for even the almighty Budokan is not exempt from the exorbitant taxes that come with owning 10,830 square meters of prime Tokyo real estate.

The Nippon Budokan building serves as the headquarters for the Nippon Budokan Foundation, which is recognized as the government-endorsed caretaker of budo culture. It was pivotal in the inauguration of the Japanese Academy of Budo in 1968. The academy, in which I currently serve as a director, is an academic society that promotes scholarly inquiry into budo. The Budokan also functions as an umbrella organization for the nine modern budo federations affiliated with the Japanese Budo Association (JBA), a union that was established on April 23, 1977.[2] According to the JBA's founding statutes, it was set up as a roundtable consortium of the nine federations and the Budokan to facilitate interaction between the groups and to promote the "spirit of each art to benefit the physical and mental well-being of the nation's people." In particular, it was stressed that youth education in budo was indispensable to creating "a strong Japan" and nurturing the wherewithal to contribute altruistically to the "welfare of the whole world."

In reality, there are more than nine modern budo in Japan. Modern martial arts similar to karate, such as *Nihon kenpō* and *taidō,* for example, are not included in this fellowship, as they either were not around when the JBA was formed or did not possess enough political punch at the time to secure inclusion. Some modern budo have related offshoot groups that are not acknowledged by the JBA. For example, the Kōdōkan operates independently of the All Japan Judo Federation, albeit while retaining a close and cooperative relationship. In the world of karate there are prominent autonomous organizations such as Kyokushin (and its many derivative groups) that have little or nothing to do with the JBA's affiliated karate body, the Japan Karatedo Federation. Another example would be Shōdōkan and Yōshinkan, independent splinter groups of aikido that do not fall under the auspices of the Aikikai Foundation.

There are also several, typically right-wing, peripheral confederacies composed of minority or fringe martial art groups. Some have been known to derisively assert their ideological and technical purity vis-à-vis the mainstream federations. Examples of societies representing alternative and sometimes radical budo creeds include the postwar reincarnation of the Dai-Nippon Butokukai and the kendo-specific Nihon Kendō Kyōkai (Japanese Kendo Association). Their main point of contention with mainstream budo is what they perceive as the overt "sportification" and compromising of martial and cultural veracity. Purists in mainstream budo, however, share similar concerns and see preoccupation with competitiveness as the double-edged sword of internationalization.

Anxious to mitigate the negative effects of globalization on traditional Japanese culture, the JBA promulgated a sweeping definition of budo ideals in its "Budo Charter" of 1977. Made up of six short articles, the document functions as a collective statement of belief, ideologically binding the eclectic mix of member federations. The opening section draws attention to how the recent trend of obsessing over technical skill, compounded by an excessive concern with winning at all costs, shown by both practitioners and instructors, is a "severe threat to the essence of budo."

I was appointed by the Budokan in 2004 to make significant revisions to the original 1977 English translation of the charter. The text intimates that the erosion of budo's cultural integrity was partly catalyzed by its growing popularity overseas. For the sake of international goodwill, I convinced the Budokan to allow me to gloss over this sentiment in my revision. Nevertheless, as I demonstrate in the final chapter of this book, the perceived connection between globalization and the cultural deterioration of budo is still prevalent. This belief was expressed unambiguously during the 2012 London Olympic Games by the jingoistic commentary of Ishihara Shintarō, who was the governor of Tokyo at the time: "Westerners practicing judo resemble beasts fighting. Internationalized judo has lost its appeal. . . . In Brazil they put chocolate in *norimaki,* but I wouldn't call it sushi. Judo has gone the same way."[3]

The release of a more recent and succinct JBA document, the "Philosophy of Budo," was announced in 2008, and I crafted the official English translation in 2010. Both the "Budo Charter" and the "Philosophy of Budo" were formulated consensually by JBA member organizations to define what true budo is ideologically and to advise how its integrity should be defended and conveyed in its "correct form" to future generations both in and outside of Japan.

Although I was eager to help promote budo, I had reservations about the content of the document. I sensed that tradition was being invented before my eyes and that in a small way I was playing a complicit role in the process. However, I was obliged to keep my misgivings in check as I translated the text. It is precisely the clash between my emotional—and therefore subjective—attachment to budo as a practitioner and the objectivity required as a rational scholar of budo that motivated me to write this book. I'll introduce the "Philosophy of Budo" before offering a cursory outline of the heterogeneous features of each of the nine budo.

> *Budō,* the martial ways of Japan, have their origins in the traditions of *bushidō*—the way of the warrior. *Budō* is a time-honoured form of physical culture comprising of *jūdō, kendō, kyūdō, sumō, karatedō, aikidō, shōrinji kempō, naginata* and *jūkendō.* Practitioners study the skills while striving to unify mind, technique and body; develop his or her character; enhance their sense of morality; and to cultivate a respectful and courteous demeanor. Practiced steadfastly, these admirable traits become intrinsic to the character of the practitioner. The *budō* arts serve as a path to self-perfection. This elevation of the human spirit will contribute to social prosperity and harmony, and ultimately, benefit the people of the world.[4]

Noble ideals indeed, but how accurate can a single manifesto meant to represent nine completely different budo really be? In terms of their similarities, the budo all emphasize etiquette and courteous behavior. All have developed systemized and safe technical curricula as well as modern rules and sets of kata. They all hold competitions (or demonstrations), award dan ranks, and have a professed focus on education and character development. All except jukendo currently have international federations.

There are also substantial differences in their historical development and the values that they hold. Some budo are predominantly competition oriented (judo, sumo, karate, jukendo); some are focused more on culture and spirituality (kyudo, aikido); and some fall somewhere in-between (kendo, naginata, shorinji kempo). Some have talismanic founders with cultlike status (aikido, shorinji kempo, judo). Some utilize weapons and protective equipment (jukendo, kendo, kyudo, naginata), while others use nothing but bare hands and feet (judo, sumo, karate, aikido, shorinji kempo).

Knowing a little about the other modern budo may help the reader contextualize my forthcoming discourse and purpose for authoring this volume. I will start with the unarmed budo.

UNARMED BUDO

Judo

Of the nine budo, judo (the gentle way) is the one that provided the blueprint for martial art modernization. Training in the *jūjutsu* schools of Tenjin Shin'yō-ryū and Kitō-ryū, the diminutive and polymathic Kanō Jigorō (1860–1938) discovered that his physical and mental strength vastly improved, not to mention his ability to fight off bullies. He also realized that, with a bit of tweaking, the principles of combat could be applied to modern education and used to enhance life in general. After graduating from the forerunner to the University of Tokyo, he created his own style of *jūjutsu* in 1882 as a means of promoting physical education, competition, and intellectual and moral development. He named his school Nihon-den Kōdōkan judo, choosing the suffix -*dō* (way) instead of -*jutsu* (techniques) to distance his activities from thuggish *jūjutsu* street fighters and highlight his educational objectives.

He adapted traditional *jūjutsu* techniques, systemizing them into logical sequences for learning and developing safe methods for free-practice sparring (*randori*). He eliminated perilous techniques from *randori* but recognized their cultural and combat value and thus preserved them in kata forms. He also created competition rules and refereeing protocols and pioneered the now-ubiquitous kyu and dan ranking system (5-kyu being the lowest and

10-dan being the highest). Kanō borrowed the idea of dan ranks from the grading system introduced in the board game Go during the early Tokugawa period. These modifications gave learners tangible goals to strive for, and those who passed the 1-dan rank (*shodan*) were awarded the distinction of being allowed to wear black sashes to secure their training tops.

Kanō was a prolific writer and exploited his high-society network and standing as a prominent educator to promote judo throughout Japan and the world. He made over ten overseas trips to inspect educational facilities during his career and took advantage of every opportunity to introduce judo to foreign audiences with evangelistic verve, explaining the principles in impeccable "headmaster's English." He also dispatched some of his top students abroad for prolonged periods to instruct. For example, Yamashita Yoshitsugu (also known as Yamashita Yoshiaki, 1865–1935), one of his greatest disciples and Kōdōkan's first 10-dan, was sent to the United States in 1903, where he taught at such esteemed institutions as the US Naval Academy, and he even instructed President Theodore Roosevelt in the White House in 1904. Furthermore, firm in his belief that the benefits of judo were equally efficacious for both sexes, Kanō allowed women to train under him as early as 1893 and formally launched the Kōdōkan's women's division in 1926.

Kanō continued developing judo's philosophy throughout his life. Inspired by Baron Pierre de Coubertin's notions of Olympism, Kanō established the combined ideals of *seiryoku-zen'yō* (the best use of energy to maximum efficiency) and *jita-kyōei* (mutual prosperity for self and others). In other words, train hard to become a good judoka—a first-rate citizen who is sound in body and mind—and employ this strength to contribute to society at large.

Kanō was a tireless advocate for athletics in general and was lauded as Japan's "father of sports." He founded the Japan Amateur Athletic Association (today's Japan Sports Association) in July 1911. As the first Asian member of the International Olympic Committee, he served as Japan's Olympic delegation leader in 1912, accompanying the country's two athletes when Japan took part in the Olympic Games for the first time at the fifth Olympiad in Stockholm. With some deft politicking, he even managed almost singlehandedly to convince the IOC to hold the 1940 Olympic Games in Tokyo. However, the militaristic Japanese government ended up forfeiting the games in July 1938. Kanō died a little before this turn of events on May 4, 1938, on a boat bound for Japan via North America following the IOC meeting in Cairo, where the Tokyo bid was ratified.

Judo as an Olympic sport is often derided by budo pedants who view it as having sold its soul to the doctrine of "victory for victory's sake," something that ran counter to Kanō's educational doctrine. Kanō was initially opposed to judo's inclusion in the Olympics, an idea that was championed by German judoka. He wrote to Pierre de Coubertin stating that judo would be an inappropriate inclusion because it was not a game, but instead was like a church, in that "it teaches a man a moral sense."[5] In 1936, however, he showed a more ambivalent attitude when he shared his thoughts on the issue with Koizumi Gunji (1885–1965), a Japanese *jūjutsu* expert in England who converted to Kōdōkan: "My view on the matter, at present, is rather passive. If it be the desire of other member countries I have no objection. But I do not feel inclined to take any initiative. For one thing, judo, in reality, is not a mere sport or game. I regard it as a principle of life, art and science. In fact it is a means for personal cultural attainment."[6]

Given the profound influence Kanō and judo had on the modernization of other martial arts in terms of organization, pedagogical processes and content, educational ideology, and even nomenclature (with his prophetic implementation of the suffix –*dō*), he can arguably be called the father of modern budo. He was one of the staunchest campaigners for budo's inclusion in the physical education curriculum of Japan's schools, and he incrementally adapted judo to fit all of the educational criteria the Ministry of Education generated through its surveys of martial arts. He highlighted the importance of being able to explain techniques rationally and scientifically and took pains to introduce verbal instruction to supplement the customary hermetic approach in which students persevered until they "got it." Judo represents a patent example of invented tradition in that *jūjutsu* techniques were redefined and combined with principally Western educational ideas and developed with universal participation in mind.

Sumo

Sumo has two distinct categories: the professional sport of *ōzumō,* which is governed by the Japan Sumo Association, and amateur sumo, a budo administered by the JBA-affiliated Japan Sumo Federation. Sumo is referred to as Japan's national sport because of its association with medieval samurai culture, and its connection with the imperial family, Shinto and the founding myths of Japan, and agrarian rites.

The sumo of today is markedly different from the popular sumo entertainment of the Tokugawa period, which was in turn nothing like the wrestling of the medieval and ancient periods. In his chapter on the invention of the *yokozuna* (grand champion) title in professional sumo in Stephen Vlastos's edited volume *Mirror of Modernity: Invented Tradition of Modern Japan*, Lee Thompson argues that "sumo as we know it today developed during the Edo period as a spectator sport while the elements that emphasized the martial arts were later refashioned into judo by Kanō Jigorō" (p. 175). In other words, the medieval form of sumo patronized by warriors involved throwing the opponent to the ground, just as judoka do today. This changed during the Tokugawa period, when a ring defined by straw bales was introduced to separate spectators and wrestlers and bouts were decided by pushing the opponent out of the ring.

A highly regulated form of professional entertainment (not a martial art) enjoyed by pleasure-seeking townsmen, Tokugawa-era sumo started to evolve into a modern sport at the end of the Meiji period. Influenced by principles of Western athleticism, sumo became a popular amateur sport among schoolboys and university students. Although rarely referred to as such today, it was even called *sumō-dō* during the war years to accentuate its spiritual value. Distinct from *ōzumō* in many ways, amateur sumo has weight divisions and a dan ranking system, and it does away with some of the distinctive and colorful Shinto-based rituals seen before and after bouts in professional sumo, such as throwing salt to purify the mound.

Following the formation of the International Sumo Federation in 1992, amateur sumo became ideologically aligned with Olympic ideals. A short and whimsical explanation titled "You think you know sumo?" on the international federation's homepage reveals the changes amateur sumo is still undergoing. "It's a 1,500 years old Japanese martial art, steeped in the Shinto religion. It's a fast and exciting sport with simple, easy to understand rules. It's part of the World Games, and is on track for inclusion in the Olympics. At last count, 84 nations have joined the International Sumo Federation, so it has evolved far beyond its Japanese origins."

To qualify as an Olympic event, sumo is required to comply with mandatory World Anti-Doping Agency regulations and to include women in the sport. The prohibition against women is a deep-rooted and sometimes controversial taboo highly unlikely to be broken in professional sumo. Thus, the traditions of amateur sumo are still in a state of flux, especially as it seeks

Olympic induction. Professional sumo, meanwhile, faces a different challenge. The media and general public in Japan lament the fact that, as of September 2014, no Japanese has been promoted to the rank of *yokozuna* since Takanohana retired in 2003. The current three active *yokozuna* are foreigners, and foreign wrestlers have incontrovertibly dominated the top division in recent years, winning every one of the six annual tournaments since March 2006.

Karate

Of all the budo arts, karate (the way of the empty hand) is the most popular internationally. The Japanese Ministry of Foreign Affairs declares that there are fifty million karate practitioners worldwide, while the World Karate Federation declares audaciously that there are over one hundred million. Obviously, such disparity indicates that the exact number is not known. Any sports organization aspiring for Olympic inclusion may succumb to the temptation to embellish membership statistics, but even a conservative estimate of ten million people would still make karate phenomenal. In comparison, according to the Japanese Ministry of Foreign Affairs, judo claims five million participants worldwide.

Karate developed in Okinawa, based on fighting techniques introduced by Chinese immigrants and traders in the fourteenth century. When the Satsuma clan appropriated the Ryukyu Islands in 1609, weapons were confiscated from the general populace and all forms of hand-to-hand combat (*te*) became hidden arts, practiced furtively until Japan modernized centuries later. In the early 1900s, public karate demonstrations were held in Naha, and classes were offered at some public schools by Itosu Ankō (1831–1915), who modified some of the traditional kata forms for this purpose. However, karate was not seen in mainland Japan until 1922, when Funakoshi Gichin (1868–1957) was invited by the Japanese Ministry of Education (MOE) to demonstrate the art. He was sponsored by Kanō Jigorō, who even allotted him time and space to teach karate at the Kōdōkan.

With Kanō's counsel, the transformation of karate also involved the adoption of white uniforms and colored belt ranks. It was accepted by the Dai-Nippon Butokukai in 1933—assimilating it into the pantheon of Japanese budo—and its kanji was changed from "Chinese [*kara*] hand [*te*]" to "empty [*kara*] hand [*te*]," both of which happen to be pronounced *karate*, with the *-dō* suffix appended to underscore moral education and "Japaneseness." Karate saw rapid growth in Japan only in the postwar period, and it may come as a surprise that it is still a minority budo there compared to kendo and judo, with approximately three hundred thousand registered dan rank holders.

Like the Japanese and international sumo federations, the Japan Karatedo Federation and the World Karatedo Federation are seeking Olympic inclusion. Karate was being considered for the 2020 Olympic Games but failed to receive enough votes at the IOC's executive board meeting in Russia on May 29, 2013. Tokyo was selected as the host city for the 2020 Olympic Games, so it is possible that karate and other budo could be selected as demonstration sports. Karate's appeal for last minute inclusion as an official event is pending.

Aikido

Probably the most esoteric of the budo arts is aikido (the way of unifying with life energy). At the heart of aikido is the concept of *ki,* or "life-force," which was described by founder Ueshiba Morihei (1883–1969) as "love." Ueshiba learned *jūjutsu* from the famous practitioner of Daitō-ryū *aiki-jūjutsu,* Takeda Sōkaku (1859–1943), but Ueshiba's pacifistic leaning left him ill at ease with the violent tone underlying *bujutsu.* He had an epiphany that it was not violence but rather peace that characterizes true budo.

> The moment I was awoken to the idea that the source of budo is the spirit of divine love and protection for everything I couldn't stop the tears flowing down my cheeks. Since that awakening, I have come to consider the whole world to be my home. I feel the sun, moon the stars are all mine. Desire for status, honor and worldly goods has completely disappeared. I realized that, "Budo is not about destroying other human beings with one's strength or weapons, or annihilating the world by force of arms. True budo is channeling the universal energy (*ki*) to protect world peace, to engender all things fittingly, nurture them and save them from harm." In other words, "budo training is to protect all things and nurture the power of unconditional divine love within."[7]

After hearing rumors of the miraculous healing powers displayed by Deguchi Onisaburō (1871–1948), the spiritual leader of a small Shinto-derived Ōmoto-kyō religious movement, Ueshiba became a follower, hoping these powers would benefit his ailing father. This served to intensify his fascination with spirituality. He continued teaching the techniques of *jūjutsu* but simultaneously developed a dogma centered on harmony rather than destruction. He initially taught his art to select individuals of standing but not to the general public, out of fear that the techniques would be misused for nefarious purposes.

He called his art *aiki-jūjutsu, Ueshiba-jūjutsu, aiki-budō,* and *aiki-bujutsu,* but he changed the name to aikido in 1942, when his group affiliated with the Dai-Nippon Butokukai. (All martial art organizations were appropriated by the Butokukai in 1942, when it was commandeered by the government, as described in chapter 4.) Aikido became a mainstream art in the postwar period, but few people had heard of or seen it before this. Aikido philosophy is opposed to initiating aggression, and therefore competition is seen as the antithesis of its objective of harmony. The style of aikido taught by the JBA-affiliated Aikikai Foundation is distinguished by the absence of competition, although it does hold large demonstrations (*enbu*).

Ueshiba asserted that the highest teachings in aikido are "to purge the self of maliciousness; to find harmony with the natural order of the universe; and to be at one with the universe." This philosophy exhibits the culmination of aikido ideals, of which the most important is to rid oneself of enmity and the urge to trounce one's opponent.

> It is a grave mistake to think that budo is about being stronger than your partner or opponent and that you have to defeat him. In true budo, there is no partner. There is no enemy. True budo is to become one with the universe. It is to be united with the universe's center. In aikido, we do not train to become strong or to defeat opponents, but to make even a small contribution to peace for all people in the world. To that purpose we must strive to harmonize with the center of the universe.[8]

The Aikikai Foundation is the largest aikido organization, although there are splinter groups that operate independently from it. The Shōdōkan, founded by Tomiki Kenji (1900–1979) in 1967, promotes "sport aikido," and in 1955, Shioda Gōzō (1915–94) created the Yōshinkan style, which is considered to be more in line with the rigorous prewar techniques of Ueshiba. After Ueshiba's death in 1969, his son, Kisshōmaru (1921–99), took over as head of the Aikikai Foundation. Due to a disagreement on the role of *ki* in aikido training, one of the foundation's head instructors, Tōhei Kōichi (1920–2011), broke away and started Shin Shin Tōitsu Aikido in 1974. Another splinter group, teaching what is known as the Iwama style, was developed by one of Morihei's students, Saitō Morihiro (1928–2002), who trained under him in the Iwama dojo. It is considered to be more "functional" than the Aikikai style and is purported to reflect the kind of techniques Ueshiba taught when he retired to Iwama to engage in ascetic training, from about 1946 to 1955.

The Aikikai Foundation is unique from the other mainstream budo in that it adopts the practice of hereditary transmission for the head of the organization. Currently, Morihei's grandson, Ueshiba Moriteru, is the third *dōshu*, meaning "master of the way."

Shorinji Kempo

The most recent of the nine budo is shorinji kempo, founded in 1947 by Sō Dōshin (Nakano Michiomi, 1911–80). In 1925, Sō Dōshin left Japan to live in Manchuria with his grandfather, Sō Shigetō, who was skilled in *kenjutsu* (sword work), *sōjutsu* (spear), and *jūjutsu*. Sō Shigetō apparently taught his grandson the basics of these arts.

After the deaths of his mother in 1926 and of his two sisters and grandfather in 1927, Sō Dōshin joined the right-wing Black Dragon Society and enlisted in the Imperial Army under the command of General Doihara Kenji in Manchuria. The degree of Sō Dōshin's involvement in military operations in China during the 1930s is unclear, but the dust jacket of his book *What Is Shorinji Kempo?* indicates that he operated as an "intelligence gatherer," or spy. To facilitate his covert activities, he became a disciple of Taoist priest Lian Chen, who was a master of Báilián Mén Quán, a branch of hand-to-hand combat with origins in the Shaolin Temple. Later Chen introduced him to Taizong Wen, grandmaster of another Shaolin Quán Fa derivative known as Yihe Mén Quán. Sō Dōshin inherited the headmastership of this style in 1936.

He traveled extensively throughout China during the 1930s on geographical surveys. Shorinji kempo lore has it that when he visited the White Robe Hall at the Shaolin Monastery, he was inspired by a famous mural depicting dark-skinned Indian monks engaged in fighting arts with light-skinned Chinese monks. He understood the importance of training with a partner rather than individually, as was the norm in Chinese martial arts.

He was repatriated to Japan in 1946 after surviving the Soviet invasion of Manchuria and settled in Tadotsu in Kagawa Prefecture. There he lamented the decayed state of Japanese Buddhism and the waywardness of dissolute youth. This compelled him to start teaching his own Buddhist philosophy. Guided by the spirit of the Bodhidharma, a Buddhist monk who lived during the fifth or sixth century, Sō Dōshin claims to have received divine inspiration to teach the ancient art of *arahan-no-ken,* which was what he had seen depicted in the mural at the Shaolin Monastery. He hoped that teaching martial arts would also attract interest in his ideas for improving society, although initially few were concerned with what he had to say. His oft-quoted mantra was, "The person, the person, the person—everything depends on the quality of the person."

Starting in 1947, he proceeded to codify the techniques he had learned in China—kicks, strikes, throws, and holds—and added a religious and educational dimension, thus creating his own distinct style of martial art, which he called shorinji kempo. In 1948, he founded the Japan True Transmission of Northern Shaolin Kenpō Association (Nihon Seitō Hoppa Shōrinji Kenpō Kai), and, as his reputation in the community grew, an influx of new students followed. To evade the suspicious eyes of the Occupation authorities, he registered his group as a religious organization and justified the training of combat techniques as observance of Buddhist dancing practices.

For legal reasons, the group was renamed Kongō Zen Sōhonzan Shōrinji in 1951. In 1963, the Japan Shorinji Kempo Federation was established (now referred to as the Shorinji Kempo Federation Foundation). The World Shorinji Kempo Organization (WSKO) was inaugurated in 1974.

Zen and religious teachings are important aspects of shorinji kempo, and the federation even offers priesthood qualifications for Kongō Zen. Kongō Zen represents the religious ideals of Sō Dōshin and the philosophy underlying the techniques of shorinji kempo. It was inspired by the universal law of Buddhism (dharma) and the ideal of body-mind unification. As part of their study of shorinji kempo, practitioners engage in zazen (seated meditation) to contemplate these ideals and their application. The principles of training are expressed as *kenzen-ichinyo,* meaning that *ken* and *zen* are one and the same, where *ken* refers to training in the physical techniques and *zen* to the spiritual. The swastika, or *manji* in Japanese, was the original emblem for shorinji kempo because of its dharmic affiliation. Symbolic of Kongō Zen teachings, the swastika signifies love (when it is left-facing) and strength (when it is right-facing). However, due to the irrevocable association with Nazism, a new insignia was introduced in 2005—a double circle created through two interwoven swastikas.

Sō Dōshin died in May 1980. His daughter from his third marriage, Sō Yūki, now heads the shorinji kempo organizations. Although a comparatively new martial art, shorinji kempo has continued to gain in popularity over the past six decades, and it is estimated that there are over one hundred forty thousand members worldwide, with 2,950 branches in Japan and 33 in other countries. Due to the international popularity of the art, especially in Indonesia, where it has an estimated membership of eighty thousand, "Shorinji Kempo" was made a licensed international trademark, and all branches and instructors are now closely regulated by the Japan-based WSKO. This move was also made in order for the WSKO to distinguish itself from the hordes of unrelated groups that use the Shaolin name.

Even though it is included in the nine budo, shorinji kempo is distinctive in terms of the monk-like uniforms donned by advanced practitioners and the use of the *gasshō-rei* style of greeting (both palms put together and raised in front of the face—a Buddhist gesture of piety) as opposed to bowing, which is the norm in other budo.

ARMED BUDO

Jukendo

Jukendo, the "way of the bayonet," was first demonstrated in Japan in 1841 by the musketeer Takashima Shūhan (1798–1866), who had learned the techniques through his contact with the Dutch in Nagasaki. It was not until after the Meiji Restoration in 1868 that the bayonet became a part of Japanese military culture. Although connected loosely with classical schools of spearmanship (*sōjutsu*), jukendo is mostly a modern contrivance from the Meiji era. French military instructor François Ducros first introduced Western-style fencing and bayonet practice into the physical training curriculum of the Toyama Military Academy in 1874. In 1884, two more French military officers, Étienne de Villaret and Joseph Kiehl, were invited to the school to teach Western fencing.

Dissatisfaction prevailed with regard to fully adopting French military practices. However, given the proven effectiveness of the bayonet in modern warfare, the school continued to research new techniques. In 1892, the chief instructor of calisthenics at the Toyama Military Academy and successor of the Tsuda Ichiden-ryū tradition of martial arts, Tsuda Takamichi (reading of name uncertain; 1850–1907), referred to texts on Hōzōin-ryū and Saburi-ryū *sōjutsu* to adapt Japanese spear techniques for bayonet usage. These new methods were formalized and became the new martial art of *jūken-jutsu*, which was taught at the academy from 1894.

Jūken-jutsu was officially accepted into the Dai-Nippon Butokukai in 1925, but its designation was changed to jukendo in 1941, when a special promotion section was established in the Butokukai. It was not until 1998 that jukendo's governing body introduced traditional navy blue *hakama* and training tops (like those worn in kendo). Before that, the conventional uniform in jukendo consisted of white shirts and trousers reminiscent of military physical exercise uniforms. Jukendo armor is very similar to kendo armor, with the addition of a large pad protecting the torso from thrusts aimed at the heart and throat. The weapon used is called a *mokujū,* which is made from wood in the shape of a rifle, with a rubber cap covering the blunted bayonet at the end.

Falling under the auspices of the All Japan Jukendo Federation is a subsidiary sport called tankendo (the way of the short sword) that is also very similar to kendo in terms of equipment but uses a one-handed short sword with a straight blade, that is, a detached bayonet. Although stabs to the body and throat make up the bulk of offensive techniques, *men* and *kote* are also valid striking targets. The standard method for cutting the *men* involves a flat striking movement over the top of the head to ensure that as much surface of the cutting edge as possible comes into contact with the target. Traditionally, the short one-handed *shinai* used in tankendo represented a straight bayonet, but it is now widely considered to represent a traditional Japanese short-sword—a *kodachi*—with its distinctively curved blade. Thus, although the *shinai* is straight, the conventional method for making a valid strike is being questioned given the hypothetical curved shape of the blade; and even the kata now uses exactly the same wooden *kodachi* as those utilized in kendo kata.

The Jukendo Federation is still battling to overcome lingering images of militarism and make itself more convincingly Japanese in appearance and modus operandi. Despite the various struggles it faces, jukendo is currently preparing to launch an international federation. On the home front, the vast majority of the approximately forty thousand practitioners are members of Japan's Self-Defense Forces, or JSDF. However, as the JSDF has become more diversified in recent years, the number of personnel training in jukendo has decreased steadily and karate is becoming more popular for practical reasons.

Kyudo

Kyudo (the way of the bow) is seeing a surge in popularity in Japan, especially among university students. The bow was the predominant weapon of the samurai more or less until the introduction of firearms in the sixteenth century. Influenced by Chinese ideals from around the sixth century, Japanese archery consisted of two categories: ceremonial (standing) and military (mounted). The former placed emphasis on correct physical and mental posture, and the latter focused on efficacy. The earliest distinct systems of archery were the Takeda-ryū and the Ogasawara-ryū, developed in the twelfth and thirteenth centuries, respectively. In the latter part of the fifteenth century, Heki Masatsugu (1444–1502) transformed traditional methods with a new style of foot soldier archery called Heki-ryū, of which some offshoots survive today.

The peaceful Tokugawa period saw archery thrive as a spiritual pursuit and a competitive sport. With the onset of the Meiji period, traditional archery (*kyūjutsu*) fell into decline. Amid vehement protestations from purists, Honda Toshizane (1836–1917) combined military and ceremonial shooting styles to form a hybrid version that became known as Honda-ryū. Honda initially taught his style to university students, but it soon spread among the general public. He is thus sometimes credited as being the savior of kyudo in the modern era, wresting it from the firm grip of traditional archery families and giving it wide popular appeal.

As the gatekeeper of prewar martial arts, the Dai-Nippon Butokukai saw the need to create a national standard for shooting protocols. They invited several archery experts to represent their schools in a controversial attempt to form a synthesized model that transcended ryu affiliation. This is especially in reference to the Heki-ryū-based methods, which employed angled bow-raising (*naname-uchi-okoshi*) before releasing, and Ogasawara-ryū- and Honda-ryū-based styles, which used front bow-raising (*mae-uchi-okoshi*). A standard was finally established in 1934, although the principal schools took little notice of the Butokukai's "meddling."

During the postwar budo ban, kyudo was able to reform and the All Nippon Kyudo Federation was inaugurated in 1949. It published the *Kyūdō kyōhon* (1953) an instruction manual outlining the standard shooting method called *shahō-hassetsu* (eight-step shooting method). This became the common procedure, which allowed practitioners of diverse school affiliations to participate in tournaments and examinations together, although a certain degree of leeway was provided to allow for *ryūha* idiosyncrasies. Many archers now practice only the *shahō-hassetsu* method.

The manual also stipulated that the objective of kyudo is the pursuit of "truth, goodness, and beauty" (*shin-zen-bi*), but the origin of this principle is not clear. *Shin-zen-bi* does not feature in any traditional Japanese *kyūjutsu* teachings. A recent feature of kyudo is its tenuous association with Zen. This relationship was greatly influenced by the book *Zen in the Art of Archery*, written by the German philosopher Eugen Herrigel (1884–1955). Herrigel studied kyudo for six years in Japan under the tutelage of the eccentric master Awa Kenzō (1880–1939). Yamada Shōji postulates that Herrigel misinterpreted the Zen epiphany he thought he was experiencing under his master's guidance.[9] However, when Herrigel's book was translated into Japanese in 1956, its impact on the perception of Zen in Japanese kyudo circles was massive, amounting to a "reverse import" of ideology.

Kyudo is now studied widely among high school and university students in Japan. As of 2012, there were approximately 140,000 registered practitioners in Japan, nearly half of whom are women.

Naginata

The only modern budo in which women make up the clear majority of aficionados is naginata. *Naginata* refers to both the martial art and the weapon used. The *naginata*—a glaive over two meters in length—was the principal weapon of foot soldiers from the eleventh to the fifteenth century and was also widely used by warrior-monks, perhaps the most celebrated being the fabled Musashibō Benkei. It was eventually made obsolete on the battlefields of the fifteenth century with the introduction of easier-to-use spears called *yari*. With the onset of peace in the seventeenth century, *naginata-jutsu* became established as a concealed martial art primarily studied by women of warrior families.

Irrespective of the Ministry of Education's initial reluctance to include *naginata-jutsu* and other martial arts in the regular school curriculum in the Meiji period, a few schools independently taught the art to girls. For example, Hoshino Shinnosuke, a well-known advocate of *bujutsu* education, started teaching *naginata-jutsu* forms from the Hokushin Ittō-ryū and Yagyū-ryū traditions at the Meiji Girls' School in Tokyo as early as 1889.

In 1910, five sports suitable as extracurricular subjects for girls were recommended in a MOE-sanctioned report for normal school principals. *Naginata-jutsu* was included, along with ice skating, swimming, tennis, and archery. In the "School Gymnastics Teaching Syllabus" released by the MOE in 1913, *naginata-jutsu* was listed as one of the exercises acceptable for girls as an extracurricular subject.

Naginata-dō, as the art became known after 1919, became an elective subject (along with kyudo) for girls undertaking tertiary education in 1936. Further reforms to the education system saw girls in elementary schools receive compulsory *naginata-dō* training beginning in 1942. The Butokukai had already created a teacher's training course in 1934 in which Mitamura Kunihiko, Mitamura Chiyo, and Nishigaki Kin taught Tendō-ryū techniques. Similarly, a rival Jikishin Kage-ryū training college called the Shūtokukan was formed in 1936 by Sonobe Hideo. These two schools were responsible for training the bulk of *naginata-dō* teachers until the end of the war, but there was no amalgamated style the like of which had been developed for kendo. Attempts had been made to come up with one, but nothing was implemented before the end of the war.

For the most part, training before and during the war years was centered on kata that involved *naginata* versus sword. As *naginata-dō's* popularity increased, so did the desire of younger practitioners to engage in competitive bouts. A light wooden *naginata* with the blade sheathed in impact-softening leather was devised for this purpose. This was eventually replaced with a bamboo blade attached to the end of a wooden shaft. Match rules based on kendo's model were adopted, but almost all bouts were conducted against a kendo opponent rather than another naginata practitioner.

After Japan's defeat in 1945, *naginata-dō* was banned until the 1950s. Following kendo's lead, a research committee of eight experts and a number of education officials was formed in 1954 to explore a unified, modern style of naginata for dissemination. Nineteen meetings later, the committee created a sporting version of naginata with an entirely new corpus of techniques and training methodology that transcended ryu affiliation. The All Japan Naginata Federation was inaugurated in Kyoto on May 4, 1955.

In 1959, a proposal to reinstate naginata in schools was accepted by the MOE, and the sport was approved as an extracurricular club activity for girls in junior high school and above. A hybrid sporting version called "school naginata" (*gakkō naginata*), later changed to "new naginata" (*atarashii naginata*), was introduced. The MOE advised the All Japan Naginata Federation to promote the sport using phonetic hiragana characters rather than Chinese characters, as the kanji used to write *naginata* was not included in the "list of kanji for general use" (*tōyō* kanji) circulated by the ministry in reforms carried out to simplify the written language in 1946. This was not the only reason. According to my former naginata teacher, the late Tokunaga Chiyoko, who was directly involved in negotiating with the MOE for the reinstatement of naginata in schools in the 1950s, the ministry was still wary of perceived militaristic connotations associated with the kanji, especially as it included the character for "katana." Kanji characters are, however, still used for classical naginata styles such as Tendō-ryū and Jikishin Kage-ryū. The MOE also directed the federation not to use the suffix *–dō,* to circumvent any correlation with wartime moral education in the new style of sport naginata.

The postwar style of naginata is similar in many ways to kendo. Although a longer weapon is used and ambidextrous side-on stances are featured, the protective equipment (*bōgu*) is basically the same, with the addition of a *suneate* to protect the shins and split-finger gauntlets (*kote*) to allow easier manipulation of the weapon.

Nowadays, most practitioners train primarily in new naginata. Currently, naginata is reputedly practiced by over forty thousand people in Japan. The vast majority of participants are women, but the number of men taking up the sport has increased in recent years. The annual All Japan Men's Naginata Championships commenced in 2002, and the Naginata World Championships are held every four years. The International Naginata Federation—for which I currently serve as vice president—was launched in 1990 and now has fifteen affiliated countries. More countries are in the process of becoming affiliated, but naginata remains a comparatively minor budo in terms of population and recognition, even in Japan.

. . .

The kendo experience overlaps with the other eight mainstream modern budo in terms of its pattern of modernization. In sheer numbers, karate and judo are by far the most ubiquitous martial arts internationally. Kendo is the most widely practiced martial art in Japan at the school and community club level. This is due in part to deeply entrenched notions that kendo is the purest of the martial arts—being easily linked to the honorable sword-wielding samurai heroes of yesteryear.

What most people overlook is that the form of kendo practiced today is in many ways a very modern contrivance. The word "kendo" itself only came into popular use around 1920. Early usage of the designation *kendō* was popularized by a swordsman of the Chikuzen domain, Abe Munetō (1624–93), in his 1667 document outlining his school, *Abe-ryū kendō denshi.* This was a rare exception, however, and appellations such as *gekitō, gekiken, tachi-uchi, kenpō,* and *kenjutsu* were more common.

Starting in the mid-nineteenth century, as Japan modernized and began to assert its uniqueness, a notion that the Japanese people and their virtues emanated from samurai culture became prevalent. As Harumi Befu points out, "Japan's modernization coincided with the samuraization process—the spread of the ideology of the ruling warrior class."[10] This was accomplished over several decades through such means as introducing a modified warrior ideology in the Civil Code (1898) and modifying the school curricula to celebrate warrior customs and myths.

Newly created notions of bushido and ideas of a glorious warrior past were propagated vigorously from the 1890s onward, and many of the national myths created during this epoch became so strongly entrenched in the Japanese psyche that they remain largely unquestioned to this day. Basil Hall Chamberlain (1850–1936), a renowned English Japanologist, made the following cynical but astute observations about bushido and the burgeoning Japanese nationalism of the later Meiji period.

The twentieth-century Japanese religion of loyalty and patriotism is quite new, for in it pre-existing ideas have been sifted, altered, freshly compounded, turned to new uses, and have found a new center of gravity. Not only is it new, it is not yet completed; it is still in process of being consciously or semi-consciously put together by the official class, in order to serve the interests of that class, and, incidentally, the interests of the nation at large.[11]

Kendo represents a fine example of an "invented tradition" that was "freshly compounded" during the period of modernization to cultivate national partisanship. To be sure, kendo's lineage can be traced directly back to the warriors of the medieval period. However, its teaching and training methodology, match rules, philosophical concepts, and so on were, for the most part, developed or reformulated in the twentieth century. From the late Meiji period until Japan's defeat in the Second World War, kendo was increasingly utilized as an educational tool to infuse nationalistic doctrines of self-sacrifice and bolster ideas of the Japanese being a powerful warrior race with a courageous spirit that was unsurpassed in the world.

Kendo's technical evolution continues into the twenty-first century, as does the official insistence that practitioners follow the same righteous path that samurai trod before them to rectify the self and, by extension, the societal and ethical ills of the present to create a brighter future. This is indicative of what Matthew Levinger and Paula Lytle describe as "nostalgic nationalism." In other words, a "triadic structure of nationalistic rhetoric" is evident in which kendo connects the glorious past with the degraded present and ultimately the utopian future.[12]

Actually, it is the cultural link with samurai culture that provides significant appeal for non-Japanese practitioners, although there is a latent supposition among the Japanese kendo fraternity that non-Japanese are unlikely to ever fully understand what they consider to be the essence of kendo. Such views are usually motivated by ethno-cultural pride rather than nationalistic or jingoistic sentiments. Brian McVeigh also contends that the difficulty in internationalizing Japanese culture "is attributed, sometimes with a measure of pride, to how inscrutable Japanese culture is, to insiders as well as outsiders."[13] Nevertheless, this patronizing attitude does not inhibit the labors of Japanese kendoists at all levels, as well as the government, to propagate the culture of kendo and other budo internationally as their "gift" to the world—one that can even contribute to world peace, as the rhetoric often goes.

Misunderstandings abound in Japan and elsewhere regarding the evolution of kendo and the other martial arts and the cultural and political forces that shaped them. To date, there are few books in English that plot in detail their development from the Japanese martial arts of the medieval period to the international combat sports of today. Although there are abundant works in Japanese on the history of swordsmanship, few offer more than a cursory analysis of kendo and nationalism in the modern era. Thus, curiously, the correlation between martial arts and nationalism remains a poorly explored area in both Japanese and Western academia.

A growing number of English books about traditional Japanese swordsmanship are on the market. Most of them, however, are how-to manuals, biographies of master swordsmen, or translations and commentaries on classic texts—often historically naïve, mixing fact with fiction. Books on modern swordsmanship are primarily technical manuals that offer only rudimentary outlines of the history, with little or no analysis. Sasamori Junzō and Gordon Warner's classic book *This is Kendo: The Art of Japanese Fencing* is a good example.

Among the most extensive studies of the evolution of Japanese martial art systems are Cameron Hurst's *Armed Martial Arts of Japan: Swordsmanship and Archery* and Donn Draeger's *Classical Bujutsu, Classical Budo,* and *Modern Bujutsu and Budo.* Draeger's books have long been considered required reading among Western martial artists who want to understand Japanese martial culture and swordsmanship. They were pioneering works when they were published in the 1970s and valuable contributions to Westerners' understanding of the field, but they lack scholarly rigor and adequate social analysis, relying too much on simplistic notions of how the martial arts transformed from techniques for killing (*bujutsu*), to arts (*bugei*), and then to martial paths to self-perfection (*budō*). There is little scrutiny of the complex social forces underpinning these historical transformations.

Hurst's highly accessible book is superior in terms of scholarly analysis, giving an overview of both swordsmanship and archery from ancient times to the present day. He analyzes the nationalization of martial arts in the post-Meiji era and discusses the influence of Western athletic tradition on the modernization of budo, detailing the characteristics that have remained markedly Japanese. He also ponders misconceptions of budo in both the West and Japan, especially with regards to how Zen Buddhism has become synonymous with the martial ways.

Karl Friday's excellent book *Legacies of the Sword: The Kashima-Shinryu and Samurai Martial Culture* explores the historical, philosophical, and pedagogical dynamics of the Kashima Shin-ryū as a case study of classical swordsmanship. A groundbreaking book, Friday's discourse is, however, generally restricted to one tradition and does not delve into the far-reaching political and social implications of kendo in the modern era.

A recent work that also raises the bar in understanding budo culture in the modern context is Denis Gainty's *Martial Arts and the Body Politic in Meiji Japan*. His study is a long-overdue examination of the Dai-Nippon Butokukai and its sponsorship of budo in modern Japanese society through the end of the Second World War. It is an important contribution to Western analysis of the sociopolitical significance of budo in Japan from the late Meiji up to the immediate postwar era.

In contrast to these works, I will focus on kendo as Japan's most prevalent domestic martial art, taking a macro approach in my historiography in order to contextualize kendo's evolution and a micro perspective to illuminate its cultural and political significance.

To date, there has been little discourse considering nationalist sentiment as a driving force behind efforts to diffuse kendo domestically and then internationally. Moreover, although no one is in denial or oblivious to the connection, underscoring the relationship between kendo and militarism has been treated either as taboo or as not worthy of in-depth scholarly investigation by the majority of scholars in Japan. This is understandable, given that budo researchers are typically practitioners as well. Abiding by the unspoken rule that it is best to let sleeping dogs lie, budo scholars tend to sidestep such issues.

Negative aspects of kendo's modern history and certain inconvenient truths, particularly about kendo's wartime militarization, have been largely swept under the carpet in ways that I expand upon in chapter 5. The propensity to overlook the wartime experience of kendo as an undeniably important phase in its gradual transformation into a postwar democratic sport has left huge gaps in our understanding of its social, cultural, and political relevance today.

To make sense of how traditional swordsmanship could feature in militaristic machinations in the twentieth century, we must first plot its fascinating evolutionary process, starting with the rise of the warriors. Chapter 1 outlines the historical process that led to the appearance of professional warriors and the emergence of the role of the sword in medieval warfare. This will entail an explanation of how *ryūha* (distinct martial traditions) evolved, as well as a discussion of the rise of the "sword cult" and its symbolism.

Chapter 2 plots the transition of *kenjutsu* from a combat art to a combat sport. I look at the maturation of *kenjutsu* as an example of a "civilizing process" and consider how the invention of safety training equipment led to the art's "sportification." This important turn of events enabled the samurai's social inferiors to take up and even excel in early modern fencing. To the samurai, the intellectualization and spiritual refinement of *kenjutsu* filled a vacuum in his self-identity and bolstered sentiments of cultural elitism—a sentiment that was to reveal itself again in the Meiji period among the citizens of modern Japan.

The third chapter inquires into the temporary fading of *kenjutsu,* followed by its reinvention in the Meiji period with the modernization of social systems and the creation of national identity. In particular, I assess Sakakibara Kenkichi and the *gekiken-kōgyō* (public martial art shows) that he initiated to revive public interest and provide swordsmen with a source of income. I also consider the new niches that were devised for *kenjutsu,* both as an indigenous form of physical education and as a way to keep the police fighting fit. Of particular significance in the modernization of swordsmanship was the formation of the Dai-Nippon Butokukai—the self-appointed guardian of Japan's martial arts—and its contributions to the standardization of budo for national dissemination on an unprecedented scale.

Following this formative period of martial art exploitation in modern popular and state nationalistic agendas, chapter 4 will map the state's appropriation of kendo in the 1930s and 1940s. Kendo became a compulsory subject in schools and underwent what could be described as a process of de-civilization as the techniques, rules, and methods of training were brutalized to inculcate fighting spirit in the youth and prepare them for the rigors of war.

State control of budo for militaristic purposes during the Second World War led to a blanket ban on martial arts in the postwar period. The budo arts, particularly kendo, were viewed by the Occupation forces as potent weapons for brainwashing gullible minds. The main theme of the penultimate chapter, therefore, is the sanitization or re-civilizing of kendo into a democratic sport, separated from state control and exorcised of any hint of militarism. This process involved the invention of *shinai-kyōgi* (a hybrid Westernized version of kendo) and the subsequent formation of the All Japan Kendo Federation as the new gatekeeper of kendo culture. The second theme addresses kendo's ongoing identity crisis, or the clash between traditional values and overt competitiveness. What makes kendo distinctive— that is, culturally superior—to other sports?

The final chapter investigates the early international propagation of kendo in Europe and the Americas, as well as in Japan's former colonies of Korea and Taiwan. Each region has well-established kendo communities, but for varying reasons, each has different views on the cultural ownership of kendo.

The international dissemination of kendo is seen as a double-edged sword. On the one hand, it is considered by the AJKF and the Japanese government as a contribution to world culture and a way to affirm Japanese soft power at an individual and organizational level. It also facilitates a self-affirmation of what it is to be Japanese in the international community and is a fountainhead of national pride for those directly involved. On the other hand, retaining control over the destiny of kendo as it spreads throughout the world is a source of cultural anxiety in Japan. The issue of "who owns the culture?" is examined in chapter 6.

Collectively these chapters will illustrate the socio-historical evolution of Japanese swordsmanship and its correlation with perceptions of tradition, cultural nationalism, and "Japaneseness."

CHAPTER 1

The Art of Killing

SWORDSMANSHIP IN MEDIEVAL JAPAN

WHENCE THEY CAME

To the samurai, martial ability was an expression of individual strength and valor, symbolizing their distinctive subculture as specialist men-at-arms. Starting in the ninth century (or arguably even earlier), Japanese warriors developed and cultivated an idiosyncratic culture based largely on their ability to utilize violence. Warrior ideals evolved over many centuries and were imbued with idioms of honor, such as the bonds of loyalty forged between retainer and lord, for whom—as the classic war tales frequently inform us—the warrior would gladly forfeit his life.

But how accurate is our understanding of the origin of samurai culture? It seems that Japanese and Westerners alike maintain a distorted, often-romanticized view of the samurai. For example, the long-held interpretation in the West of the so-called emergence of the samurai was largely based on an economic thesis put forth by Asakawa Kan'ichi,[1] whose ideas were subsequently propagated by early generations of highly influential Western scholars of Japanese history and culture such as George Sansom and E. O. Reischauer.

In simple terms, the traditional view presents an unambiguous interpretation of the events that led to the appearance of powerful provincial warrior families in the late Heian period (794–1185). In Sansom's classic three-volume treatise of Japanese history, *The History of Japan to 1334*, he states that "the gradual collapse of the civil power after the decline of the Fujiwara dictators was accompanied by a rise in the influence of warrior clans."[2]

Oppressed by high taxes, many peasants deserted their fields for other occupations, adversely impacting the Heian government's income and influence. This caused instability and tension throughout the land, and landowners in the provinces were compelled to fortify their holdings to protect them from marauding bands of belligerents who had become disconnected from their familial connections in the capital and engaged in acts of brigandry to expand their own estates.

Even the court found itself unable to protect its assets in the provinces, and its economic base was significantly weakened as a result. Newly formed alliances of provincial warriors were able to gather political momentum and assert their power through the use of military force. Eventually, these provincial warriors became economically dominant as well. After the Genpei Disturbance (1180–85) and the abdication of the ineffectual nobles (*kuge*), the samurai were able to elevate themselves to powerful positions in society simply by filling the political holes that appeared. Their influence burgeoned with the formation of the Kamakura shogunate in 1189 by Minamoto Yoritomo (1147–99).

More recently, however, this interpretation of the rise of warriors to political dominance has been substantively amended. Among Western scholars, prominent theorists include J. W. Hall, Jeffrey Mass, and Marius B. Jansen. They refute the simplistic idea of *kuge* powerlessness in the face of warrior ascension. The contemporary consensus is that *kuge* actually maintained a significant degree of control and certainly did not hand political power over to the provincial samurai; by the time of the establishment of the first warrior government at the end of the twelfth century, the samurai remained relatively politically immature.

New theories of how the samurai rose to prominence have been postulated in Japan and the West from many different angles, especially in the last two decades. Some of the representative works in English include William Wayne Farris's *Heavenly Warriors*, Karl Friday's *Hired Swords*, and Eiko Ikegami's *The Taming of the Samurai*.

Farris's book avoids the term "emergence" and instead promotes the idea that the warriors "evolved" in an ongoing process spanning many centuries, before the eventual consolidation of a unified warrior power structure with the formation of the Kamakura shogunate. Farris also contests the "Western analogue theorists" who forcibly apply a Western model of feudalism to the samurai experience. He divides his analysis of samurai evolution into sections extending back to approximately 500 AD. He draws our attention to the culture of mounted archers—not uncommon throughout Asia—who were organized into an imperial army by Emperor Tenmu (?–686), whose name means "heavenly warrior," hence the title of Farris's book.

He conjectures that the aristocratic warriors of the Heian period did not suddenly appear and fill a political vacuum but rather inherited a much older culture that continued to develop over time. He argues that mounted warriors had become the main strike force on battlefields by the ninth century and that "many soldiers organized themselves into houses with the exclusive right to practice the martial arts, either as local aristocrats or local strongmen."[3] During the period extending from 500 to 1300, warriors were not pitted against the courtiers but instead acted as shields for them until the samurai asserted their political independence over the court starting in the thirteenth century.

Karl Friday also questions the perceived impotence of the court. Through a detailed analysis of the military technology and motivations of the imperial army and conscripts, he contends that the warriors at court and those stationed in the provinces were in fact allied. Furthermore, the court actively made use of provincial warriors to upgrade its military and policing system.

There were instances in which certain warriors exerted palpable influence, such as Taira Kiyomori (1118–81), who rose to dominate court politics and even enthroned his infant grandson Antoku (1178–85) as emperor. Nevertheless, Friday argues that for the most part the evolution of military institutions between the seventh and twelfth centuries followed a consistent pattern that relied on the military abilities of the provincial elites and lower members of the aristocracy.

Eiko Ikegami's *The Taming of the Samurai* focuses on violence as the decisive factor in the rise of the samurai. She highlights this as a distinguishing raison d'être among the Japanese warrior subculture and also mentions the clashes between violent groups of eastern warriors and the indigenous Emishi people of northeastern Honshū. Central to her argument is the concept of honor (*na*), and the bonds of loyalty that were formed between the warrior and his lord through combat experience.

Ikegami contends that the gradual rise of the samurai to political prominence on a national scale was prompted by the dismantling of the military obligations that had previously been forced upon the general populace under the *ritsuryō* system. This culminated in certain offices, such as guard and military posts, becoming hereditary among a small, select group of nobles. Determined to maintain their monopoly over government positions, these noble families increasingly sought affiliation with warriors and even created their own private armies. This in turn provided an opportunity for career advancement among the middle- to lower-ranked nobles, who realized that martial ability could be their ticket to a successful career.

As Friday points out, "by the tenth century, military service at court and service as a provincial official had become parallel and mutually supportive careers for the members of several middle-ranked courtier houses collectively known as the *miyako no musha*, or 'warriors of the capital.'"[4] The best-known warriors were members of the houses of the Minamoto (Genji) and the Taira (Heiji or Heike). These two great warrior clans provide the heroes (and anti-heroes) of many of Japan's war tales. Their feats in battle, particularly in the Hōgen (1156) and Heiji (1160) Disturbances and the Taira-Minamoto War (the Genpei Disturbance of 1180–85), were recorded for posterity in all their embellished gore and glory.

Although these war tales (*gunki monogatari*) provide valuable insights into samurai culture, they have also been at the root of the glorification and misconceptualization of samurai culture, even among warriors themselves. The war tales describing the rise to supremacy of Minamoto Yoritomo (1147–99) and the establishment of the first warrior government (*bakufu*) in Kamakura highlight a pivotal time in the evolution of the samurai. The formation of a warrior government did not spell the end of court authority, but it did signify the beginning of new conventions and rules that instilled new notions of warrior self-identity.

Yoritomo's initiatives included legally elevating trustworthy vassals to the status of privileged housemen (*gokenin*), who were obligated to show loyalty to him. He also ensured that he was the only agent connecting his vassals with the court, which rendered warriors stationed in the capital ineffectual. In 1185 he rewarded his vassals with the titles and privileges of governor (*shugo*) and land steward (*jitō*). He successfully created a warrior union with "new mechanisms for organizing and directing its housemen, as well as an unprecedented clarity to the reciprocal obligations that bound them."[5] By and large, by the Kamakura period (1189–1333) "reciprocal obligation" meant the idealization of martyrdom as the definitive show of fidelity and personal honor.

Motoki Yasuo proposes a useful description of how samurai can be distinguished from other combatants who have been active throughout Japanese history:

> *Bushi* [samurai] refers to the professional warriors who wielded political authority in medieval [*chūsei*] and early modern [*kinsei*] Japan. As professional warriors, they were distinctive from peasant or civilian conscript soldiers of the ancient [*kodai*] and modern [*kindai*] periods. In the sense of being hereditary, their existence differed greatly to the officials who were merely assigned military duty in ancient times, and also to the modern career soldier.[6]

Toyotomi Hideyoshi (1537–98) attempted to segregate warriors from non-combatants through the introduction of decrees defining occupation. Separation of farming and military functions was intended to get warriors off the land and drive a wedge between fickle vassals and volatile peasants lest they combine forces to overthrow their superiors. Hideyoshi's diktats were not entirely unprecedented, nor were they obeyed particularly closely. Other daimyo, notably Oda Nobunaga (1534–82), also tried to consolidate occupational roles within the four spheres of agriculture, production, commerce, and military in their provinces. Although impossible to enforce to the letter, such measures did facilitate the rise of castle towns. Sustained by the surrounding farmlands, castle towns functioned as administrative, economic, and military bases for daimyo.

With Hideyoshi's nationwide Sword Hunt Edict (Katanagari-rei) of 1588, farmers were obliged to relinquish their weapons. Although the disarmament of non-warrior groups has been overstated in spite of considerable evidence to the contrary, it can at least be concluded that government-sanctioned attempts at occupational segregation sought to make martial training formally the sole prerogative and responsibility of samurai from the end of the sixteenth century.

PRAGMATISM CLOAKED IN ROMANTICISM

If we buy into the larger-than-life accounts of warrior feats as they are recorded in the war tales, warfare could be construed as a well-ordered and noble pursuit. However, the battles portrayed in popular literature through the centuries—such as the *Heike monogatari* (The tale of the Heike, early thirteenth century) and *Taiheiki* (Chronicle of great pacification, c. 1370)—are renowned for distorting the truth.

The typical battle scene portrayed in the war tales, although thoroughly bloody and violent, is regularly depicted as conforming to the following formula: mutual agreement on the time and place of battle; safe passage of emissaries as both armies face off; release of arrows to signal commencement; gradual advancement as increasingly accurate volleys of arrows are released; careful opponent selection, self-introduction, and combat at close quarters using bladed weapons; and guaranteed safety of noncombatants such as women and children.

Notwithstanding some genuine acts of gallantry and extraordinary valor, real battles rarely played out according to this blueprint, and the archetype of the romantic, glamorous, gentlemanly, and noble samurai is mostly farcical. Winning was everything. If underhanded methods were necessary to accomplish a gruesome task, so be it. One does not need to read between the lines in the old war tales to find accounts of blatant treachery, trickery, and what can essentially be described as far-from-gentlemanly deportment. Night attacks, hostage taking, broken promises, and espionage were commonplace and acceptable in pursuit of victory.

Interesting tenets of rational battle wisdom can be found in *Kōyō-gunkan*, a chronicle recording the exploits of the Takeda clan.[7] For instance, according to transcriptions of his conversations on military affairs, the daimyo Takeda Shingen (1521–73) maintained a policy of attempting to win only six or seven battles out of ten. Attempting to win all ten would result in heavy casualties. In this fashion, while he might succeed in winning each individual battle, he would eventually lose the war. As survival of the clan was at stake, the samurai's greatest weapon was a deep-rooted mastery of strategy in which the underlying ideology was pluck bolstered with cunning, deception, duplicity, and even retreat, if that was the smartest option.

To be sure, a samurai would forfeit his life in battle if trapped, and he believed his cherished reputation would live on. This is often interpreted as validating the strong bonds of loyalty between a lord and his stalwarts. The samurai ethos has even been described as "the moral of selfless dedication" (*kenshin-no-dōtoku*).[8] Allegiance to one's overlord was unquestionably an important component of warrior ethics, but there was also a very calculated side to this emotional connection. Although loyalty is championed as the adhesive for samurai hierarchical relationships (and also serves as one of the most moving themes in the literature), it could be adjusted according to convenience. History abounds with examples of warriors who readily changed allegiance if circumstances were better elsewhere. It was not until the Tokugawa period that the ideal of unfaltering loyalty to one lord became hereditary and resolute. But even then, scores of disenfranchised samurai (*rōnin*) roamed the countryside looking for new masters in the wake of some indiscretion, or even out of contempt for their reckless lord.

Ideally, however, the medieval warrior was expected to repay his lord's special favor (*go'on*) with servitude (*hōkō*). This meant the warrior could be mobilized for military campaigns and was expected to perform valiantly and to the death if required. Battle provided an opportunity for the warrior to showcase his prowess. If he triumphantly took a number of heads from the enemy (preferably those of rank), he would be rewarded. If he were killed, his death would be commended as a spirited demise. Although he would not benefit directly, he would die assured that his lord would continue bestowing favor on his descendants. The notion of loyalty to the death was most often pragmatism cloaked in romanticism rather than a pure human bond, as it is usually portrayed.

The intangible benefit gained from gallantry was the currency of honor. A deceased samurai's honor would be inherited by his sons and grandsons, and his feats of valor would be recounted as family lore. Conversely, if a samurai was deemed guilty of cowardice, his good name—and that of his ancestors and descendants—would be irreconcilably tarnished. While a European knight may have fought courageously to justify his posthumous place in God's Kingdom, the samurai, who was resigned to the belief that his destiny ultimately lay in one of the hundreds of Buddhist hells before eventual rebirth, fought boldly to ensure the perpetual prosperity of his family line.

A paradox existed with regard to a warrior's martial ability, especially in the Warring States period (1467–1568). The more valiant and skilled a warrior was at his craft, the more likely a rival daimyo army would be to try to poach him. Loyalty was a transferable bond. However, the provincial laws of this chaotic era urged warriors to remain faithful and true to their lords.

The onus was on a lord to lead his men in a manner that inspired fidelity. He was burdened with the delicate task of keeping his warriors in line while at the same time emboldening their independent spirit. Failure to keep the balance could result in dissension and the defection of his warriors, ultimately leading to the extinction of his entire house or clan.

"House codes" (*buke kakun*) were precepts recorded for posterity by warrior family patriarchs to guide the clan scion and collateral descendants in appropriate behavior. A common tenet in various house codes was advice not to stifle the individual attributes of each warrior and to reward valiant service. House codes also placed weight on training in military arts. This was the samurai's vehicle for accruing honor. Fighting was his vocation and weapons were the tools of his trade, but what did belonging to the profession-of-arms involve? Apart from actual combat experience, by what means did the samurai hone his military skills?

Early medieval period battles were primarily contested by mounted archers, foot soldiers with shock weapons such as *naginata* and pole arms, and archers on foot. According to Karl Friday, early medieval clashes "tended to be aggregates of lesser combats: melees of archery duels, and brawls between small groups, punctuated by general advances and retreats, and by volleys of arrows launched by bowmen on foot, protected by portable walls of shields."[9]

Starting in the Nanbokuchō period (1337–92) battle strategies shifted away from the skills of individual mounted warriors to tactics based on organized group attacks. This was concurrent with a change in the motivations for war, where the goal became the acquisition of vast territories. To achieve this objective, a warlord needed specialist platoons that could work as cogs in a highly regimented war machine.

Eiko Ikegami lists the following changes in the method of warfare by the late medieval period: "(1) the increased amount of manpower mobilized in battle; (2) strategic shift away from fights between individual champions, to planned collective movements of armies; (3) the rise of strong fortified castles; (4) the emergence of foot soldiers as a significant strike force; and (5) the introduction of firearms."[10]

The tools of warfare were also continually being adapted. In the case of swords, straight, double-edged blades (*tsurugi* or *chokutō*) were brought to Japan from China during the Kofun period (300–710). Curved single-edged *tachi* swords were fashioned beginning in the ninth century and became more stylized as forging methods advanced. Short swords with curved blades (*uchigatana*) appeared around the twelfth century; these were inserted with the blade upward through sashes at the waist as opposed to the now-customary *tachi*, which dangled blade-down at the side. Both the *tachi* and the *uchigatana* were generally worn together. By the fourteenth century *uchi-gatana* were lengthened and eventually replaced the *tachi* as the standard bladed weapon. The *uchi-gatana* was henceforth simply termed katana and used as both a cutting and a thrusting weapon. A shorter sword—the *wakizashi*—complemented the katana, and both were inserted through the waist sash to complete what became the standard two-sword set.

The adjustment in the preferred way of wearing swords—that is, on the left at the waist with the blade facing upward instead of dangling down—was concurrent with a transformation in the style of armor worn. Heian and Kamakura warriors donned grand but cumbersome sets of armor known as *ō-yoroi*. With moveable protective panels, *ō-yoroi* provided the mounted archer with ample protection as well as enough flexibility to release his arrows, but it hampered his maneuverability when he was forced to fight on foot.

From the late thirteenth through to the mid-fourteenth century, a gradual transition was made to a cheaper, lighter wraparound style of armor called *hara-maki*. This suggested a shift away from mounted archers as the dominant factor in battle. The simpler armor offered foot soldiers stability and the option of using longer weapons such as *yari* (spears) without impediment.

There was also a noticeable rise in the number of swordsmiths around this time. In the late Heian period, Shimokawa Ushio records references to 450 smiths, compared to 1,550 in the Kamakura period and 3,550 in the Muromachi period.[11] This is not to say that archers, both mounted and on foot, were obsolete just yet. In fact, records of battle wounds analyzed by historians Thomas Conlan, Suzuki Masaya, and others show that in the Nanbokuchō period arrow wounds were more prevalent than any other battle injury. Trawling through 175 documents, Suzuki found 554 identifiable injuries in addition to 44 fatalities. Of the injuries, 480 (86.6 percent) were caused by arrows; 46 (8.3 percent) by bladed weapons; 15 (2.6 percent) by rocks hurled by sling or rolled from hilltops or fortresses; and 6 (1.1 percent) by spears.[12] Suzuki postulated that even during the Nanbokuchō period sword use was much less a factor in battle than projectile weapons.

Some scholars suggest that the sword starred more in battle following the introduction of firearms in the sixteenth century. Musket balls, they argue, could penetrate even the heaviest armor. Given the futility of heavy armor against guns, less unwieldy suits were adopted for maneuverability, but this left warriors more susceptible to blades. Moreover, vulnerability to volleys of musket balls also incited warriors to engage at close quarters with more rapidity.[13] Although it is an interesting theory, it is negated by documentary evidence. Suzuki Masaya's research reveals that of the 584 wounds logged in war records from 1563 to 1600, 263 were inflicted by guns, 126 by arrows, 99 by spears, and 30 by rocks. Only forty warriors suffered sword lacerations, and twenty-six were felled by a combination of weapons.[14] On the basis of this analysis Suzuki contends that although swords were certainly brandished in the fray, they were more useful for removing the heads of fallen foe (*kubi-tori*) than engaging in actual combat. The heads were cleaned up and presented for inspection as "invoices for payment" for services rendered. Skullduggery was rampant, and samurai often picked through battlefields, claiming crowns off cadavers that they had not even felled.

Suzuki also points out the impracticality of the sword as a battlefield weapon, an observation based in part on the work of katana expert Naruse Sekanji (1888–1948). Blades bend easily when cuts are made with imprecise trajectory or angle, and the katana was known to snap when struck on the flat of the blade by spears or staffs. Of 1,681 blades that Naruse repaired personally, 30 percent had been smashed in duels and the remaining 70 percent were damaged through inadequate cleaning and care or reckless cutting practice (*tameshi-giri*).[15]

Although by no means a completely ineffectual weapon, the sword's practical value in a violent free-for-all was less than that of the sturdy, versatile, and easier-to-use *yari*. As a weapon for self-defense in the course of daily life, however, the sword was indispensable. Naruse's findings corroborate this: although they were easily damaged, swords were the weapon of choice in duels, executions, and assassinations.

Apart from its use in duels or other acts of violence committed beyond the field of battle, what elevated the sword to the emblematic position it attained among warriors? While the katana was irrefutably a lethal weapon, it retained an important and peculiar quality beyond being a simple implement of war. Starting with the first straight, double-edged iron swords imported from China that marked Japan's entry into the Iron Age, the shiny, hard quality of the metal created through advanced Chinese technology gave swords a perceived mystical quality. Although used as weapons, they also fulfilled an important symbolic function in religious ceremonies. In line with ancient Chinese ideals, swords were believed to contain magical powers with the ability to ward off evil.[16] After taking root in Japan, these beliefs matured into a distinctive Japanese ethos that came to feature prominently in national mythology.

A good example of this can be found in the tale of the eight-headed serpent Yamata-no-Orochi. The story describes capricious young Susanoo, who had been thrown out of Heaven for tricking his sister, the sun goddess Amaterasu Ōmikami. He then recovers a mythical sword from the tail of an eight-headed serpent and presents it to her as an act of placation. Generations later, the same sword is presented for protection to the great warrior Yamato Takeru by his aunt, Yamato-hime of the Ise Shrine. When he is lured into an open field by a treacherous warlord who then sets the grass on fire, Yamato Takeru uses the sword to cut the grass and stop the spread of flames, discovering in the process that the weapon is magical. After exacting revenge, he names the blade Kusanagi-no-Tsurugi (literally "grass-cutting sword").

Today the sword is housed in the Atsuta Shrine as one of the Three Sacred Treasures that make up the imperial regalia, along with a mirror (*yata-no-kagami*) and the *magatama* bead. In other words, the sword became symbolic of imperial authority.

The mythological associations and belief in certain magical qualities of swords are manifest in a curious samurai custom. The term *meitō* refers to a sword of special significance. A sword was recognized as extraordinary if it had been made by a legendary smith, had an awe-inspiring cutting quality, or belonged to a historical figure. Although an inanimate object, a *meitō* would be given a name.

Records for appraising the value of swords were kept from as early as the reign of Ashikaga Yoshimasa (1436–90), the eighth shogun of the Muromachi period. It can be inferred that at this time swords were emblematic of their owner's authority as well as important items of exchange. In addition to deriving narcissistic satisfaction from owning a *meitō,* owners of swords of worth used them as a form of currency. Warriors fought for prizes. Ideally, they would receive parcels of land from their lord as a reward for heroism, but they could also be rewarded with money or valuable artifacts such as antique tea utensils or a remarkable sword.[17]

Swords were not the primary frontline weapon. Other than for the ignoble task of headhunting, they were used only as sidearms to supplement principal battlefield armaments, namely missile weapons such as arrows—and later musket balls—and long, sturdy thrusting weapons such as *yari*. However, off the battlefield was a different matter, where the sword proved its worth in brawls, duels, and other homicidal encounters.

THE AESTHETICIZATION OF VIOLENCE

What, then, was the impetus behind the rise of specialist martial art schools that tended to focus on swordsmanship from as early as the late fourteenth and fifteenth centuries? Karl Friday maintains that the creation of styles or schools of martial arts (*ryūha*) "constituted a new phenomenon—a derivative, not a linear improvement, of earlier, more prosaic military training."[18] The Muromachi period was key in terms of samurai aesthetic development, so it should come as no surprise that the art of swordsmanship was inspired by the systematization of other, more advanced, art forms.

What political forces facilitated martial aestheticization in the Muromachi period? In 1333, after a period of exile for a plot to overthrow the weakening Kamakura shogunate in 1324, the emperor Go-Daigo (1288–1339) returned to Kyoto more determined than ever to restore imperial power. His objective was realized with the aid of renegade shogunate generals Ashikaga Takauji (1305–58) and Nitta Yoshisada (1301–38). This led to Go-Daigo's Kemmu Restoration (1333–36), but the alliance between these men was short-lived, ending when Yoshisada joined forces with Go-Daigo to overthrow Takauji's authority. Go-Daigo then fled to Yoshino (Nara) and established the Southern Court in 1337, while Takauji, who backed the north, formed the Muromachi shogunate (1338–1573) in Kyoto. This started a war of legitimacy between the Northern and Southern Courts that lasted from 1337 to 1392.

Takauji established his regime in Kyoto rather than in Kamakura to the east to keep tabs on the *kuge* political machinations and to circumvent any potential uprising. This move generated a massive influx of samurai from the provinces into the capital, where they rapidly began to influence political and cultural life. As they replaced nobles in positions of authority, they felt pressure to behave in an appropriate fashion and break away from the rustic mannerisms that had earned them the scorn of refined aristocrats.

Samurai concern for propriety is evident in two trends in the Muromachi period: the proliferation of house codes (*buke kakun*); and the circulation of texts outlining unique samurai ceremonies, rules and customs (*buke kojitsu*)—adapted from the protocols of the ancient imperial court (*yūsoku kojitsu*).

Warriors started developing their own forms of etiquette in the Kamakura period. At the onset of the Muromachi period, the study of cultural and ceremonial standards set by the court took on more urgency among the warrior subculture as they asserted their cultural equality and political superiority. There were protocols for court ceremonies, religious rituals, appropriate attire, daily interactions, and the treatment and use of arms and armor, especially with regard to archery. The two main authorities that ordained *kojitsu* norms for samurai were the Ogasawara and the Ise families.

House codes of the Muromachi period exhibit a newfound concern for balancing martial aptitude with refinement in the genteel arts and civility; namely an equilibrium between *bu* (military arts) and *bun* (civil arts and letters). It was no longer appropriate for warriors to be seen as brawny, bucolic bumpkins with no sense of decorum or edification. They needed to be worthy rulers by virtue of both intellect and violence, when necessary. Samurai had long felt culturally inferior to the nobles, and now they sought to cover themselves with a mantle of equality, or even to assert their superiority.

There are a number of well-known house codes from this period, such as *Chikubasho* (Selected precepts for young generations, ca. 1383) by Shiba Yoshimasa (1350–1410) and *Imagawa ryōshin seishi* (The regulations of Imagawa Ryōshun) by Imagawa Ryōshun (also known as Sadayo, 1325–1420). They stood the test of time and were still studied enthusiastically, with a sense of nostalgia, by warriors of the Tokugawa era. Apart from military strategy, these house codes offered meticulous advice on proper social deportment, such as where to sit at a banquet and how to exchange sake cups, and guidance on cleaning, travel etiquette, and manner of speech.

The *buke kojitsu* texts were more detailed with regard to etiquette and applied to all warriors, whereas the *kakun* were more specific and applied only to the warriors of a particular family or clan. Primarily written by the head of a clan to ensure that his sons or retainers did not incur shame in their persnickety honor-driven community, the articles accentuated the right mindset rather than just the right form.

Ashikaga Takauji wrote a celebrated set of house rules—*Takauji-kyō goisho* (Testament of lord Takauji). The thirteenth article demonstrates the value placed on *bunbu-ryōdō* (the two ways of the civil and martial arts). "*Bu* and *bun* are like two wheels of a cart. If one wheel is missing, the cart will not move."[19] Living up to the ideal of *bunbu-ryōdō* espoused in the house codes, it should be pointed out, was primarily the responsibility of the upper echelons of warrior society. In his *kakun* of 1412, Imagawa Ryōshun advised, "It is natural that the samurai learns the ways of war, and applies himself to the acquisition of the basic fighting skills needed for his occupation. . . . Without applying oneself to study [*bun*], however, it is impossible to be a worthy ruler."[20]

Another *tour de force* in *kakun*, Shiba Yoshimasa's *Chikubasho,* also admonishes the ruling class to pay attention to propriety and self-cultivation. "Have a mind to improve one step at a time, and take care in speech so as not to be thought a fool by others."[21] "All things should be done with single-minded intent. . . . Warriors must have a calm mind, and the ability to understand the measure of other people. This is crucial to success in military matters."[22] With regard to balance in the military and civil arts, the code states, "In this world, honor and reputation are valued above all else. As a man is able to enhance his standing by virtue of competence in the arts, he should try to excel in these too, irrespective of whether he has instinctive talent or not. . . . Naturally, a warrior should be skilled in using the bow and arrow in such practices as *mato, kasagake,* and *inu ou mono.*"[23]

Yoshimasa states the importance of being au fait with arts such as linked verse and music in addition to the military arts. He alludes to military training with the bow and horse, but swordsmanship was also essential for self-defense in the course of daily activities. This is mentioned in the *Yoshisada-ki* (Records of Nitta Yoshisada), around the first half of the fourteenth century.

> Our house records admonish that when you walk along the road and see someone, pass by with an arrow fixed to your bow, or with your hand on the long sword's hilt. These are customs of the past. Our times are not that hard and these [specific] customs are outdated and ridiculous, but in your heart you should treat every person [you meet in the street] as your enemy. Even if you do not reveal this state of alertness in your outward appearance, people will certainly know it.[24]

The elevation of swordsmanship into an art coincides with samurai involvement in other traditional artistic disciplines (*geidō*), which included calligraphy and painting (*shodō*), theater (Noh), flower arrangement (*kadō*), tea ceremony (*sadō*), dance (*mai*), and various forms of poetry (such as *renga* and *waka*). These civil arts inspired the aesthetic development of swordsmanship. Swordsmanship was practical but could also be theatrical, and it was easily adapted to fit the philosophies being embraced in performing arts like Noh. Like masters of other arts, a virtuoso in the art of swordsmanship stood to gain high social standing and patronage and hence honor, employment, and wealth.

The word *geidō* first appeared in *Kyoraika* (1433), a famous treatise by the renowned Noh master Zeami (1363–1443). He considered Noh and the other arts to be "ways" (*michi* or *dō*) for seeking perfection. The suffix -*dō* had been attached to the names of various occupations from before the Heian period, but it simply designated the specialization in, and transmission of, specific skills without necessarily containing the spiritual connotations implied in the term *geidō*.

Geidō became permeated with deeply spiritual meaning, and prodigies who reached a certain level of mastery would receive accolades and patronage from members of high society. To enhance and maintain their prestige, the masters of these arts codified their techniques and arcane knowledge (*hiden*) into systems and conveyed it only to select disciples. Furtiveness about the hidden *hiden* teachings gave the master an air of mystique as well as an aura of cultural authority. Disciples' reputations also benefited through association with the exclusive culture club.

Although practical combat application and effectiveness were always considerations in the development of the martial arts, infatuation with the artistic excellence of technique was clearly an important factor in the genesis of *ryūha*. The martial arts were, as Friday contends, an "abstraction of military science, not merely an application of it."[25] Furthermore, the sword, with its long history entrenched in Japan's ancient myths, ties to mysticism, and exterior beauty, was the perfect weapon for an art that went beyond just combat concerns. A fixation with questions of life and death that were stimulated through the experience of war set swordsmanship and its secrets apart from all of the other *geidō*.

THE GENESIS OF HOLISTIC MARTIAL ART SCHOOLS

The medieval battlefields of Japan were not simply settings for murderous intent; the reality was far more complicated. As historian Futaki Ken'ichi observed, "It was a world both religious and artistic in nature, where men demonstrated their physical and spiritual prowess bolstered by resourcefulness and strategy, and ultimately decided by the will of heaven."[26] Superstition, divination, and religious beliefs played just as important a role in the way battle was waged as the martial skills of the individual warriors and the military tactics of the commander.

Although certain traditions of archery and horsemanship, such as the Ogasawara school, had already established well-defined protocols during the Kamakura period, it is difficult to identify organized schools of swordsmanship before the fourteenth century. What sources can be found are generally scant and open to conjecture. The earliest sword styles were probably developed as family affairs, passed on from father to son but not divulged to outsiders.

There are some descriptions in the old war tales of what appear to be distinctive styles of swordsmanship with specified techniques. For example, the *Heike monogatari* depicts the exploits of the warrior-monk Jōmyō Meishū. In the section titled "Battle on the Bridge," this fearsome fighter kills twelve men and wounds eleven others with twenty-four arrows. He then battles on with his *naginata,* which snaps after he engages his sixth enemy. Finally, he pulls out his sword as a last resort: "Hard-pressed by the enemy host, he slashed in every direction, using the zigzag, interlacing, crosswise, dragonfly reverse, and waterwheel maneuvers. After cutting down eight men on the spot, he struck the helmet top of a ninth so hard that the blade snapped at the hilt rivet, slipped loose, and splashed into the river. Then he fought on desperately with a dirk as his sole resource."[27]

Although the *Heike monogatari,* which is thought to have been written sometime in the early thirteenth century, predates the earliest known schools of swordsmanship, such as the Kage-ryū or the Nen-ryū, passages such as this one indicate the existence of distinctive sword techniques. It also suggests that martial systems that included an array of weaponry can be traced back to the twelfth century, although they were probably comparatively basic at this time. During the Muromachi period, more sophisticated and comprehensive martial systems emerged, but at this early point in history the profession of arms was still mostly taught within the confines of families or clans.

The kind of training warriors engaged in varied depending on the period, and even their rank. For example, when mounted archery was considered the supreme form of combat during the Kamakura period, elite warriors would hone their skills through *yabusame, inu ou mono,* and *kasagake.*[28] Lower-ranked warriors practiced foot archery and fighting with weapons such as glaives and polearms. However, regardless of his specialty, a warrior needed to be familiar with a variety of different weapons. When his arrows ran out, he would use his sword or *naginata;* when that broke, he would use his dirk or resort to barehanded grappling and even biting. Dealing with adversaries who were equipped with various weapons required that a warrior have at least a fundamental understanding of how they were utilized in order to defend himself against them.

Numerous political, social, cultural, and military factors eventually led to the rise of specialist schools of swordsmanship, and certain criteria were indispensable to ensure perpetuation. The weak hold the Ashikaga shogunate had on its vassals at the middle of the Muromachi period gave rise to powerful military rivals, militant monasteries, and bands of riotous outlaws. Japan was a perilous place in which to live at the time, and not just for warriors. Peasants were motivated to learn martial skills for the sake of self-preservation, and as the scale of war increased they were increasingly press-ganged into the swelling daimyo armies on a seasonal basis and needed training.

Itinerant warriors sought to catch the eyes of daimyo willing to secure their services, as either mercenaries or instructors for their part-time peasant armies. Also, as horses were being used proportionally less in the large, regimented battles that were waged in the late medieval period, more urgency was placed on developing infantry tactics and close-quarter combat skills. Systemized martial curricula became necessary to facilitate military instruction, with the added ingredient of *hiden* power for good measure. I have already outlined the current theory that the sword was only a secondary weapon in battle. All the same, sword usage became more "cutting-edge" through combat experience, and some warriors began to formulate their own styles of sword work. This led to the rise of those swordsmen who established their own sword art schools and reaped the benefits as combat celebrities.

Karl Friday maintains that swordsmen, even during the turbulent Sengoku era (sixteenth century), "had more in common with Olympic marksmanship competitors—training with specialized weapons to develop esoteric levels of skill under particularized conditions—than with Marine riflemen."[29] I tend to agree with this analogy at one level: martial artistry and soldiery required different skills. Then again, the swordsman was a soldier as well as a martial artist and, depending on the circumstances, there was always going to be a degree of overlap in core skills and mindset, even if the actual combat techniques were poles apart.

A successful martial artist needed a proven record in pitched battle; the reputation he garnered in war augmented the legitimacy of his art. It should also be added that a number of martial *ryūha* were based more on armored soldiery than naked-blade dueling, or at least included techniques that took into account the differences between "art" and "war." The illustration of a medieval battleground in figure 5 shows warriors engaged in a frenzied free-for-all at close quarters. It is hard to imagine combatants being too concerned with aesthetic matters of beauty in form as they cut and thrust at each other for all their worth. Note the severed head—an apparent trophy—at the lower left.

The prototypical *ryūha* of swordsmanship started evolving around the fourteenth and fifteenth centuries. The founders drew inspiration from artistic concepts centering on ideals of perfection, infused with instinctive discernment gleaned from thrashing about in battle. The juxtaposition of aesthetic and religious paradigms with empirical knowledge is what gave each of these schools their signature qualities.

Not just any warrior could create a school on a whim. He needed combat experience and a reputation for indomitability. Charisma and proven techni-

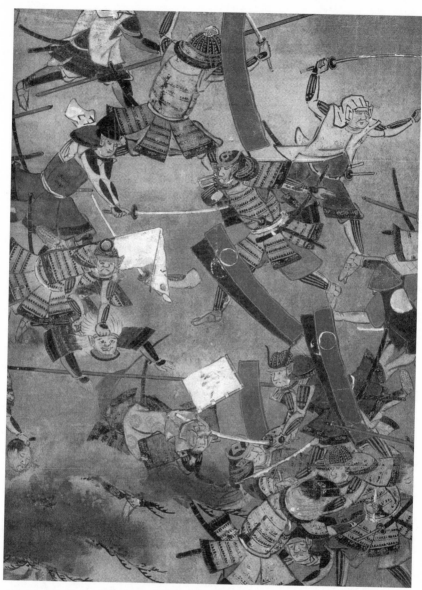

FIGURE 5. The brutality of the medieval battlefield, shown in this depiction of a battle between Uesugi Kenshin and Takeda Shingen at Kawanakajima in the mid-1500s. (Courtesy of Bunkasha International)

cal proficiency were requisite for attracting students. Furthermore, the techniques developed by the progenitor (*ryūso*) had to be learnable. Additionally, a system for imparting the knowledge to disciples was necessary to ensure continuity. The kanji for *ryū* means to flow or cascade, and in the context of the arts it inferred the flow of knowledge from one generation to the next.

Instruction would typically involve one-on-one techniques taught using predetermined patterns of movements (kata), oral teachings (*kuden*), and, later on in the Tokugawa period, written teachings (*densho*) in the form of cryptic handwritten scrolls that transmitted the higher principles of the school. These scrolls were often purposefully vague to safeguard "trade secrets" from outsiders.

Fear greatly weakens combat competence. A warrior who does not quiver in the face of death or injury is a formidable foe indeed. Having had experience fighting to the death, the founders of *ryūha* in the medieval period incorporated into their curricula the psychological lessons they had learned. Typically, the highest level of *hiden* teachings was simultaneously esoteric and pragmatic. Ideally, *hiden* held the key to the "holy grail" of combat—a superlative combination of body and mind, attained by transcending concerns for life and death, that was believed to make the warrior unassailable. These teachings were jealously guarded by adherents of the *ryūha*.

As I will expand upon in the following chapter, during the Tokugawa period the content of *ryūha* doctrines became increasingly esoteric and mystical, and new kata were being invented at a prolific rate. More than anything, it was kata that represented the lifeblood of the *ryūha* throughout the history of martial arts. Synergy of body and mind were taught through kata, which were usually performed in pairs. Martial arts in China and Korea also incorporated kata training, but the exercises were mainly performed alone. Through practicing kata with a partner, a Japanese warrior was able to learn the significance of timing and distance (*maai*), breathing (*kokyū*), apposite attacking opportunities, and posture, as well as to develop his mental strength.

The forms and process for learning kata are different in each tradition. However, one concept is applied to all of the traditional Japanese arts, not just martial: *shu-ha-ri* (maintain-break-separate). Scrolls of the Ono-ha Ittō-ryū, a traditional and highly influential school of swordsmanship during the Tokugawa period, explain that a student must follow three steps to learn martial techniques. First, the teachings of a master must be strictly adhered to without deviation (*shu*). Then, after the student has absorbed everything he can from his master, he breaks the ideas down to try to acquire a higher understanding of the principles (*ha*). Last, after testing and enhancing his basic knowledge, the warrior aims to acquire an even deeper understanding of the teachings, one that is in fact so profound that he essentially creates his own path (*ri*).[30]

There are other, similar terms that describe the process of learning the basic moves, improving on them, and finally achieving a transcendent state in which the techniques become an expression of the warrior's very being, and his being becomes an expression of the techniques. This ultimate state of "martial enlightenment" occurs supposedly when a new *ryūha* is born. It represents a perfect union of technique and mind, reinforced by a spiritual dogma and schematized into a curriculum to pass on to disciples.

Kata can be defined as a type of "death ritual," configured as prearranged mock combat that provides an encoded scheme for technical improvement and spiritual growth through flirting with mortality. In almost all kata, one adept—usually the senior one—is allegorically killed, with the blade stopping just millimeters from a vital spot as the symbolic death blow is delivered. In this role-play of death, the junior adept aspires to seamlessly unify mind, technique, and precision of execution. The senior "sacrifices" himself to teach his partner the correct instant and method for capitalizing on physical and psychological weakness, while contemplating the "virtual reality" of his own demise.

Practicing each different kata over and over, the samurai trained his mind to enter what is commonly referred to now as "the zone," and he programed his body to react instinctively to myriad technical possibilities, rising above concerns for self-preservation. Training was far more than a physical pursuit; it was a kind of religious exercise encapsulated in the notion of *shugyō* (ascetic training)—a term utilized in the worlds of both samurai and Buddhist monks that is still used today to denote the study of modern martial arts as opposed to purely athletic training.

Karl Friday contends that the martial arts were "fundamentally secular arts in which pietistic-sounding locutions often mask entirely down-to-earth pieces of information."[31] Undeniably, the use of Shinto, Buddhist, Taoist, and Confucian terms and constructs to give techniques an air of divine infallibility was commonplace, but the religious aspect of martial arts cannot be written off so easily. Cultural anthropologist Clifford Geertz formulated a definition for religion that is, I believe, wholly applicable to martial art *ryūha* and the warriors who studied in them. According to Geertz, a religion is: "(1) A system of symbols which acts to (2) establish powerful, pervasive, and long lasting moods and motivations in men by (3) formulating conceptions of a general order of existence and (4) clothing these conceptions with such an aura of factuality that (5) the moods and motivations seem uniquely realistic."[32] My point here is that almost all the martial *ryūha* that developed in the late medieval period orbited around the ideological crux of life and death. The emphasis on highly symbolic rituals and divinely inspired techniques, combined with a medley of magical and polytheistic beliefs, sustained warriors in their quest for technical excellence and spiritual enlightenment. Furthermore, idiosyncratic *hiden* teachings inculcated in the adept a comprehension of cosmic principles of universal order and his transient existence. It also encouraged a connection with mythical tradition, which in turn bestowed on the disciple an air of uniqueness and supreme confidence. Although warriors typically adhered to a specific religious affiliation, such as one of the various sects of Buddhism, the martial *ryūha* was akin to a religious cult in its own right.

The warrior trained "religiously" to the extent that the techniques became a part of his very being, helping him to reach a transcendent state of selflessness that came to be defined with various terms of Buddhist origin such as *muga* (no-self) or *mushin* (no-mind). It should also be pointed out that although Zen Buddhism was an important element in many schools, it was not *the* defining influence. For sure, scores of warriors were attracted to Zen ideals and practiced the religion as a way to detach from mundane concerns and accept impermanency. As Peter Haskel eloquently expressed, Zen's attractiveness to martial artists was in "its stress on directness and instantaneousness of response, on immediately 'sizing up' others' capabilities; and its insistence on flexibility, on meeting each situation free of preconceptions and expectations, even in the face of death."[33]

Many Zen-based terms are prevalent in the classical schools of swordsmanship and the lexicon of modern budo. In most cases, however, the terms were simply borrowed and adapted to the context of martial arts. Esoteric forms of Buddhism, Taoism, Confucianism, Shinto, and indigenous regional folk beliefs are all featured, to varying degrees and forms, in the eclectic mix of martial philosophy. This is illustrative of Japan's long tradition of polytheistic, syncretic religious culture.

THE "THREE GREAT SCHOOLS" OF SWORDSMANSHIP

Three main traditions provided the core teachings for hundreds of offshoot schools: the Tenshinshō-den Katori Shintō-ryū (Direct and correct teachings from the deity of the Katori Shrine), the Nen-ryū (School of perception), and the Kage-ryū (Shadow school). In particular, the regions of Kashima and Katori were central to the development of the sword arts since ancient times.[34] Kashima-no-Tachi (the Sword [style] of Kashima) is a hallowed tradition that was established by Kuninazu-no-Mahito, a priestly celebrant at the Kashima Shrine. After receiving divine inspiration from the deity Takemikazuchi-no-Mikoto, he transformed the sword rituals for purification ceremonies into combat techniques. There are various hypotheses about when Kuninazu-no-Mahito lived, but the standard theory indicates that it was sometime in the seventh century. He was guided by the deity to the secret technique known as *hitotsu-no-tachi* (the foremost sword) or *shinmyō-ken* (the divinely inspired sword), which became the foundation technique for his clan-based tradition.

Beginning during the reign of Emperor Sutoku, from 1123 to 1142, Kashima-no-Tachi (the Sword of Kashima) was referred to as Kashima Shichi-ryū (seven schools of Kashima), suggestive of the seven families that were closely associated with the Kashima Shrine and the secret teachings passed on by Kuninazu-no-Mahito. At some stage during the twelfth and fourteenth centuries, Kashima-no-Tachi was divided into the two categories of Jōko-ryū (ancient-period style) and the Chūko-ryū (middle-period style). The latter was revised by Tsukahara Bokuden (1489–1571), a descendent of the Yoshikawa family of Kashima, into the Shintō-ryū around the beginning of the sixteenth century.

Table 3 shows how Tokugawa-period scholars categorized the various schools. Given the close geographical proximity of Katori and Kashima, sword traditions from these regions were usually considered to be principally the same in terms of origin, or at least with significant overlap among their progenitors. The Tenshinshō-den Katori Shintō-ryū is often abbreviated to the Katori-ryū or even Shintō-ryū, which can cause confusion with the Shintō-ryū (which is written with different characters) created by Tsukahara Bokuden.

The origins of most of these early traditions are unclear and shrouded in mythical claims alluding to divine inspiration. For example, the lore of the Tenshinshō-den Katori Shintō-ryū, which is considered one of the oldest extant schools of swordsmanship in Japan, has it that at the age of sixty, founder Iizasa Chōisai (1387–1488) endured a harsh one-thousand-day training regime of fasting and prayer in the Katori Shrine. One night the shrine deity, Futsunushi-no-Kami, appeared to him as a small boy standing on top

TABLE 3 Japan's first schools of swordsmanship, as defined by Tokugawa-period scholars

Name of school	Description
Tenshinshō-den Katori	The Tenshinshō-den Katori Shintō-ryū was founded by Iizasa Chōisai (1387–1488). Foremost offshoots from this school include the Bokuden-ryū (Shintō-ryū) and the Arima-ryū.
Shintō-ryū	The Kashima Shin-ryū was founded by Matsumoto Bizen-no-Kami (dates unknown).
Kashima Shin-ryū	According to some sources, Iizasa Chōisai was Matsumoto's teacher. Others, however, indicate that Tsukahara Bokuden was actually Matsumoto's student instead of Iizasa Chōisai's. Clearly, there was considerable overlap in the earliest schools, especially as they originated in the same locality.
Nen-ryū	Created by the monk Jion (1351–?).
Chūjō-ryū	The Chūjō school traces its origins back to the monk Jion. Related splinter schools include Toda-ryū and the well-known Ittō-ryū.
Kage-ryū	Formed by Aisu Ikōsai (1452–1538), the Kage-ryū line of schools became increasingly influential in the Tokugawa period with the shogunate's patronage of the Yagyū branch of Kamiizumi Ise-no-Kami's Shinkage-ryū (New shadow school).
Kashima Shichi-ryū (Seven Schools of Kashima; also referred to as the Seven Schools of Kantō) 1. Kashima 2. Katori 3. Honshin-ryū 4. Bokuden-ryū 5. Shintō-ryū 6. Yamato-ryū 7. Ryōi-ryū	Scholars in the Tokugawa period devised this classification of schools to represent the main lines that evolved in the eastern provinces.
Kyō Hachi-ryū (Eight Schools of Kyoto) 1. Kiichi-ryū 2. Yoshitsune-ryū 3. Masakado-ryū 4. Kurama-ryū 5. Suwa-ryū 6. Kyō-ryū 7. Yoshioka-ryū 8. Hōgan-ryū	The existence of these schools is difficult to verify. They were allegedly offshoots of martial arts taught to eight monks by Kiichi Hōgan and are traditionally associated with Kyoto and the Kuramadera Temple.

of a plum tree and divulged secrets of strategy, stating, "Thou shalt be the master of all swordsmanship under the sun."[35] It was on the basis of these divine teachings that he formed his school.

Accounts of the Tenshinshō-den Katori Shintō-ryū, Nen-ryū, and Kage-ryū, as well as the stories of their respective progenitors, are found in Hinatsu Shigetaka's (1660–1731) 1716 treatise *Honchō bugei shōden* (Brief accounts of our country's military arts). This is arguably the most important work recording the history of classical schools of swordsmanship, archery, and other martial arts. Subsequent works dealing with the same topic, such as Mikami Genryū's *Gekken sōdan* (A collection of stories on swordsmanship, 1790), *Bujutsu keifu-ryaku* (Martial school genealogies, author unknown, 1790), and *Bujutsu ryūso-roku* (Record of martial school heads, author unknown, 1843) rely heavily on the information chronicled by Hinatsu. Unfortunately, much of the information in Hinatsu's work is based on conjecture and is difficult, if not impossible, for modern scholars to verify. However, his and other texts are still useful for understanding how samurai themselves interpreted the roots of their martial culture.

The description of the origins of the Tenshinshō-den Katori Shintō-ryū starts by stating that Iizasa Chōisai was born in a small village called Iizasa located in the Katori district of Shimōsa (now Chiba Prefecture). He later relocated to the nearby village of Yamazaki, where he became mesmerized by the arts of the sword and spear and quickly proved to have outstanding talent in using them. Hinatsu casts him as being "the progenitor of sword and spear arts in the middle period."[36]

Aisu Ikō (1452–1538) was the founder of the Kage-ryū (Shadow school). Little is known about him, but it is thought that his family resided in Ise, and he was engaged in piracy—an occupation that took him as far as Korea, China, and the Ryūkyū islands. Where and from whom he learned swordsmanship is the cause of much speculation, but it is plausible that his style was influenced by his sojourns in China.

In 1487, his vessel was shipwrecked off the coast of Kyushu, but he managed to make his way to shore, where he found the Udo Daigongen Shrine. Grateful to be alive, he abandoned his life at sea and spent thirty-seven days praying and fasting at the shrine. A "monkey-like apparition" appeared before him and communicated the higher secrets of combat. (One document, *Hirasawa-ke denki*, written by Ikō's descendent, Hirasawa Mondo Michiari, claims that the deity appeared as a spider.) This shrine deity instructed him to duel with a local warrior named Sumiyoshi. Empowered by his newfound knowledge, Ikō defeated his foe and became famous as he traveled throughout the land testing his skills. His illustrious student Kamiizumi Ise-no-Kami (1508–77)[37] created the Shinkage-ryū (New shadow school), which came to great prominence in the Tokugawa period through Yagyū Muneyoshi and his son Munenori.

Nen Ami Jion (c. 1350–c. 1408), formerly known as Sōma Shirō, was the founder of the Nen-ryū. Again, details of his career are sketchy and often conflicting. He was still a child when his father—a celebrated retainer of Nitta Yoshisada (1301–38)—was assassinated. His wet nurse cared for him until he was seven years old, and then he was placed in the care of a Buddhist priest at Yugōji Temple, where he became a monk and was conferred the Buddhist name Nen Ami Jion.

At age ten he transferred to the Kuramadera Temple in Kyoto, where he commenced his study of the martial arts, becoming adroit at using an assortment of weapons. He then moved to the Jufukuji Temple in Kamakura, where a priest named Eiyū taught him the highest secrets of swordsmanship. In Kyushu he received divine teachings from the Buddhist deity Marishiten via a supernatural creature known as a *tengu* while engaged in austere training at the Anryakuji Temple. These teachings formed the basis of the Nen-ryū. Other stories suggest he avenged his father's murder before taking Buddhist vows.

Chūjō Hyōgo (?–1384), one of Jion's students, created the third significant style of swordsmanship of the fourteenth century, the Chūjō-ryū. This tradition eventually gave rise to the Ittō-ryū (School of one-sword), one of the most distinguished traditions of swordsmanship in the Tokugawa period and considered to be one of the main guiding influences on the techniques and philosophy of modern kendo.

According to Hinatsu, Chūjō Hyōgo lived in Kamakura and was a parishioner of the Jufukuji Temple. He studied under Jion, who had lived in the temple for many years, and became a master of the inner secrets of sword and spear combat.

Unfortunately, there is little that can be confirmed as factual with regard to the original *ryūha*. We can only piece together tidbits of information and try to avoid the temptation of believing all that has been written by later generations of adherents. Followers were devout believers in the divine geneses of their schools and understandably had (and still have) a tendency to embellish history. Tradition was continually invented to enhance the reputation and perceived potency of a school's wisdom. These invented traditions

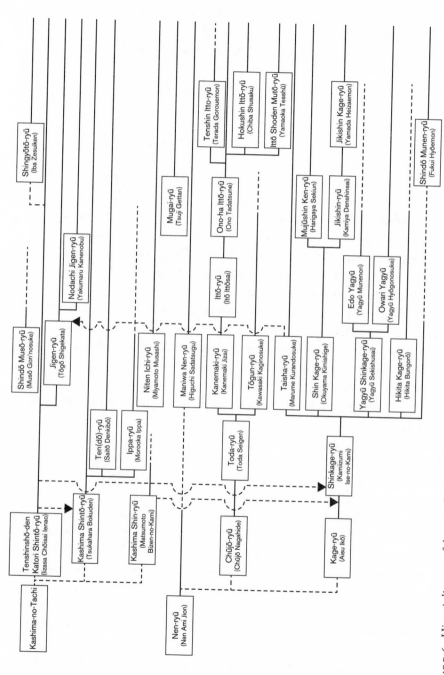

FIGURE 6. Historic lineages of the main *kenjutsu* schools. Names of the progenitors or heirs of each tradition are included in parentheses. Please note that Japanese names changed with age or status, and differ slightly depending on the historical document being referred to.

were elaborated on further over subsequent generations in offshoot schools, which developed increasing technical and spiritual sophistication.

Figure 6 outlines the main *ryū* introduced here, along with some of the splinter schools that are related to them. Although it merely scratches the surface, and some aspects are impossible to verify, it provides a visual representation of how martial schools developed and were interrelated.

NONPAREIL SWORD MASTERS

By the mid to late sixteenth century, daimyo actively pursued noteworthy instructors to train them and their men in swordsmanship. Individual warriors also sought skilled teachers to guide them to new levels of martial prowess and greater employment opportunities. This was a time when samurai roamed the countryside on ascetic martial pilgrimages for months or years at a time, engaging not only in duels but also in austere physical and spiritual training in shrine and temple precincts.

Of the three main source schools mentioned above (Tenshinshō-den Katori Shintō-ryū, Kage-ryū, and Nen-ryū), it was the second and third generations of adherents who were able to take advantage of the growing esteem that came with being a master of the sword. After absorbing the celestial knowledge of the founders, enlightened disciples crafted even more refined philosophical frameworks to supplement the evolving body of techniques.

The names of many of the distinguished swordsmen involved in this evolutionary process live on in the lore of modern kendo. Numerous schools sprang from the initial three main source *ryūha* and other lesser-known systems. I will restrict the following brief commentary to the most celebrated traditions of which the pith is still evident in modern kendo.

By founding the Shinkage-ryū, Kamiizumi Ise-no-Kami gained cult status throughout Japan.[38] He is thought to have studied under Aisu Ikō's son Koshichirō and possibly even Aisu Ikō himself. He also reputedly received instruction from other preeminent swordsmen of the time, including Matsumoto (Sugimoto) Bizen-no-Kami, Tsukahara Bokuden, Jion, and Iizasa Chōisai. Even if this was not the case, his father likely did, and so in one way or another he was versed in all of the main styles of the day.

According to the *Honchō bugei shōden,* Kamiizumi was matchless in martial skill. Having attained the uppermost level of mastery in the Kage-ryū, probably around 1540, he created his own school, which he named the Shinkage-ryū.

Kamiizumi had a dozen or so students, most of whom went on to make names for themselves and start their own schools. Among them, Hikita Bungorō (1537–1606), Marume Kurandonosuke (1540–1629), and Yagyū Tajima-no-Kami Muneyoshi (also known as Munetoshi or Sekishūsai, 1527–1606) were particularly influential. For example, Hikita Bungorō, who is said to have been Kamiizumi's nephew, was employed by the entourage of Toyotomi Hidetsugu (1568–95) and was lavished with gifts in appreciation of his skill.

Marume Kurandonosuke began his martial pilgrimage at age seventeen. During a chance meeting with Kamiizumi, he challenged the legendary warrior to a duel. Marume was soundly defeated, but his life was spared because Kamiizumi insisted on using bamboo swords (*fukuro-shinai*) instead of potentially lethal wooden swords or live blades. Although a seasoned warrior, Kamiizumi was reputedly somewhat of a pacifist, and he preferred not to slaughter his challengers if possible. The fortunate Marume immediately became Kamiizumi's disciple, and after absorbing all his secret knowledge, plus that of twenty or so other *ryūha* throughout his distinguished career, he formed the Taisha-ryū.

Yagyū Muneyoshi, yet another celebrated student of Kamiizumi's, was vastly experienced in combat and indirectly commanded considerable political sway in his later years. Kamiizumi was not his only teacher; he studied under other notable swordsmen such as Tsukahara Bokuden and Itō Ittōsai (1560?–1653?). His martial talents were evident from a young age. According to Hinatsu, "Yagyū Tajima-no-Kami Muneyoshi was born in the Yagyū village in Yamato. His family had lived in the region for generations. . . . In his youth, Muneyoshi was keen on the arts of the sword and spear. . . . Once, Kamiizumi Ise-no-Kami visited the Yagyū village escorted by his students Jingo Izu-no-Kami and Hikita Bungorō. Without delay, Muneyoshi asked the master to teach him swordsmanship, to which Kamiizumi agreed and taught him the art."[39]

Apparently, Muneyoshi was trounced in a bout with Hikita Bungorō and then by Kamiizumi himself. Kamiizumi then left the village for a period of time on other business, but Hikita remained in his stead. When Kamiizumi returned to check the progress of his new understudy he was apparently pleased with the boy's improvement: "He commended his proficiency, saying, 'Muneyoshi's swordsmanship has arrived at the apex. He has accessed the essence of the Shinkage style. His skill in swordsmanship is greater than my own.'[40] After receiving certification for his mastery after only two years, Muneyoshi was invited to serve the shogun, Ashikaga Yoshiaki, and the notorious daimyo Oda Nobunaga. He chose to serve Nobunaga, and his instruction was eagerly sought by many other personages, including Tokugawa Ieyasu after the Battle of Sekigahara in 1600. Ieyasu bestowed the highest praise upon Muneyoshi, and he was known countrywide for his consummate ability.

I will analyze the contribution made to the development of swordsmanship by Muneyoshi's son Munenori in the following chapter. Suffice it to say that the impact of the Yagyū line of the Shinkage-ryū in Tokugawa politics and swordsmanship cannot be overstated.

From the Tenshinshō-den Katori Shintō-ryū line, Matsumoto Bizen-no-Kami and Tsukahara Bokuden were exalted men in their age. Bokuden had a strong family connection with the Kashima Shrine and its sword traditions and also learned the Tenshinshō-den Katori Shintō-ryū from his adoptive father. As Bokuden journeyed the provinces, talk of his exploits spread far and wide. Hinatsu suggests that he sought instruction from Kamiizumi Ise-no-Kami and successfully mastered his teachings in swordsmanship and spearmanship. As Bokuden was approximately twenty years Kamiizumi's senior, it is more likely that the opposite is true. In any case, Bokuden then trekked to Kyoto, where he was employed as instructor to Ashikaga Yoshiharu, Ashikaga Yoshiteru, and Ashikaga Yoshiaki—three successive generations of Muromachi shoguns—as well as Takeda Shingen. Having mastered the fabled technique of *ichi-no-tachi* (foremost sword, also known as *hitotsu-no-tachi*), Bokuden gathered a massive following, and many of his students became successful in their own right. For example, Matsuoka Hyōgonosuke became shogun Tokugawa Ieyasu's teacher.

Hinatsu quotes the *Kōyō-gunkan* in his description of Bokuden's influence: "Tsukahara Bokuden was a skilled swordsman and prodigious warrior. The secret of Bokuden's swordsmanship is said to be *ichi-no-tachi*. However, this technique was created by Matsumoto Bizen-no-Kami. In the Kashima-Katori battles, Matsumoto fought with a spear 23 times and collected the heads of 25 warriors of rank and 76 common soldiers. . . . Bokuden also combatted with a spear nine times, and took 21 enemy heads. . . . He was designated 'heroic warrior.'"[41] Bokuden, as with so many swordsmen of his day, pursued divine guidance from the Katori Shrine deities. It was there that he dedicated himself to one thousand days of rigorous training, and legend has it that he gained enlightenment into the secret of *ichi-no-tachi*. Whether he actually learned it from Matsumoto Bizen-no-Kami, as the *Kōyō-gunkan* and Hinatsu claim, or from his intensive religious training at the Katori Shrine will never be known. However, it was this long-forgotten technique that was acclaimed as being at the crux of Bokuden's unmitigated skill.

This secret technique was the foundation of his new school, which he named Shintō-ryū (also referred to as Bokuden-ryū). As for the mysterious *hitotsu-no-tachi* technique, the *Honchō bugei shōden* records this enigmatic explanation: "*Hitotsu-no-tachi* is comprised of three levels of *hitotsu-no-kurai, hitotsu-no-tachi,* and *hitotsu-dachi.* The first utilizes the timing of heaven. The second uses the vantage of the earth and is the movement that connects heavenly and earthly plains. The third highly secret technique of *hitotsu-dachi* instills harmony of man and resourcefulness."[42] By the time he died at the age of eighty-three, Tsukahara Bokuden had amassed numerous followers, some ranking as high as daimyo. He was one of the most important swordsmen of his era and contributed to the status of swordsmanship as a profession.

Finally, from the Nen-ryū line, Itō Ittōsai also stands out as being a giant of his age. Little is known about him except that his legacy culminated in one of the most prominent schools of swordsmanship in Japanese history. Even Hinatsu's entry on Ittōsai is quite brief: "Itō Ittōsai Kagehisa hailed from Izu. He studied under Kanemaki Jisai and mastered the Chūjō tradition of sword and spear usage. Kagehisa journeyed throughout the country in the quest to develop his sword skills and participated in 33 duels. His techniques were godlike, and his skill so sublime that it defies words."[43] Ittōsai named his school the Ittō-ryū (One sword school), not as an allegory for using one sword, but from the Taoist philosophy that all things arise from "One" and then return to where they came from.

There were dozens of other warriors of this era, including the legendary Miyamoto Musashi (1584–1645), who could be mentioned for their contributions to the systemization of martial art schools, and who also acquired iconic status for their awe-inspiring skill in swordsmanship. Their epic feats are still lionized today in historical novels, traditional plays, manga, movies, and television dramas. Unfortunately, the distinction between fact and fiction has become too blurred over the centuries to know what kind of men they really were. It is clear, however, that swordsmanship to them was more than just a means of killing. It provided them with a life philosophy and was the cradle of their aesthetic ideals and powerful religious sentiments.

With the arrival of "The Great Peace" of Tokugawa Japan, martial arts were consciously and continuously reinvented as vehicles for holistic personal edification and growth—and later as spiritual sports. As Friday states, in many ways the adherents of these schools in their day became "military anachronisms, out of step with the changing face of warfare in their times. And in their pursuit of this quest through *musha shūgyō* and other ascetic regimens—their devotion to their arts over conventional military careers and service—they were self-indulgent and quixotic."[44]

Although not all *ryūha* were devoted solely to the sword, it was the principal weapon studied by many. Masters of the sword came to symbolize the warrior culture of the late medieval period. Infatuation with the sword became even more fervent during the peaceful Tokugawa period. An exponential proliferation of pseudo-religious *ryūha* dedicated to *kenjutsu* led to intensification in the pursuit of spiritual enlightenment through swordsmanship. The function of martial arts took on a new role as samurai tried to come to grips with and reinterpret their raison d'être in an era of relative tranquility. The spread of martial *ryūha* in the early Tokugawa period was expedited by large numbers of *rōnin* who had became disenfranchised as a result of years of conflict and were able to make a living through teaching.[45]

In the following chapter, I will investigate the transition from a time of war to one of peace and examine the advance of *kenjutsu* as a way of cultivating the self. I will also discuss the "civilizing process" and various innovations in training equipment and methodological approaches.

CHAPTER 2

The Art of Living

EARLY MODERN KENJUTSU

A NEW FUNCTION FOR MARTIAL ART SCHOOLS

With the onset of the Tokugawa period (1603–1868), centuries of turmoil were steadily supplanted by peacefulness, and opportunities for warriors to exhibit heroism in the theater of war became scarce. Nonetheless, samurai were obligated to remain combat-ready. Although the kinds of military arts that a warrior was permitted to study depended on the subclass or rank to which he belonged, all samurai studied some form of swordsmanship, and it gradually became emblematic of the samurai identity.

The culture of honor that warriors had developed over many centuries was based on, and sustained by, martial ability. However, Eiko Ikegami asserts that during this era of peace, warriors were "tamed," and their distinctive subculture was refocused with "an emphasis on the inner dimension of self-control."[1] The role that martial arts played in this process was crucial.

Norbert Elias's notion of the "civilizing process" is wholly applicable to the evolution of swordsmanship in Japan. He describes this process as one in which "the social standard of conduct and sentiment, particularly in some upper-class circles, began to change fairly drastically from the sixteenth century onwards in a particular direction," becoming "stricter, more differentiated and all-embracing, but also more even, more temperate, banishing excesses of self-castigation as well as of self-indulgence."[2] Although Elias is applying his theory to the European social experience, Japanese society experienced a similar transformation during the Tokugawa period, which coincides with the epoch Elias specifies. The advancement of swordsmanship and its many innovations in this era provide an excellent microcosmic indicator of how this process unfolded.

Sanctions imposed by the shogunate to control violence were a catalyst for the maturation of *kenjutsu* into ways of self-perfection and ultimately into what I label "spiritual sports." Participation provided a controlled release of pent-up tensions, and the excitement of mock-battle helped warriors to sustain their elite collective identity.

Four distinct trends characterize the martial arts of this period—of which swordsmanship was the most widely practiced: intellectualization, spiritualization and pacification, commercialization, and sportification. An analysis of these four broad movements in the evolution of swordsmanship will validate how it exemplifies a "civilizing process."

During centuries of conflict, samurai culture incorporated a distinctive ethos that was pragmatic and morally aloof. Peace, however, brought with it a problem. Several decades into the Tokugawa quietude, samurai began descending into a deep torpor, unsure of how to reconcile the chasm between their ideals and reality of their existence. They needed to come to grips with the vexing contradiction of being soldiers in peacetime.

There was virtually no need for a class of professional warriors during this period, but the samurai's status as men-of-arms required that they maintain at least a façade of military preparedness. Thus their dilemma was in essence one of legitimization. Wary of the volatile disposition of samurai, the shogunate and domains outlawed inter-clan dueling and other obstreperous behavior that could jeopardize the peace. Warriors were stuck between a rock and a hard place. Their customs and ethos dictated that they defend their honor at all costs, violently if need be, but their masters had ordered them not to.

By whom and by what means was the early modern samurai's contradictory lifestyle reconciled? An answer of sorts was crafted incrementally by experts in military science, including Hōjō Ujinaga (1609–70) and his students. Their collective teachings were adapted by prominent scholars such as the neo-Confucian Yamaga Sokō (1622–85) and his disciple Daidōji Yūzan (1639–1730), who set about constructing a new ideological framework for warriors that encouraged meticulous attention to matters of etiquette and duty. Martial arts played an increasingly important function in the everyday lives of samurai for reasons other than war. Before describing this function, I shall summarize some of the governmental decrees promulgated in the uneasy calm of the early Tokugawa period that were intended to keep a lid on the volatile samurai.

The introduction of a stipend system commanded allegiance, dedication to duty, and military service in return for salaries, making samurai de facto government employees who were ultimately accountable to the shogunate. The shogunate fashioned legislation to establish the responsibilities of samurai as well as to set boundaries separating them from commoners.[3]

Samurai were required to maintain their readiness to fight in case they were summoned to battle. Daimyo were duty-bound to retain a certain number of combat-ready men and equipment, commensurate to the size of their domain holdings. However, the actual details of what "military preparedness" meant were never explicitly articulated in any of the government ordinances. The concept was essentially open for interpretation, and the onus was placed on each domain to keep its retainers fit for duty on the off chance that they should need to be mobilized. Government decrees seemed to be promoting pro forma military preparedness—ready, but not too primed for action.

The principal legal documents issued by the shogunate in the early years of the Tokugawa period, namely the *Buke-shohatto* (Laws for the military houses, 1615) and the *Shoshi-shohatto* (Legal codes and guidelines for samurai of *hatamoto* and *gokenin* status—that is, the direct vassals of the shogunate, 1632), broadly state that the samurai's professional duty was to be versed in both literary and military matters. Again, though, exactly what this entailed was never explained. Moreover, few, if any, records exist of samurai having been punished for negligence or noncompliance.

The shogunate also introduced copious sumptuary laws that aimed to prevent financial excess, and they even included restrictions on ostentatious accessories, such as garishly decorated swords. Laws regarding appearance were also issued, regulating the type of attire samurai could wear, which hairstyles and grooming were acceptable, and what was off-limits to non-samurai.

However, the myriad edicts issued by the shogunate did not state what samurai were allowed to use their stipends for, only what was not permitted. In this sense, the dissemination of ethical guidelines by the shogunate, despite the outward show of authority, was actually quite laissez-faire. The guidelines that meant something in the lives of samurai were drafted chiefly by domain authorities and erudite independent Confucian or military scholars such as Yamaga Sokō, Daidōji Yūzan, Nakae Tōju, and Kumazawa Banzan. These individuals are well known to students of Japanese history, especially for their contributions in articulating the code of ethics commonly referred to today as bushido.

The shogunate also enacted a series of edicts regarding the right to bear arms. The Sword Hunt Edict (Katanagari-rei, 1588), for example, was issued by Toyotomi Hideyoshi (1537–98) to disarm commoners, but in reality they continued to carry weapons with impunity during the early years of the Tokugawa period. This and similar edicts did in fact permit commoners to carry long and short swords when they were traveling or felt the need to defend themselves. The eventual comprehensive prohibition of sword-carrying by anyone other than samurai was a protracted process that extended from the 1640s to the 1690s.

In 1668–69, the shogunate forbade commoners from carrying swords, barring special occasions like weddings and funerals, and certain emergencies such as fires.[4] Incidentally, there were no laws at this time forbidding samurai from teaching commoners swordsmanship. In 1683, the fifth Tokugawa shogun, Tsunayoshi (1646–1709), issued an ordinance unequivocally outlawing commoners from carrying swords under any circumstances. With this edict, the carrying of two swords formally became the symbolic badge of samurai status. In special circumstances, however, some commoners of high repute were allowed to insert a sword in their sash, a privilege usually paired with the right to use a surname.

Each domain still enjoyed a measure of freedom in the establishment of their own laws, but they exercised a degree of caution so as not to garner too much attention from the shogunate. Quite a few domains remained relatively lenient with regard to commoners possessing swords and other weapons, such as firearms. Noel Perrin's *Giving up the Gun: Japan's Reversion to the Sword, 1543–1879* is still oddly fashionable in Japan in spite of, or perhaps because of, the naive notion it promotes that Japanese rejected firearms—which is considered a noble precedent in our precarious age of weapons of mass destruction. Perrin's understanding, however, is simply wrong.

Guns were used to devastating effect on medieval battlefields in the later part of the sixteenth century and would surely have replaced all other weapons as the primary armament of daimyo armies if civil war had continued to rage into the seventeenth century and beyond. The bloodshed came to an end, however, so we will never know for sure; but as David Howell argues, for much of the Tokugawa period guns were perceived as farm tools and used to scare or exterminate destructive animals. The samurai elite also took pleasure in going on hunting excursions with firearms, as a display of status and masculinity. *Hōjutsu* schools continued teaching the art of gunnery, complete with rituals, kata, arcane teachings, and secret transmission scrolls. From around the 1840s, guns became weapons in the conventional sense again, flaunted by vulnerable peasants in self-defense against disenfranchised samurai, outcasts, and other unsavory elements on the fringes of society who threatened the peace.[5]

The numerous sumptuary bylaws established by the shogunate were largely pro forma and had limited effect on the way people lived their lives. Nevertheless, the content and sentiments underlying their conception does shine light on the shogunate's ideals of serene governance and the upholding of performative authority.

THE INTELLECTUALIZATION OF *KENJUTSU*

Tominaga Kengo divides the development of martial art schools during the Tokugawa period into three broad stages: early (1603–80), middle (1680–1786), and late (1787–1867).[6] These phases roughly correspond with my analysis of the intellectualization (early), spiritualization and pacification (middle), commercialization (middle to late), and sportification (late) of *kenjutsu*.

The first obvious transition in the civilizing process of swordsmanship was its "intellectualization," evidenced by a proliferation of martial art literature and by the imaginative application of combat principles to concerns other than warfare. The most representative example of intellectualization was exhibited by the Yagyū Shinkage-ryū tradition (sometimes called Shinkage Yagyū-ryū). Yagyū Munenori (1571–1646) was influential in the early Tokugawa period by virtue of his legendary father and his illustrious students. He was to have a resounding impact on the social validation of a peacetime military.

Munenori was the son of the exalted Sengoku-period (1467–1568) swordsman Yagyū Muneyoshi (1529–1606), founder of the Yagyū line of the Shinkage-ryū and student of Kamiizumi Ise-no-Kami (1508–77). Although not as battle-hardened as his father reputedly had been, he did get his hands bloody on the front lines. He once found himself surrounded by the men of Kimura Shigenari (1593–1615), a retainer of Hideyoshi, during the summer siege of Osaka Castle in 1615. He proved his worth by dispatching seven of his foes. This feat boosted his reputation, and high-ranked samurai, including daimyo and their direct retainers, sought his mentorship. More significantly, among his students were the second and third Tokugawa shoguns, Hidetada (1579–1632) and Iemitsu (1604–51).

In 1632, Munenori finished his magnum opus, the *Heihō-kadensho* (Book on family-transmitted military arts)—a complex fusion of Muneyoshi's and Kamiizumi Ise-no-Kami's technical teachings on swordsmanship, combined with borrowed wisdom from texts on both Noh and Zen ideals. The influence of celebrated Zen priest Takuan Sōhō (1573–1645) is also evident throughout the text. According to Peter Haskel's analysis, "Takuan's writings on swordsmanship focus from first to last on a single purpose—illuminating the principles of Zen through the exigencies of the warrior's art."[7]

Takuan's treatises *Fudōchi shinmyō-roku* (Record of immovable wisdom) and *Taia-ki* (Sword of Taia) offer advice for the swordsman on how to keep his mind fluid and prevent it from becoming deluded or attached to something like the opponent's sword. *Fudōchi shinmyō-roku* is a document believed to have been written by Takuan subsequent to a conversation on swordsmanship with Tokugawa Iemitsu. Although the original has long since been lost, a later version has an addendum addressed to Yagyū Munenori, who was Iemitsu's teacher. The original was most likely presented to Iemitsu, and Munenori would have been called upon to guide the shogun's understanding of how the highly philosophical content applied to swordsmanship.[8]

The document focuses on the psychological posture necessary to prevail in combat rather than on the techniques of sword fighting. Takuan contended that as soon as a swordsman's mind is distracted, an opening in his spiritual armor appears that will leave him vulnerable to physical attack. "Immovable mind" (*fudōchi*) denotes a psychological state that is resistant to becoming attached or sidetracked by an opponent's actions. Munenori incorporated some of Takuan's teachings almost verbatim in his *Heihō-kadensho*. He interprets "attachment"—where the mind stops—as a "disease" that inhibits the mind's "normal state" (*heijōshin*). Fixation on being fixated is also a "disease," so the swordsman is advised in the most Zen of ways to melt obsessions into the mind instead of dwelling on them—in other words, to just go with the flow.

Heihō-kadensho held considerable sway over Munenori's powerful disciples, providing them not only with a basis for their study of *kenjutsu* but, more importantly, with guidelines for nurturing their political acumen for governance. The book is divided into three sections: "Shinrikyō" (the shoe-offering bridge), "Setsunin-tō" (the death-dealing blade), and "Katsunin-ken" (the life-giving sword).[9] "Shinrikyō" is a catalogue of the school's principles and techniques and lists all the kata of the original Shinkage-ryū conveyed by Kamiizumi Ise-no-Kami to Yagyū Muneyoshi.[10] As techniques were generally taught directly from master to disciple, only cursory information is chronicled regarding the mechanical intricacies of sword work. The other two sections, however, discuss philosophical revelations that emphasize the importance of the mind in swordsmanship and its applicability to leadership.

Of particular relevance is the chapter titled "Setsunin-tō." Ironically, Munenori starts by pointing out that weapons of war are inherently bad, as they are meant for destructive purposes, and that killing runs counter to the "Way of Heaven" (*tendō*). He concedes, however, that there are times when the use of force is necessary in order to maintain the peace: "Killing one man's evil so that ten thousand may live peaceably."[11]

In order to "kill one man's evil," a warrior needs to be accomplished in combat, lest he be killed himself. Munenori elaborates by explaining that in individual combat, which he calls "small warcraft" (*chiisaki-heihō*), there is only one winner and one loser. Strategy for governing the realm is "great warcraft" (*dainaru-heihō*). According to Munenori, regardless of the scale of the battle, victory or defeat is determined by whether or not the warrior holds the principles of warfare in his mind. Munenori declares that the smallest encounter between two warriors with swords is strategically equivalent to a shogun who must make crucial decisions to rule the country effectively: "It is *heihō* [strategy] to be aware of disorder when ruling the country in a time of peace. Likewise, it is *heihō* to scrutinize the internal workings of the realm to understand what turmoil is, and to rule the people effectively before pandemonium breaks out." In other words, small warcraft is essentially a microcosm of statecraft.[12]

Although the martial philosophy of the Yagyū Shinkage-ryū espoused in *Heihō-kadensho* was influential in warrior high society, it had little direct impact on the rank-and-file. It was, however, one of the first important martial texts to organize a martial philosophy linking the training of body and mind into a systemized holistic corpus for combat, life, and governance. As such, it was also one of the first clear-cut examples of *kenjutsu* being associated with something other than just combat.

Probably the most celebrated warrior in Japanese history is one of Munenori's contemporaries, Miyamoto Musashi (1584–1645). There are many aspects of Musashi's life that are shrouded in mystery and continually debated by scholars. In his book *Gorin-no-sho* (Book of five rings, 1645), Musashi writes that he was born in Harima Province (present-day Hyōgo Prefecture). Born into the Tahara family, it is thought that he was adopted when he was nine by Miyamoto Munisai—a retainer of the Shinmen family in Mimasaka (present-day Okayama Prefecture)—who was an expert with various weapons, including the sword and *jutte* (truncheon). By the time he was thirty, Musashi had fought sixty or so duels, the first at the tender age of thirteen against Arima Kihei, a swordsman of the Shintō-ryū.

Even though he was victorious in all of these fights, Musashi self-effacingly confesses in *Gorin-no-sho* that his success was due more to luck than to prodigious tactics. He had reached an impasse around the age of thirty regarding his skill as a swordsman and sought something more spiritually profound. He was invited by the daimyo of the Kumamoto domain, Hosokawa Tadatoshi, to be his advisor in 1640. It was there, inside the Reigandō cave, that he wrote *Gorin-no-sho* and recorded his life lessons for posterity. He completed it just before he died in 1645, although some scholars suspect that his students actually wrote the text after he died, based on his teachings.

Musashi is credited with writing several other documents related to the martial arts, including *Hyōdōkyō* (The mirror of the way of strategy, 1605), *Hyōhō kaki-tsuke* (Notes on strategy, 1638), *Hyōhō sanjūgo-kajō* (Strategy in thirty-five articles, 1641), and *Dokkōdō* (The way to be followed alone, 1645). His most famous treatise, however, is undoubtedly *Gorin-no-sho*.[13]

Gorin-no-sho consists of five chapters: "Chi" (Earth), "Sui" (Water), "Ka" (Fire), "Fū" (Wind), and "Kū" (Void). In "Chi," Musashi documents the first half of his life. He also provides an introduction to military tactics and the metaphysics behind his school, the Niten Ichi-ryū, which was famous for teaching the strategy of using two swords simultaneously. In "Sui," Musashi explains various aspects of individual combat, such as mental and physical posture, gaze, sword manipulation, footwork, and fighting stances. In "Ka," he expounds on how to choose the best site for dueling, control the enemy by taking the initiative, and implement stratagems. In the penultimate chapter, "Fū," he critiques other schools of swordsmanship and outlines their weaknesses. The final chapter, "Kū," is a short but nebulous account of how he created the Niten Ichi-ryū based on his rich experience of conflict. In it he discloses the supreme level of combat and all arts by referring to the allegorical "void" or "emptiness," which deals with "spirit," or things that cannot be seen. He declares that people who do not understand something judge it to be unreal and incorrectly refer to it as emptiness. The true void is a realm of perfect clarity, devoid of delusion, ego, or evil. Without knowing this, it is impossible to discern what is real and what is not. Thus, to know the void, and that the void is also emptiness, is to know the true path. It is the only correct way, and applies to everything, from the way of the warrior, to the way of the carpenter.[14]

What makes Musashi's treatise distinctive is the way he endeavors to apply his philosophy to all manner of activities, such as combat, painting, carving, and even carpentry: "If you master the principles of sword, when you freely beat one man, you beat many men in the world. The spirit of defeating a man is the same for ten-million men. The strategist makes small things into big things, like building a great Buddha from a one-foot model. I cannot write in detail how this is done. The principle of strategy is having one thing, to know ten-thousand things."[15]

His overall thesis is simplistic when compared to Munenori's *Heihō-kadensho,* and he does not dwell on the underpinnings of Zen or Confucian concepts. Nevertheless, there are similarities, such as the emphasis he places on mindset in combat and how mastery of the principles of strategy is a never-ending pursuit applicable to all facets of life. Both books were written by warriors who experienced the chaos prior to Japan's unification in the Tokugawa period, as well as the ensuing peace. They provide a link between two different worlds of samurai experience, and are still widely referred to by modern practitioners of kendo.

SPIRITUALIZATION AND PACIFICATION

A noticeable trend in the middle of the Tokugawa period was the overt "spiritualization" and "pacification" of the martial arts as they adapted to a society that no longer tolerated brazen violence among its warriors. The number of martial art schools mushroomed beginning in the mid-1600s, and the new schools tended to specialize in specific weapons rather than a variety, as had been the case in more turbulent eras. The techniques and kata became progressively more ostentatious, and elaborate canons were concocted by the school heads, giving martial arts, especially *kenjutsu,* an increasingly spiritual zest.

As Friday observes, "Abstract personal education, rather than workaday military drill, was precisely the reason it [martial arts] was able to evolve so rapidly during the early decades of the Tokugawa period."[16] This is not to say that martial traditions of the fourteenth and fifteenth centuries were devoid of incorporeal principles. Far from it. Students of the earliest *ryūha* performed secret rituals and followed teachings to overcome fear, and they even practiced divination, which they believed would give them a magical aura of invincibility. The metaphysical elements of martial arts practice, however, became better defined in the Tokugawa period. The goal was not to supplement combat efficiency as much as to provide a framework for the ascetic quest for perfect unity of body and mind and the attainment of heightened spiritual awareness.

As I suggested in the previous chapter, even the earliest *kenjutsu* traditions resembled pseudo-religious cults, and the more war faded from the collective memory of warriors, the more esoteric in nature *kenjutsu* became. This may have been a result of the peacetime environment, or it may have been simply a continuation or maturation of the overt religiosity present in the teachings espoused by masters of yore. In addition to Confucian and Buddhist (especially Zen) concepts and ideals, holistic Daoist teachings of ancient Chinese philosophers such as Chuang Tse also featured in Tokugawa-era *ryūha*. Developing both mind and body as a path to spiritual liberation became the key objective in many of the schools that emerged during the middle of the early modern period.

In times of social tumult, spiritual fortitude and transcendence were ways of dealing with the reality of death. In times of peace, martial training transformed into a vehicle for nurturing individual morality and self-control; that is, it developed into something more than the ability or will to kill. Schools of all eras taught practical combat techniques as well as aspects of aesthetic beauty, the pursuit of higher mystical ideals, and self-cultivation. The degree to which these aspects were accentuated depended on circumstances.

As spirituality became more prominent in the Tokugawa period, influential tomes in the genre of "martial spiritualism" became popular, especially among samurai. Two of the most widely read were *Tengu geijutsu-ron* (Discourse on the art of the mountain demons, 1727) and *Neko-no-myōjutsu* (The cat's eerie skill, 1729), both by Niwa Jūrōzaemon Tadaaki (1659–1741), who was more commonly known by his nom de plume, Issai Chozan. Issai was a student of Zen Buddhism, Confucianism, and the Chinese classics, as well as the martial arts.

Neko-no-myōjutsu is a story of a large rat that torments local cats with its defiant behavior. Each cat tries to outdo the others and capture the bold rat, but without success. Then an elderly cat decides to take up the challenge and captures the rat with seemingly no effort. The other cats are amazed by his deftness and inquire as to how he achieved such a feat. The narrative then turns to the wise old cat educating his much younger protégés. His sermon centers on the "natural way of the universe" (*dōri*) and the use of vital force or life energy (*ki*). He explains how the warrior who can control his mind and access the very essence of his existence will be able to triumph in anything.

Issai's first book, *Tengu geijutsu-ron*, was also a popular read among samurai. It tells the story of a warrior who studied the martial arts for many years but could not see the way forward. He was inspired by the legend of how Minamoto-no-Yoshitsune (1159–89) was taught the highest secrets of strategy from the fabled *tengu*—supernatural, goblin-like creatures that were extremely skilled in the arts of war. Each night he ventures into the mountains and meditates in an attempt to summon the *tengu* for himself. He continues this ritual until eventually a *tengu* appears in a large cedar tree and answers his inquiries about the secrets of swordsmanship. The dialogue makes no mention of sword techniques per se, but instead elaborates on how the warrior should hold his mind without fixation.

The ability to harness and control the power of *ki* is a theme that both of Issai's stories have in common. The value of *Tengu geijutsu-ron*'s message is summed up in a preface written by Kanda Hakuryūshi in 1728:

> Recently there are a number of samurai who have acquired magnificent reputations through their expertise in swordsmanship. Each school divides into 10,000 more branches, and so-called masters continue to teach their students so that all blindly follow each other. Some pass on dubious theories with the promise that if the student obediently follows and masters the knowledge, he will be able to command heaven, earth, and the whole realm. They teach willing disciples to wield their blades in all directions, and how to single-handedly overcome ten adversaries simultaneously. Other teachers proclaim that by correcting the mind and developing the power of *ki* one can gain victory in any encounter, without even the need to move. Indeed, nonsensical theories abound. These "tenets of wisdom" are spurious, and by no means should be construed as acceptable in swordsmanship. Students who believe such ill-conceived fabrications will pass them on to their own disciples; just as one dog barks a lie, 10,000 more will convey it as the "truth." This is a reprehensible state of affairs.[17]

He concludes by stating how Issai's text will keep students on the correct path of swordsmanship, preventing them from straying off into the mists of obscurity and seeking knowledge of frivolities instead of the true principles of the martial arts.

What were considered to be "true principles" varied depending on the school, but even the most prestigious *kenjutsu* schools, such as the Ittō-ryū, increasingly incorporated Daoist sword rituals and religio-magic practices related to esoteric Buddhism, ancient Chinese cosmic theories, and spiritual training.

Heihō michi shirube (A guide to the martial arts, 1834) by Shirai Tōru Yoshinori (1781–1843) is one of the most celebrated spiritual treatises about swordsmanship. In it Shirai explains the secret Daoist respiratory methods employed in his style of fencing, the Nakanishi-ha Ittō-ryū. He divulges in rather abstract terms how *ki* should be circulated in the lower abdomen (*tanden*) in accordance with the teachings of the Daoist deity Tenshin (Heavenly Truth). These conceptions of *ki* and the importance of the *tanden* are still regarded as fundamental considerations in modern kendo.

Alongside developing "life energy," the matter of how to live one's life was a central consideration for samurai. Even without war, they were obligated to maintain military readiness as "keepers of the peace." The warrior ideal also encouraged samurai to cultivate their humanity and be paragons of moral perfection as they fulfilled their duty. At least that was the ideal, according to fashionable books by Yamaga Sokō, Daidōji Yūzan, and many other scholars of the day.

The nature of martial arts of the Tokugawa period has been described as embodying a spirit of nonlethality, which accords perfectly with the features of the civilizing process. Although very much a romanticized notion by the eighteenth century, death remained a central concern in the warrior ethos and could be re-enacted through continued training in the martial arts.[18] To this day, the vast majority of martial art kata sequences end in the theoretical defeat of one of the participants. As explained in chapter 1, this represents the moment in the performance of mock combat at which the adept confronts his mortality. This ritual celebrating both death and the power to take life— or not take life despite the ability to do so—served to reinforce the identity of samurai as professional warriors.

Peace also led to the pacification of the martial arts, bringing about a conspicuous inclination toward the avoidance of confrontation altogether. Some kata developed in the Tokugawa period ended in a draw as opposed to a metaphorical death. Odagiri Ichiun (1636?–1706) was a proponent of this new leaning. Inspired by his teacher Harigaya Sekiun (1593?–1662), he wrote *Kenpō Sekiun-sensei sōden* (Sword techniques taught by master Sekiun, 1686). In it, he promotes the concept of *ai-nuke,* which refers to a confrontation in which two warriors with equal outstanding skill and a lack of concern for their own death purge "murderous intent" from their minds and end the confrontation without a coup de grâce. It was the early modern version of Mutual Assured Destruction (MAD): "When the contestants are of equal caliber and proficiency the game as it is generally played [in a fencing bout] finishes with an *ai-uchi* [mutual strike], which, when carried on with real steel, means killing each other. An *ai-nuke,* however, does not at all involve any kind of killing or hurting each other, as *nuke* means, not 'striking down' as *uchi* does, but 'passing by', or 'going through' unhurt."[19] Again, this is reminiscent of Elias's theory of the civilizing process, in which impulsive, violent tendencies are suppressed: "Part of the tensions and passions that were earlier directly released in the struggle of man and man must now be worked out within the human being."[20] No doubt, the idea of both warriors "winning" the encounter through abstention because of some lofty, self-congratulatory concurrence of mutually assured destruction was mocked as being genuinely "mad" (in the softheaded sense) by warriors of a more prag-matic disposition. It was, it could be argued, just a clever way of avoiding getting hurt or killed, albeit one premised on the pompous appeal of spiritual transcendence that neither protagonist was prepared to prove. Nevertheless, it was a trend that was no doubt welcomed by shogu-nate authorities, who were keen for temperamental warriors to avoid confrontation.

From around this time (the mid-Tokugawa era) the term *bu*, which had originally meant "war" or "martial," came to mean its antonym, "antiwar." The kanji glyph radicals for "foot" (or possibly "to walk") with "lance" in hand were originally comprehended as foot soldiers marching off to battle. The radical for "foot" is very similar in form to the glyph for "stop," and from around the middle of the Tokugawa period, the same character was pacifisti-cally construed as "to stop" fighting with the "lance."[21]

COMMERCIALIZATION

How did the martial arts reinforce a samurai's military preparedness? Certification of advancement in a martial art *ryūha* was imperative to the samurai in two ways. First, it provided them with the credentials needed to prove they were actually earning their stipends. Second, it enabled the samu-rai to see themselves as practicing warriors rather than brush-wielding bureaucrats.

Certification catalyzed market demand for expert teachers, and conse-quently the number of *ryūha* and private schools multiplied. This growth, along with competition between various *ryūha* to attract students, led to a surge in the phenomenon of "invented tradition," as each ryu attempted to legitimize its approach by associating itself loosely with a long-established school and some unfounded, mythical beginning. Enthusiasm for the martial arts temporarily declined due to the perception that quality had diminished with the rise of sham schools. Moreover, as the new schools had been created in a time of peace, their progenitors and students were untested in the cauldron of combat, and the efficacy of the techniques that they taught were seen as dubious.

Warriors could now maintain the appearance of being capable by demonstrating a refined intellectual understanding of combat in place of grit in a real fight. This was agreeable to the shogunate, which desired warriors to be ready to perform military duties if needed, but not to the extent that they would pose a threat to social stability.

According to Elias's examination of violence in European society, "If social tensions approach or reach the threshold of violence, a parliamentary regime is in danger of breaking down."[22] This was as much a point of concern for the Tokugawa shogunate in Japan as it was for European governments. Elias goes on to assert that governmental functionality depends on the control of physical violence as well as the stability of a society's internal pacification, which is in turn partially reliant on the personal restraint of the people who live in that society. This can help explain why the shogunate was not opposed to the commercialization of *kenjutsu*. After all, one of the primary objectives of *kenjutsu* schools was to teach self-restraint as a step toward self-perfection.

With the commercialization of *kenjutsu* came a longer training period for students. In the Sengoku period, apprenticeships were short, lasting from a few months to a few years. If he was accomplished enough, a student could even start his own branch of the school after receiving a license from his master.

In the Tokugawa period, proprietors of schools introduced arduous promotion systems.[23] The intricate curriculums took considerable time to master, although in many cases they lacked practicality. Many of the men who formed schools had little to no campaign experience but had been given authority by transmission documents that certified their step-by-step mastery of a school's techniques and arcane teachings (*hiden*).

To become a member of a private fencing academy, a swordsman was required to submit a letter of guarantee, give pecuniary gifts at certain times of the year, and pay monthly fees in rice. He also had to provide his own bedding and fencing equipment, and abide by strict rules of propriety forbidding the usual vices of imbibing, womanizing, borrowing money, and gambling. Students practiced *kenjutsu* techniques and, depending on the dojo, engaged in classical studies and took lessons on more politically oriented topics.

Some schools adopted the *iemoto* system, whereby succession was heredi-tary rather than based on skill; but succession of the orthodox line of the school was typically conferred on the most trusted disciple. Many domains chose to employ the services of the established hereditary master house (*shihan-ke*) of a specific *ryūha*, and clansmen were discouraged from learning different sword styles concurrently. Sometimes the entire *ryūha* in question would be contracted exclusively to the warriors of a specific domain. On the other hand, it was not uncommon for several instructors representing differ-ent *ryūha* or martial arts to be simultaneously employed within the same domain. In these cases, the master instructors were given separate facilities so that they could operate independently within the domain and keep the *hiden* teachings of their schools concealed.[24]

The position of *kenjutsu* instructor was esteemed and financially reward-ing. With high market demand for instruction and certification, new ryu continued to burgeon. According to rough estimates by Imamura Yoshio, by the late eighteenth century there were 45 schools of *kyūjutsu* (archery), 61 schools of *bajutsu* (horsemanship), 121 schools of *sōjutsu* (spearmanship), 173 schools of *hōjutsu* (gunmanship), 167 schools of *jūjutsu* (grappling), and— the most numerous by far—620 schools of *kenjutsu*.[25]

New schools developed novel and untested techniques, and kata routines became ever more flamboyant and removed from the reality of combat. Toward the end of the seventeenth century, there were few, if any, samurai who had actually risked their lives in pitched warfare. Although some *ryūha* continued to maintain battle-oriented curricula, many others emphasized abstract, occult teachings that would have been utterly useless on a battlefield.

Purists deplored this state of affairs and rather sarcastically referred to the modern practice of *kenjutsu* as "flowery swordsmanship" (*kahō kenpō*). These detractors had a romanticized notion of the "good old days," when samurai had been "real men"; they mistakenly believed that the "naked sword" schools of the previous era had been wholly focused on utilitarian combat tactics. They had forgotten that even the earliest *kenjutsu* schools had been some-what detached from practical soldiery and concerned more with the meta-physical and aesthetic aspects of the practice.

Theatrical rituals, bizarre fighting stances, and brazen sequences of tech-niques were criticized as purely decorative and superfluous. Then again, these metaphysical idiosyncrasies helped attract students. The years extending from the reign of the fourth shogun, Ietsuna (1641–80), through that of his successor, Tsunayoshi (1646–1709), were perceived as a period of stagnation in the martial arts. There was a deterioration of technical practicality and a lack of overall enthusiasm for training. This was partly due to bans the shogunate and individual domains imposed on inter-school matches out of concerns for potential escalations of violence. These bans meant that the efficacy of *ryūha* techniques remained largely unverified, and the fact that students weren't allowed to compete with other schools probably took some of the excitement out of training as well. Interaction between adepts of different *ryūha* had been a stimulating, meaningful, and sometimes fatal aspect of the itinerant warrior's lifestyle.

Attracting students was a serious issue for schools; population projections show that the martial arts market was probably close to saturation by the early 1700s.[26] This fueled a number of innovations by schools in the mid-Tokugawa period, such as the awarding of magnificent color transmission scrolls to mark progress. Some schools even opened their doors to commoners. One observer of the time made the following cynical remark: "All swordsmanship of today is almost entirely the creation of people living in a time of peace.... They make great display of their strikes, and place some primary emphasis on winning in a spectacular fashion. Some samurai [teaching the art] today do quite well for themselves and debate lofty theories. Other samurai concentrate on perfecting their choreography and gestures."[27]

Most discussion on the phenomenon of "inventing tradition" is concerned with the emergence of modern nationalism and perceptions of national culture and identity around the nineteenth century. I will address this issue in the next chapter. It is important to note here, however, that the many schools of *kenjutsu* that arose in the Tokugawa period were invented entities that were purposefully elitist and exhibited an impression of uniqueness. Although the standard conception of tradition hinges on the oppositional condition of modernity, the evolution of Japanese swordsmanship reveals a deliberate molding of practices drawn from a mythical historical past and, significantly, from the purview of scholarly discourse, such a phenomenon indicates the components of "modernity" well before the nineteenth century, the period on which most debate on the subject is typically focused. In other words, the process of change in Japanese *kenjutsu* shows that temporal boundaries usually linked with modernity and tradition are too constricting.

The progenitors of new schools endeavored to substantiate their connection with a mythical historic past by linking themselves to legendary warriors and prototypical *ryūha* from centuries earlier. These ties were often fanciful and tenuous, but they became increasingly important as samurai became further removed from the field of battle. To use Ikegami's term, the fast growth of *kenjutsu* schools was a consequence of "refocusing" the warrior culture of honor. Samurai were disillusioned with the status quo and longed to forge a nostalgic connection with the past. *Kenjutsu* and the various *ryūha* provided this, while helping samurai maintain a sense of their own exclusivity.

SPORTIFICATION

The late-seventeenth-century deterioration of *kenjutsu* into "flowery" performances with swords culminated in its sportification, with the introduction of protective training equipment (now called *kendō-gu*) and bamboo swords (*shinai*) in the early eighteenth century. The training method utilizing this equipment was known as *shinai-uchikomi-geiko* ("*shinai*-striking practice method," hereafter referred to as "fencing").

Dissatisfaction with what some perceived as pretentious kata-centric *kenjutsu* provided the initial motivation for developing this new method. Another incentive was the hunger for excitement among a warrior class who yearned for the thrill of action, albeit in a more civilized form. As Elias observes with regard to the rise of sports in Europe, "a phase of struggle, of battle-tension and excitement which may be demanding in terms of physical exertion and skill but which can be exhilarating in its own right as a liberation from the routines and stress-tensions of non-leisure life, is usually followed by a phase of decision and release from battle-tension either in triumph and victory or in disappointment and defeat."[28]

Fueled by a centuries-old subculture based on honor earned through contests of strength, a samurai's instinctual drive to defend his reputation was not something that could be quelled easily. A consciously pacified society had to figure out how to mollify this urge. The question was how to make physical, combat-based activities safe but still charged with the buzz of battle. Protective fencing equipment provided the answer, as it enabled participants to safely engage in full-contact fencing bouts.

Exactly how and when *kenjutsu* schools started to use such equipment is uncertain. Schools of *sōjutsu* (spearmanship) used full-contact training methods before they became popular in *kenjutsu*. Bamboo practice swords

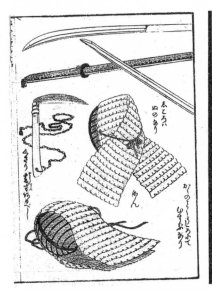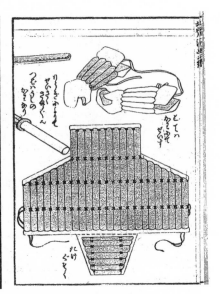

FIGURE 7. An illustration of early fencing equipment from the *Hokusai manga* sketches, early nineteenth century. (Courtesy of Bunkasha International)

covered in leather sheaths (*fukuro-shinai*) were employed in duels by Yagyū Muneyoshi toward the end of the sixteenth century, and the Maniwa Nenryū was using padded head protectors in the early seventeenth century.

The implementation of protective equipment in mainstream *kenjutsu* (figure 7) was a gradual process in which Yamada Heizaemon Mitsunori (1639–1716) of the Jikishin Kage-ryū played a pivotal role. He suffered a serious injury at the age of eighteen in a match fought with wooden swords. He resumed his training wearing rudimentary armor for safety and later developed the equipment further so that vigorous full-contact attacks could be made without injuring, or even killing, one's opponent. His third son, Naganuma Shirōzaemon Kunisato (1688–1767), improved on his father's design, and the family's armored training method became established in the Jikishin Kage-ryū.

Nakanishi Tsugutake of the Nakanishi-ha Ittō-ryū tradition also introduced armor in training sessions from 1751 to 1764. His disciples donned protective masks complete with metal face grills, plastrons, and gauntlets, and used bamboo swords.

Although the use of armor signified a revolutionary way of training in swordsmanship, its introduction was not without controversy. There was a fixation in some schools with preserving conventional methods and maintaining all-important links with the past. Even within a single *ryu* there were differences of opinion about the preferred training methodology. There were those who stubbornly clung to the customary method of kata practice and those who sought to undertake training that was both safe and competitive. A well-known and often-quoted exchange of letters on the subject between Ono Tadayoshi of the Ono-ha Ittō-ryū, and Yamaga Hachirōzaemon Takami and Nakanishi Chūzō Tsugutake of the Nakanishi-ha Ittō-ryū offers interesting insights into the dilemma faced by schools regarding the development of fencing equipment.

Yamaga Hachirōzaemon was an Ittō-ryū swordsman of the Tsugaru domain. He questioned the validity of Nakanishi Chūzō's use of protective equipment and bamboo swords and brushed a letter consisting of eleven articles to his master Ono Tadayoshi, the seventh-generation head of the Ono-ha Ittō-ryū, for his take on the matter. Tadayoshi was less than enthusiastic: "When using a wooden sword, you strike the enemy's *ki* (spirit) first, and then attain victory. With the *shinai,* you strike at the enemy's body first in order to win."[29] He also condemned the *shinai* by saying, "the strikes are weak," and that "it is nothing more than child's play." He claimed that training with a *shinai* would actually teach swordsmen a distaste for mortal combat; in other words, it would make him weak in mind. Yamaga passed on his master's response to Nakanishi, who, obviously chagrined by these condemnations, crafted a reply to silence his doubters. He first acknowledged why some would consider the training method problematic:

I believe that it is virtually impossible to attack with sacrificial conviction when training with a blunt or wooden sword. This is precisely the reason why men who are skilled [and don't hold back] are more likely to be victorious. When people train with bamboo swords and protective equipment, weaker or technically inept swordsmen can attack with full force, without fear [of injury] and it is difficult to foretell who will prevail... This method of training causes a distorted view of the bout, in which the swordsman does not feel he has been truly defeated unless the blow is strong and telling.[30]

Nakanishi then offered solutions for these problems by emphasizing that the trainee should always use a *shinai* as if it were a wooden or blunted sword and concede defeat in good conscience, even if the blow was light. In addition, he stated that the warrior should approach each opponent as if he were a prodigious swordsman, so as to give the bout a sense of veracity and tension. In this way, training with bamboo swords and protective equipment would,

FIGURE 8. An illustration of fencing with *shinai* and *yari* from the *Hokusai manga* sketches, early nineteenth century. (Courtesy of Bunkasha International)

he contended, expedite improvement in the art of swordsmanship as if it were actual combat (figure 8).

The two camps remained opposed for some time. However, by the end of the eighteenth century, most *kenjutsu* schools had merged both methods into their curricula to differing degrees, but it was the new schools that centered on fencing rather than kata attracted the most students. As Anatoliy Anshin points out, this leads to the conclusion that the promoters of the full-contact fencing method of training were "converting the most fundamental element of the intangible warrior culture into a profitable sport."[31]

At the end of the seventeenth century, there was a rise in the number of commercial dojos. Being private, these fencing academies (*shijuku*) differed from domain sponsored schools (*hankō*), where retainers and their children were instructed in the martial arts, as they were open to samurai (and even commoners) of any affiliation.[32] They operated independently from the government and the various domains, and some became very prosperous, particularly toward the end of the Tokugawa period. According to John Rogers, "This emphasis on rough-and-ready sparring shifted the focus from hereditary sword masters to rising young stars—popular teachers at well-known training halls who commanded attention not only as pontifical grandmasters but as great competitive fencers."[33]

There were seven core *ryūha* that became prominent in the early 1800s with the expansion of fencing. They were the Shingyōtō-ryū, the Nakanishi-ha Ittō-ryū, the Hokushin Ittō-ryū, the Kōgen Ittō-ryū, the Shintō Munen-ryū, the Jikishin Kage-ryū, and the Kyōshin Meichi-ryū. Fencing enabled swordsmen to safely engage in matches with students of other schools, and this subsequently revived interest in *musha-shugyō*, a practice in which swordsmen traveled the provinces visiting domain schools and private dojos to test their skills.

Nagai Yoshio analyzed the fascinating diary of Muta Bunnosuke Takaatsu (1831–90), a warrior of the Saga domain who embarked on a national tour of fencing schools from September 1853 to September 1855.[34] Bunnosuke was experienced in several styles, including Taisha-ryū, Jikishin Kage Toda-ryū, and Tetsujin-ryū (a derivative of Miyamoto Musashi's two-sword school). He visited both private fencing academies and domain school dojos (figure 9). An observation he made in his diary that stands out is the palpable fun warriors experienced when crossing swords. The whole experience is reminiscent of a modern academic going on a year's sabbatical to get away from mundane chores, and see a bit of the world while deepening his or her international network in the field. Bunnosuke was even given a special stipend to cover his costs.

To tour the provinces, Bunnosuke secured a *tefuda,* a kind of passport that gave him access to domain school dojos. Representatives from his domain sent introductory letters to his intended stops in advance, providing his credentials and approximate dates of arrival. Along the way he stayed at inns in castle towns that operated expressly for swordsmen on their journeys. Such was the conviviality that accommodation costs were even paid for by the host domain, as was the custom. Once he had checked in, the inn's proprietor would notify the domain administrators and dojo leaders, who would come to greet him and then escort him to the training venue. During his stay, he could expect to fight up to eighty bouts with the academy students in a single day. He would be treated to lunch, and after the day's training was over he might enjoy a soak in the local hot springs followed by a sociable drinking party in the evening.

However, not all academy heads were so welcoming. Sometimes Bunnosuke's request for a visit would be denied by the master, who would cite such reasons as being absent on official business, illness, or because his *ryūha* did not engage in fencing free-for-alls with outsiders, or simply because

FIGURE 9. A scene depicting warriors engaged in rigorous fencing bouts, probably in a domain school dojo, with the local daimyo watching attentively. (From *Chiyoda no onomote–bujutsu jōran,* 1897; courtesy of Bunkasha International)

FIGURE 10. An early Meiji-era photograph of a swordsman heading to the dojo. Note the two types of *dō* (breastplate) he is carrying at either end of his *shinai*. The bamboo variety of *dō* could be rolled up, making it easier to carry on longer journeys. (The Mainichi Newspapers)

it did not teach fencing. Sometimes these reasons were legitimate, but Bunnosuke was not always convinced.

Matches were decided by conscience rather than by the judgment of referees. Of course, that meant that verdicts of victory were a subjective matter, and interpretations of the outcome were not always consensual. Bunnosuke was obviously a confident fellow, estimating his own win rate at around 70 to 80 percent. Perhaps that was an acceptable scorecard to present to his superiors when they reviewed his activities upon his return.

Although fencing was popular in the provinces, the city of Edo (present-day Tokyo) was considered a mecca for ambitious swordsmen. While in the city, wayfaring fencers, much like the warrior depicted in figure 10, stayed at their domain's dedicated Edo residence, but they frequently spent time with samurai from other parts of the country at various fencing academies, or went out sightseeing with new friends and old fencing acquaintances. Although different domains were wary of each other, *kenjutsu* seemed to provide an amicable conduit for inter-domain interaction between rival samurai.

Of the hundreds of fencing academies, the so-called three great dojos of Edo stood out: Chiba Shūsaku's (1794–1856) Genbukan (Hokushin Ittō-ryū), established in 1820; Saitō Yakurō's (1798–1871) Renpeikan (Shintō Munen-ryū), started in 1826; and Momonoi Shunzō's (1825–85) Shigakkan (Kyōshin Meichi-ryū), founded in 1849. Each boasted thousands of students. Their respective masters were charismatic and enjoyed celebrity status. Chiba Shūsaku was known for his technical dexterity, Saitō Yakurō for his power, and Momonoi Shunzō for his elegant style of fencing. Calling on these iconic dojos of Edo was a highlight of Bunnosuke's tour. His visit to Saitō Yakurō's dojo was eye opening. He was most impressed by the fencing skills of Yakurō's students, and especially by his two sons, Kannosuke and Shintarō. He became a good friend of the latter. Momonoi Shunzō declined to fight Bunnosuke himself as he was feeling "under the weather," but he allowed a bout with his top student, Ueda Umanosuke (1831–90)—against whom Bunnosuke believed he gave a good account of himself.

Chiba Shūsaku's Genbukan was an anticlimax. Repeated requests made to Shūsaku's son Eijirō (1833–62) were turned down with all manner of "excuses." Bunnosuke was finally given permission to fight with twelve of the dojo members, but he was unable to challenge Eijirō himself, who was, predictably, "not feeling so well." Bunnosuke sardonically records that of the approximately one hundred fencers in the dojo, only two stood out as being worth their salt. He slates Eijirō as "a supreme coward."

In total, Bunnosuke visited approximately seventy *kenjutsu* schools around Japan, and his diary was submitted to domain officials as a chronicle of his trip. The record was undoubtedly a vital source of intelligence for the domain.

Marius B. Jansen observes that, toward the end of the Tokugawa period in particular, fencing academies, which were "filled to overflowing with ambitious and restless samurai, became the centers of extremist and obscurantist thought and action."[35] For example, among the estimated three thousand students of Saitō Yakurō's Renpeikan were renowned swordsmen reactionaries, such as Takasagi Shinsaku, Kido Kōin, and Shinagawa Yajirō, all from the Chōshū domain. I will expand on this important point in the next chapter.

Although the shogunate issued several perfunctory prohibitions after 1805 that banned commoners from participating in martial arts, the decrees were never forcibly upheld. The legendary Saitō Yakurō himself was the son of a farmer, but he took advantage of the open-door policies of private academies to study Confucianism, military tactics, and *kenjutsu*. He opened the Renpeikan when he was twenty-eight. The number of commoners participating in *kenjutsu* depended by and large on the discretion of each domain or individual school. The saturation of the martial arts market in the eighteenth century pressed the proprietors of many schools to enroll their social inferiors even before the 1800s, but the sportive style of *kenjutsu* (commonly referred to as *gekiken* or *gekken*—"battling swords") was particularly attractive to wealthy townsmen and villagers who took pleasure in emulating samurai culture.

It may come as a surprise to some readers that non-samurai played a sizable role in popularizing this prototype of modern kendo. A number of the most celebrated fencers from the early nineteenth century were in fact not of warrior stock. Match records that survive from the 1840s from the region that makes up modern-day Saitama Prefecture reveal that commoners (farmers, deputy administrators, village headmen, and merchants) made up 81 percent of notable fencers, while samurai amounted to only 19 percent of the total. Yamamoto Kunio gives several plausible reasons for this, including the abolishment of shogunate retainer demesne in the region, which led to a diminished presence of samurai, causing the task of maintaining safety to fall on the shoulders of village officers and the community; economic destitution among the warrior class, which led to a clouding of class distinction; close proximity to Edo, which enabled commoners to frequent private fencing academies and even copy the samurai way of life; and the increasing inclination of farmers in the early nineteenth century to seek a life away from agriculture.[36]

Thus, depending on the time and place, a certain degree of tolerance with regard to commoners studying martial arts was not unknown. Not all of Yamamoto's observations regarding Saitama were relevant to other parts of the country, but commoner involvement became prevalent countrywide—especially when martial arts became commercialized—and in provincial areas, where class lines between rustic samurai and farmers were blurred. Some schools were made up almost entirely of commoners. The Maniwa Nen-ryū, for example, was predominantly practiced by farmers and villagers in the Maniwa region.

To generalize in the most sweeping terms, the main difference between the attitude of samurai and non-samurai *kenjutsu* exponents, notwithstanding the many cases in which class distinction was vague, was that swordsmanship played an important symbolic role in the construction of samurai identity. Commoners were as dedicated to the art as the samurai, and it must have been more than just an exhilarating pastime to many. Nevertheless, from the perspective of more class-conscious middle- to upper-level samurai, the difference lay in the "samurai spirit"—something that a non-samurai could never embody, regardless of how skillful he was with a sword. I base this assumption on examples of sniping remarks to that effect in historical documentation, and on my experiences as a non-Japanese doing kendo in Japan. I expound on some of the interesting parallels in chapter 6.

What then was the "samurai spirit," and how did it and *kenjutsu* feature in the construct of samurai identity? The consideration of death was central to samurai subculture, albeit in a rather abstract, nostalgic, and philosophical way. The strength to embrace death was at the core of the existential samurai ethical code known as *shidō,* or bushido—moral principles that were emphasized in domain school education. *Kenjutsu* provided samurai with a way to prove their worth as warriors. Elias observed, "Fighting, in games of war, was centered on the ostentatious display of the warrior virtues which gained for a man the highest praise and honor among other members of his own group."[37] Fencing provided samurai with a "game of war" for accruing honor and accolades.

Although commoners were undoubtedly serious in their undertaking and enjoyed the thrill of victory, it was not necessarily a crucial factor in their social raison d'être—at least not before the 1800s, when skilled fencers became celebrities, irrespective of class affiliation. Even though commoners became increasingly prominent in fencing circles, conservative samurai were still condescending toward them, considering their social inferiors to be masquerading as pseudo-warriors on the basis of their fencing skills. They were acknowledged for their ability in the sporting sense, but it was not believed that they could ever truly embody the mind of a warrior. Skilled fencing masters not of warrior stock, for example, were snubbed for positions in the shogunate's military academy—the Kōbusho, which was established in 1856.

While on the topic of *kenjutsu*'s sportification, another interesting trend can be seen with the systemization of unified fencing techniques. Kōsaka Masataka's *Chiba Shūsaku jikiden kenjutsu meijin-hō* (Master Chiba Shūsaku's direct transmissions for mastery of *kenjutsu,* 1884) contains a detailed explanation of the sixty-eight fencing techniques Chiba Shūsaku created for the Hokushin Ittō-ryū. These techniques became decidedly influential in mid-nineteenth century fencing and now constitute the fundamental modus operandi of modern kendo (figure 11). The techniques break down as follows: head (*men*), twenty techniques; wrists (*kote*), twelve; thrusts to the face or throat (*tsuki*), eighteen; body strikes (*dō*), seven; and combinations (*renzoku-waza*), eighteen. Although it is unclear exactly when Chiba Shūsaku systemized these techniques, it must have been before Kōsaka entered his tutelage in 1844. It was from around this time that the *men* strike became the most coveted target for its decisiveness—an attitude that is still prevalent in modern kendo.

Fencers at Chiba Shūsaku's dojo were also known to strike opponent's legs, although there is only one recorded technique categorized as such. The Ryūgō-ryū also taught leg-striking techniques. However, these strikes were uncommon and disappeared completely from the technical repertoire of fencers by the Meiji period, as rules for engagement became more unified. This systemization is concurrent with similar modifications to combat sports being made in Europe. Elias observes of boxing: "Like many other bodily contests, fighting with bare knuckles assumed the characteristics of a sport in England where it was first subjected to a tighter set of rules which, inter alia, totally eliminated the use of legs as a weapon."[38]

This trend, seen in boxing in the West and *kenjutsu* in Japan, is indicative of the degree to which both had become "gentlemen's sports," or at least imbued with notions of "fair play," since in real combat one would resort to kicking or cutting any part of the body that was exposed.

One notable swordsman who pushed the envelope with regard to what was considered sportsmanlike was Ōishi Susumu (1797–1863), a fencing instructor for the Yanagawa domain. Ōishi was a certified *sōjutsu* master of both the Ōshima-ryū and of his own style, Ōishi Shinkage-ryū. Accounts suggest that he was tall, had freakishly long arms, and was a southpaw.[39] He put these attributes to good use by creating a technique that involved a one-handed thrust to the throat or torso with the left hand, hitherto unseen in fencing. His skill, and the fact that his *shinai* was much longer than most at 5-*shaku* 3-*sun* (approx. 167cm), made him a formidable opponent in fencing matches.

During the Tempo era (1830–44), Ōishi made his way to Edo, where he engaged in numerous bouts, including fights against such notables as Chiba Shūsaku and Otani Seiichirō (1798–1864). He believed that he won these

FIGURE 11. A rare specimen of mid-nineteenth century *dō* and *men*. Note the pronounced throat protector, which indicates that thrusting techniques to the throat had become common. (Courtesy of Gakken)

two matches, although differing interpretations of what rules were applicable left his two illustrious opponents unconvinced of their defeats. In any case, his success, and, by some opinions, unfairly long *shinai,* caused quite a commotion.

By the *bakumatsu* era, concerns were raised once again about the practical effectiveness of *kenjutsu* and the other martial arts as Japan faced the threat of foreign intrusion. Reliance on the traditional martial arts as a defense was questioned even before the unwelcome arrival of the steam-driven "black ships" of the American naval officer Commodore Perry, who arrived in Japanese waters in 1853 in pursuit of a trade treaty. When it came to a fight, Japan found itself to be outdated, outgunned, and out of its depth when pitted against Western powers. Although *kenjutsu* and the other martial arts had developed into fascinating martial sports that were rich in ritualistic symbolism and spiritualism, they were no match for the devastating fire-power backing up the Western nation's demands that Japan open her ports.

Amid the political unease, however, *kenjutsu* schools functioned as venues where anti-shogunate dissidents could gather and exchange information. As Jansen notes, "Tournaments and conventions provided ideal opportunities to refresh contact and friendships made in Edo fencing centers, and as the time for action neared, the swordsmen tested their ability by domestic disorder and political assassination."[40] The fencing network connected like-minded, politically active swordsmen, and dojos became support bases for the champions of the Meiji era. The role and destiny of *kenjutsu* in the Meiji period will be the topic of the next chapter.

CHAPTER 3

The Fall and Rise of Samurai Culture

KENJUTSU'S NATIONALIZATION

Men of Satsuma, behold the blade that hangs on this warrior of
the east; see for yourselves—is it dull or is it sharp?

YAMAKAWA HIROSHI, AIZU WARRIOR, 1845–98

DISMANTLING THE CENTURIES-OLD
WARRIOR HEGEMONY

The British envoy Thomas McClatchie (1852–86) was a great aficionado of
the Japanese sword. He even studied swordsmanship under the famous
master swordsman Sakakibara Kenkichi (1830–94) during his sojourn in
Meiji Japan. McClatchie underscored the relevance of the sword in Japanese
culture in a speech he gave to the Asiatic Society of Japan in 1873: "There is
no country in the world where the sword has received as much honor and
renown as in Japan. Regarded as of divine origin, dear to the general as a
symbol of authority, cherished by the samurai as a part of himself, considered
by the common people as their protection against violence, how can we
wonder to find it called the living soul of the samurai?"[1] The idea that
commoners regarded the sword as "protection against violence" was an arguably condescending construal that McClatchie presumably gleaned from his
dealings with former samurai. Nevertheless, as I have detailed in previous
chapters, reverence of the sword was most certainly a feature of Japan's early
modern warrior culture. With the arrival of the modern era, however, notions
of the sword and the traditional martial arts such as *kenjutsu* were subject to
a significant change in symbolic value. Immediately after the Meiji
Restoration in 1868, enthusiasm for the weapon ebbed. This was followed by
a full recovery, or, more precisely, a reinvention of its emblematic function.
The sword came to represent Japanese spiritual culture—an association that
has survived to this day.

During this period, *kenjutsu* transitioned from a form of culture largely associated with a particular social class to one that the entire nation could embody. In this way, *kenjutsu* as a legacy of traditional samurai culture was adopted in the process of inventing a new, nationalized cultural identity. According to Eric Hobsbawm, coeditor with T. O. Ranger of the 1983 book that brought the concept into prominence, "invented traditions" are "set[s] of practices, normally governed by overtly or tacitly accepted rules and of a ritual or symbolic nature, which seek to inculcate certain values and norms of behavior by repetition, which automatically implies continuity with the past."[2] As Japan strived to modernize itself, certain elements of its traditional culture were shed for the sake of social and economic advancement. In 1873, the imperial government established a modern conscript army, and *kenjutsu* and the other martial arts gave way to modern methods of warfare. Nevertheless, centuries of sword worship could not be so easily done away with: the sword's symbolic potency continued to make it irresistible. After a short lapse in popularity, swordsmanship was reinstated in society on an even greater scale than before, catalyzed by a number of fortuitous conjunctures, such as the advent of fencing shows (*gekiken-kōgyō*) and the introduction of *kenjutsu* into the police force and later the national education system.[3]

The evolution of the culture of swordsmanship was facilitated by a paradigm shift as to who owned it. To borrow one of Pierre Bourdieu's widely quoted concepts, the cultural field—which he defines as "a series of institutions, rules, rituals, conventions, categories, designations and appointments which constitutes an objective hierarchy, and which produce and authorize certain discourses and activities"[4]—contains cultural capital or culturally authorized attributes that confer power and status on the individual or group. As demonstrated in the previous chapter, fencing had become a captivating divertissement for townsmen and farmers, especially toward the early to mid-nineteenth century. Although authorities generally turned a blind eye to this imitation of samurai culture, *kenjutsu* was the exclusive "cultural capital" of warriors within their specific "cultural field."

According to Bourdieu, society considers "symbolic goods, especially those regarded as the attributes of excellence, . . . [as] the ideal weapon in strategies of distinction."[5] Cultural elements or aesthetic preferences thought to be particularly distinguished are incorporated into the cultural capital of the dominating class so that the differences in cultural capital mark the distinctions between the classes. With the resurgence of *kenjutsu* in the mid-Meiji era (1868–1912), the idea that the martial arts were representative of a noble warrior past, and therefore a marker of national superiority, was reinforced and increasingly exploited. Although not concerned with class elitism per se, the adoption of samurai cultural capital into the experience of a burgeoning modern Japanese national elitism, in relation to other cultures and nations, fits this paradigm. *Kenjutsu* came to be known not simply as fencing, but as "Japanese fencing," making tangible the implicit conditions of what it meant to be Japanese. As *kenjutsu* was gradually introduced into the national education system at the end of the Meiji period, its core principles, which were based on revived and contrived notions of bushido, and its physical manifestation, as represented by a newly created standardized version of *kenjutsu,* had become firmly consecrated as symbolic cultural capital for all Japanese.

As Carol Gluck observed of Japan's burgeoning nationalism, "National spirit, national thought, national doctrine, national essence, nationality— this outburst of nation-mindedness included explorations of national character, reassertions of indigenous ways, and projections of Japan into the world order as the nineteenth-century West defined it."[6] Within the paradigm of popular nationalism (vis-à-vis statist nationalism) *kenjutsu* as an "indigenous way" came to represent a continuous social and cultural history that linked the past with the present, thus connecting all Japanese. *Kenjutsu* was seen as something inherently good, the essence of which was curiously entrenched in the psyche of all citizens simply by virtue of their being born Japanese. Anthony Smith asserts that nations "provide individuals with 'sacred centers,' objects of spiritual and historical pilgrimage that reveal the uniqueness of their nation's 'moral geography',"[7] and this is precisely the role that *kenjutsu* increasingly played in Japan in the modern era.

Preceding this development, why and how did seven centuries of warrior hegemony get replaced by an imperial government? What were the motivations of the samurai who drove Japan's furious modernization? What did their championing of "functional equality" achieve in the ethno-symbolic reconstruction of the Japanese people and society? Answers to these questions will establish how and why *kenjutsu* was nationalized in the process of modernization.

Commodore Matthew C. Perry navigated his American flotilla of four steam ships, armed with the latest Paixhans guns and highly explosive shells, to the shores of Japan in 1853. The shogunate was panned as being ineffectual in the face of potential foreign incursion, and the foundations for a monumental social revolution were laid, mainly by seditious samurai from the Satsuma and Chōshū domains.

Ii Naosuke was appointed as Tairō (Great Elder) by the shogunate to help restore its dwindling authority. He facilitated many of the unpopular "unequal treaties" with Western powers, starting with the Harris Treaty of 1858. He also ordered the Ansei Purge in 1858 to quash opposition to shogunate policy. This served only to further politicize the lower-ranking, reactionary samurai, who were agitated at the shogunate's weak handling of the "foreign barbarians."

Various dojo records from this period show a huge increase in the number of visiting swordsmen, indicating that dissident warriors known as *shishi,* or "men of high purpose," were doing the rounds and using fencing venues as places to exchange information. As Marius Jansen points out, "Lacking responsibility for negotiation and government, full of enthusiasm for the martial values of their own culture without being encumbered by much knowledge about the strength of the West, these loyalists were willing to trust in the strength of the sword and spirit to repel the hated Westerners."[8] They resented the fact that their lowly ranks in the scheme of the samurai hierarchy hindered them from exerting influence on government policy, and mutinous aspirations were bolstered by the ideals of *sonnō-jōi*—"Revere the emperor, expel the barbarians."

Supported by anti-shogunate domains and Kyoto-based nobles, the *shishi* busied themselves with hatching subversive plans to rid Japan of foreigners and certain government officials, including Ii Naosuke, who they successfully assassinated in 1860 in front of Edo Castle. Zealous advocates of the *sonnō-jōi* doctrine included Yoshida Shōin (1830–59) and a handful of his followers, such as Kusaka Genzui (1840–64), the celebrated swordsmen Kido Kōin (also known as Katsura Kogorō, 1833–77) and Takasugi Shinsaku (1839–67; figure 12) of the Shintō Munen-ryū, and Itō Hirobumi (1841–1901) and Yamagata Aritomo (1838–1922), who were to become leading statesmen in the new Meiji government. Itō and Yamagata even had connections with the Dai-Nippon Butokukai, which I will look at later in this chapter.

Takechi Zuizan (1829–65) of the Kyōshin Meichi-ryū in the Tosa domain was another outstanding swordsman and a charismatic advocate of revolution. Nakaoka Shintarō (1838–67) and Sakamoto Ryōma (1836–67), who studied the Nakanishi-ha Ittō-ryū, were his followers. Together they traveled throughout the country, stopping at various dojos to participate in fencing

FIGURE 12. A photograph of Takasugi Shinsaku (1839–67), a samurai from the Chōshū domain. His skills with the sword were legendary, as was his contribution to the *shishi* movement. (Courtesy of Bunkasha International)

bouts and mixed training. Through crossing *shinai,* they formed an extensive network of anti-shogunate swordsmen. These dissidents flocked to fencing halls across Japan to feed off one another's antipathy for the government, and to prepare for action.

Supporters of revolution were not limited to samurai. Saitō Yakurō—the farmer turned iconic Edo fencing master—was also a strong advocate of *sonnō-jōi* ideology. Some of his estimated three thousand students would eventually feature among the most influential statesmen in the Meiji government. The *sonnō-jōi* movement not only spurned the shogunate but also condemned Western "barbarians" and included foreigners as targets of their murderous wrath. The Dutchman Henry Conrad Joannes Heusken, who translated for Townsend Harris when the Harris treaty was signed, was cut down in 1861 by Kiyokawa Hachirō (1830–63), a well-known radical swordsman of the Hokushin Ittō-ryū and student of the Genbukan. In September 1862, retainers of Satsuma's Shimazu Hisamitsu murdered a British merchant and seriously injured two of his companions for not showing respect to the daimyo's procession. Resident foreigners grew fearful of any samurai they happened to pass in the street, wondering if the last thing they would hear would be the swish of a *shishi* blade.

Although anti-shogunate sentiment had been simmering for generations, it was the last shogun, Tokugawa Yoshinobu (1837–1913), who brought dissatisfaction to a head due to his feeble response to the threat of foreign irruption. The Tosa domain recommended that he abdicate in favor of restoring imperial governance. They also suggested a compromise devised by Sakamoto Ryōma in which Yoshinobu would lead a bicameral legislature, possibly consisting of daimyo and prominent vassals.

Toward the end of 1867, Yoshinobu accepted the proposal; however, on January 3, 1868, Chōshū and Satsuma forces expedited the process by announcing the restoration of imperial rule as they surrounded the palace in Kyoto. Narrowly defined, this coup d'état represents what is known as the Meiji Restoration. Yoshinobu then sent his forces from Osaka Castle in response to demands that he surrender all of his land and offices. They were attacked by the imperialists, starting the Boshin War (1868–69). The imperialists prevailed, and Japan embarked on a frenzied path of modernization under Emperor Meiji (1852–1912).

Prior to the Meiji Restoration, samurai society had been fraught with complicated dichotomies generated by powerful notions of autonomy and duty. Although there were clear institutional mechanisms that allowed samurai to rise up the ranks within the context of hierarchical stratification, with some even reaching the lofty heights of clan elder or daimyo confidant, most were destined to remain in the position they had been born into. Imperialist supporters championed the idea of creating a modern army and navy that would match any power in the West and pondered the adoption of a new social system in which men with merit, regardless of class background, would be afforded opportunities to engage in careers previously closed to them.

Following the Meiji Restoration, traditional domains were abolished in favor of a progressive prefectural system supervised by governors who were selected by the central government. Furthermore, from 1869, the old class distinctions were replaced with the new categories of *kazoku* (nobles), *shizoku* (former samurai), and *heimin* (commoners including farmers, merchants, artisans, and certain outcast groups).[9] Although *shizoku* were initially afforded special treatment, such as government-issued stipends, up until 1877, their political, economic, and social privileges and symbols of rank were systematically abolished during the 1870s. While social status was still generally fixed, the lines separating *heimin* and *shizoku* became progressively obscured through governmental consent to such matters as interclass marriage, the right for commoners to take surnames, and occupational freedom.

Sonoda Hidehiro observed that in the dismantling of social status in Europe, the more closely high status was related to the center of the state apparatus, the harder it was to establish ideas of equality. He argues that in the case of Japan, the samurai instigated a type of self-revolution, enabling an accelerated formation of ideals of "functional egalitarianism."[10] In other words, the old system of samurai government was not replaced as a reaction to revolting peasants, but rather by the will of the samurai themselves. It was the samurai's specialized military duty as professional warriors that drove them to initiate a revolutionary social overhaul to prevent Japan from becoming a victim of powerful Western nations, as had happened to the once-almighty China a few years before. Ironically, it was recognition of the need for a renaissance in the military profession that played a part in the dismantling of the samurai as a social class.

As described in the previous chapter, the military arts had evolved into pursuits that were, for the most part, removed from the realities of modern war. Far from being battle-hardened warriors, samurai had become salaried bureaucrats and duty-bound servants. With the exception of the odd skirmish or vendetta, and a degree of inter-domain rivalry and tension that characterized Edo society, war had become an abstract concept. Martial arts continued to function as a symbolic locus for warrior identity, but they turned into what can essentially be called spiritual sports. Samurai were judged by their peers on their intangible projection of inner strength, the number or level of licenses they managed to procure, and their demeanor and gravitas during training.

By the time Perry's ships arrived in Japan, it was evident that skill in the martial arts would not be enough to defend the country from potential

FIGURE 13. A European drawing of samurai engaged in training with spears and swords at the Kōbusho. (From *Le Japon illustré*, 1866)

intrusion. A revolutionary new military system was needed to save Japan. After the Meiji Restoration, the latest weaponry was imported from the West, and a conscript army was established to train common men as soldiers in the art of modern warfare.

In 1856, prior to the restoration, the shogunate had attempted to strengthen its defensive capabilities by establishing the Kōbusho (figure 13), a military academy that was based on maintaining traditional values of civil and martial arts (*bun-bu*). Its purpose was to instruct Tokugawa retainers, and although it was closed a decade later, in 1866, in its heyday it employed over five hundred instructors (mainly assistants) of *kenjutsu*, *sōjutsu*, and *kyūjutsu*. Cursory lessons were also offered in *jūjutsu* and firearms, but over two-thirds of the instructors taught sword or spear usage. The curriculum was largely a stubborn reaffirmation of traditional rather than modern combat. As Karl Friday maintains, "*Bushi*, who had not made or even trained seriously for war in generations, had lost sight of any separation between martial art and military training. . . . There was but one form of sophisticated combative training: the individual-centered, self-development-oriented arts of the various *ryūha*."[11]

Even so, it is possible to detect a smidgen of progressiveness in the way the Kōbusho was organized. For instance, its regulations, which consisted of forty-two articles, stipulated that matches (sparring) would be the core of training. Interestingly, Article 13 makes reference to the fact that numerous schools of the spear and sword rely on kata practice. From this we can infer that, although full-contact fencing with protective armor was popular in the *bakumatsu* era, traditionalists still preferred practicing choreographed sequences of techniques. The regulations warn, however, that such methods only "lower morale." All trainees, even those from the illustrious Yagyū Shinkage-ryū, were required to participate in sparring, which the Kōbusho deemed "clearly more practical."[12]

A fencer who defeated a ranked opponent from an established school of swordsmanship could formally request that the Kōbusho bestow upon him a comparable rank. This was radical in that it rewarded practitioners for their actual ability rather than the length of time they studied under a *ryūha* master. The Kōbusho also introduced other avant-garde changes in swordsmanship, such as the introduction of fixed-length bamboo practice swords and match rules to adjudicate contests. In other words, the academy authorities experimented with a style of fencing that rose above *ryūha* rivalries and prejudices. This was the first government attempt at a nationally unified style of swordsmanship.

Nevertheless, in the final analysis, Kōbusho instruction clung closely to conventional techniques and the idea of *kenjutsu* as a medium for spiritual and moral training. The shogunate was not alone in its conservatism. The Hikone domain, for example, was adamant that military training for its warriors should revolve around archery, horse riding, swordsmanship, and spearmanship, and should foster a "sense of shame"—a clear indication that self-cultivation and traditionalism were still cornerstone considerations in martial art training.[13]

In spite of Japan's precarious state of national security, a degree of sentimental attachment to the symbolic value of the sword was inevitable. Even Mori Arinori (1847–89), one of the chief advocates for the 1876 edict forbidding the wearing of swords in public (*Haitō-rei*), championed traditional concepts of balancing the literary and military arts. Nevertheless, the necessity to keep pace with Western military practices eventually trumped nostalgic cultural sensitivities. The katana was functional against sword-wielding foes, but Mori argued that Japan as a nation needed to adopt and master the latest Western technology to defend itself against foreign powers.

There was growing acceptance of the idea that firepower was needed to ensure Japan's continued existence. The abscission of traditional patterns of behavior was unavoidable. The martial arts entered a temporary period of hibernation but would eventually evolve into an ideological vehicle utilizing powerful notions of tradition to supplement modernity.

Between 1868 and 1871, feudal domains were dismantled and the Imperial Army and police force were formed, shifting the responsibility for civil defense. Instigated by the Chōshū samurai Ōmura Masajurō, Japan's modern army was established in 1869 and was formulated largely on the French model. Nationwide conscription was established in 1873, although the question still remained of who would be allowed to hold which rank in the new army. Would officer positions be reserved for former samurai, or would the job be open to anyone with the right stuff?

Motivated by functionalism and their sense of duty as warriors and protectors of the nation, former samurai initiated a renovation of the out-of-date hierarchical, class-based system. Reforms were made during the early years of the Meiji government, giving bureaucratic and military posts to men with ability rather than those with hereditary status. Entrance examinations for the army and navy were open to all, as were institutions of higher education, through a new policy premised on "functional equality."[14]

In the years following the promulgation of the Conscription Ordinance of 1873, all men over the age of twenty were expected to complete three years of military training, unless they had the wherewithal to buy their way out. The Hair Cut Edict (Danpatsu-rei) of 1871 forced former samurai (*shizoku*) to cut off their now passé topknots (*mage*). The Sword Abolishment Edict (Haitō-rei), issued in 1876, forbade *shizoku* from carrying swords, transferring this right to military officers and policemen, whose ranks were made up of men from a mix of class backgrounds. To use Anthony Smith's words, these changes required "ethno-symbolic reconstruction," a concept that he defines as "the reselection, recombination and recodification of previously existing values, symbols, memories and the like, as well as the addition of new cultural elements by each generation."[15]

To make the transition less excruciating, the government gave stipends to the *shizoku* beginning in 1869. However, due to the massive financial burden on the nation's coffers, measures introduced in 1873 resulted in the taxation of income, and *shizoku* were eventually forced to exchange their stipends for government bonds in 1876, leading to the impoverishment of many of them. A considerable number of *shizoku* were able to reestablish themselves in new careers—91 percent of Meiji political leaders were from samurai stock, as were 70 percent of cultural leaders, and 23 percent of business leaders.[16] Some, however, lacking tangible skills suited to the world modernizing around them, became destitute.

Inspired by the *shishi* of a generation before, rebellious groups made up of forlorn *shizoku* participated in assassinations and rioting. Influential Meiji leaders, such as Ōmura Masajurō and Ōkubo Toshimichi, assassinated in 1896 and 1878, respectively, were notable victims of these extremists. Indignant *shizoku* also led several violent revolts, including the Saga Rebellion (February 1874), the Hagi Rebellion (October 1876), the Shinpūren Rebellion (October 1876), and the Satsuma Rebellion (1877).

THE REINVENTION OF *KENJUTSU*

How did *kenjutsu* survive this period of tumultuous social change to become an integral medium for imparting ideas of "Japaneseness"? Some chance events kept the martial arts, and especially *kenjutsu,* in a position to be capitalized upon as Japan's modern nationalism began to flourish. Prominent swordsman Sakakibara Kenkichi organized an intriguing source of income for poverty-stricken fencers. Using the sumo tournament model, Sakakibara initiated public fencing shows called *gekiken-kōgyō* that gave swordsmen a chance to earn money by displaying their talents in demonstration matches (figure 14).

Sakakibara's father served the shogunate as a direct retainer (*hatamoto*). It was clear from a young age that Sakakibara was gifted in the martial arts, and his father entrusted his fencing tuition to Inoue Denbei—a master of the Jikishin Kage-ryū. Inoue was assassinated in 1838, possibly by Honjō Moheiji to stop Inoue from divulging details about a murderous scheme that he refused to lend a hand with. Sakakibara then entered the tutelage of another Jikishin Kage-ryū master, Otani Seiichirō Nobutomo (1798–1864), who awarded him a teaching license in the tradition in 1856. In March of that year, Otani recommended that his protégé be appointed as one of the assistant instructors at the Kōbusho. He became a head instructor in 1858. That year, he also married Taka, the niece of the celebrated Meiji statesman and naval engineer Katsu Kaishū. In addition to being the captain of the first modern Japanese ship to sail across the Pacific in 1860, chief negotiator for the Tokugawa shogunate in the events surrounding the Meiji Restoration, and minister of the Meiji government's Navy Ministry, Katsu was also Sakakibara's benefactor, helping him out financially when he lost his source of income as a fencing instructor.

FIGURE 14. An illustration of matches at a *gekiken-kōgyō* meet. The names of the featured swordsmen are written in the upper background. (From *Sakakibara gekiken-kai no nishiki-e,* 1873; courtesy of Bunkasha International)

Lamenting both the decline of *kenjutsu* and the impecuniousness of once-venerated swordsmen in the post-restoration era, Sakakibara vowed to remedy the situation. He initially organized open training sessions and demonstrations at his training hall in Shitaya Kurumasaka, Tokyo, in February 1873. Exponents from all fencing styles were invited to attend and members of the public were also allowed to observe the proceedings.

Among the spectators were a priest named Tanuma Toshiaki and a wealthy teahouse proprietor named Yakataya Naojirō. Both men proposed commercializing the event on a grand scale. Sakakibara was quick to see the financial potential of such a venture, and he also realized that this might be his chance to save *kenjutsu* from its downward spiral. He filed an application to the Tokyo Metropolitan Government to hold a public display of fencing, which was sanctioned on March 8, 1873.

Sakakibara then issued a statement concerning the method in which the matches would be conducted. The participants were to follow the Kōbusho style of competition in using a *shinai* no longer than approximately 115 cm. Matches would be decided by the best of three points (*sanbon-shōbu*), judged by neutral adjudicators rather than the fencers themselves. Members of the public were even given an opportunity to challenge the fencers by registering a day before; equipment could be leased for a fee.

Newspapers were enthusiastic, and information about the demonstrations quickly spread. The first event lasted twelve days, opening on April 26, 1873, and continuing until May 5. Each day, hundreds of people lined up outside the makeshift arena near the riverbank in Asakusa, and many were turned away disappointed due to the restricted space inside the venue. It was originally scheduled to last ten days but continued by popular demand, only coming to an abrupt end because of a sudden dictate halting all entertainment in Tokyo because of an outbreak of fire in the imperial palace.

According to Ishigaki Yasuzō, a raised earthen mound measuring 27.4 × 24.3 meters was prepared inside the enclosure. It was not an oval-shaped mound like that used in sumo, although contemporary illustrations of the event depict it as such. Positioned in the middle of the mound, a wooden floor measuring 7.3 × 5.5 meters served as the match court. Encircling the mound was a 46 × 46 meter space for spectators. All of these dimensions vary slightly from those stated in Sakakibara's initial application to hold the event. Furthermore, as the arena was packed beyond capacity on the first day, the bleachers were widened to approximately 64 × 64 meters on the second day. I cannot find any record indicating the actual number of spectators. However, based on rough calculations of the space around the mound, with an average of 1 meter squared per person, it is plausible that up to four thousand people sat inside to watch the spectacle each day.

The matches started at eight o'clock each morning, and eighty-eight demonstration fighters were divided into three ranks. The "first class" group consisted of ten elite Jikishin Kage-ryū fencers, whose matches featured at the end of the day. There were thirty-six "second class" fencers, who were mainly students of Sakakibara. The "third class" group was made up of forty fighters, including women, who competed with *naginata*. There was even an exponent of the *kusarigama* (sickle and chain) and a couple of foreigners. British envoy Thomas McClatchie and another Englishman named Jack Vince (or Binns) were also students of Sakakibara, and it must have been a sight to behold for Japanese, who were not accustomed to seeing martial art contests, not to mention foreigners.

Following this remarkable success, Sakakibara convened a second martial arts gala a few weeks later in Yokohama, and this one was attended by fencers from other schools. The Yokohama amphitheater was surrounded by red and white drapes, the traditional colors used to symbolize opposing teams in Japan.[17] Within two months, the shows had become immensely popular in Tokyo, and they began spreading throughout the provinces. Troupes sprouted up all over the country to take advantage of public interest.

Were the events profitable for the participants? Okada Kazuo's research shows that in the big tournaments organized by Sakakibara, well-known fencers could receive the modern equivalent of ¥20,000–30,000 for an appearance (US$160–250). Lesser fighters received only one-tenth of that amount, but daily matches over a week would nonetheless bring in a welcome sum of cash.[18] Given the moneymaking potential, some of the fighters within Sakakibara's company broke away, some to design their own shows, while others simply copied his model, and in one case, even his name.

It is impossible to know exactly how many martial artists participated in *gekiken* tournaments, as records are too scant. Newspaper articles from the period indicate how the sudden rise in the number of companies organizing events led to a decline in quality and, subsequently, a gradual loss of interest among the paying public. To counter falling patronage, proprietors attempted to make their shows more entertaining and dynamic. At first, these ostentatious spectacles rekindled excitement, but the enthusiasm was short-lived. The media began to take an increasingly critical stance. Editorials and magazine articles lambasted the swordsmen as being nothing more than cheap performers who pawned their once-sacred samurai honor for cash to spend on booze and women. They were criticized for sullying the integrity of their swords, which had once signified the pride and reputation of the adherents of bushido.

The government had no inkling that the *gekiken-kōgyō* meets would become such a sensation. Had officials known, they would probably not have allowed them to go ahead in the first place. Featuring Japan's "greatest warriors" in a carnival-like atmosphere was probably a source of embarrassment to them as the country sought parity with the West. On July 15, 1873, no more than three months after the first *gekiken-kōgyō* meet was authorized, the Ministry of Finance issued a decree banning the gatherings in Tokyo, effective July 31. Other regions soon followed suit, reasoning that the exhibitions were "impeding the productivity" of the people.

The bans were undoubtedly motivated more by politics than by economic concerns. As demonstrated later, by the outbreak of the Satsuma Rebellion in 1877, Japan was politically volatile, and authorities saw the *gekiken-kōgyō* venues as potential hotbeds for disgruntled *shizoku* to congregate and engage in subversive plotting, just as private fencing academies had been for the *shishi* in the twilight years of the Tokugawa era.

Penalties for violating the bans were strict in most parts of the country. For example, the Kyoto prefectural government warned that offenders would be incarcerated for six months in Nijō Castle. However, the restrictions became less stringently enforced in eastern Japan, and even though hostility between government forces and Satsuma rebels in Kyushu had reached a crescendo, the national government allowed fencing exhibitions to be held in Tokyo once again in 1877.

This may seem to be an odd reversal of policy given the political situation in Japan at the time. However, as I will explain shortly, it had become clear over the course of the Satsuma Rebellion that swords did have a use on the modern battlefield after all. The government most likely sanctioned the exhibition matches as they would provide a handy arena for scouting recruits into the police and army. Thus Sakakibara was permitted to organize a demonstration of fencing in Ueno on March 2 and 3, 1877. An article reporting his exhibition matches using *yamato-zue* (literally, "Japanese sticks") appeared in the *Yomiuri Newspaper* on April 17, 1877. Interestingly, Sakakibara judiciously avoided using the word *ken* (sword) this time.

Still, one can sense the changing attitude authorities and the general public had toward the value of martial arts in another *Yomiuri Newspaper* article with a humorous twist: "We reported previously how, sparked by the exploits of the Battōtai police unit in the Satsuma Rebellion, *kenjutsu* had become popular far and wide. Apparently, Sakakibara Kenkichi has accepted a number of young women aged 7 to 16 into his tutelage. They are studying the martial arts enthusiastically, and have formed a group of formidable *naginata* exponents ready to cut the testicles off Saigō [Takamori] and his henchmen" (August 18, 1877).

It is unlikely that *kenjutsu* would have disappeared completely without *gekiken-kōgyō,* but the demonstrations certainly contributed to its successful adaptation in the modern era. This was further helped by a rather peculiar incident during the Satsuma Rebellion involving the abovementioned Battōtai (Bare Blade Brigade). The Battōtai was a government police unit made up of one hundred former samurai from the pro-shogunate Aizu domain. These skilled swordsmen contributed to a hard-fought victory against the Satsuma rebels at the Battle of Tabaruzaka, which took place in Kumamoto Prefecture in March 1877. Aizu *shizoku* harbored an intense hatred for the warriors of Satsuma, who had humiliated them in the Boshin Civil War (1868–69) that followed the restoration. They were crushed as enemies of the court and shown no clemency by the pro-imperial forces. In a curious quirk of fate, those same Aizu *warriors* found themselves in the ranks of the imperial government forces fighting against their avowed enemy Saigō Takamori, who, in turn, was battling against the very regime he had helped install.

The Aizu soldiers were ordered to take only their swords with them to the front. The reason for this is not clear, but I surmise that it was a kind of punishment for their allegiance to the shogunate a decade before. Perhaps the directive was welcomed by the Aizu men themselves, who wanted to commit the ultimate act of retribution by traditional means. The *Yūbin hōchi* newspaper published future prime minister Inukai Tsuyoshi's firsthand account of the conflict. In it, he relates an Aizu battle cry that attests to the warriors' conviction that revenge is a dish best served with cold steel: "A former Aizu soldier put himself in bodily danger and charged forward, immediately cutting down the thirteen rebels. As he slashed about, he called out loudly, 'Remember the Boshin, remember the Boshin!' This may sound like a work of fiction but it is by no means made up. It is said that this Aizu man suffered only slight wounds."[19]

He was lucky. Two days of bloody close-quarter combat saw twenty-five of the one hundred members of the Battōtai unit killed and fifty-four injured. Close inspection of documents reveals that their victory was facilitated by Satsuma rebel miscalculations: a series of tactical blunders, a shortage of food and munitions, and a lack of vigilance.[20] Nonetheless, this hard-fought victory was eulogized in the media, and the incident retrospectively proved to be a turning point for *kenjutsu,* as well as for elite swordsmen. Unbelievable as the triumph must have seemed to the world at large, it is not difficult to fathom how the bare blades of the Battōtai could have prevailed when the opposing forces suddenly found themselves in close proximity. Satsuma warriors were cut down as they frantically tried to reload, or when they had run out of munitions altogether.

In any case, the victory proved to be a tremendous windfall for many of the *gekiken-kōgyō* fighters who had managed to solidify their reputations as the country's most celebrated fencers, ultimately fortifying an allegorical bridge that let obsolescent martial arts enter the modern world. It also denoted the start of an era in which the martial arts became popular among the masses on a scale never seen before: "In recent times, one can hear the battle cries of many people, including farmers, engaging in *kenjutsu* practice in the mountains on moonlit evenings, and in temple gardens. Could this be the far-reaching inspiration of the Battōtai?" (*Yomiuri Newspaper,* May 16, 1877). Indeed a pertinent, if not rhetorical, question.

After the battle, Kawaji Toshiyoshi (1829–79), a former Satsuma warrior and commissioner of the newly formed national police, expressed his unreserved admiration for the Battōtai and their exploits. Notions of nostalgic romanticism—albeit inspired by his former enemies' victory against his former clansmen—most likely encouraged him to write "Gekiken Saikō-ron" (Revitalizing swordsmanship) in November 1878, before departing on an inspection tour of European police forces in 1879. The gist was that *kenjutsu* should no longer be disregarded as an antiquated remnant of a bygone era; it had proved itself irrefutably in the theater of modern warfare. It would, he maintained, surely provide an excellent means for training the nation's patrolmen, improving both their physical strength and their powers of perception, while simultaneously providing them with some necessary skills for self-defense.

> Swordsmanship is studied with much enthusiasm in the West. If we in Japan lose our way of fencing, we will be forced to learn it off them in the future. The Western sabre is not nearly as sharp as the Japanese sword [*nihontō*]. If we do away with our style of swordsmanship [*kenpō*] and take up the Western sabre, this is analogous to discarding gold and replacing it with clay roof tiles. Although we live in an era in which guns are predominant, we have seen proof of the efficacy of swordsmanship through the great exploits of the Battōtai in the Satsuma Rebellion. Furthermore, *kenjutsu* is particularly useful for developing individual character and encouraging discipline.[21]

Curriculum guidelines for the newly constructed Patrolman's Training Institute (Junsa Kyōshūjo), founded in 1879, recommended that cadets study *kenjutsu* in their off-hours. Although the institute was closed in 1881 as part of an overhaul of the national police system in which training responsibilities were allocated to regional departments, *kenjutsu* continued to flourish in the police, demonstrated by this comment made by a policeman to the *Yomiuri Newspaper* in 1882: "I continue to train diligently in *gekiken* as it is indispensable for policing. Yesterday, a police sergeant urged patrolmen at each police station to keep practicing swordsmanship, even when they are off-duty" (October 10, 1882). The Tokyo Metropolitan Police continued to support *gekiken* tournaments, which were publicized in local newspapers. These tournaments were frequented by policemen from other parts of the country, and the Tokyo department became established as the principal advocate for *bujutsu* in the force. This legacy is still very much alive today, with many of the strongest kendoka in Japan hailing from the Keishichō (Tokyo Metropolitan Police Department).

The police attended private *gekiken* meets as competitors, but with the ulterior motive of recruiting star fighters as department instructors. Consequently, the fencing shows became depleted of talent, and public interest waned once again. Some troupes of fighters, such as the one led by Satake Kanryūsai, continued their traveling martial art extravaganzas in the provinces, but the majority had disappeared by 1890.[22]

The Keishichō started to convene its own *bujutsu* tournaments, the first of which was held in November 1882. (This tournament proved auspicious for Kanō Jigorō, when his judo students famously overwhelmed police *jūjutsu* experts, giving his Kōdōkan a formidable reputation.) In August 1885, police *kenjutsu* guidelines were established, limiting *shinai*-length to less than 4 *shaku* (approximately 121 cm), and a national police *kenjutsu* promotion system was introduced.

To further standardize police *kenjutsu*, representatives from several influential *ryūha* contributed to the creation of a unified kata at a *bujutsu* tournament in June 1886. This formed the basis for a new *kenjutsu ryūha* (the Keishiryū), which is still practiced today by some officers in the Tokyo Police. A total of ten techniques were eventually adapted for the *kenjutsu* kata from the Jikishin Kage-ryū, Kurama-ryū, Hōzan-ryū, Tatsumi-ryū, Hokushin Ittō-ryū, Asayama Ichiden-ryū, Jigen-ryū, Shintō Munen-ryū, Yagyū-ryū, and Kyōshin Meichi-ryū. Five kata were borrowed from five different *ryūha* to form the Keishi-ryū standing *iaidō* (solo sword-drawing forms performed against an imaginary opponent). Also introduced were sixteen techniques for *jūjutsu* (which was eventually rendered obsolete by Kōdōkan judo) and seven methods for rope tying (*hojōjutsu*).

Cherry-picking techniques from various *ryūha* was a progressive step toward creating a standardized hybrid curriculum for nationwide diffusion. Comparable attempts to unify fencing conventions (*shinai* length, etc.) had been experimented with in the now-defunct Kōbusho and Sakakibara's *gekiken-kōgyō* matches, but *ryūha* differences and preferences precluded the creation of a truly uniform style of *kenjutsu*.

The army also tested *kenjustu* at the Toyama Military Academy, but it primarily employed techniques based on French and German one-handed fencing introduced by foreign instructors commissioned to bring Japan's military up to speed with powerful Western nations. Japanese-style two-handed fencing was not introduced until 1915, in the third revision of the military's *Kenjutsu kyōhan* (Fencing textbook). Other developments worthy of mention were the inauguration of *kenjutsu* training for the Imperial Guards (Kōgū Keisatsu) in 1881 and the erection of their Saineikan martial training hall in 1883. The Imperial Guard fencers were led by ten notable swordsmen, including Watanabe Noboru (1838–1913) of the Shintō Munen-ryū and the eminent Meiji statesman and swordsman Yamaoka Tesshū (1836–88).

Tesshū was a retainer of the Tokugawa shogunate when imperial forces entered Edo in 1868 under the command of Saigō Takamori. The acting commandant of the shogunate forces, Katsu Kaishū, relied on Tesshū's diplomatic savoir-faire to help stave off a bloody confrontation between the two forces, ultimately negotiating the nonviolent surrender of Edo Castle. After the restoration, Tesshū served as a trusted aide to Emperor Meiji, and taught his brand of unforgiving *kenjutsu* to the Imperial Guards.

The life of Tesshū is shrouded in myth, and it is often difficult to separate fact from fiction owing to his virtual deification by future generations of followers of his school. His skills in calligraphy (he apparently sold tens of thousands of examples of his work) and his dedication to Zen represent his tranquil side, but he had a fearsome reputation in the dojo. As a child he studied a number of different styles of *kenjutsu,* eventually becoming a disciple of Asari Yoshiaki (1822–94) of the Nakanishi-ha Ittō-ryū. In 1885, he created his own school, the Ittō-shōden Mutō-ryū. He died in 1888 of stomach cancer. Apparently he always took sips of the highly carcinogenic charcoal ink before brushing his calligraphy, which was the probable cause of his illness.

Tesshū was a great proponent of fencing, but he was a fundamentalist who advocated the arduous training methods of "old-style" *kenjutsu*. Although he was not directly involved in lobbying activities to include *bujutsu* in the education system, many of his influential students were at the vanguard. These included Kagawa Senjirō (1848–1921), who became the second head of the Mutō-ryū and held the title of *hanshi* in the Dai-Nippon Butokukai; Koteda Yasusada (1840–99), an elder statesman who served as the governor of Shiga, Shimane, and Niigata prefectures and was a member of the House of Peers; and Kitagaki Kunimichi (1836–1916), who was also a member of the House of Peers as well as an official in the Butokukai, serving in the committee that formed the "Greater-Japan Imperial Kenjutsu Kata" in 1912. Tesshū also taught Nishikubo Hiromichi (1863–1930) and Takano Sasaburō (1862–1950), who were of particular importance to the nationalization of kendo.

The following quote from Takano Sasaburō recalling one of the infamous *tachikiri* training sessions is lengthy, but it will give the reader a vivid image of the merciless training endured by the men who became the most influential kendo masters of the twentieth century.

Once, Takahashi Kyūtarō, Kawasaki Zenzaburō and I did "day and night *tachikiri-geiko,*" where we kept fencing nonstop throughout the night. For the policemen from the Keishichō who participated, those who lasted this grueling exercise were selected to travel around the country to promote kendo. At that time, in addition to the three of us, ten prominent *kenshi* were chosen to practice without any break from 18:00 through to 6:00 the next morning. The session took place at the Azumabashi Police Station in Tokyo, and "assistants" who were willing came from various stations to beat us to a pulp. By midnight, my senses were completely numbed. If we stood in the middle of the dojo in such a dazed state, the assistants would throw us down and hammer us. We would not pass the test if we did not hang on until the bitter end, but around 2:00 it became so excruciating that I really felt like quitting. Still, there were four or five of us still standing. If we stood with our backs against the wall with our *shinai* upright, they would drag us out to the center by force, and strike and thrust at us making it hard to carry on. The more we persevered, the drowsier we became because of the onset of fatigue. We became as tottery as carp in rough waters. Nevertheless, the human spirit is an amazing thing. A big chicken coop was situated beside the police station, and when the first cock started crowing, somehow we were reenergized. With the growing light of dawn we came to our senses again, and we sought out the individuals who were pounding us a short while ago and gave them a taste of their own medicine. In the end, the three of us managed to survive until the end. Nonetheless, training from 18:00 until 6:00 was a truly miserable experience. We were able to eat three helpings of rice gruel over the twelve hours, and visited the washroom three times. My body did not return to normal for a whole week. Although I snored loudly, my head did not sleep at all. All I could see in my dreams for the week ahead were images of fighting with a *shinai*. Although crude to mention, my pee was bright red for a week as well because of the blood in my urine. Those were the toughest days of training in my life.[23]

To this day, kendo practices are typically grueling—even seemingly violent in many respects—especially at high school and university club level (although instruction is less demanding in PE classes). The police are also renowned for their ruthless training regimes. Kendo training sessions are rarely as inhuman as Tesshū's trademark *tachikiri-geiko,* but pushing oneself to the brink of physical and mental discombobulation (and beyond) in a way that would make a rational sports trainer cringe in disbelief is commonplace, and considered to be essential to freeing the mind.

Aside from the police department and *gekiken* events, *kenjutsu* was also featured at some of the Popular Rights Movement (*jiyū minken undō*) rallies. The movement consisted of loosely allied, nonconformist popular nationalist groups known as *kessha*, which were made up of former samurai and commoners. They had a common purpose of encouraging reform in the Meiji government along the lines of Western democracy. Kevin Doak suggests that the movement's spirit of individualistic patriotism "was increasingly engulfed by a romantic, historicist nationalism that asserted the particularity of the Japanese ethnic nation."[24] It is estimated that there were 255 Popular Rights groups in Japan at the movement's zenith. However, measures such as the Peace Preservation Law of 1887, which was designed to thwart political opposition, and the promulgation of the Constitution of the Empire of Japan in 1889 essentially spelled the end for this group, as its prominent leaders either bowed out or found new roles in the government.

Little research has been done on the extent of *kenjutsu*'s role in this early Meiji-era political movement, but, according to Yuasa Akira, *kenjutsu* clearly served an important purpose. Displays of swordsmanship that "lifted spirits and heightened the tension" were conducted before political speeches to intensify opposition to the government manifesto.[25] Participants in these events engaged in a variety of matches, including individual contests and large-scale, free-for-all battles with the aim of appropriating the opposition's flag. Such melees nurtured leadership, fighting spirit, and teamwork for a collective cause.

The authorities were watchful of these political meetings, aware of the precedent set by *shishi* a few generations before and apprehensive about the rebellious *shizoku* still looking for trouble. This was possibly another reason why the police started endorsing *kenjutsu* in earnest. It would not only help them spy on treasonable political groups but also provide employment to the charismatic sword experts who might otherwise lead them. Although these aims were never stated explicitly, an article in the *Yomiuri Newspaper* on May 27, 1888, reported that "three police officers skilled in the art of *kenjutsu*" were sent on an extended period of *musha-shugyō* (traveling to engage in matches) in the provinces. Surely there were ulterior motives for the trip.

Sheldon Garon observes that by the late 1880s, "intellectuals, local elites, and officials broadly agreed on the need to foster 'a sense of nation' in the masses if Japan were to modernize and compete with Western rivals."[26] It is precisely in this period that questions of Japaneseness—the essence of what it meant to be Japanese—became a widespread matter of deliberation. In many respects, the Japanese were feeling their way as they formed a national identity, and, according to Doak, this epoch represented the "first important moment in Japanese nationalism when culture, as a code for conceptualizing the collective identity of the Japanese as a single people, was mobilized in agendas that spanned the political spectrum."[27]

With momentous popular and symbolic appeal, *kenjutsu* and other martial arts seemed an irresistible, albeit highly romanticized, feature of Japan's cultural makeup. Harumi Befu referred to this phenomenon as the "samuraization" of the Japanese people, in which "characteristics such as loyalty, perseverance, and diligence said to be held by a small (but elite) segment of the population—the samurai—were gradually extended through propaganda, education, and regulation to cover the whole of the population."[28]

Although more attention was being directed at the martial arts in the 1880s than ever before, it was too early to refer to the "reinvention" of *kenjutsu* as national myth, accepted by citizens as part of their everyday lives. The process was underway, though, and the next phase of *kenjutsu*'s modernization would ensure that it became engrained in Japan's cultural fabric and esteemed as representative of the spiritual, aesthetic, and hardy splendor of the nation.

Despite the interest shown at the popular level, the government consistently showed caution in utilizing martial arts outright for educational purposes. This was most likely due to a number of factors: a degree of cultural elitism among former samurai in officialdom, who opposed the idea of popularizing what they felt was their exclusive traditional heritage; apathy among anti-traditionalist government officials, who advocated modern Western knowledge and methods; and the existence of intense *ryūha* dogmatism, which opposed the idea of creating a unified form of *kenjutsu* that would supersede individual *ryūha* identity. Of course there was also the pressing matter of physical danger to children.

The governor of Kyoto at the time, Makimura Masanao, was opposed to adopting *kenjutsu* into the national education curriculum. In his essay "Kenjutsu yūgai-ron" (The harmful effects of *kenjutsu*), written in 1878, he outlines how *kenjutsu* could be detrimental to the balanced growth of youth.

> Recently *gekiken* is seen everywhere as our country navigates a cultural swing. But it is highly unlikely that *gekiken* will be successful as it makes people aggressive and it may lead to hurting others as sword practitioners fool themselves. As the old saying goes, "A little learning is a dangerous thing." Moreover, it damages health, rattles the brain, dangerous thrusts to the chest, throat or face can affect respiratory function, and randomly jumping around causes painful palpations. Yelling and the like are all excessive actions detrimental to one's wellbeing. Rather than spending valuable time engrossed in such harmful activities and making the mind and body suffer, if we are committed to other jobs and work hard, we can help our country and families prosper far more effectively. Please understand what this means, and by no means allow yourself to be misled.[29]

Advocates for *bujutsu* education nonetheless continued to champion their cause. The process of inducting *bujutsu* into schools passed through three stages. The first was in 1883–84, when the Ministry of Education (MOE) commissioned the National Institute of Gymnastics (Taisō Denshūsho) to conduct a survey on the merits and shortcomings of martial arts in education. The second came in 1886, when the School Hygiene Advisory Board (Gakkō Eisei Komonkai) conducted a similar investigation and reported findings to the MOE. The third was the period extending from the turn of the century to 1911, when enthusiastic lobbying by martial arts experts, educators, and politicians finally culminated in approval for the martial arts to be introduced in middle and normal schools.[30] Table 4 pinpoints the main events in this process.

Gellner observes that modern societies "possess a very homogenous educational system which provides a basically common generic training for the whole population, or for as much of it as possible, and on the basis of which a more specialized and extraordinarily diversified system of occupations is erected, as a kind of second stage."[31] With the enactment of the Education Order in 1872, the Meiji government formulated its first modern school

TABLE 4 Key events leading to the introduction of *bujutsu*
into the school system

Year	Event
1872	Physical exercise and hygiene are included as subjects in the elementary school curriculum with the enactment of the Education Order.
1875	Sakatani Shiroshi publishes articles in the *Meiroku zasshi* advocating *bujutsu* as spiritual education for youth.
1878	The National Gymnastics Institute (Taisō Denshūjo, hereafter referred to as the NGI) is established by the Ministry of Education (MOE).
1879	With the Education Order of 1879, gymnastics is introduced into schools as an optional subject.
1880	An unsuccessful petition is submitted to the Council of Elders (Genrōin) to include *bugi* (martial technique) as physical education.
1881	*Kenjutsu* is taught as a subject at the Peers School (Gakūshuin).
1882	Kanō Jigorō forms Nihon-den Kōdōkan Jūdō.
1883	The MOE commissions the NGI to conduct a survey on the merits of including *bujutsu* in the school gymnastics curriculum.
1884	NGI announces the findings of its survey, recommending that *kenjutsu* and *jūjutsu* not be included in the education system. A debate rages in the *Tōkyō iji shinshi* (*Tokyo Medical Journal*) about the advantages of *bujutsu* education.
1889	A *kenjutsu* society is established at the First Higher Middle School in Tokyo.
1893	Seki Jūrōji becomes the first private citizen to petition the MOE to adopt *kenjutsu* into the school curriculum.
1896	The MOE commissions the School Hygiene Advisory Board to conduct another survey to investigate the benefits of introducing *gekiken* and *jūjutsu* into the school curriculum. The findings recommend the sports as extracurricular activities for boys who are over the age of fifteen and of good health.
1897	Seki Jūrōji submits another petition to the Tenth Imperial Diet House of Representatives Session, which is forwarded to the government for deliberation. His application is rejected by the government, but Seki continues making the same petition annually, without success.
1898	The MOE declines to accept *bujutsu* as regular subjects in middle and normal schools.
1900	Educator and martial artist Shibata Kokki submits a petition at the Fourteenth Imperial Diet House of Representatives Session arguing for the addition of *bujutsu* as a regular school subject. The petition is forwarded to the government for consideration but is ultimately rejected. Shibata, like Seki, continues to submit his petition annually.
1901	Ozawa Ichirō and Takano Sasaburō initiate an annual petition to the MOE to introduce *kenjutsu* to schools.
1905	The notable fencer Hoshino Senzō submits a petition to the Twenty-First Imperial Diet House of Representatives Session, but it is rejected.
1906	Hoshino Senzō presents a petition to the Twenty-Second Imperial Diet House of Representatives Session. Five officials from the MOE decide to visit Kawagoe Middle School to observe martial art classes run by Hoshino as extracurricular activities. Dai-Nippon Butokukai creates a set of three *kenjutsu* kata for national instruction.

(continued)

TABLE 4 *(continued)*

Year	Event
1907	Normal school principals discuss a proposal to allow *gekiken* and *jūjutsu* to be taught to boys at schools. It is agreed upon in principle following some amendments.
1908	Hoshino Senzō makes yet another proposal regarding physical education, to the Twenty-Fourth Imperial Diet House of Representatives Session.
1910	At a national meeting for normal school principals, it is decided to introduce *gekiken* and *jūjutsu* as regular curriculum subjects for boys and to promote naginata and *kyūjutsu* for girls as extracurricular subjects.
1911	In Article 13 of the revised "Curriculum Regulations for Middle and Higher Schools," it is announced that "*gekiken* and *jūjutsu* may be added to the regular program of study." Although recognized as regular subjects, in reality they remain extracurricular activities in most schools. A small number of schools (especially those that originated from feudal domain schools) do incorporate *bujutsu* as official subjects. An MOE-sponsored national seminar to unify martial arts instruction, presided over by Kanō Jigorō, is held at the Tokyo Higher Normal School.
1912	Naitō Takaharu from the Butokukai is invited to teach *kenjutsu* at the second MOE national instruction seminar, which lasts for four weeks. Martial art instruction for boys at normal schools is officially ratified after some amendments are made to the statutes. The Butokukai creates a set of unified kata (Dai-Nippon Teikoku Kenjutsu Kata) to replace the standardized forms created in 1906.
1913	The MOE mandates that *gekiken* and *jūjutsu* be taught to boys at middle and normal schools as regular subjects with the promulgation of the "School Gymnastics Teaching Syllabus." Naginata and *kyūjutsu* remain extracurricular activities for girls.

SOURCES: Bennett and Yamada, *Nihon no kyōiku ni budō wo*, 57–58; Bennett, *Budō*, 294–98.

system, which included physical education based on Western-style gymnastics. Predictably, however, there were educators and politicians who were reluctant to totally westernize the school curriculum, and they pushed to retain a certain amount of Japaneseness. Sakatani Shiroshi (1822–81) was one such proponent, who yearned not only to include bujutsu in the school curriculum but also to make it compulsory study. He was a member of the Meirokusha, an influential intellectual society established in 1873 for "promoting civilization and enlightenment." In its journal, the *Meiroku zasshi*, he wrote the following entreaty in 1876:

> What I would stress here is reviving the military arts. Of course gymnastics are all right, but we have already attained proficiency in our traditional training in the use of swords, spears, cudgels, and *jūjutsu*. Actually, it is only bar-

barism to reject these skills because they did not emerge in the West. There are now many from the former warrior classes who are expert in these arts. We should invite these former samurai into the lower and middle schools and into the police and the military where they should be encouraged to practice their skills energetically during their free time.[32]

Despite Sakatani's passionate plea, many education experts remained opposed to the introduction of the martial arts. *Kenjutsu* was condemned as being utterly unsuitable for young children due to the possibility of cerebral damage from repeated strikes. Sakatani died before he could offer counterarguments, but the debate continued to rage after his death. Proponents of Sakatani's point of view saw the need to nurture feelings of "patriotism" in Japan's youth, as well as to produce healthy minds and bodies fit for military service. To this end, introducing *kenjutsu* into schools was viewed as a practical exercise that would stimulate mental and physical growth, foster a greater appreciation of Japan, and give youth the skills needed to defend their country. Opponents argued that the martial arts had little cultural or practical worth, and even less benefit in terms of physical education. This argument was amplified by the potential health risks.

One of the first serious parliamentary debates to tackle the suggested inclusion of *bujutsu* into the national school curriculum was conducted by the Council of Elders (Genrōin) in 1880. The councilor who initiated the discussion was Kusumoto Masataka (1838–1902). He and his supporters were in favor of including martial techniques (*bugi*) in the Education Code as simple military training rather than as a holistic form of physical education. Their proposal was defeated in a twelve to seven vote.

The thrust of the investigation was to ascertain exactly what physical effects learning *kenjutsu* would have on a boy's growth and maturation. The NGI contracted medical experts at the Tokyo Imperial University to conduct the assessment. Among them were two German doctors, Erwin Bälz and Julius Scriba. Diaries written by Bälz reveal that he was enthusiastic about the use of Japan's traditional swordsmanship as a form of exercise, especially given the poor physical state of students at the Imperial University of Tokyo, who "often broke down and sometimes actually died" due to their arduous academic programs.

> Recognizing that *kenjutsu*, the old Japanese sword-fencing, was an excellent gymnastic method, I recommended its revival, but it was discountenanced as a rough and even dangerous sport. Not until, in order to overcome this

prejudice, I myself took lessons from the most famous fencing master of the day, Sakakibara [Kenkichi], and secured a little publicity for the fact in the newspapers, did interest in this old method of fencing revive. It was felt that, if a foreigner, and, what was more, a professor of medicine at what was then the only university in the country, was studying this art, it was impossible to suppose that Westerners could regard it as barbarous or dangerous.[33]

The NGI's findings regarding *kenjutsu* and *jūjutsu* (for boys) were submitted to the MOE in October 1884 after reaching the following conclusions:

Benefits

1. An effective means of enhancing physical development.
2. Develops stamina.
3. Rouses the spirit and boosts morale.
4. Expurgates spinelessness and replaces it with vigor.
5. Arms the exponent with techniques for self-defense in times of danger.

Disadvantages

1. May cause unbalanced physical development.
2. Always an imminent danger present in training.
3. Difficult to determine the appropriate degree of exercise, especially as physically strong boys must train together with weaker individuals.
4. Could encourage violent behavior due to the rousing of the spirit.
5. Exhilarates the will to fight, which could manifest into an attitude of winning at all costs.
6. There is a danger of encouraging a warped sense of competitiveness to the extent that boys could even resort to dishonest tactics.
7. Difficult to sustain unified instructional methodology for large numbers of students.
8. Requires a large area to conduct training.
9. Even though *jūjutsu* requires only a *keiko-gi* (training wear) *kenjutsu* requires the use of armor and other special equipment, which would be expensive and difficult to keep hygienic.[34]

Thus, the survey reached the conclusion that *kenjutsu* could be hazardous without adequate protection, and heated arguments ensued after the results were publicized. It could be scientifically proved, opponents to *bujutsu* education maintained, that continuous strikes to the head with bamboo *shinai* were injurious to the brain. Practitioners retorted that it had never done them any harm, and, considering the number of Diet members who were former samurai who had studied *kenjutsu* as children, this particular concern was probably not well received.

Notwithstanding, the NGI recommended that *bujutsu* not be included as a regular subject in schools, although it was acknowledged that it could potentially supplement an academically oriented curriculum. It was still not readily accepted, however, that it provided substantial physiological benefits, and the idea that *kenjutsu* could be detrimental to balanced physical growth prevailed. It was also supposed that *kenjutsu* could nurture undesirable aggression and violent behavior. From a logistical perspective, the most critical problem was the lack of a unified teaching methodology due to the greatly divergent technical curriculums of the different *ryūha*. Besides, *kenjutsu* had the added disadvantage of requiring expensive equipment.

The Home Ministry—backed by the Greater-Japan Society of Hygiene (Dai-Nippon Shiritsu Eiseikai, established in 1883)—also entered the debate. Their position was propelled by the growing number of vociferous martial arts advocates in the community and the fact that many schools were starting to introduce extracurricular *bujutsu* education of their own volition. They considered both Western gymnastics and martial arts but found that one disadvantage of the former was that it did not cultivate "Japanese spirit" (*yamato damashii*) or provide pupils with skills in self-defense. However, with respect to *bujutsu,* the society, like the NGI, was concerned about balanced physical development, the potential for cerebral damage, and the difficulty of teaching large classes of students simultaneously. Accordingly, the introduction of *bujutsu* education was shelved once more.

The issue was addressed yet again when the School Hygiene Advisory Board (Gakkō Eisei Komonkai) was established in May 1896. The physiological demerits of *kenjutsu* remained a reason for resistance, but the board found no reason to prevent adolescents over the age of fifteen from participating in the martial arts as an extracurricular activity.

Bujutsu's eventual introduction into the national curriculum was aided by "*bujutsu* calisthenics" (*bujutsu-taisō*), which was developed specifically to overcome the problems cited in government surveys. Following the lead of a teacher, groups of students would simultaneously perform what could be described as "pumped up kata," or dance routines with sticks. The idea soon caught on, and before long, schools throughout Japan allowed pupils to participate in newly developed callisthenic exercises using wooden replicas of weapons such as swords and *naginata* (for girls).

One of the masterminds of the method was Ozawa Unosuke (1865–1927). He declared that *bujutsu* calisthenics was designed as an educational tool for boys and girls in order to "nurture a nation of people with physiques by no means inferior to Westerners."[35] Others experimented with the development of an indigenous system of gymnastic exercises based on *kenjutsu*. Of particular note was Nakajima Kenzō (1868–1925), who had studied the Jikishin Kage-ryū tradition in his childhood. It is unknown whether or not Ozawa and Nakajima ever collaborated; however, the efforts of both men saw their initiatives spread nationwide, with seminars held at various localities.

Despite a fair amount of support for Ozawa and Nakajima's ideas, there were also those who vehemently opposed them. Reasons varied, but the most common criticisms were that the techniques were unrealistic and ineffective, paid little attention to the cutting direction of the blade, and involved too much twisting and turning. Detractors claimed they could not see the difference between *bujutsu* calisthenics and another form of exercise, baton twirling.

Books introducing *bujutsu* calisthenics started to appear in the 1890s. Several publications were written as collaborations between educators and martial artists. It was not until 1904 that the first pure *bujutsu* textbooks for teaching novices and children were published, but even these were heavily influenced by the calisthenics style and its methodology of group work.

With the promulgation of the first national "School Gymnastics Curriculum Guidelines" in 1911, the Lingian approach to gymnastics, a system developed by the Swede Per Henrik Ling to strengthen the body without the use of apparatuses, was prescribed in accordance with trends in Great Britain, America, and Scandinavia. This was supplemented with military drills and games (*yūgi*). Schools were expected to devise their own curriculum based on the MOE's guidelines. For the first time, both *kenjutsu* (referred to as *gekiken*) and *jūjutsu* were elevated to the status of optional subjects (*zuika*) in the government guidelines, becoming regular subjects (*seika*) for boys in middle and normal schools in 1913. This meant that they would be assessed as a regular course of study if the school chose to include the martial arts in its curriculum. Girls were allowed to study naginata and traditional archery.

Although the 1911 guidelines spelled the end of *bujutsu* calisthenics, the method had proved that the martial arts could be practiced in large groups easily and without expensive equipment, contrary to previous beliefs. From this standpoint, it is fair to say that it had a profound effect on teaching approaches adopted in modern budo, but martial artists avoided the term "*bujutsu* calisthenics," instead describing their initiatives as "group teaching methodology."

THE DAI-NIPPON BUTOKUKAI: SELF-APPOINTED GATEKEEPER OF BUJUTSU

According to Garon, by the late 1880s, "intellectuals, local elites, and officials broadly agreed on the need to foster 'a sense of nation' in the masses if Japan were to modernize and compete with Western rivals."[36] They attempted to achieve this by "promoting, preserving, and in general renovating an immutable Japaneseness."[37]

State nationalists (*kokka-shugi*) were insistent that citizens revere the state as the highest object of loyalty, whereas popular nationalists (*minzoku-shugi*) emphasized notions of Japaneseness based on common history, language, customs, traditions, and morality. State nationalism was spread through decrees such as the Imperial Rescript on Education (1890) and though various other means, culminating in the ultranationalist and militaristic dogmas of the 1930s. Although there is a degree of overlap, popular nationalism revolved around intellectual movements such as pan-Asianism and Japanism (*Nihon-shugi*) and was prevalent among groups that believed the state was kowtowing to Western powers instead of asserting its own influence, especially in the period extending from the Sino-Japanese war (1894–95) to the Russo-Japanese war (1904–5).

Benedict Anderson contends that in addition to states being able to activate their resources in order to piece together socially constructed community, there are other organizations that are also capable of utilizing these same methods to create alternative nationalistic interpretations at a popular level. In some instances, these interpretations and the organizations that championed them could even rival the state in defining and constructing the essential elements of nationality.[38] The Dai-Nippon Butokukai fits this description well. It was a private society formed in 1895 to reify a sense of Japanese pride through the preservation and promotion of traditional martial arts, and was absolutely instrumental in the establishment of *bujutsu* in the regular school curriculum.

As Dennis Gainty remarks, the Butokukai made itself the "guardian of elite ideas and symbols" by "locating itself in Kyōto, gathering support from notables in government, asserting the complex of samurai/martial arts values and claiming the endorsement of the Imperial institution past and present."[39] Gainty also points out that many historians show a tendency to "simplify the moment of the Butokukai's creation as a point of sharp transition between two opposing worldviews: that of an early Meiji mix of fascination with Western modernity and learning coupled with a concomitant weakening of the Japanese spirit to a subsequent return to Japanese tradition and martial self-sufficiency."[40] Indeed, the transition cannot be attributed to one point in time, but the Butokukai's influence in elevating *kenjutsu* to a symbolic agent representative of the fusion of tradition and modernity was profound.

The Butokukai was the brainchild of Torinoumi Kōki (1849–1914), a Kyoto tax collector with a proclivity for the martial arts. The Heian Shrine was built in Kyoto in 1895 to celebrate the 1,100th anniversary of Emperor Kammu's decision to relocate the capital to Heian in 794. Torinoumi was disgruntled because, in his opinion, the planning of festivities marking this momentous occasion was below par. He joined forces with Konishi Shin'emon—an enthusiastic swordsman and wealthy brewery owner of the sake brand Shirayuki—in 1893, and together they planned a martial arts exhibition for the celebration.[41]

Few people gave Torinoumi and Konishi's ideas much credence at first. Nevertheless, their enthusiasm was infectious, and Niwa Keisuke, a local kimono maker, together with Kyoto District Police Commissioner Sasa Kumatarō, suggested that Torinoumi go a considerable step further and establish an organization to promote the martial arts in the community, rather than limit his efforts to a one-off event. Before long, momentum for his project began to snowball.

These developments were contemporaneous with growing nationalistic sentiments, which were especially strong following Japan's triumphant victory against China in the Sino-Japanese War. This achievement made Japan the dominant power in Asia, and the only one that was afforded much in the way of respect from Western colonialist nations. The Japanese were understandably proud of their country's success, and around this time a broader appreciation of traditional culture began to flourish. The culture, ideals, and masculinity of the samurai were particularly alluring.

It was the perfect timing for Torinoumi to create his martial art society. He was able to solicit the assistance of Kyoto governor Watanabe Chiaki, who, wielding his political influence, recruited Mibu Motonaga, the head priest of Heian Shrine, and Tanaka Kidō, the Kyoto Prefecture police chief, as officers. Thus, from its earliest stages, the organization had ties with the police force and the Home Ministry, as well as other government offices, through the patronage of Watanabe Chiaki.

The men met for the first time on April 3, 1895, and a general assembly was convened shortly thereafter, on April 17, to communicate the founding principles of the organization, which now bore the name Dai-Nippon Butokukai. A proposal was agreed upon to reconstruct Emperor Kammu's ancient Hall of Martial Virtue (Butokuden) near the Heian Shrine for use as their main dojo, and the Butokukai was officially launched. Following its inauguration, the Butokukai gradually extended its network throughout the country to unify isolated pockets of martial arts experts, and preserve and promote the various *ryūha* still in existence. Another objective was to gather data pertaining to overseas military technology and systems and publish periodicals related to the culture of war. According to the articles of the association (which was written in both Japanese and English):

Article 1

The Butokukwai shall undertake to accomplish the following works with object of encouraging military arts and diffusing martial spirit and virtue:

1. To build Butokuden within the Heianjingu grounds.
2. To observe Butokusai festival.
3. To hold grand match at the Butokukwai with a view of preserving martial virtue.
4. To establish schools for the training of military arts.
5. To provide for the preservation of old military arts deemed worthy of preservation.
6. To construct an arsenal for the collection of ancient and modern arms and weapons of both home and foreign origins.
7. To publish ancient and modern histories of wars and campaigns, military arts, and arms and weapons of our Empire and foreign countries.[42]

The successful appointment of Prince Komatsu-no-Miya Akihito on May 28, 1895, as superintendent of the organization gave it the powerful legitimacy of imperial benefaction. Many other influential government and military leaders were appointed as officials. Notable among them were Itō

Hirobumi, four-time prime minister of Japan; Yamagata Aritomo, field marshal and two-time prime minister; and Saigō Tsugumichi, politician and admiral. As the Butokukai network grew, prefectural governors were appointed as branch chairmen, senior prefectural officials served as secretaries, and committees were composed of mayors and other willing dignitaries from each locality.

Before long, area offices of the Butokukai had been established in each prefecture, with the first new affiliate being created in Toyama Prefecture on February 25, 1896. By 1909, the organization had amassed a membership of one and a half million. In 1895, the Butokukai founded the celebrated Martial Virtue Festival, an annual martial arts tournament that continues today, and in 1902, it established an award system to commend individuals who had made significant contributions to the promotion of *bujutsu*. In 1905, a section for training instructors (Bujutsu Shidōin Yōsei-ka) was established. The Butoku School (Butoku Gakkō) was launched in 1911, although its name was changed to the Bujutsu Vocational College (Bujutsu Senmon Gakkō) the same year and then to the Budo Vocational College (Budō Senmon Gakkō) in 1919, for reasons I will explain in the following chapter.

The inaugural issue of *Butokushi,* the Butokukai's official publication, lays out the various activities the society planned on promoting: athletics, target shooting, horsemanship, bayonet practice, fencing, *jūjutsu,* swimming, rowing, archery, and classical military arts. With regard to fencing, the text is blatantly or, more accurately, nationalistically, biased and also conveniently includes an accompanying English translation (left as in the original):

> Fencing is practiced in every country though differing more or less in the instruments used and the ways of using them. Yet we believe ours is highly superior to that of any country, with the sword of one sided blade so sharp and deadly in offense and defense. When this art is mastered, one can foil his enemy even with a piece of stick. Moreover, it inspires one with chivalric spirit, which enables him to stand fearlessly against any odds. As soon as the Gymnasium [Butokuden] is ready we shall at once open the school, with masters of this art for its teachers, and by examination shall classify the pupils according to the degrees of their skill.[43]

In 1906, Watanabe Noboru (1838–1913) chaired the first Butokukai committee tasked with formulating a set of generic kata for disseminating standardized *kenjutsu* in schools nationwide. The committee was appointed on May 7 and consisted of Watanabe and six other *kenjutsu* experts from various *ryūha,* all of whom were recipients of the Butokukai's honorary title of *han-shi,* the highest honor awarded to outstanding martial artists. In July, a further seven "younger experts," who held the lesser title of *kyōshi,* were invited onto the committee. The results were presented to the president of the Butokukai on August 13, 1906.[44] The committee had crafted a set of kata they called the Dai-Nippon Butokukai Seitei Kenjutsu Kata. It was comprised of three forms: *jōdan* (heaven), *chūdan* (earth), and *gedan* (man).

Once the Butokukai kata were released, reaction ranged from lukewarm to out-and-out disapproval. Due to the hastiness of the process—only about three months had passed from the committee's inception to the presentation of the new kata—there had been very little opportunity for discussion about the concept and forms. Watanabe's high social standing and authoritarian approach seem to have thwarted any meaningful dialogue between the illustrious swordsmen on the committee and others who were not consulted.

One of the main complaints concerned the nomenclature of the fighting stances (*kamae*) used in the kata. For example, a stance that resembled *hassō* (sword held vertically at the right side of the face) in most traditional *ryūha* was confusingly labeled as *chūdan* (the middle stance with the sword held out in front of the body). The radical shift away from orthodoxy also invited the scorn of traditionalists. Due to such hostility toward the kata—especially from one member of the committee itself, a somewhat sullen Negishi Shingorō (1844–1913)—they were not widely circulated.

Following the modifications made to physical education guidelines in 1911, the MOE sponsored an intensive, five-week *bujutsu* seminar at the Tokyo Higher Normal School (Tōkyō Kōtō Shihan Gakkō) to determine procedures and teaching methodology for instruction in schools. Kanō Jigorō, the founder of modern judo as well as the principal of the school, oversaw the first seminar, at which the Butokukai's kata problems were openly reviewed. It was decided that the three kata created in 1906 were altogether unsuitable. Negishi Shingorō, Takano Sasaburō, and Kimura Nobuhide, assisted by ten other *kenjutsu* experts, began devising a different set of three kata that would be more aligned with the requirements of *kenjutsu's* nationalization. The Butokukai contested this slight to its authority, but the MOE was adamant, and the protests amounted to nothing.

The Butokukai convened an extraordinary meeting in December 1911 to assess its predicament, and another committee was convened to develop yet another set of kata.[45] The committee was assisted by twenty *kenjutsu* instructors from around the country and completed its project at the Myōdenji

Temple in Kyoto in the summer of 1912. The result was the Dai-Nippon Teikoku Kenjutsu Kata (Greater-Japan Imperial Kenjutsu Kata), which consisted of the three kata formulated during the MOE-sponsored *bujutsu* seminar plus four new forms, totaling seven kata of *tachi* (long sword) versus *tachi*. Three more kata of *tachi* versus *kodachi* (short sword) were also created. The honor of the MOE and the Butokukai was maintained, and the full set of ten kata was ratified on October 16, 1912. Frequent modifications were made to the original version in the following years, but it essentially constituted what modern exponents still practice as the Nippon Kendo Kata.[46]

The MOE *bujutsu* seminars were an important step in gaining the consensus necessary to nationalize the martial arts. There were ten seminars for *kenjutsu* instruction, attended by over four hundred teachers, who then conveyed the content to the schools in their own prefectures. Negishi Shingorō was assigned to lecture on the unified principles of *kenjutsu* at the first seminar. Nakayama Hakudō (Hiromichi) later published Negishi's principles in *Kendō kōwa* (Kendo lectures, 1914). He also included chapters to be taught in schools as one-hour lectures concerning the "greater meaning of kendo" as well as various philosophical and technical concepts.

Takano Sasaburō and Kimura Nobuhide were responsible for lecturing specifically on teaching methodology for groups and on technical content, which included kata and fencing techniques with protective equipment. Broadly speaking, the teaching methodology curriculum consisted of a regimented system of warm-up exercises, etiquette and ritual formalities, fighting stances, basic striking techniques to the designated targets of head, wrists, and torso as well as thrusts to the throat, and other applied techniques. These techniques were published in two monumental textbooks: *Kendō* (1915), by Takano Sasaburō of the Tokyo Higher Normal School, and *Kendō kihon kyōju-hō* (Teaching kendo fundamentals, publication date unknown), by Naitō Takaharu of the Butokukai's Bujutsu Vocational College.

An important achievement in the creation of modern kendo was the consolidation of ritual forms of etiquette, which are an integral part of training to this day. All traditional *ryūha* maintained their own special rituals, which differed in form and ideology. The development of a nationalized form of kendo included the introduction of a standard sequence of movements: standing and bowing to the opponent with the sword (*shinai* or *bokutō*) held in the left hand at the waist with the blade facing up (*teitō*); drawing the sword and crouching into the *sonkyo* position; commencement of the bout; sheathing the sword in *sonkyo* after the bout; and standing and bowing from *teitō* to conclude. Furthermore, at the commencement and conclusion of each lesson, all students were required to bow simultaneously to the teacher as a sign of respect as well as to a Shinto altar (*shinzen*) in the training hall.

Naitō Takaharu, head kendo instructor of the Butokukai, is credited with further refining the ritual of bowing by determining three different objects of respect: "the *shinzen,* or emperor," "the instructor," and "one's training partners."[47] Thus, from the outset, the newly formed nationalized methodology incorporated notions of state Shinto that were to become even more stringent in the militaristic 1930s.

The decision to make the martial arts regular subjects in the national school curriculum spurred the creation of a uniform style of *kenjutsu* for the masses. It came complete with a unified technical prospectus, an ideology that confirmed the connection between the Japanese people and the samurai, and a rich framework of symbolic meaning and rituals that promoted a sense of Japaneseness. But, more important, *kenjutsu* now had the backing of the government to ensure its rapid and effective dissemination.

Smith states in his seminal work on nationalism that "it is through a shared, unique culture that we are enabled to know 'who we are' in the contemporary world. By rediscovering that culture we rediscover ourselves, the 'authentic self,' or so it has appeared to many divided and disoriented individuals who have had to contend with the vast changes and uncertainties of the modern world."[48] After *kenjutsu* had been nationalized, it would go on to fulfill an important function for this very reason.

With respect to the adopted or created paradigms used to formulate a common cultural and national identity, Hobsbawm proposes, "so much of what subjectively makes up the modern 'nation' consists of such constructs and is associated with appropriate and, in general, fairly recent symbols or suitably tailored discourse (such as 'national' history), the national phenomenon cannot be adequately investigated without careful attention to the 'invention of tradition.'"[49] The time it took for the Meiji modernization to run its course corresponds exactly with the time frame in which *kenjutsu* was reinvented. It evolved from a multi-styled, arcane medieval combat art that symbolized samurai culture into a one-size-fits-all national sport that symbolized Japanese culture.

To return to Thomas McClatchie's 1873 speech regarding the symbolic significance of the sword in Japan during the Meiji era:

It is gratifying to find the Japanese themselves so far awakened to a sense to the uselessness of their once dearly-cherished swords as to actually ridicule, in the public press, the few who still adhere to the old custom. Honesty of purpose and firmness in action,—straightforward dealing and steadfast endeavor will do far more to help on this country to her rightful place in the world than could ever have been achieved by means of her formerly much-prized possession, "the girded sword of Great Japan."[50]

Retrospectively it could be argued that there was a major flaw in his commentary. As his observations were tendered in the dormant stage of *kenjutsu*'s transition, however, there was no way he could foresee how the art would, over the subsequent four decades, become a means through which Japanese citizens learned the ideals of "honesty of purpose and firmness in action." After the edict prohibiting the wearing of swords in public was enacted, the katana became a symbolic tool for spiritual education that conveyed ideals of nationalism and enabled the Japanese people to "touch the samurai soul."[51] A new nationalistic education regime popularized the idea that the Japanese people were the "inheritors" of samurai culture.

Newly created notions of bushido and images of a glorious warrior past were propagated vigorously from the 1890s, and many of the national myths created during this period became so strongly entrenched in the Japanese psyche that they remain virtually unquestioned essentials of Japaneseness even today. To be sure, kendo's lineage can be traced directly back to the warriors of old, but the actual techniques, ideals, equipment, teaching and training methodology, educational concepts, and so on were for the most part shaped in the early twentieth century. I should add that Western influence in nationalizing *kenjutsu* and other martial arts—either as a catalyst, an antithesis, or a paradigm for modern pedagogy or athletic discourse at various junctures along the way—should not be overlooked, although it often is.

CHAPTER 4

Sharpening the Empire's Claws

Kenjutsu is the product of centuries of risking life and limb by the Japanese people [*Yamato minzoku*]. The essence of the Yamato spirit is manifest in Japanese *kenjutsu*. It represents the blossoming of the Yamato soul.

SUGAHARA TŌRU, 1939

TEACHING THE TEACHERS

Although *bujutsu* was brought into the national curriculum under the rubric of physical education (*taiiku*), from the outset the underlying motivation of the introduction was to instill a sense of Japaneseness in students as a counterbalance to the unbridled importation of Western ideals and teaching content. As Yuko Kikuchi states, "the main concern of the intellectuals was to define the originality and identity of the Japanese, and [to promote the] actual realization of *wakon-yōsai* (Japanese mind with Occidental knowledge). They struggled to retain intrinsic qualities while not denying the need for Westernization."[1] Kendo, with its connection to Japan's noble warrior culture, proved to be the perfect agent for imparting traditional values.

To the youth who took up kendo, it was an exciting sport where the thrill of competition was the main attraction. As with other sports, the competitive aspects of kendo were accentuated, especially during the Taishō period, from 1912 to 1926. However, the 1930s saw a systematic appropriation of kendo by the wartime government as a way to prepare young men for the rigors of modern war. Although there is some evidence of opposition to the government's commandeering of the martial arts for overtly militaristic purposes, kendo was swept away by a powerful riptide into what is now widely considered to be the darkest period in its history.

Ivan Morris's definition of nationalism in imperial Japan perfectly contextualizes the social, political, and cultural climate of the 1930s and 1940s that facilitated kendo's militarization:

(1) precedence of loyalty to the nation over every form of loyalty;

(2) hostility towards any extension of democratic rights and towards international socialism;

(3) support of militarism and opposition to pacifist movements;

(4) glorification of a national "mission";

(5) appeal to protect national traditions and culture from sinister outside influences;

(6) emphasis on duties as opposed to rights, on order as opposed to freedom;

(7) stress on the individual's family and birthplace as the fundamental bonds of social cohesion;

(8) tendency towards the authoritarian regimentation of all human relationships;

(9) integration of the national spirit in support of orthodox ideas;

(10) tendency to be especially vigilant and suspicious in regard to intellectuals and members of the free professions, on the grounds that they are apt to become the disseminators of "subversive thoughts."[2]

Although it may seem fanciful that the government entertained the idea that kendo could be useful to the militaristic cause, mystical allusions to the spiritual superiority of kendo over Western sports—and, by implication, the superiority of the Japanese people—typically colored the lofty rhetoric that was used to promote the virtues of kendo and its inextricable connection with being Japanese. As the American wartime observer C. N. Spinks reported, "the Japanese warrior sought to acquire through the sports he practiced perfection in the art of *kiai,* or psychic equilibrium, which affords mental composure and supreme confidence in one's own spiritual superiority."[3]

The wartime periodical *Nippon Budō* contributed to the immense body of jingoistic literature devoted to the study of kendo and the self-denial and self-sacrifice that could be nurtured through training. As one contributor wrote in January 1941, "The objectives of the practice of kendo are not only [to master] the techniques, but to become aware of the national essence (*kokutai*) and conscious of the national spirit, showing total loyalty to the emperor, and developing a preparedness to die for one's country."[4]

Plotting the path of the militaristic development of kendo from the Taishō period to the early Shōwa—up through 1945—shows how kendo transformed from the "cultural capital" of popular nationalists, represented mainly by the Dai-Nippon Butokukai, to a tool adopted by the agents of state nationalism during the intensification of the war effort. Through this process of appropriation, kendo changed in terms of technical form and objectives to become overtly combative and violent. Contemporary scholars and kendo experts are wont to refer to this era as a dismal exploitation of kendo culture by the state, but such critics are neglecting to acknowledge that combat always was, and still is, an intrinsic part of kendo. It can therefore be argued that this period was not a repugnant deviation from the fundamentally peaceful nature of kendo, but rather a swing of the pendulum back in the direction whence *kenjutsu* came—the reverse of Norbert Elias's concept of a movement toward a "de-civilizing" process.

What exactly was this process, and how did it unfold? How did the state manage to appropriate kendo, and what were its intentions? In what ways does this process inform our understanding of ultranationalism in imperial Japan? As we will see, the answers are based on three basic and traditional concepts of Japanese ultranationalism—"the divinity of the Emperor, the superiority of the Japanese people, and the sacredness of Japanese soil"[5]—kendo in schools and in the community had several different functions: to cultivate a sense of ethnicity ("Japaneseness") and patriotism, to promote the virtue of martyrdom for emperor and country, and, as ludicrous as it may seem in the theater of modern warfare, to equip the nation with the practical combat skills and indomitable spirit to prevail on the battlefield in defense of the sacred empire.

There was a shortage of equipment and suitable facilities for training, but the biggest problem for the introduction of an obligatory nationwide martial arts program was a dearth of teachers. Until there were enough qualified teachers to fill instructional positions in the country's schools, martial arts would remain optional subjects. The two main colleges to produce expert martial art instructors from the Taishō years were the Dai-Nippon Butokukai's specialist teacher training college in Kyoto and the Tokyo Higher Normal School (Tōkyō Kōtō Shihan Gakkō), which was headed by the progenitor of Kōdōkan judo, Kanō Jigorō.[6]

The Butokukai first created a martial art instructor training department (Bujutsu Kyōin Yōseijo) in 1905. This was closed in 1911 and replaced by the School of Martial Virtue (Butoku Gakkō), following modifications to the Private School Edict (Shiritsu gakkō-rei). Coinciding with the MOE's decision to make *bujutsu* a regular school subject, the Butokukai made an application to elevate its school to the status of "vocational college"; permission was granted in 1912. The Butoku School thus became the Bujutsu Vocational College (Bujutsu Senmon Gakkō), which allowed it to offer a more intensive three-year course specializing in martial arts.

In 1916, the MOE issued a further directive stating that physical education teaching licenses would be classified into three specific categories: calisthenics, *gekiken,* and *jūjutsu.* This prompted the Bujutsu Vocational College to increase its course length by one year in 1917. Beginning in 1918, graduates automatically received certification to teach martial arts without needing to take the national teacher qualification examinations.

Around this time, the Bujutsu Vocational College compiled a standard manual for teaching kendo in schools titled *Kendō kihon kyōju-hō* (Teaching kendo fundamentals). The content paralleled the subject matter taught at the national *bujutsu* seminars, which were sponsored by the MOE and conducted at the Bujutsu Vocational College's rival school, the Tokyo Higher Normal School. *Kendō kihon kyōju-hō* was published in response to the Tokyo Higher Normal School's earlier book *Kendō,* written by Takano Sasaburō in 1915, which is still considered a classic by kendo enthusiasts.

In 1919, the Dai-Nippon Butokukai officially changed the terminology for the martial arts by adopting the suffix *-dō* (way) in place of *-jutsu* (techniques). Nishikubo Hiromichi (1863–1930), vice president of the Butokukai and principal of the Bujutsu Vocational College, announced the change, declaring that *bujutsu* would be referred to thereafter as *budō, kenjutsu* as *kendō, jūjutsu* as *jūdō,* and so on.[7] He had delivered a series of lectures to the police in 1914 arguing for the switch and is widely attributed with bringing about the new nomenclature, although the precedent had been set long before, in 1882, with Kanō Jigorō's Kōdōkan *jū-dō.*[8] Subsequently, Bujutsu Vocational College changed its name to Budo Vocational College (often abbreviated to Busen). The MOE, however, did not officially change its terminology until 1926.

The reason for the shift was to emphasize the important cultural and spiritual heritage of the martial arts. The new terms represented a kind of purism and highlighted the uniqueness of the Japanese. Moreover, the changes were motivated by the rampant competitiveness that had developed in the martial arts, especially among student practitioners.

Contemporary debates about Japaneseness, as Tessa Morris-Suzuki points out, "were compounded by problems of terminology. Was the defining characteristic of Japaneseness to be looked for in 'national character' (*kokuminsei*), in ethical systems like Bushidō, or (as Nishida Kitarō had suggested) in distinctive perceptions of reality?"[9] The Butokukai elected to accentuate the spirituality of the martial arts and to use this attribute as the cornerstone of their educational and promotional policies. This was certainly meant to draw attention to notions of Japaneseness and the spiritual superiority of Japan's physical pursuits over Western sports, which were, in contrast, fixated on matters of victory or defeat.

Although the Butokukai is frequently extolled as having been the principal promoter of *bujutsu* from the end of the Meiji period onward, the Bujutsu Vocational College's equal in the field of specialist instructor education was undoubtedly the Tokyo Higher Normal School, which, as I have alluded to, actually established educational standards for *bujutsu* much earlier. The highly influential educator and martial artist Kanō Jigorō became the school's president in 1893, and he immediately set about promoting physical education (including the martial arts) at this prestigious institution.

He created five sports clubs in 1896, including one for judo, which he instructed himself, and one for *gekiken* (kendo). After a slow start, the *gekiken* club was invigorated by the appointment of Kimura Nobuhide (1855–1924) of the Jikishin Kage-ryū as the head teacher. (Now known as the University of Tsukuba, the club remains one of the powerhouses in Japanese college kendo.) After a number of changes to the teaching staff, Takano Sasaburō was eventually named supervising instructor of the club and made responsible for implementing the dan and kyu system of ranking in 1908. The police were already utilizing a kyu system to designate rank, and Kanō Jigorō had started using a similar system in judo, but this was the first time that dan grades had been used in kendo. The Butokukai was initially opposed to the grades, but the society eventually adopted the system in 1917, and it became standardized throughout Japan.

Kanō successfully elevated judo, kendo, and calisthenics to regular subjects of study at the Tokyo Higher Normal School in 1906. Starting in 1913, they were divided into three separate courses, each of which granted graduates a nationally recognized teaching license. This specialist martial art teaching qualification was approved by the government and preceded that of the Bujutsu Vocational College. However, the first graduates of the Bujutsu Vocational College's four-year course were conferred a Bachelor of Budo degree, the first of its type in Japan.

With the decision to allow *bujutsu* education in schools, the MOE sponsored national *bujutsu* seminars with the purpose of standardizing teaching content and improving the competence of teachers. The first such seminar (there were ten in total) commenced on November 6, 1911, and ran for five weeks. The instructor for kendo theory was Negishi Shingorō (1844–1913).

Takano Sasaburō and Kimura Nobuhide from Tokyo Higher Normal School were allotted the task of tutoring participants in kata and *shiai* (match) methodology. Given that the seminar was held at the Tokyo Higher Normal School and that most of the instructors for kendo and judo were teachers at the college, its dominant position in early budo education cannot be overstated. A Bujutsu Vocational College professor was asked to teach only from the third seminar, when Naitō Takaharu (1862–1929) took over Negishi Shingorō's lecturing duties.

As explained in the previous chapter, one of the important accomplishments of the early seminars was the creation of a unified set of kata to propagate nationally. Another significant development was the refinement of group teaching methods. The syllabi and group training methodology outlined in the aforementioned books published by the Tokyo Higher Normal School and Bujutsu Vocational College are very similar to what was discussed at the seminars, judging by notes taken by Sugiyama Kiyosaku.

The tone was set for the nationwide dissemination of a standardized form of kendo. Armed with a modern pedagogical methodology, a cohesive unified curriculum, and a growing number of qualified teachers, and boosted by state sanctioning and mounting popular enthusiasm, kendo was on the verge of being propagated more broadly than ever before.

MILITARIZATION AND COMPULSORY KENDO EDUCATION

Stuck between the tumultuous Meiji period and the militant early Shōwa era, the Taishō period was an ambiguous epoch of conflicting ideologies representing all colors of the political spectrum. It was a time of national discovery, with experimentation in Marxism, ultranationalism, liberalism, and hedonism, underscored by a shift in political power from oligarchic Meiji imperialism to party politics of "democracy" in the Diet and then back to a doctrine of ultraconservatism.

The First World War proved to be a windfall for Japan. Perfectly positioned to take advantage of disrupted markets around the world, Japan's industry thrived in many different sectors, including iron, textiles, chemicals, and machinery. Investors and entrepreneurs made fortunes overnight, giving rise to the term *narikin,* or "nouveau riche." Domestic consumption soared, *moga* (modern girls) copied Western fashions, the number of factory workers swelled and their wages increased, and demand for agricultural produce kept farmers wealthier and happier than they had ever been before.

With the sudden rise in prosperity, however, came vociferous calls for workers' rights, and labor disputes over benefits and acknowledgment erupted nationwide with increasing frequency. Perhaps the most venomous disturbances were the rice riots (*kome sōdō*) of 1918, which broke out in reaction to the extortionate elevation of prices for Japan's staple crop.

The end of the war in Europe did not bring worldwide democratic emancipation, and Japan's economic prosperity plummeted with the collapse of markets overseas. Suddenly, the short-lived era of opulence was replaced with one of debt, bankruptcy, and unemployment. A potent mix of intellectuals, students, activist workers, and unionists demonstrated in favor of replacing what they saw as privileged politics with universal manhood suffrage, which would give all men, irrespective of wealth or standing, a say in the running of the country. However, their calls to Prime Minister Hara Takashi's cabinet in 1920 for equality were in vain, leading only to more widespread demonstrations among revolutionary syndicalists, Marxists, democratic socialists, and other popular groups.

Although born into a samurai family, Hara Takashi renounced his status as *shizoku* (former samurai), preferring instead to be classified as a commoner. Thus, he became the first commoner (and Christian) to serve as Japan's prime minister. In many ways he epitomized what came to be known as Taishō democracy, which was a movement toward a broader representational government, but he could not stop the growing social unrest and wound up being scorned by both ends of the political gamut. He met a macabre end, stabbed to death by a disgruntled right-wing railroad worker in 1921.[10]

Strikes became commonplace throughout the country, and when the Japanese Communist Party was inaugurated in 1922, alarm bells rang through the institutions of the conservative government. With the upsurge of left-wing ideologues in Japan came the rise of right-wing, nationalistic, imperialist traditionalists. Militant organizations, such as the Dai-Nihon Kokusuikai (Greater-Japan National Essence Association), a network made up of two hundred thousand yakuza, prominent politicians, like Suzuki Kisaburō, and a gallimaufry of militant mossbacks, justified violence as a means to purify the nation of the influx of dangerous "foreign contagion." Their "prescribed bulwark against the corruption of Japan's civilization and national essence," according to Eiko Maruko Siniawer, "was none other than 'the way of the warrior.'"[11]

Universal suffrage was eventually ratified in 1925, but so too was the infamous Peace Preservation Law, which was conceived to monitor the activities of seditious groups critical of the state. Through the government's "thought police," the law was used to crack down on radicals and communists, and, later on, opponents of Japan's war machine.

The MOE, concerned with the alarming propensity of students to sympathize with left-wing or liberalist ideals, formed a student section in 1924. One of the section's main tasks was to investigate methods of thwarting adherence to undesirable ideologies. The Physical Education and Exercise Deliberation council (Taiiku Undō Shingikai) was inaugurated to devise approaches for utilizing sports for this purpose.

According to a report written by the Supreme Command Allied Powers (SCAP) in the postwar period on the topic of the Butokukai's historical development, "when ultra-nationalistic development got underway [in the Taishō period], the leaders of the school system directed a 'thought war' against all forms of this dissident philosophy [leftist or liberal idealism]. Liberal student organizations and activities were put down, while substitutes that were congenial to nationalistic ideology were encouraged."[12]

One strategy conceived in 1924 to fight this "thought war" was the Meiji Shrine Sports Tournament (Meiji Jingū Taikai)—an annual event held on the date of the Meiji emperor's birthday, November 3, at the Meiji Shrine. The celebrated tournament featured fourteen events, including kendo, and the objective was to use sports to mobilize youth and nurture loyalty to the state and emperor. Interestingly, the Dai-Nippon Butokukai refused to participate in the tournament despite repeated pleas, stating that the idea of competition for self-gratification ran counter to the organization's ideals of spiritual and moral development. The state's appropriation of sports would become an effective means of exerting ideological control and instilling nationalistic fervor, but there was clearly an ideological schism between the Dai-Nippon Butokukai, a private organization and popular caretaker of budo, and the government, which had political incentives to exert ideological control.

A few primary schools started introducing martial art classes after they were designated as regular subjects in middle schools. The MOE commissioned the School Hygiene Board (Gakkō Eiseikai) to investigate whether budo should be included in primary education. They published their findings in 1918 and concluded that inclusion as an optional subject would be acceptable. The number of primary school kendo courses increased markedly after this. According to research by Nakamura Tamio, 957 of a total of 21,006 primary schools nationwide chose to offer kendo in 1917. In just over two decades, by 1938, this number had grown to 5,908 primary schools out of 20,308, with 5,001 instructors holding dan ranks.[13]

The momentum to bring kendo fully into the primary and middle school curricula continued to build. In 1925, a petition was submitted to the Fiftieth Imperial Diet House of Representatives Plenary Session to make budo a regular subject in primary schools and a compulsory subject in middle schools. Deliberations were generally favorable toward the propositions, but it was decided that the elevation of martial arts to regular subjects of study in primary schools was premature.

During this period, kendo's extracurricular clubs were helping it gain an enthusiastic following among university students, who enjoyed participating in competitions and tournaments throughout the country. Although the popularity of kendo among this demographic was applauded as demonstrating successful nationwide dissemination, pedants were critical of the penchant shown by students to "corrupt" the spirit and techniques of kendo for the sake of winning matches and appeasing their own egotistical desires. This clash of values continued into the Shōwa period, but kendo would take an altogether different route with the onset of the militaristic 1930s, culminating in nearly total state arrogation.

Sakaue Yasuhiro and Ōtsuka Tadayoshi identify three stages in the state-driven militarization of kendo.[14] These phases were aligned with three of Irie Katsumi's four stages of "fascist" development in Japanese physical education, which he labeled: "germination" (1917–31), when the MOE introduced policies to discourage liberalism; "shift" (1931–37), corresponding to the Japanese invasion of Manchuria and the rise of militarism; "control" (1937–41), when the government commandeered physical education in schools and the community following the outbreak of the second Sino-Japanese war; and "culmination" (1941–45), when all physical education was restructured for the exigency of war.[15]

The first stage in Sakaue and Ōtsuka's thesis lasted from 1931 to 1937—a period in which a thorough reassessment was made of the competitive nature of kendo and its suitability for combat. By this time, kendo had become immensely popular among male students, and events such as intercollegiate competitions and the prestigious Tenran-jiai (a judo and kendo tournament conducted before the emperor) accentuated the competitive dimension of kendo as a sport.[16]

It was the growing "sportification" of kendo at the popular level that cha-grined militarists and ultranationalists. They interpreted this evolution as proof of the polluting influences of Westernization and sought the "purifica-tion" of traditional budo in order to keep it indicative of the "Japanese spirit." As Abe Ikuo, Kiyohara Yasuharu, and Nakajima Ken argue, "Contests and games were ritualized to indoctrinate militarism, patriotism, and above all, the ideology of the Emperor System. All kinds of physical activities were colored by notions of bushido and *Yamato-damashii* (Japanese soul). Meanwhile play elements and the liberalism of sports were decolorized."[17]

With the "decolorization" of kendo, we see a massive surge in bombastic expressions connecting kendo with concepts of the "indomitable Japanese spirit." This proclivity was evident at the time of the Dai-Nippon Butokukai's foundation, but it escalated in the 1930s. The following declaration by the Butokukai in 1930 is a clear indication of nascent militaristic sentiment:

> Our current army is not made up of a distinct class of warriors. All the peo-ple of the nation are soldiers. The nation is the army. The way of the warrior [bushido] is the way of the citizen [*kokumindō*]. Bushido education must be the moral education of the people. Therefore the people must know the his-tory of the *bushi*, study the spirit of martial virtue [*butoku*], and aspire to be like the warriors of old by being good citizens at home and good soldiers in the army.[18]

There was considerable reinterpreting and refining of competition rules, ranks, and techniques, as well as new motivations for training and teaching. Kendo was torn between conflicting definitions of a hedonistic competitive sport and the stoic life-or-death legacy of samurai combat. The principle of *butoku* (martial virtue) espoused by the Butokukai—the "great spirit that protects world peace" and augments the "welfare of the people"—encouraged practitioners to think of the *shinai* as a sword and to develop an affinity with samurai and the bushido ethos. Given such considerations, it was preposter-ous to celebrate upon scoring a point or to execute showy or aberrant tech-niques with the *shinai* that could never be successfully accomplished with a real sword. Such "corruption" of swordsmanship had already become quite commonplace among fencers in university and community clubs.[19]

Of all the private kendo organizations that existed during the Taishō and early Shōwa periods, the Butokukai saw itself as representing the moral high ground in terms of what was ideal. In Butokukai matches, competitors were given scores based on their attacks, posture, attitude, and spirit, and those who were recognized as upholding the principles of the katana scored highly. This system of scoring continued for eight years, until 1927, when unified criteria to decide points were devised by the Butokukai. A valid strike (*yūkō-datotsu*) required an attack to be executed with full spirit, correct blade angle, and correct posture.

Conservatives felt that the first of the three Tenran competitions held in Kyoto in 1929 to decide the "best fencer in Japan" threatened the demise of kendo, irrespective of the great honor of competing before the emperor himself. Opposition to such an exalted tournament may seem odd, but it was indicative of the antagonism between populists and statists, along similar lines as the Butokukai's earlier opposition to the Meiji Shrine sports tournament. The Tenran tournament employed, for the first time, a five-minute time limit for each bout. This encouraged cowardly behavior in some competitors, who, after scoring the first point in the best of three, would attempt to avoid further confrontation until the time was up, thereby holding onto victory by virtue of the sole point scored in the match. Nevertheless, despite a raft of criticism, the method of competition used in the Tenran matches provided a model for tournaments in other sectors of the kendo community.

A turning point in the move away from competitive kendo to something more warlike was the Manchurian Incident. On September 18, 1931, an explosion damaged a section of Japanese-owned railway track near Mukden in China. This act of sabotage was blamed on Chinese nationalists, and the Japanese used it as justification to retaliate and invade Manchuria. There were suspicions around the world that the explosion was in fact caused by mid-level officers in the Imperial Japanese Army as a pretext for the invasion. The Japanese army proceeded to take control of the region, which was rich in natural resources, and declared it to be the new "autonomous" state of Manchukuo, albeit under the control of Japan.

In the Manchurian Incident, cold steel was actually used in battle.[20] After this, government and military officials began to criticize the practice of kendo as a sport and sought to draw attention to practical applications of the sword, as well as to ways to use it to promote patriotism.[21] The government had taken the first step in this direction in 1929, when the Bunsei Shingikai (Educational and Cultural Policy Council) was created under the supervision of the prime minister to respond to important matters of educational and cultural policy (*bunsei*). In 1930, the council published a report outlining the necessity of finding a rational or moral approach to promoting physical education among youth, and budo, rather than Western sports. This was touted as the most expedient way to indoctrinate the "Japanese spirit" and foster patriotism.

The MOE decided that budo would become a compulsory subject in all middle and normal schools beginning in 1931. It was announced that boys would study kendo or judo, and girls would take classes in naginata or kyudo. Due to the hurried introduction of this policy, the outline for teaching content was not issued until years later, in 1936. When finally released, the "Middle School Kendo Description" (*Chūgakō kendō kaisetsu*) itemized in great detail the techniques and mindset expected in kendo instruction. At this stage, the recommended teaching content was still focused on character development rather than the practical combat application of the sword. The virtues expected to be cultivated in compulsory kendo education in middle schools were presented as follows:

1. There are many ways in which agile and stable [physical] movement extends to spiritual movement [*seishin undō*].
2. It is suitable for nurturing powers of discernment and the ability to accomplish tasks.
3. It can be helpful in forging courage and grit.
4. It increases self-confidence and creates a calm demeanor.
5. Students can learn the spirit of bushido, and, through rigorous training, will nurture the admirable qualities of liveliness, fortitude, perseverance, endurance and diligence.
6. Students will come to understand the fine points of etiquette [*reigi-sahō*], with composure in deportment, and grace.
7. The student will learn respectability, and his character will be refined with a robust sense of honor.
8. In short, kendo will serve to cultivate broad-minded Japanese people with human qualities of wisdom, compassion, and feelings.[22]

Compared to the violent makeup of the militarized kendo that would soon be developed, the expectations outlined here seem perfectly civilized and in line with holistic individual growth. The text states that kendo's ultimate purpose is one of "peace" but that it can be used for "self-defense should the need arise." It also equates the "spirit of kendo" with the "spirit of bushido" and ultimately the "soul of Japan," which is defined as the "unique spirit of the Japanese people which places loyalty and filial piety above all else, and resonates with the spirit of self-sacrifice."[23] The tone of the text is nationalistic in a popular sense, but it is a far cry from the militaristic pitch that would become a feature of kendo instruction a year later, when war broke out with China in 1937.

It was not until the Seventieth Imperial Diet House of Representatives Plenary Session in 1937, around the outbreak of the second Sino-Japanese war (1937–1945), that the proposal by Imai Shinzō (1894–1962) to include budo as a regular subject in primary and "youth schools" (secondary education facilities that operated between 1935 and 1947 for working boys and girls) was approved. This signified a sudden intensification of interest from various sectors for a fiercer cultural-political role for kendo. For example, in 1938, the prominent nationalist Ishii Saburō (1880–1948) of the Kōdō Gikai, together with renowned kendo instructors of the day, such as Takano Sasaburō and Naitō Takaharu, were involved in the establishment of the Kendo Deliberation Council (Kendō Shingikai), a consulting body to the MOE. Their goal was to facilitate a greater understanding of the effectiveness of kendo as a means to instill national spirit and thereby encourage the government to support a policy of wider sponsorship of kendo in education and the community.

In 1938, the Kendo Deliberation Council announced its desire for kendo to be recognized as a "source of spiritual strength" that would help the nation's people endure the hard times ahead. It also urged the government to become more involved in the dissemination of kendo: "If the nation embodies the spirit of kendo, and it is propagated to the extent that there are no Japanese who do not study kendo, this would indeed be a wonderful accomplishment from the state's point of view. This great objective will be exceedingly difficult to achieve without the active cooperation of the state. . . . The spirit of kendo will return to the apex of devotion and sacrifice for the emperor."[24] The council also advocated the creation of a central government-controlled training institution for kendo teachers, which would be founded in 1942.

Apart from the Kendo Deliberation Council, other groups and individuals intensified the push for a more extensive role for budo. Of particular consequence were the twenty-two proposals submitted by parliamentarian Fujio Yasutarō (1895–1971) and others concerning budo education in primary, youth, and girls' schools. The thrust of his argument was that budo would help cultivate "national morality" (kokumin dōtoku), which would ensure Japan's survival as it headed into what threatened to be an extended period of hostility. Physical fitness was seen as one key to success, as one observer noted: "Regardless of country or ethnicity, final victory is determined by the health of the nation's people and the training they engage in to maintain it."[25] These propositions had a resounding effect on the implementation of budo education.

Fujio suggested that budo, as it was so valuable for enhancing the physical and mental strength of the nation's people, be considered seriously as a compulsory form of physical education—distinct from Western-style physical education—for all Japanese youth. Kendo and the other martial arts promised to contribute to this goal.

Fujio's proposals were tendered with a number of other propositions, which were combined into one submission consisting of nine articles. They included the following suggestions: construct a martial arts hall in the precincts of the Meiji Shrine; launch an institution to be called the Budō Deliberation Council (Budō Shingikai, later to be established as the Budō Shinkō Iinkai); promote sumo(-dō); construct municipal martial art training halls in cities and towns; create a budo section or department in the Ministry of Health and Welfare (Kōseishō); include budo education as a regular subject in all primary, youth, and girls' schools; create more institutions to train budo instructors; establish a system of school inspectors to oversee budo; and afford special privileges to budo instructors. Fujio's suggestions were endorsed by lawmakers, signifying the culmination of many years of petitioning the government by Fujio and others to take a more active stance on supporting budo as a cultural vehicle for educating the people. These developments will be discussed in more depth below.

Although it is not always clear how implicated a state is in the use of culture for political means, officialdom does influence the role of culture in society through its mandates of legitimization. The early Shōwa era marks the beginning of the Japanese state's endeavor to use the martial arts for national advancement and to imbue the people with pride and a sense of Japaneseness as the country prepared for war.

Some populist advocates proclaimed that it had taken too long for authorities to recognize the crucial role kendo could play in primary education to counter the pervasive and detrimental influence of Western ideals. The reasons it finally became possible to introduce kendo into the primary education curriculum, according to one kendoka of the time, Watanabe Sakae, were threefold: first, the Japanese people recognized that kendo was the national sport of Japan and that it formed the basis for national ideals (kokumin shisō); second, children had the right mind to learn the spirit of kendo properly; and third, there was an acknowledgement that kendo could further facilitate optimal physical and mental development in children.[26]

Satō Ukichi (1895–1975) was a leading kendo master and professor at the Tokyo Higher Normal School.[27] In 1928, he published his now-classic book *Kendō,* in which he wrote that extolling the spirit of true patriotism as represented in the "one-nation, one-state" of Japan would convince individual Japanese people to avoid the insalubrious ideals of foreign countries and to instead connect with the spirit of the Japanese people (*Yamato minzoku*) through kendo. In the same year he wrote a paper in the educational journal *Taiiku to kyōgi* (Physical education and sport) about the importance of cultivating state and ethnic consciousness—that is to say, a sense of Japaneseness— through kendo.[28] This demonstrates the considerable overlap and ambiguity between so-called statist and nonstatist nationalists in Japan at the time.

Implanting "Japaneseness" took on more urgency after the Manchurian Incident, when absolute state values were attached to kendo—an activity viewed as morally superior to Western sports and thereby useful for nurturing not so much "good individuals" as "good imperial subjects." Given the exigency of war, educators and kendo instructors acquiesced to the state's agenda with little open resistance.

Another way in which kendo was linked to state machinations was through a government decree that ordered the installation of *kamidana* (Shinto altars, literally "god-shelves") in all dojo and in school halls where kendo was practiced. Items of worship, such as scrolls, had decorated training venues since the Tokugawa period, but there were few examples of Shinto altars. As Nakamura Tamio points out, Shinto altars started to show up in martial art halls from the end of the Meiji period and became more common around the beginning of the Showa period as a contrivance of the "national reinforcement policy," which fused imperialism with fascist militarism. A survey conducted in 1932 found that 47.2 percent of middle schools had *kamidana* in their dojo, a figure that was decried as totally unacceptable by nationalists. This was discussed at a meeting of regional heads of physical education and exercise convened by the MOE in 1936, who decreed: "The sanctity of the dojo must always be maintained.... All dojo will be furnished with a *kamidana.*"[29]

This edict effectively forced a direct relationship between kendo and *kōdō*—or reverence toward the imperial way. Whenever a training session commenced or finished, all students would bow to the *kamidana* as a sign of deep respect to state Shinto deities and, concomitantly, to the emperor and the state itself. It was obviously meant as a way of indoctrinating youth with nationalistic ideals through the use of symbols and invented protocols of propriety.

In another pivotal development in the state's takeover of kendo, the Army Ministry proposed in 1937 that a Ministry of Health and Welfare (Kōseishō) be established in order to bolster the war effort. The ministry was inaugurated in January 1938, and under its auspices was the Board of Physical Fitness (Tairyoku-kyoku). This board was tasked with overseeing all aspects of public health and well-being, and its jurisdiction even extended to previously independent sports organizations. The only area of consequence it did not regulate was physical education in schools, which was the domain of its rival ministry, the MOE.

The Ministry of Health and Welfare also requisitioned the annual Meiji Shrine Tournament and renamed it the Meiji Shrine Citizens Training Tournament (Meiji Jingū Kokumin Rensei Taikai). A patently militaristic program was introduced, which included calisthenics, air raid drills, martial arts, and combat drills. Western sports were excluded. Thus, through its various ministries, the government tightened its multipronged grip on all physical activity in Japan and set up a framework to wrest administrative control from private sports bodies. Furthermore, militarists began to "Japanize" Western sports, attaching the suffix -dō to their names to create new terms, such as taiiku-dō (the way of physical education). This represents the "budofication" of sports as opposed to the "sportification" of budo.

Sakaue and Ōtsuka plotted the following key points in the progression of kendo's fusion with state cultural policy: the inclusion of the Butokukai in the Central League for the Mobilization of National Spirit (Kokumin Seishin Sōdōin Chūō Renmei) in 1937; the inauguration of the Budo Promotion Council (Budō Shinkō Iinkai) in 1939; and the elevation of budo to become a provisional regular subject (jun-seika) in primary schools in 1939 and then a full regular subject in 1941. They contend that kendo lost its "life force" for internal development as a result of being coerced into serving as a tool for the promotion of nationalism and militarism.[30]

I would argue that it was not a case of kendo losing its "life force" but rather of another intrinsic aspect of the sport coming to the fore. Postwar Japanese scholars tend to bemoan the state's appropriation of kendo as a reprehensible abuse. They are missing two points: first, it was not only the state that was at the forefront of this movement, but also former popular nationalists; and second, as I have already noted, despite the many historical expressions for attaining individual spiritual peace through kendo, it is fundamentally a fighting art. The intrinsic qualities that characterize kendo—its DNA—are combat-derived. A martial art contains the building blocks for military training. It is the nature of the beast. Kendoka do not compete to put a ball in the back of a net; they vie to cleave the other asunder, albeit metaphorically, but the action and intent can easily be twisted to fit the exigency of times of war.

There was a process in which kendo was made more violent in the late 1930s. It essentially involved downplaying kendo as a way of self-development in the traditional, holistic sense and promoting nationalistic agendas through state-sanctioned, forced martial arts participation, mainly in schools. The Butokukai often used the phrase "spirit of self-sacrifice" (*gisei-teki seishin*) in reference to kendo, which suggests that the sport was being employed to produce cogs to power the national machine of emperor and state, in compliance with the ideals promulgated in the *Kokutai no hongi* (Cardinal Principles of the National Entity of Japan): "To give up one's life for the sake of the Emperor cannot be called self-sacrifice. Rather, it is a discarding of one's lesser self to live in the great Imperial Virtue, and the exalting of one's true life as a national subject."[31]

After the commencement of the second Sino-Japanese War in 1937 and the subsequent buildup to Japan's involvement in the Second World War, even popular nationalist kendo experts, such as Watanabe Sakae, began promoting the correlation between kendo, the state, and its citizens. In Watanabe's words: "As the national sport of Japan, the spirit of kendo lies at the root of the spirit of the nation, and the promotion of the national spirit is tantamount to the promotion of the spirit of kendo. The spirit of kendo and the current situation [with the war in China] are inseparably linked. In recent times we have endorsed the ideal of patriotic kendo, and this is going to become even more important from now."[32]

The jingoistic rhetoric used to evoke cultural pride and associate kendo with the samurai value of self-sacrifice was further reinforced by contrasting kendo with Western sword arts: "Western swordsmanship was developed in accompaniment with the shield, which was used for protection while trying to kill the enemy. Self-defense and safety are the primary concerns. In the case of Japanese *kenjutsu,* protecting the self is never a consideration. If there is an opportunity to cut or thrust, all of one's energy is put into a committed attack, and it is unpardonable to think of anything else."[33]

Western sports in general were seen as "liberal" and perilous to the cause. In 1938, the Ministry of Health and Welfare even went so far as to brand athleticism a "germ of Western self-pride." It enforced a policy requiring all sports organizations to comply with the government's initiatives for improving physical well-being. Intimately linked with a glorious warrior past, in addition to being a way to cultivate physical fitness, mental toughness, discipline, combat preparedness, and national morality, kendo was the ultimate tool for the diffusion of militarism.

FROM SELF-PERFECTION TO SELF-SACRIFICE

The second stage of kendo's militaristic development, according to Sakaue and Ōtsuka, was the period falling between the Second Sino-Japanese War and the Pacific War, 1938–41. This was the most concentrated period of kendo's militarization. With the implementation of the National Mobilization Law in 1938, numerous aspects of Japanese society were modified to support the war effort, and kendo was restructured to be more combat-oriented through changes to match rules and teaching methodology. The following excerpt from a report by the Budo Promotion Council is telling: "As budo inspires the Imperial Way [kōdō] and aims to protect and develop the Japanese empire, its study should not be limited to being a vehicle for individual character cultivation, but viewed as a means to directly strengthen the nation to sustain the national polity."[34]

Nakayama Hakudō (1872–1958), one of the most famous twentieth-century masters of kendo and iaidō (the art of sword drawing), inadvertently demonstrated how markedly the philosophy of kendo changed as Japan became ensconced in war. Interviewed in the Japan Times and Mail on July 25, 1926, about the philosophy of kendo, he is reported as saying: "The ethics of swordsmanship, Mr. Nakayama wishes to clarify, is not in aggressive manslaughter. It lies primarily in psychic training. . . . The instrument, the sword, is necessary to give that serious frame of mind. What is more serious than life as forfeit for mistakes or inattention? The cold, mirror-like glimmer of the blade facing you, you cannot but be serious." However, a few years later he showed his warrior colors regarding the role of the sword in the modern theater of battle: "It is fighting with cold steel that makes the enemy petrified of our Japanese army and is our greatest weapon and strongest point. The idea of using one's own body to attack the enemy in hand-to-hand combat is the quintessence of the Japanese spirit."[35]

Such parti pris was also endorsed by other prominent kendo teachers, and the Kendo Deliberation Council petition of 1938 stated that, although modern warfare is fought with "science and technology," final victory is attained only by soldiers "facing the enemy front on, and stabbing and cutting them."[36] Modern kendo practitioners will know at least some of the seven signatories: Ishii Saburō, Takano Sasaburō, Nakayama Hakudō, Ogawa Kin'nosuke, Ōshima Jikita, Saimura Gorō, and Mochida Moriji.

Charles Nelson Spinks also observed an arrogantly aggressive attitude in Japanese military men and their fetish for swords: "General Sadao Araki once boasted that Japan was not greatly concerned about the standards of her material weapons, that if imbued with the real Japanese spirit, her soldiers could defeat the world with bamboo swords."[37]

Given the militaristic and statist ideologies engulfing Japan, it is hardly surprising that leading figures in martial arts education followed suit and assisted in the exploitation of kendo for violent means. By 1942, all physical training, not just budo, had militaristic objectives. Cultivating steadfastness in the face of danger surpassed matters of athletic prowess and well-being. Kendo and the other martial arts were taught with the aim of encouraging bellicosity in Japanese youth and glorifying martyrdom. Watari Shōzaburō, a teacher at the Tokyo Higher Normal School, expressed the following expectations for budo education.

This is the unique spirit of our country. It is the Japanese spirit. This spirit experienced remarkable development as bushido, so the phrase "*mononofu no Yamato-damashii*" [Japanese spirit of the warrior] means that the spirit of the *bushi* and the spirit of Japan are the same thing. With the advance of bushido came the parallel development of the techniques of fighting, or budo. Our country, martial Japan, a nation without peer in the world, is looked up to by all others because of the Japanese spirit and Japanese budo. Budo is represented by the virtue of valor [*buyū*]. How is this virtue manifest in the Japanese spirit? (1) A brimming attacking spirit [*kōgeki-seishin*].... (2) This fighting spirit becomes even more resolute in the face of a strong enemy and amid adversity.... (3) The tenacity to keep fighting to the bitter end regardless of the outlook.... (4) The fighting spirit is so overflowing with vim and vigor, that even in death the enemy will ultimately also be destroyed.... (5) In the throes of combat with the enemy, the mind is stolidly calm and able to move freely.[38]

In 1939, a monumental measure in terms of governmental control of sports was announced: the introduction of mandatory martial art classes in primary schools. This was, for all intents and purposes, designed to educate young soldiers prior to formal military training.

The MOE elevated budo to the status of a provisional regular subject (*junseika*) in May 1939 and simultaneously released the "Primary School Budo

Instruction Guidelines" (*Shōgakkō budō shidō yōmoku*). Instructions for how classes were to be structured and carried out were somewhat vague at first but were clarified in an explanatory text, "Primary School Budo Explanation" (*Shōgakkō budō kaisetsu*), which was published by the ministry in December of that year. The stated objective of these guidelines was to "encourage academic studies and martial practice [*shūbun-renbu*] from childhood, nurture a strong mind, and reap the fruits of practical disciplined education while cultivating a loyal and patriotic Japanese character" (p. 2). Classes were to be conducted two times a week outside of regular school hours, and, in the case of kendo, *shinai* or wooden swords were to be utilized but not protective armor—probably because the resources were not available to supply equipment to schools nationwide.

The promotion of budo from a provisional to a regular subject was generally welcomed. For example, Abe Mamoru, a teacher at the Ibaraki Prefecture Normal School, was representative of many educators who supported the policy because children could be "nurtured in accordance with the way of the Japanese Empire."[39] Also in 1939, Nakayama Hakudō described the value of this policy in terms of the limits of compulsory education (*gimu-kyōiku*), which extended only to the end of primary school.

> Not all primary school students continue through to higher education. Actually, of one hundred children, sixty or seventy will be unable to continue due to their home situation, and only one-quarter or one-third will be able to receive higher education. Many will enter society after receiving only primary education. These children will not be given the opportunity to study budo. . . . What a decrepit state of affairs if our nation's soldiers, born and bred in Japan, go through life without knowing budo. Looking at the kind of kendo practiced at universities and vocational colleges nowadays, students seek only to compete with taps of the bamboo sword. They engage in matches for the sake of competing rather than to learn the spirit of budo. To equate this condition with pot plants or *bonsai* trees, it is like fussing over the shape of the branches, but not paying any attention to the roots. This cannot be regarded as an ideal order of development. Why would such kendo arise (not that it should be called kendo) in which the practitioners vie to hit each other with *shinai* without forging the gut. This is the destructive influence of foreign sports.[40]

Still, there remained the problem of who was going to teach the classes. At a national meeting of normal school principals, held in June 1939, those present were urged to make an effort to foster capable budo teachers. The need for these teachers would become even more acute with the impending introduction of compulsory budo education in primary schools.

FIGURE 15. A group of children from Mito doing their bit to cheer on the war effort in front of the Yasukuni Shrine in 1941. (The Mainichi Newspapers)

With the National People's School Order (Kokumin gakkō-rei) of 1941, primary schools were renamed National People's schools, and the duration of compulsory education was lengthened from six years to eight. The school curriculum was designed to educate pupils who would embody the spirit of the nation (*kokumin seishin*), follow the "imperial way," and have resolute faith in the government's ability to "fulfill the mandates of the empire." Article 10 of the order stated that nurturing citizens with a strong physique and vigorous spirit would enhance the strength of the nation, and this was perceived as necessary for the defense of the homeland (figure 15). The ordinance also made budo a compulsory subject for all school children starting in the fifth year of primary school.

The physical education curriculum (*taisō*) was renamed physical training (*tairen*), increased from three to six hours a week, and divided into two sections of calisthenics (military drills and marching) and budo. Apart from physical training, pupils also had to take classes in citizenship, science and mathematics, and art. Citizenship classes included moral education, which

complemented budo classes with themes of military heroism and the glorification of war. Kendo was required for all boys in year five and above. Girls
were given the option of doing naginata. The new *tairen* curriculum was
designed to prime youth for war, and thus the style of kendo education
was aggressive and militaristic. Children were taught that the essence of budo
was to attack without concern for the outcome. They were supposed to continue budo in the seventh and eighth grades with full implementation of the
curriculum planned for 1944, but this proved unfeasible due to the strain on
resources caused by the war, and the extra two years were never realized.

After the enactment of the National People's School Order, procedures for
middle, higher, and other school categories were also issued, and budo education was intensified beginning in early 1943. For example, Article 5 of the
Chūgaku kitei, which provided guidelines for budo lessons in middle schools,
stipulated that "bodies will be strengthened and spirits forged to raise
unyielding reserves for augmenting the nation's capacity for defense and loyal
service." The following objectives were given for normal school budo
education:

1. We must induce [our students] to master our nation's unique martial
   arts, and train healthy, vigorous minds and bodies.
2. As well as nourishing a disposition to hone a martial spirit, esteem
   propriety, and value modesty, we must encourage an aggressive spirit and
   a confidence in certain victory.
3. We must inculcate a spirit of self-sacrifice and train a fighting mentality.[41]

Lectures outlining the objectives of training, the structure of the Japanese
sword, and the way that budo was intimately linked with the Japanese psyche
were an important characteristic of budo classes. In fact, the lecture portion
of the syllabus was taught in correlation with moral education (*shūshin*),
national language studies, national history, and geography, closely associating
budo with Japanese identity.

The Ministry of Health and Welfare also became particularly active in
pushing budo after establishing the Budo Promotion Council in 1939. A
minor jurisdictional conflict ensued between the Ministry of Health and
Welfare and the Home Ministry's Police Bureau, which had a long association with budo. In the end, however, the Minister of Health and Welfare was
appointed chair of the committee, which comprised the Minister of
Education, around thirty senior government officials, and a handful of budo
experts.

The first meeting of the Budo Promotion Council was convened in February 1940 to establish the basic direction budo promotion should take. The only kendo representative was Takano Sasaburō, who reportedly sat in the room but rarely contributed to the discussions. The reason for his passivity at the inaugural meeting remains a mystery, but perhaps it was due to his age—he was seventy-seven at the time—or maybe his presence was meant to be no more than token. In any case, the budo experts in attendance were not afforded the same liberty to express themselves as the bureaucrats. One of the outcomes of the five meetings was the creation of a central government body to administer budo. According to the official committee mandate:

> Budo as it stands now is either fixed on competition, or taught simply as an activity for physical education. To instill the true spirit of bushido and revive the special characteristics of budo that make it an effective means to vanquish enemies, we are resolved to creating a composite form of budo to meet the challenges our nation faces now. We propose to adopt components from judo, kendo, kyudo, *kidō* [horse-riding], and *suiei* [swimming] into a functional style of budo, giving youth the skills they need to meet the responsibility of universal conscription [*kokumin-kaihei*]. In accordance with the ideal of both literary and military paths [*bunbu-ryōdō*], the aim is to stir the national spirit and augment national strength. To facilitate this, each budo society will be assimilated into a central body supervised by the government. Instructors will be trained, and a supreme organization for budo education will be established.[42]

The Dai-Nippon Butokukai was restructured into an extragovernmental organization in 1942 to become the central body the Budo Promotion Council was looking for. This would have far-reaching consequences for the fate of budo after the war. The style of budo being promoted by the government was not yet pragmatic enough for some advocates. For example, a kendo instructor named Takayama Masayoshi lamented that budo was in a state of disarray, focused more on spirituality than utility. He argued that teaching children that it was okay to lose as long as they tried their best and played fairly would lead to a distorted, pusillanimous view of budo.

Furthermore, according to Takayama, the very attributes that had been touted so zealously to get budo taught in schools were now superfluous inconsequentialities that had no function in wartime. He complained that the elevation of budo as the spiritual core of the Japanese and the elegant lexicon used to this end without an understanding of "true bushido" had led to budo's "emasculation."

His scathing appraisal of budo in general was that it was completely removed from the realism of bloody war and little more than "puppet theater." Takayama felt the need to move away from using budo for moral development and argued for adopting a policy that reinforced budo's usefulness in the thick of the fray. He believed that only through studying the way of *kami* (deities), *waza* (techniques), and death would one be able to sacrifice oneself in service of the emperor. Serving the emperor with purity of mind would cause *Yamato-damashii* to manifest itself and loyalty and heroism to radiate from within.

He loathed the "weak-willed, spiritless armchair intellectuals" who were involved in concocting teaching guidelines: "Current budo education does not teach how to kill. . . . Surely, this amounts to no more than salt that is not salty, sugar that is not sweet, or *senpuri* [*Swertia japonica*] that is not bitter."[43] Although Takayama could be categorized as representing one extreme, he was certainly not alone in his thinking. Budo education in schools and in the community would gradually conform to his ideals.

Nakayama Hakudō took a different position on how kendo should be taught at the National People's Schools once instruction commenced in 1941. He believed that the purpose of kendo was to make human beings burly both in "bone and spirit." He bewailed the fact that the "spirit of bushido" was barely understood by Japan's youth. According to Nakayama, youth were not given enough opportunity to cultivate purity of spirit through kendo.

At first glance, it appears that Nakayama's position, which advocated personal cultivation, was the opposite of Takayama's. However, this was not exactly the case. The issue of functionality was, in fact, very much on Nakayama's mind. He relays chilling information about the war in China that was divulged to him by one of his students, Terada Kanzō, a deft kendo and *iaidō* expert. At the end of a battle between six hundred Chinese soldiers and two hundred Japanese, the Japanese soldiers asked each other how many of the enemy each had cut down:

Terada reported to his peers that he had cut off the right hands or left feet of his enemies, and that they should go and count. It turned out that there were sixty-six enemy bodies without a right hand or left foot, and there wasn't a single chip on his blade. However, others who boasted of their skill in kendo claimed ten or twenty kills, but their *guntō* [military-issue katana] were completely bent; the blades were so chipped that they looked like saws, and the men themselves were exhausted. I view this as symptomatic of the colossal divide separating those who have learnt kendo properly, and those who have not. This is something that I admonish all primary school kendo teachers to consider carefully.[44]

Could true combat ability realistically be cultivated through kendo instruction in schools? Ishida Ichirō, a school inspector in Tokyo, suggested that kendo be regarded as *kenjutsu*. He implored students to imagine that they were training with live blades and to be relentless in their attacks during practice. Only then would they develop strength and learn to use a *nihontō* (Japanese sword) properly.[45] This was the premise, but how exactly were these goals to be activated on a national scale?

STICKS AND STONES AND BREAKING BONES

The zenith of kendo's militarization came in what Sakaue and Ōtsuka label the third stage, 1942–45, which was an era of unprecedented policies aimed at militarizing martial art education. The government explored a proposal to incorporate all budo organizations under the auspices of one state-governed umbrella organization. In December 1941, the Budo Promotion Council was restructured for this purpose, becoming the Budo Training Division (Renbu-ka) of the Ministry of Health and Welfare's Population Bureau (Jinkō-kyoku, originally Kokumin Tairyoku Shingikai, or National Physical Strength Council). A year later, in 1942, it was renamed the Training Division (Tanren-ka), and it took over administration of all budo activities except for university clubs.

The National Physical Strength Council created a subcommittee headed by General Nara Takeji and thirteen other officials. They recommended that an all-encompassing organization be formed with connections between the Home Ministry and the ministries of Health and Welfare, Education (MOE), the Army, and the Navy to spur budo in all walks of society. With this aim, the Dai-Nippon Butokukai was restructured on March 21, 1942. The Butokukai headquarters was relocated inside the Ministry of Health and Welfare's Tokyo office, and its original Kyoto base was designated a regional branch. The Ministry of Health and Welfare's Student Physical Education Promotion Committee became a division inside the Butokukai, and its role was to administer the five budo arts of kendo (which included naginata), judo, kyudo, jukendo, and *shagekidō* (the way of marksmanship). Other private associations, such as the Kōdōkan (judo institute), the Nippon Kobudō Shinkōkai (Classical Martial Arts Promotion Society), and the Shiseikai and the Dai-Nippon Kendokai (private kendo societies), were also supervised by the Butokukai.[46] The following declaration made the state's motivations abundantly clear: "Subjects of the Japanese empire learn budo to cultivate loyalty, bravery, and heroism to bolster the spirit of the nation and personify the virtues of fidelity and honor. The essence of budo must be exemplified in the lifestyle of the nation, and when danger threatens, all should embrace the idea of martyrdom out of duty to the emperor."[47] The process of the Butokukai's arrogation by the militaristic government was reported in detail in SCAP documents concerning the postwar purge of militaristic officials:

> It appears that a critical phase in the society's change into a militaristic organ took place under government pressure. This pressure was said to have been exercised by the army every [sic] since the Manchurian incident but the conservative element in the society was able to resist until 1942 when the organization was finally forced to change its rules to the effect that the prime minister was to be its president ex-officio and the ministers of the army, navy, education welfare and home ex-officio vice presidents. For this reason General Senjuro Hayashi resigned on March 5, 1942, and on 21 March when the new by-laws were put into force General Tojo as Premier and Minister of War assumed the presidency. This ended an eleven year struggle (according to these government spokesmen) in which the army had consistently tried to infiltrate army methods of judo, kendo, and kyudo as against the conservative purely athletic method which was taught by the organization since its inception.[48]

The appropriation of the Butokukai was not without controversy. It reportedly took twenty months to complete the integration of the organization's prefectural branches into the new government organ. This may have been due to the antipathy of some popular nationalists toward the state or simply the inevitable logistical difficulties of taking control of a nationwide organization with millions of members. Nevertheless, in 1943, the newly reorganized Dai-Nippon Butokukai issued guidelines on how kendo training would be conducted under its watch. It listed unambiguous practical directives from the outset:

1. A reasonable understanding of sword usage [tōhō] is expected to be acquired. This includes the execution of basic cuts and thrusts, and correct kirikaeshi [repetitive striking practice].
2. Ample training should be conducted outdoors. Attire will consist of trousers, wrap-around leggings and shoes so that attacks can be practiced while running.
3. The length of the shinai will be regulated. Shinai shall be no longer than 3-shaku 6-sun [109 cm]. The tsuka [hilt] should be less than 1-shaku [30.3 cm]

with 9-*sun* [27.2 cm] under the *tsuba* [hand guard; these measurements are in line with standard issue military swords].

4. Matches against a variety of weapons should be conducted. Sword versus sword; sword versus *jūken* [rifle and bayonet]; sword versus short sword; one person versus multiple opponents; group matches.

5. Test cutting [*tameshi-giri*] is to be encouraged.

6. Kendo instructors should also study jukendo, and instruct it at a basic level.[49]

The new rules and guidelines set the tone for the introduction of militarized (*sengi*) kendo, in which the sole objective was to teach participants the skills to kill in a fearless death frenzy.

Even once the Butokukai came under the administrative wing of several ministries, the MOE and the Ministry of Health and Welfare continued to administer their own programs for kendo. In 1943, as the war effort intensified, the MOE promulgated the "Guidelines for Wartime Physical Education Training Implementation for Students" (*Senji gakuto taiiku kunren jisshi yōkō*), which introduced "militarized budo" for university and vocational school students. Kendo was included in the basic training section to promote combat readiness to go with student mobilization, which was initiated in the same year.

Toward the end of the war, the MOE put out "Important Aims for Preparing Citizen Combat Capability" (*Kokumin tōryoku rensei yōkō*), which was devised mainly by Ōtani Takeichi, a professor at the Tokyo Specialist College of Physical Education (amalgamated with the Tokyo University of Education at the end of the war). The following translation is from the preamble:

> The war situation has become dire, and a corner of our sacred empire has been defiled by the callous enemy. The time has come for the people to rise and protect the homeland. To meet this heavy burden of responsibility, the citizens of Japan must first be armed with a vigorous fighting spirit and master the fundamentals of combat. Through the coalescence of skill and spirit, the people can attain a high level of military preparedness. The purpose of the items outlined herein is to augment the fighting capacity of the Japanese people.[50]

The text reveals signs of desperation as the war worsened for the Japanese. The threat of foreign invasion had become a real possibility. It was seen as imperative that every Japanese citizen be ready to fight to the last if Allied forces landed in Japan.[51] The next section in the text outlines the type of

TABLE 5 Militarized budo content

Males	
Topic	*Content*
Running (*hosō*)	1–2 km dash
Body blows (*taiatari*)	Punches and kicks
	Throws
	Holds
Cuts and thrusts (*zantotsu*)	Cutting training (*tanren-zangeki*)
	Fundamental cutting and thrusting, including bayonet practice (*kihon-zantotsu*)
	Vertical and horizontal cutting practice
Throwing (*tōteki*)	Catching ball
	Short-staff throwing

Females	
Topic	*Content*
Running (*hosō*)	1 km dash or 2 km fast walking
Self-defense (*goshin*)	Punches
	Kicks
Throwing (*tōteki*)	Catching ball
	Short-staff throwing

SOURCE: Japanese Ministry of Education, "Important Aims for Preparing Citizen Combat Capability" (*Kokumin tōryoku rensei yōkō*).

training that citizens would be subjected to: "The public must be proficient in two aspects of combat: the first is maneuverability developed through walking and running exercises, and the other is actual fighting skills involving training in hand-to-hand combat and with weapons. The weapons are wooden staves (katana), bamboo spears (bayonet), and rocks (grenades). These cover the essential techniques for action, and are simple to learn and apply. Nurturing the crucial element of individual fighting spirit can be accomplished through rigorous training" (p. 52). The syllabus consisted of exercises that sought to enhance fitness and hone basic skills of self-defense (table 5).

The objective of the "cuts and thrusts" section was to cultivate an indomitable fighting spirit and learn to execute decisive cuts with the sword (figure 16). The training involved the frenzied striking of bundled sticks on a stand at least one hundred times, which was probably inspired by the classical school of swordsmanship known as Jigen-ryū.[52] The instructional content

FIGURE 16. A 1943 photograph of military cadets honing their sword and bayonet skills against hit dummies made to resemble Churchill and Roosevelt. (The Mainichi Newspapers)

includes details for correct cutting technique, particularly underscoring correct blade trajectory, stable posture, and continued physical and mental vigilance after the cuts.

In addition to smashing a stand with staffs or sticks, trainees engaged in matches wearing protective armor. For the sake of authenticity, much of the training was conducted outdoors with the participants wearing shoes. The *shinai* was shortened to 3-*shaku 6-sun* (109 cm). Bouts were conducted in rectangular areas twenty meters in length so that competitors were compelled to charge each other head on, or in the center of a circle formed by all the participants so that when one person was defeated another would rush in to challenge.

In 1943, the Ministry of Health and Welfare implemented a similar training policy for community physical education (*shakai taiiku*) that included kendo, jukendo, and *shagekidō*. Back in 1938, the ministry had created the Physical Fitness Badge Test for males aged fifteen to twenty-five. They planned a similar program for the martial arts in 1943 called the Budo Proficiency Awards (*budō-shō kentei*), in which badges, not unlike those awarded by the Boy Scouts, were issued to individuals who successfully completed a series of tasks designed to enhance combat ability.

In March 1944, the Ministry of Health and Welfare rolled out a more comprehensive outline for nationwide participation in militarized budo. The ministry published the "National Military Budo Fundamentals Training Manual" (*Kokumin sengi budō kihon kunren yōkō*), which provided guidelines for drilling citizens in traditional and modern martial skills. The booklet outlined the four combat arts of jukendo, kendo, *shagekidō,* and judo. It opens with the following statement of intent: "Conditions are becoming critical as we enter the third year of the Greater East Asian War. When the time comes for deployment, it behooves imperial subjects to be imbued with the traditional spirit of budo. Now is the time to acquire the fundamentals of combat through daily budo training. This booklet outlines the kind of budo training citizens must engage in to annihilate the enemy using all of the physical and mental attributes they possess." In Article 3, the nexus between the "spirit of budo" and the sacred Japanese empire is rationalized: "Important considerations in budo are reverence of *kami* and veneration of our ancestors, and the spirit of loyalty and patriotism based on all of one's might. . . . A crucial aspect of budo training is constant repetition [to master the basic skills], and to exemplify the essence of martial virtue (*butoku*) at all times." The syllabus for kendo was more comprehensive and pragmatic than the one defined in the MOE's 1943 "Guidelines for Wartime Physical Education Training Implementation for Students" (table 6). Although procedures of etiquette (*reihō*) were included, the Ministry of Health and Welfare's training did away with traditional forms that involved squatting down (*sonkyo*) as a sign of respect and replaced them with the battle-ready standing bow (*ritsurei*).

Militarized budo techniques will be totally unfamiliar to the modern kendoka because they were specifically designed for combat. For example, the idea of "charging in" (*totsunyū*) is to storm the enemy from any spatial inter-

TABLE 6   Militarized budo teaching content

Topic	Content
Etiquette protocol (*reihō*)	Standing bow (*ritsurei*)
Fighting posture or stance (*kamae*)	Sword in the sheathed position (*taitō*), sword in the ready position (*kamae-tō*)
Application of the sword	Vertical cut, right to left diagonal cut, right to left diagonal cut from below, right to left horizontal cut, thrust (*tsuki*)
Cutting and thrusting (*zantotsu*)	Cut to the head (*men-no-zangeki*), left to right cut to the head or torso (*men-no-zangeki* and *dō-no-zangeki*), thrust to the throat or chest (*tsuki*)
Continuous cutting (*aikiri*)	Continuous left to right strikes to the head (*men*)
Rushing in to cut (*totsunyū-zangeki*)	Charging in to cut *men* (*totsunyū-men-zangeki*), running in to cut the left diagonal (*totsunyū-hidari-kesa-zangeki*), running in to thrust (*totsunyū-tsuki*)
Respiration (*chōsoku*)	Prolonged respiration

SOURCE: Ministry of Health and Welfare, "National Military Budo Fundamentals Training Manual" (*Kokumin sengi budō kihon kunren yōkō*).

val and unleash a crude but effective barrage of cuts and slashes rather than the purposefully decisive single blow that is sought after in modern kendo. The terminology is deliberately militaristic. "Cut and thrust" (*zantotsu*) uses the Chinese character denoting an actual "cut" as opposed to the previous and currently used term *datotsu,* which means "strike and thrust." Students were taught to maintain the mindset that they were using a live blade, even though the sword or stick they were training with was wooden.

Furthermore, many of the techniques outlined in the syllabus were executed with one hand, differing from the standard two-handed style of fencing. This was due to the need to maintain balance while running and wielding a sword at the same time. The syllabus also advised that the right foot should be forward when cutting with the right hand (the opposite was true when cutting with the left hand). This was a safety measure in case the swipe at the opponent missed. The sword was usually held with the right hand, and if the left foot was forward the wielder put himself in danger of accidentally cutting his own leg on the follow through.

In short, militarized kendo was not intended to be sophisticated. It was battlefield preparation for brandishing cold steel, or anything that could be used as a weapon. Although it was still called kendo, it was essentially a reversion to medieval battlefield *kenjutsu.* There were target areas, but the objective was

FIGURE 17. Schoolboys practicing with wooden swords outside in a schoolyard, 1944. (The Mainichi Newspapers)

not to score points; the goal of militarized kendo was to learn how to wield a sword effectively while cutting along various trajectories and targets that were not usually employed in standard kendo, such as the neck and legs. In spite of its intention to fortify Japan's war effort, the system, although implemented in some regions, never reached full swing before the war ended. Still, as figure 17 shows, by the end of the war, most children in the school system were engaged in the study of budo in some form or another to prepare for the ultimate sacrifice.

DEFEAT AND FALLING ON THE SWORD

By 1945, the Japanese were tired of the incessant warfare, which had started in 1937, but martial art training became increasingly desperate as the inevitable confrontation with an enemy on home soil neared. As the Americans fought their way up through Okinawa and the southern islands, the Japanese vowed to fight to the last, using whatever they could get their hands on to ward off the invaders. Nobody, however, could foresee the utter futility of such diehard determination. The *Enola Gay* dropped "Little Boy" on the city of Hiroshima on August 6, 1945. The destruction was immediate and complete. In a flash, an estimated eighty thousand people were killed. Tens of thousands more would die slow deaths in the months and years to follow. Then, on August 9, another B-29, *Bockscar,* dropped "Fat Man" on the city of Nagasaki, killing roughly sixty thousand more. The wretched war for Japan was thus brought to an end, with an ethically untenable coup de grâce.

The Japanese were now at the mercy of the Allies. The United States led the Allies in Japan's occupation until it came to an end in 1952. Headed by General Douglas A. MacArthur, the occupying forces instigated extensive political, economic, educational, social, and military reforms. One of the first objectives was to punish or remove former militarists from engaging in public service by implementing what was called "the purge."

The purge directives contained in SCAPIN 548 ("Abolition of Certain Political Parties, Associations, Societies, and Other Organizations") dictated that ultranationalistic or militaristic social, political, professional, and commercial societies and institutions be disbanded.[53] The other directive often quoted apropos of the Butokukai is SCAPIN 550, "Removal and Exclusion of Undesirable Personnel from Public Office," which states, "Persons who have been active exponents of militarism and militant nationalism will be removed and excluded from public office and from any positions of public or substantial private responsibility."[54]

This meant that anybody who was a member of a militaristic or ultranationalistic organization, such as the Dai-Nippon Butokukai, would be removed, or disallowed from taking up positions in the bureaucracy. Given that a fair proportion of the Butokukai's hierarchy were already prominent men in various echelons of Japanese officialdom, this meant that many careers were in danger of coming to an abrupt end.

Thus, a memorandum was recommended to the Chief of Staff, General MacArthur: "Dissolution of Dai Nippon Butokukai by order to the Imperial Japanese Government is recommended in accordance with the provisions of SCAPIN 548 Paragraph 'I-f' on the grounds that this is an organization 'affording military or quasi-military training' and which provides for the 'perpetuation of militarism' or a martial spirit in Japan."[55] Interestingly, however, this recommendation was not acted on, and neither was a subsequent one prepared for the imperial government. Had either of these memorandums been followed up, the fate of the Butokukai and its officers would have been clear under Paragraph C of the purge directive categories: all would have been expunged without question.

Hans Baerwald, a second lieutenant posted to the Government Section in General Douglas MacArthur's GHQ, reports that the content of the recommendations was relayed verbally as the imperial Japanese government assured them that verbal ultimatums would suffice. Before any action was taken by the government to follow the recommendations, the Butokukai set about creating what one could cynically term "a façade of repentance" in the immediate postwar period.

Jukendo and *shagekidō* were removed from the Butokukai's curriculum, leaving only kendo, judo, and kyudo. Nakayama Hakudō was appointed as head of the kendo division in early 1946, and the Butokukai sought funding from private sources in order to disassociate itself from the government and make its former officers less conspicuous. Negotiations were held between the Japanese government and SCAP regarding the future of the society and the degree to which it would be subjected to the purge. A SCAP report outlined the debate as follows:

> The society rid itself of all its characteristics as an auxiliary organ of the government in March this year [1946]. Since then it has become a purely people's corporation, changing its system and organization along democratic lines, and endeavoring to regenerate and develop fencing, judo and archery as national sports for the establishment of a peaceful and well-cultured Japan. But in view of circumstances and with the object of fully attaining the above-mentioned intentions, it was found suitable to throw away all connections, create fresh atmosphere all over the country, and form new autonomous organizations for every branch of the sports. Thus on Sept. 13 [1946], a meeting of the directors was held and the liquidation of the society was decided upon.[56]

The main point of contention was whether the Butokukai would be classed as "ultranationalistic" or "militaristic" from the time of its inception in 1895 or only after it was appropriated by the government in 1942. General Willoughby, Chief of Intelligence during the Allied occupation of Japan, recommended to the Government Section in November 1946 that if the Butokukai were to be included under the provisions stipulated in SCAPIN 550, the beginning date for applying sanctions against any of its main officers should be no earlier than January 1942 and no later than September 1945—in other words, for the period in which the Butokukai was controlled by the government. He also relayed his concern that dismantling the Butokukai and purging all of its officers would have an adverse effect on the incumbent government. Three members of the Yoshida Shigeru cabinet and the director of the Bureau of Public Safety of the Home Ministry would ultimately be ousted from their posts, destabilizing the government at a critical time before the introduction of the new constitution.

Other SCAP officials took a similar, almost sympathetic stance. Of particular note was the Government Section's Political Affairs Division Chief, P. K. Roest, who wrote in a report, "At no time did the Butoku Kai have a special section or group in charge of 'spiritual' training. The 'spiritual' counterpart of the sports taught had been an integral element of the teaching itself for every one of these sports. It was reiterated that until the out-break of the Pacific War these so-called military arts were practiced as athletics, a physical training only, which at the same time developed worthy moral qualities." He also tried to justify the role played by military elites in the Butokukai as a passive one and even argued that the society was opposed to military and governmental interference, especially with regard to army training, including shooting and bayonet practice.

He concludes his report with the following statement: "From the material submitted by the Home Ministry it appears that the Butoku Kai could not be considered as an instrument of ultra-nationalism and militarism until the beginning of 1942, unless the athletics taught by the organization in connection with the Samurai code are in themselves considered as evil. If that extreme position is taken the organization stands condemned from its inception in 1895."[57]

Hans Baerwald witnessed the Butokukai leadership's gradual escape off the proverbial hook, and he viewed the light-handed treatment with skepticism. He surmised that Home Ministry bureaucrats had intentionally misled prominent SCAP officials to ensure that the Butokukai's officers escaped severe punishment in the purge.

The incumbent president of the Butokukai, Fujinuma Shōhei (1883–1962), sent a report to SCAP's Civil Intelligence Section outlining the organization's decision to break away from governmental control in March 1946 and to subsequently operate as an "independent organization" in a "democratic manner." Fujinuma stressed that the Butokukai's avowed objective was to contribute to the rebuilding of a peaceful Japan by improving the national sports of kendo, judo, and kyudo for the welfare of the public. Nonetheless, it was decided at a Butokukai director's meeting convened on September 13, 1946, that it would be better to disband the society and encourage enthusiasts to inaugurate their own independent "democratic societies" to promote the martial arts.

An application for dissolution was lodged with the MOE on November 2, 1946, and ratified on November 7 with a directive stipulating which measures the MOE intended to take regarding the Butokukai's assets. The dissolution was finalized by the Home Ministry on November 9. In addition to officially announcing the dissolution of the Dai-Nippon Butokukai and its branches, the directive stated that the Butokuden in Kyoto (the main dojo of the Butokukai, built in 1899) would be used as a venue for cultural and athletic activities.

Baerwald claims that the Government Section of SCAP was unaware until January 1947 that the Butokukai had dissolved of its own volition, and he interpreted the concealment as a subterfuge by the Butokukai, intended to avoid culpability and evade the purge. After the issuance of repeated requests by the Government Section asking the Japanese government to add the Butokukai to the purge, the Minister of Home Affairs, Uehara Etsujirō, sent a petition to General Courtney Whitney, a senior official of the Allied occupation, on February 24, 1947, stressing that the Butokukai was concerned only with promoting traditional sports and that the government had coerced it against its will to coordinate military exercises, such as bayonet training and shooting. Whitney issued the following response to Uehara's appeal on March 13, 1947:

1. I have carefully considered your memorandum concerning the status of the Great Japan Military Virtue Association (Dai Nippon Butoku Kai). This association was dissolved and its funds and other property seized under a Home Ministry Ordinance dated 8 November 1946 because during the war the association became an instrument of the militarists.

2. I am advising State Minister Kanamori that in the administration of Imperial Ordinance No. 1, dated 4 January 1947, all influential members of this association or any branch thereof within the period 6 December 1941 and 2 September 1945 will be treated as falling within the provisions of Category "G", Appendix "A" SCAPIN 550, in the absence of satisfactory proof to the contrary. (HBP 2–11)

Category "G," as opposed to "C," meant that the criteria for the purge were vague and that a time-consuming process of individual assessment would be required to judge each member of the society. Once the case of the Butokukai had reached this point, the Government Section and the Home Ministry

TABLE 7 Butokukai purge statistics

	Passed (released from purge category)	Removed (stripped of public office)	Barred (provisionally designated with purge status and barred from public office)	Previously designated (designated purgeable due to participation in the war)	Deceased (at the time of purge)	Total
National HQ officials	5	4	19	21	10	**59**
Prefectural officials (chiefs, vice chiefs, and chief directors)	67	40	182	62	17	**368**
Directors and chiefs of sections	169	8	128	—	21	**326**
Chiefs of sub-branches	416	381	462	5	56	**1,320**
Total	**657**	**433**	**791**	**88**	**104**	**2,073**

commenced with the adjudication process. As Baerwald points out, however, it was in fact bureaucrats in the Home Ministry (especially the police) who stood to be adversely affected by the proceedings, thereby prompting the ministry to take measures to protect its own officials. In the final analysis, only the local branch chiefs were declared purgeable. Baerwald describes this result as a substantial victory for the Home Ministry and rather wryly alludes to the Japanese bureaucracy's adeptness at deflecting blame and avoiding culpability.

In essence, the purge criteria for the Butokukai were not finalized until August 1947. Whereas all of the career officers in the army were designated "purgees" immediately after the war, preparation for the Butokukai purge took over two years. As laid out in table 7, of the 2,073 officials targeted (out of around three million members in 1942), 1,312 (63.3 percent) were barred from taking up any official office, 657 (31.6 percent) were passed, and 104 (5.1 percent) were deceased by the time of the proceedings. A minuscule 0.6 percent was classified "purgees."[58]

In light of the role the Butokukai played in indoctrinating nationalistic spirit and training the populace for war beginning in 1942 (and arguably before), its officials got off rather lightly. The following six observations made by Hans Baerwald reveal how the Butokukai managed to duck the brunt of the purge compared to other ultranationalistic societies and military-affiliated organizations.

> First, competing characterizations of the society's basic nature created an aura of ambiguity. Second, SCAP officials obtained contradictory information from Japanese Government officials. Third, there was a growing lack of consensus inside SCAP, especially after General Willoughby changed his mind. Fourth, both SCAP and Japanese Government officials began to give precedence to the impact that the Butokukai's inclusion in the Purge might have on incumbent holders of high office, instead of being primarily concerned with the implementation of basic Occupation policy. Fifth, SCAP's decision to exercise its control through the existing structure of the Japanese Government provided the bureaucracy—especially the Home Ministry—an opportunity to protect its career officials. Sixth, the Japanese Government's tactics of delay and obfuscation resulted in the Butokukai's purge being implemented during the period when basic Occupation policy began to shift from reform to recovery.[59]

Before the Butokukai was abolished, a proclamation was issued on November 6, 1945, banning all budo education in schools. Budo instructors were to teach other subjects if they were qualified. This ban applied not only to classes but was later applied to extracurricular club activities and the use of school facilities by private citizens.

However, the MOE had no intention of enforcing a full-scale ban on kendo (or other budo). It continued to negotiate with the Civil Informational and Education Section (CIE) of SCAP to no avail. An MOE ordinance issued on December 26, 1945, required all traces of military training to be erased from schools and the community, and all military training equipment to be destroyed. Sets of armor were taken into schoolyards and burned, and books related to budo were removed from library shelves and destroyed.

SCAP released a directive in 1947 that completed the sanitizing of any reminders of militarism in schools:

> In all educational organizations, the teaching of military curriculum must be forbidden. The wearing of student military uniforms must also be forbidden. Traditional activities like kendo, which foster the fighting spirit, must be abolished, too. Physical education must no longer be linked to "spiritual education." You must put more emphasis upon purely physical exercise; games that are not military training, and recreational activities. If instructors wearing military-type uniforms are employed as physical education instructors

or engage in sports and physical education activities, they must have their qualifications examined.[60]

Graduates of the Budo Vocational College, Tokyo Higher Normal School, Kokushikan, and other educational institutions who held national teaching qualifications for the martial arts were left jobless. Their fortunes, however, were to change in less than a decade, when the budo arts were reinstated as democratized sports. Kendo's return to the mainstream came after the revival of other budo, as it was viewed with the most suspicion by the occupation authorities.

Why was this so? Kendo had been hyped as a practical means of combat that nurtured a strong body and indomitable fighting spirit and taught practitioners how to use the cherished *nihontō*. In essence, wartime kendo was a return to *kenjutsu,* where the aim in battle was to kill, and outside of battle was to provide the Japanese people with an emotional bond to a warrior past, hence fostering collective national identity and strengthening their relationship with the emperor and the state. The "spirit of kendo" was lauded as epitomizing the spiritual and historical adhesive that aligned everybody.

At least that was the theory. How successful this ideological control through kendo actually was is difficult to ascertain due to the barrage of chauvinistic, fascist budo propaganda that was constantly regurgitated by high-level educators and military and government officials during the war. One thing is certain: as the "fun-and-games" aspect of kendo was eliminated, the sport underwent a distinct de-civilizing process, both technically and philosophically, and techniques and pedagogical methodology became focused almost entirely on encouraging self-sacrificial fighting to the death.

Preparation for war was the only concern when kendo was declared a compulsory subject in the secondary school curriculum in the 1930s, and then in National People's Schools (primary school level) in 1941–42, and other school categories thereafter. Indeed, kendo was undeniably used to help the statist cause in a variety of different ways.

The militarized kendo that was devised by the Ministry of Health and Welfare and the MOE and promoted through the Butokukai called for combat practicality. The *shinai* was shortened to the length of a real sword so that students were forced to practice true cutting action rather than relying on leverage. Matches were decided by *ippon-shōbu* (first valid cut), which represented actual mortal combat. Powerful, aggressive techniques were given greater value than subtle techniques that emphasized striking designated areas. Traditional apparel was replaced with shirts, trousers, and shoes for convenience and simplicity, as well the fact that it enabled training outside in conditions that were more realistic for combat. Students were trained to fight to the death.

These reasons made it inevitable that the occupation authorities would ban kendo after Japan's surrender. *Nihontō* were seen as a symbol of Japanese militarism and nationalism and were therefore confiscated and destroyed in massive numbers, maybe as many as five million, in what is referred to as the postwar *katana-gari* (sword hunt). The swords were detested by the Allied soldiers who had been terrorized by them during the war. The haunting photo of the execution of Australian POW Leonard George Siffleet (1916–43), who was captured and beheaded by a Japanese officer on Papua New Guinea, was found on the body of a dead Japanese soldier near Hollandia in 1944. It was published widely in Australian newspapers, as well as the extremely popular American weekly magazine *Life* on May 14, 1945. The caption read, "The Japanese are strangely sentimental and moral about this form of murder, finding it in accordance with the compassionate mercy of bushido" (p. 97). The image became an iconic representation of Japanese atrocities committed with "samurai swords."

By extension, kendo was treated with the same animosity. Even now, the wartime history of kendo and its connection with ultranationalism and militarism is awkward for kendo practitioners. Nobody denies that kendo was used in the war effort, or that more than a few of the respected elderly instructors today may have employed their kendo skills on enemy soldiers, or even innocent civilians, during the war. I personally have received kendo instruction from a handful of such individuals, and I have been party to private discussions of exploits with real swords.

But the pendulum swing in the direction of de-civilization stops here. There was a moment of suspended animation before it started moving back in the direction disapproved of only a generation before, toward a completely democratized form of "sports kendo."

CHAPTER 5

Kendo and Sports

PATH OF REASON OR CULTURAL TREASON?

The time has come for Japan to decide whether she will continue
to be controlled by those self-willed militaristic advisers whose
unintelligent calculations have brought the Empire of Japan to
the threshold of annihilation, or whether she will follow the
path of reason.

The Potsdam Declaration, July 26, 1945

STERILIZING THE SHINAI

Japan's defeat in the Second World War changed everything for the martial
arts. After it was rejected as a militaristic contrivance, kendo underwent a
painful period of introspection before embarking on a process of "recivilizing." To be accepted back into the education system and mainstream society,
kendo had to be purged of the violent, vilifying elements of ultranationalism
and militarism.

What was the process through which kendo was "recivilized"? As we have
seen, wartime martial arts education in schools was officially stopped on
November 6, 1945. The Ministry of Health and Welfare moved to promote
budo as democratic sports, distancing them from their wartime state-sponsored
antitypes. However, in June 1946, after all physical education jurisdiction had
been transferred from the Ministry of Health and Welfare to the Ministry of
Education, the Civil Information and Education Section (CIE) of SCAP
demanded strict control of budo activities, and on August 25 of that year, the
MOE issued a notification stating that use of the collective term "budo" would
no longer be permitted because of militaristic associations.

Contrary to popular belief, however, kendo did not completely disappear
in the immediate postwar period. Many small, private groups of enthusiasts
continued practicing away from the watchful eye of the occupying authorities, and police kendo was in a gray area. Although not initially prohibited, it

eventually came under the ban as an afterthought. In fact, the police held a kendo tournament in 1946, and all police instructors, including the renowned Saimura Gorō (1887–1969) and Mochida Moriji (1885–1974), were allowed to retain their posts. The allied powers officially reinstated police kendo in 1948, not long after the powerful Home Ministry (Naimushō) was abolished in December 1947, and the police system was decentralized. Another temporary ban was placed on police department kendo in 1949 following Communist May Day demonstrations, in which the baton-wielding policemen had their own weapons turned against them, but it was lifted later that same year. According to the American kendo pioneer Benjamin Hazard (1920–2011), who was training with the Tokyo police at the time, "When practice resumed, those elements in kendo which were clearly associated with a real sword, such as the slicing movement after the cut, [were missing], nor were blows delivered with as much strength as they had been prior to the ban."[1]

Kendo was severely restricted in other walks of society, however, and after prohibiting it in schools and dissolving the Dai-Nippon Butokukai, next on the occupational authority's agenda was dealing with kendo in the community. The extent to which members of the general public were permitted to practice kendo in any given area depended largely on the military overseer in charge of that particular locale. Some regions were relatively lax in the enforcement of restrictions, whereas others were more stringent. This disparity allowed small private groups to operate in pockets throughout the country, although the scale of their activities was limited and is not well documented.

Sasamori Junzō (1886–1976), a member of the House of Councilors, a Christian, and a prominent kendo practitioner, petitioned SCAP in 1946 not to instigate a blanket ban on kendo. He was successful in retaining the right of individuals to manage private dojos and clubs. In the "Report Regarding the Procedure for the Liquidation of the Dai-Nippon Butoku Kai," authorities indicated that while they did not condone kendo in the community, they did grudgingly put up with it to a certain extent, so long as it maintained a very low profile.

> It is considered advisable that in the future those who like fencing, judo, archery etc. should locally form new organizations on a democratic and autonomic basis in order to develop these sports as cheerful and liberal national ones. Accordingly the system and structure of these organizations should be free from any tendency towards centralization, while any one imbued with militarism and ultra-nationalism should be absolutely disqualified for leaders.[2]

The budo arts were seen as potentially dangerous activities by SCAP and repentant Japanese educators. The spiritual aspects of budo that had been hailed for so long were now considered to be a subversive force. The question being asked around the country was whether the martial arts should be revived at all, and, if so, which aspects of their technical and theoretical makeup could be "purified"? The following excerpt from the minutes of the "General Meeting of the Directors, Secretaries and Instructors of Butoku Kai, Concerning Dissolution of the Society" (October 30, 1946) is illustrative of the debates that occurred in official circles:

> A representative from Gunma Prefecture asked if, in the opinion of the Physical Education officer, the games should be purified. Major Norviel stated that the question was difficult to answer, because although one might understand the peaceful appearance of the sports, it is difficult to tell what is going on in the mind of the individual participating. The danger is not in the budo games alone, but rather in the spirit of combat and conquest that has been put into them. If we knew that this attitude could be completely changed, we could feel sure that there was no harm in the sports themselves. But that big a transformation cannot be done overnight, by edict or order. A philosophy cannot be eliminated by legislation.[3]

Although there was vociferous opposition among Japanese educators and officials to revivifying budo, enthusiasts persevered. Of course, there was a substantial amount of skepticism shown by SCAP, but the meeting minutes indicate that the Occupation authorities were not as adamantly opposed to citizen participation in the budo arts as they are usually portrayed:

> The Japanese again questioned the differences in prefectures concerning permission to practice budo socially. Major Norviel: That is not too hard to explain. When there are different commanders in different areas, there will be some differences in interpretation.... My suggestion, if you feel that it is not militaristic, endeavor to prove to your local MG officer, that it is not. After all, they are in charge and you have to get along with them. A Japanese ventured to guess that kendo could not be cleaned up and made a good sport.... A Japanese suggested that kendo and kyudo were similar, but to consider such games as a military activity in [the] scientific and atomic age was foolish. It is when some individual with evil intent inserts the idea of "dying for old Japan" and the spirit involved, into the games, that the bad influence begins.[4]

It was clear was that there was a certain degree of leeway regarding the restoration of kendo, but any hint of ultranationalism and related teachings would need to be attentively eradicated. Still, a modified version of kendo was possible, as American physical education consultant William Neufeld advised in 1948: "Kendo—A questionable activity due to the opportunity for injuries. If war cries are eliminated, it would possibly be on the same level with our foils, sabre, and épée. This sport might possibly be suitable for men at the university and college level."[5]

Starting in 1946, petitions to reinstate kendo and other budo were submitted to CIE from various groups. The following is an excerpt from an impassioned plea from 1,344 students representing eleven universities in Tokyo seeking permission to allow their clubs to practice kendo as an "elective scholastic sport." Being involved with student kendo in Japan myself for many years, I can empathize with the signatories' anguish.

> Kendo during the war had its entire structure changed in conformance to the expressed demands of the government and military ultra-nationalists. Although this fact was in direct contradiction to the wishes of we lovers of the sport, it presented the outward appearance of being a militaristic exercise and subsequently after the termination of the war, the Education Ministry was pressed to banish Kendo from the schools. The abovementioned fact was indeed of the greatest regret as well as a surprise to we Kendo enthusiasts. . . . The reason we love Kendo is simply because we love sports and competition and as every individual has his own particular taste and interest we follow Kendo for the simple enjoyment of it. . . . As we have just mentioned, we students do not believe that scholastically practiced Kendo was ever militaristic or warlike in its true nature; on the contrary we firmly believe that it has always been a wholesome and peaceful sport. It goes without saying that combat style Kendo formulated by the Army and Navy should be thrown out. On the other hand it is of the deepest regret to us that our Kendo had gone through such a process to become banished from the schools. Even though prewar Kendo was abused by the militarists, the fact that it was utilized by them may have been because of the deficiencies embodied within it. We shall endeavor to correct these deficiencies in order to rebuild a new Kendo worthy of a peace loving Japan.[6]

Nevertheless, until an acceptable alternative variant was devised, teaching kendo in schools was out of the question, even if it was tolerated in small doses in the community. An orchestrated "civilizing process" would be required to disarm its combativeness and revive it as a sport deemed suitable for a modern democratic society. An attempt was made to create a hybrid version of kendo known as *shinai-kyōgi,* which superficially crossed kendo with Western fencing. This form has since been swept out the dojo door, so to speak, and is now, by and large, looked upon with contempt by kendo traditionalists. Old-timers who lived through these events considered *shinai-kyōgi* an abomination, and most young kendoists today have never even heard of it.

Shinai-kyōgi was the brainchild of alumni who had come together from various university and college kendo clubs in Tokyo in 1946 to create the Hatsuka-kai (Twentieth-day Society) and the Tokyo Kendo Club. They congregated on the twentieth day of each month to discuss measures to foster kendo in the community. These meetings culminated in the formation of the Tokyo Kendo Sport Union (Tōkyō Kendō Kyōgi Rengōkai). They mulled over various tactics to reintroduce kendo to the community and schools and courteously engaged with CIE to convince the authorities to permit their activities.

On October 30, 1949, they sponsored the first National Kendo Sport Championship in Tokyo, and they formed the All Japan Kendo Sport Federation (Zen-Nihon Kendō Kyōgi Renmei) on March 5, 1950. CIE was opposed to the use of the term "kendo," so the federation simply changed its name to the All Japan Shinai-kyōgi Federation. *Shinai* was written with the innocuous kanji meaning "flexible," as opposed to the customary character signifying "bamboo katana." Thus, literally translated, *shinai-kyōgi* means "flexible [bamboo] sport."

The federation promoted *shinai-kyōgi* as a way of circumventing Occupation-imposed kendo restrictions. *Shinai-kyōgi* retained certain elements of kendo proper but was closer to a "pure" sport that would be accepted in schools. Not long after the federation's inception, there were thirty-two affiliated groups nationwide, with a total membership of over 20,300 people.[7]

According to a manual published by the All Japan Shinai-kyōgi Federation, the match area was a rectangle marked by white line tape, and measuring 7 meters in length by 6 meters in width. (Match courts had not been clearly defined in prewar kendo competitions.) The apparel consisted of a "durable material top and trousers," which could be any color, but most practitioners chose to wear white. As can be seen in figure 18, shoes were permitted both indoors and outdoors.[8]

The *shinai* was 1.5 meters in length, consisting of four slats of bamboo joined at the hilt, which were split into eight slats, and then into sixteen slats at the top third, and covered by a leather sheath. It was not dissimilar to the early *fukuro-shinai* used by the classical school of swordsmanship, the Yagyū Shinkage-ryū. They were more pliable and lighter than the standard *shinai* used in kendo, weighing from 300 to 450 grams. The protective equipment

FIGURE 18. A 1953 photograph of a *shinai-kyōgi* match about to commence. (The Mainichi Newspapers)

closely resembled that of Western fencing—undoubtedly fashioned to appeal to SCAP and to highlight a conscious move away from traditional kendo to a modern democratic version of the sport.

Another revolutionary aspect of *shinai-kyōgi* match rules was the strict enforcement of a designated time limit for bouts. Although kendo matches in the prewar era usually lasted four to five minutes, the length depended on the whim of the referee, who would keep the match going for as long as he deemed appropriate. Instead of having one referee, as was the case in prewar kendo competitions, *shinai-kyōgi* instigated a system in which three referees adjudicated each match, all with equal judicial power. Matches were not decided by *ippon-shōbu* (first point wins) or *sanbon-shōbu* (best of three points, the system used today). Instead, each competitor vied to score as many valid points as possible within the time limit, and the one who accrued the most points was the winner. The target areas for striking were the head, both wrists, and the torso, and thrusts to the throat were also permitted.

Shinai-kyōgi rules demonstrated a shift away from the overt aggressiveness that previously characterized kendo. Any vocalization other than a natural grunt when striking was forbidden, as were foot trips and body clashes, all of which were features of prewar and wartime kendo. A handwritten appeal by Sasamori Junzō to have *shinai-kyōgi* included in the National Sports Meet outlined the benefits to be gained from the sport, which he translated as "Pliant Staff Play," and defined as being neither "kendo nor Occidental fencing."[9] In rather strained English, he summarized the "meritorious qualities" that justified *shinai-kyōgi* as a legitimate sport that was conducive to the improvement of health and wellbeing among practitioners of all ages, particularly children.

a. Physical Qualities: Viewing from the standpoint of physical development, it calls for much leg movement of considerable tempo, contraction and expansion of the breast, and varied use of the arm muscles, all which is extremely effective in developing the lungs and the chest, at the same time helping to build a strong heart, not to speak of its contribution to muscular development of the limbs.

b. Mental Training: Accomplishment in this sport is more dependent upon the psychological reaction and power of concentration of the individual rather than upon the physical differences of the participants. The exercise develops powers of concentration and decision and trains the mind to react without hesitation. It inculculates [sic] the ability to change perception into action instantaneously.

c. Qualities Favorable to Health: Although it calls for a considerable amount of instantaneous bodily movement, such movement are not necessarily continuous, there being frequent natural intermittences of action which, therefore, makes it a sport with the following favorable health qualities. Both sexes of all ages, from about eight years old to about eighty years of age, can engage in the sport.[10]

Unsurprisingly, we find absolutely no mention of "Japanese spirit" or "traditional Japanese culture." Furthermore, no allusion is made to the protocols of etiquette and morality that featured in similar explanations of the values of kendo. A progressive aspect of his explanation was the view that *shinai-kyōgi* was suitable for "men and women." Women had never been openly encouraged to participate in Japanese fencing before, and this symbolized a radical change, probably as a concession to modern and foreign sporting sensibilities. The elimination of intimidating vocalizations, in addition to proscribing unnecessary roughness or violence by threat of penalization, is indicative of the great lengths supporters were prepared to go to in order to bring kendo back to the mainstream.

At a meeting convened by the MOE on December 18, 1951, the proposal to introduce *shinai-kyōgi* into schools was presented by Secondary Education Bureau Secretary Sasaki:

> Recently, *shinai-kyōgi* has been widely disseminated throughout the country [as an extra-curricular activity], and following a request by the Japan Shinai-kyōgi Federation, a meeting was held on December 4 at the MOE. In attendance were approximately forty representatives from universities, high and middle schools, physical education administrators and instructors, and officers of the Shinai-kyōgi Federation. A discussion was conducted in which all present agreed that contingent on certain conditions, *"shinai-kyōgi* may be suitable for inclusion in school PE classes." Therefore, in this meeting, the following items need to be discussed: 1. Should *shinai-kyōgi* be considered a new sport distinct from kendo, or as a new style of kendo? 2. Should *shinai-kyōgi* be taught in schools? 3. Opinions concerning the introduction of *shinai-kyōgi* into schools.[11]

Following this introductory statement, representatives offered their thoughts on the matter. The Saitama Prefecture chief administrator of physical education voiced a comment that illustrated the general sentiment:

> There seem to be two trains of thought of either treating *shinai-kyōgi* as new kendo, or as a completely new sport. This suggests that there may be some confrontation or confusion in the future. I am of the belief that in the course of transforming sports, some aspects need to be deconstructed and then rebuilt. I see *shinai-kyōgi* as a part of the process of kendo's transition, and it will become one entity again in the future without doubt. Considering the current situation of kendo, I am in support of including *shinai-kyōgi* in school physical education programs.[12]

Although some present cautioned that vigilance was warranted to retain the good aspects of kendo and eliminate elements reminiscent of militarism, the chairman concluded that the MOE should endorse *shinai-kyōgi* as a valid physical education activity. All agreed without objection.

The MOE did just that, and in a notification published on April 10, 1952, the ministry announced that *shinai-kyōgi* would "fill a gap" in the physical education curriculum. There was one condition: that instructors undergo training at official federation or MOE seminars, as was the case with kyudo and judo, which had already been reinstated.

The introduction of strict rules to curb violent inclinations, the policy of including women, and various other innovations were to have a profound effect on the evolution of conventional kendo into a modern sport. The invention of *shinai-kyōgi* is a concise example of a sport going through the civilizing process in a very short span of time.

THE AJKF: THE NEW GATEKEEPER OF KENDO

While some members of the kendo fraternity were creating *shinai-kyōgi*, others were furtively persevering with traditional kendo in the hope of reinstating it under the auspices of a decentralized national body. Two groups in Tokyo formed the core of this movement—the Shiseikai and the Dōshikai. The former had been created before the war in 1940 as the Tengukai, a small society of young kendo enthusiasts from various walks of life. At the second of their monthly meetings in February 1941, Kimura Tokutarō (1886–1982) was appointed president, and the group's name was changed to Shiseikai.[13]

The designated objectives of the Shiseikai were to meet regularly to practice and discuss kendo, produce related publications, and travel to engage in training with other groups in an exercise they called *musha-shugyō,* named after the samurai practice of ascetic errantry. The members of the Shiseikai formed an elite group of practitioners that would prove to be the mainstay of the postwar revival of kendo in terms of experience, knowledge, national network, political sway, and, most of all, enthusiasm.

The Dōshikai included now-legendary twentieth-century kendoka, such as Saimura Gorō, Nakano Yasoji, Morishima Tateo, and Haga Jun'ichi. As police participation in kendo was only cursorily prohibited, members of the Dōshikai trained together at the Waseda and Totsuka Police Departments and at private dojos, such as the Shōdōkan in Tokyo.

Other coteries were also practicing kendo throughout Japan. For example, enthusiasts in Ibaraki Prefecture were quite active and held a celebrated kendo tournament at the Nikkō Tōshōgū Shrine. The Osaka Kendo Club was established in 1950 and became a key association in the Kansai region, arranging tournament events such as the Akō Gishi Festival Tournament (in honor of the "Forty-Seven Ronin") in December 1950 and the Nishinomiya Kendo Tournament in March 1951. Small kendo groups sprouted up in most prefectures in central Japan, Shikoku, and Kyushu.

After the signing of the San Francisco Peace Treaty in 1951, local kendo federations started to form without restriction. Tokyo had forty-three kendo cliques, which amalgamated to become the Tokyo Kendo Federation in May

FIGURE 19. Sakakibara Tadashi (middle) from Aichi Prefecture, winner of the first All Japan Kendo Championship title on November 8, 1953. (The Mainichi Newspapers)

1951. In March of that year, the Osaka group joined forces with the Kyoto and Hyogo clubs to create the Kinki Kendo Federation. These two federations became hubs for linking other local groups that were spread around the country.

The first talks aimed at launching a national governing body for kendo were held at the Nikkō Tōshōgū Shrine. This had been a stronghold for kendo before the war, and a popular annual tournament was held there every summer after a Butokuden branch was built on the site in 1930. After a temporary hiatus due to the ban on budo, the competition was revived as the Nikkō Tournament in August 1951.

Before long, support to build a national body intensified. A meeting was held between representatives from all of the abovementioned groups on October 13 and 14, 1952, and the All Japan Kendo Federation was officially launched on October 14, with Kimura Tokutarō appointed as its first president. The new gatekeeper for postwar kendo was born. The first All Japan Kendo Championship was contested in Nagoya the following year (figure 19).

In a conscious effort to remove the stigma of militarism from kendo, the AJKF announced that kendo would be reestablished as a form of physical education and sport. To this end, a complete overhaul of competition and referee rules was undertaken and completed in March 1953. The main differences between the new rules and those of the prewar era were as follows:

1. A court area was defined, and penalties were given to any player who stepped out of bounds.
2. Limits were placed on the permissible length and weight of *shinai*.
3. Match time was specified. If a bout was not decided within the stipulated time, the match would go into extra time (*enchō*), or a draw could be called.
4. Excessive body clashes (*taiatari*), violent behavior, and foot-tripping became punishable offences.
5. Three referees (*shinpan*) presided over matches, each with equal authority. Decisions were indicated by raising a red or white flag.

Many modifications were made to these regulations over time, but the implementation of item 4 in this list was probably the most noteworthy in terms of taming the violent nature of prewar kendo.[14] A quick comparison with the rules that were applied by the All Japan Shinai-kyōgi Federation show that *shinai-kyōgi* clearly provided a blueprint for the reinstatement of kendo proper, in spite of the censorious attitudes kendo traditionalists held toward the sport and its proponents, and it should be acknowledged as a crucial factor in the evolution of postwar kendo.

Following the creation of the AJKF, numerous suborganizations representing various groups, such as the All Japan Students' Kendo Federation, were also launched (figure 20). There was a degree of internal factionalism within the AJKF between officials affiliated with the police and officials who were educators (mainly university academics). This rivalry still exists to a certain extent today, but it has never hampered the AJKF's efforts to popularize kendo.

PENANCE COMPLETE—BACK TO SCHOOL

Soon after the AJKF was established, it began lobbying the MOE to reinstate kendo in schools. Judo had already been reintroduced in 1950, but kendo's reestablishment was a drawn-out process that did not bear fruit until several

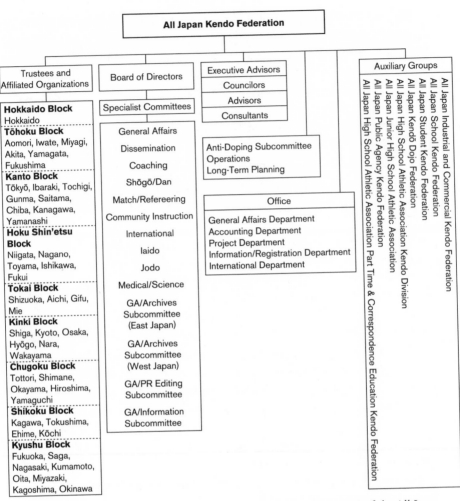

FIGURE 20. Chart outlining the structure and auxiliary organizations of the All Japan Kendo Federation (comprising kendo, *iaido,* and *jodo*). The federation has a domestic membership of 1,529,391 and an overseas membership of approximately 700,000.

years later. The MOE conducted frequent consultations to discuss kendo's path back into the national curriculum. Several main points required clarification before this could be seriously considered: 1) the AJKF needed to elucidate kendo's characteristics as a sport; 2) there needed to be a suitable competition method and content to facilitate growth in pupils; 3) it had to be disseminated widely among youth in the community; and 4) the AJKF had to prove it was an organization that was administered democratically. Only when these criteria had been satisfied could kendo make a full comeback.

The "School Course Guidelines" (*Gakushū shidō yōryō*) dictated the role and form kendo would take in the school curriculum. The guidelines affirmed the content, objectives, and teaching methodology for each subject taught in Japanese schools at each year level. The MOE first announced the guidelines in 1947 as a complete reformation of prewar education, and they continue to be revised approximately every decade to keep in touch with current educational needs and to fit political agendas.

The first period of change corresponds to adjustments enacted in 1947, 1949, and 1953, when the focus of PE moved from "teaching of physical activities" to "educating through physical activities."[15] The second phase includes modifications made in 1958 and 1968, which concentrated on building "stronger bodies" and improving overall sporting ability. This was partially a response to Japan's poor performances in the international sporting arena and to the changing lifestyle habits of the Japanese. The third period encompasses changes implemented in 1977, 1988, 1998, and 2008. In particular, lifestyle shifts resulting from Japan's postwar industrial boom triggered shifts in social attitudes and aspirations. The government reevaluated the role of sports in society and decided to introduce the "sports-for-all" movement in the 1960s that was prevalent in Europe at the time. This catalyzed the idea of "education in movement: education in sport," with particular emphasis placed on the three pillars of technical, physical, and social objectives.

In 1988, the MOE turned its attention to cultivating in students the will to "participate in lifelong sports." In 1998, it targeted the ideal of "mind and body as one." In 2008, previous goals were incorporated into a three-category agenda consisting of "technique," "attitude," and "cognitive ability, decisiveness, and expression."

In the context of evolving objectives of sport in schools and the community, kendo was formally acknowledged as a "social sport" (*shakai taiiku*) at a meeting of physical education officials on May 1, 1953: "That kendo was taught during the war years as a weapon is an undeniable fact. As such, we must now expediently eliminate any militaristic elements it may harbor.... All public and private organizations must positively engage in teaching kendo in its *proper* form.... Efforts must also be made to research ways in which kendo can be steered in the same direction as other sports."[16] Following this statement, the MOE sent out a notification on July 7, 1953, to all of the regional education boards, lifting the ban on kendo in schools and announcing that it could be practiced in high schools or universities just like any other sport, although preferably as an extracurricular club activity at first.

A specialist group called the School Kendo Research Society (Gakkō Kendō Kenkyū-kai) was assembled to deliberate on problematic issues and establish a new approach for teaching kendo in schools. The goal was to teach it in the same manner as other sports and physical education for pupils in secondary schools, rather than as budo in the conventional sense. The group was made up of educators, of which approximately half were nonpractitioners, for the sake of impartiality.

The MOE published a basic guidebook for kendo instruction in high schools in 1953, titled "Instructional Handbook for School Kendo" (*Gakkō kendō no shidō tebiki*). The document described the characteristics of so-called new kendo (*atarashii kendō*) as follows:

> The first condition for school kendo is that it must be structured as a combative sport [*kakugi*]. Kendo as a sport is not the same as kendo as a means for fighting. Even though it takes the form of combat, the relationship between both competitors is not one of antagonism. The interaction represents an affirmation of each other's existence, and a recognition of the common thread of humanity. In other words, competitors collaborate with each other as they engage in a kendo bout. The objective is to mutually improve technical skills. Participating in kendo must be enjoyable, and participants should be passionate about improving their ability. The basis for kendo as a sport is found in the cooperative relationship between the players. So long as this is maintained, respect and good deportment will manifest as a matter of course. Even if the exercise looks combative, amicable human relations will always be preserved. (p. 2)

The desired benefits of school kendo were no different from those of judo and *shinai-kyōgi,* sports that were already being taught in schools. The benefits were classified into five instructional objectives in the MOE handbook. The first objective was physical development, which included encouraging a good attitude and posture while maintaining healthy internal and sensory organs to facilitate bodily functions, such as respiration, circulation, digestion, and even excretion. Other fundamental goals were the improvement of muscle elasticity and joint movement, the development of quick and powerful muscle reflexes and endurance, the facilitation of neuromuscular coordination, and the creation of a resolute body in which movements are precise, prompt, dexterous, and "rhythmic."

The second objective was intellectual and emotional development. Pupils would improve their ability to judge an opponent's movements calmly, swiftly, and accurately and develop the capacity to act decisively. They would also learn to meet any situation with a "stable emotional response."

The third objective was social development. Kendo would teach pupils how to avoid being manipulated. They would develop leadership skills and be able to function independently. Ideally, pupils would learn to empathize with others, exhibit good manners, and show obedience to authority. Doing their best at all times, pupils would cultivate an understanding of "fairness" and the facility to "compete admirably."

The fourth was safety. It was expected that kendo would help pupils and instructors alike to learn to avoid hazardous situations. The fifth, leisure-time activity, was aimed to show pupils how to spend their free time productively and enjoy the acquisition of general kendo knowledge and skills.[17]

These objectives were predicated on maintaining physical health and honing pupils' sensibilities to serve them well in a modern democratic society. The content was directed at the wellbeing of the individual, and the fact that kendo would also ultimately benefit the state and society at large was not signposted directly. Nor, for that matter, was the correlation between kendo (as traditional culture) and Japanese identity.

Although the objectives were described in detail, the actual teaching content and methodology outlined in the MOE handbook were vague. To fill in the gaps, the MOE commissioned the AJKF to produce a supplementary text, "School Kendo: An Explanation of the Instruction Handbook" (*Gakkō kendō: shidō no tebiki kaisetsu*), which was published the same year, in 1953. In its opening pages, the authors remark that school kendo represents the fruit of considerable efforts made by kendo experts since the end of the war. They also mention that schoolteachers had been frustrated by the lack of technical guidance in the MOE handbook, as it spotlighted the educational objectives of kendo rather than the nuts and bolts of teaching the sport.

The AJKF publication was a comprehensive volume that outlined the history of kendo from medieval times through to the present day. Numerous Western authorities on physical education and sports were cited to give the text an air of scientific legitimacy and help detach kendo from its tainted wartime image. It is stressed in the foreword that comprehensive theoretical studies had been conducted in the postwar period, resulting in the discovery of a "new way for kendo education in schools." The text explains that the redirection of kendo necessitated its repackaging as a sport, although the intrinsic cultural attributes that made it conducive to "human growth" would be retained. The authors went to great lengths to posit kendo within the constructs of modern sport and tone down its ascetic image.

> When kendo is exploited as a means of combat, the opponent is attacked and killed. Those who practiced kendo with this as the primary objective were intent on dispatching their adversary at all costs. Kendo was but one way to accomplish this task.... When kendo was pushed as military training [in schools during the war], participation was mandatory. Pupils had no option to abstain. Soldierly kendo was engineered in accordance with state agendas.... Should sports kendo be considered in the same light? (p. 6)

This rhetorical question provided a platform to expound in great depth on how kendo as a sport was fundamentally opposed to wartime rationales: "Individuals take part in sporting activities for personal enjoyment.... The same can be said of those who engage in kendo as a sport. They do it because they like it." According to the authors, "the point is to do kendo for no other reason than for the sake of kendo itself." Even though mental or spiritual growth were byproducts of studying kendo, they were not the chief purpose: "People who take up kendo as a sport enjoy the path of learning, and endeavor to improve their technical skill and ability. Facing off against their training partners with this ambition in mind, all participants are essentially working together in the quest for improvement. The relationship between the protagonists is one of affirmative collaboration."

The key concern of sport kendo, according to the AJKF's narrative, was enjoyment, not training for training's sake. In the age of militarism, "if one was to declare 'I am doing kendo only because I enjoy it,' such a statement would surely have earned the wrath of the instructor. Kendo was for emperor, for country, for moral cultivation [shūyō] as a loyal subject, and for imparting manners and discipline." When pupils were coerced into doing kendo during the war, enjoyment was of no consequence whatsoever.[18]

The first section of the book continues in this vein, sketching the scientific value of physical education in rational (Western) terms. The remainder consists of detailed explanations of techniques and recommended course structures for PE classes.

By this point, the foundations were well and truly established for a wide-scale proliferation of a model of school kendo that had been exorcised of spiritual and nationalistic rhetoric. It was a compromise, but a necessary one to get kendo legitimized in mainstream society again. Kendo had been reduced—or elevated, depending on one's point of view—into a

FIGURE 21. A rare photograph of the third National High School Kendo and Shinai-kyōgi Championships, held August 11, 1956. A *shinai-kyōgi* match is pictured in the foreground, and kendo matches, which were being held simultaneously, can be seen in the background. (The Mainichi Newspapers)

leisure activity leading to self-satisfaction and harmonious relations. Participants were to learn about the enjoyment of sport—nothing more, and nothing less.

The revival of kendo in schools raised the question of whether it and *shinai-kyōgi* should be continued as separate sports, or combined into one (figure 21). This issue required swift resolution, as it was connected to the pressing matters of kendo's pending application to the Japan Amateur Sports Association (JASA) and entry as an event at the National Sports Meet.[19] Both federations held negotiations, and on March 14, 1954, they amalgamated into one body, keeping the name All Japan Kendo Federation. The new AJKF affiliated with JASA in 1955, and kendo made its debut as an official event at the National Sports Meet the same year. At an organizational level, the two sports were combined under one administrative umbrella, but *shinai-kyōgi* and kendo continued to be taught as separate subjects in schools. High schools could teach either sport, but junior high schools were restricted to offering *shinai-kyōgi*.

The MOE eventually acknowledged the unification of the two sports. In 1957, amendments to the junior and senior high school course guidelines for

PE announced that *shinai-kyōgi* and kendo would be melded into one style of "school kendo" that would be taught at both levels. Furthermore, it was stipulated that the government would arrange teaching manuals and seminars for instructor training. To further distance kendo and budo education from the past, the term *kakugi* (combative sport) was coined as the collective appellation for the martial arts in schools, in place of *budō*. *Kakugi* remained the official designation until May 15, 1989, when the MOE brought the term *budō* back to life.

Still, the nature of kendo as an allegory of nationalistic sentiment was never completely eradicated—it was merely put on hold. As Maruyama Masao explains of Japan in the immediate postwar period, "The spiritual structure of past nationalism did not become extinct, nor did it undergo a qualitative change; rather, it would be correct to say that the change was quantitative: nationalist feelings were atomized, disappearing from the political surface and becoming embedded in the lower strata of national life."[20]

In the case of kendo, the recivilizing process was successful in expunging the sport's potent militaristic symbolism. Nevertheless, although the bond between kendo and "Japaneseness" had been laid by the wayside, it had not broken. Kendo was the "spiritual sport" that epitomized samurai culture—a motif that was later to represent the stoic recovery of Japan's economy and society from the ashes of war.

The AJKF's School Kendo Research Society published another explanatory booklet called "Teaching School Kendo: An Explanation of the Instruction Handbook" (*Gakkō kendō no shidō: Shidō no tebiki kaisetsu*) on May 5, 1958, to supplement the MOE's teaching manual. In the foreword, Miyahata Torahiko, school inspector for the MOE, stated the cautious policy of the ministry: "I hope that the readers of this text will be able to view kendo in its naked form. That is, to see kendo as an exercise in which people strike each other, without paying heed to its traditional and spiritual peculiarities." Miyahata stressed that this would be the only way to gauge kendo's true worth for the physical development of children. Kendo could serve as a litmus test to see how children competed in accordance with rules and how they interacted with others. "Only then will we truly be able to see the benefits to be gained from kendo as PE, and as a sport."

Interestingly though, the AJKF takes a much stronger stance in this publication than the MOE with regard to kendo's "special qualities," indicating a clear difference in approach between the two bodies. For example, in the section explaining kendo's history and role in society, the AJKF authors make the following claim, which is suggestive of the nationalistic language used to promote kendo during the war: "As a competitive sport, kendo has specific characteristics and benefits which are wanting in other sports. Kendo was conceived by our ancestors, and has been a part of the time-honored history of the Japanese people. In concert with the advancement of Japan, kendo has progressed in its own distinct way. Therefore, the blood of the Japanese people flows uninterrupted within kendo, which is suited both spiritually and technically to our fundamental national traits. This is one of the important characteristics of kendo" (p. 10). This statement runs counter to the measured rhetoric of the MOE and the overall tone of the first explanatory book published in 1953. However, the fact that the MOE authorized the text indicates at least an embryonic desire to assert the connection between national identity and kendo.

Another section of the manual concerns the issue of how to teach the values of kendo to pupils in the limited time available for classes: "At first, kendo lessons should be fun and pleasant, making sure that lessons are not so exacting as to cause any suffering. Increase the intensity as pupils improve, and embolden them to revel in more challenging trainings. Finally, the instructor must make pupils relish the harshness and wait in anticipation to train" (p. 52).

In 1966, the MOE published yet another manual called "A Guidebook for Teaching Kendo in Schools" (*Gakkō ni okeru kendō shidō no tebiki*). What made this manual different from previous ones was that more prominence was given to class planning and technical explanations. With further amendments to course guidelines for junior and senior high schools in 1969 and 1970, kendo became an integral component in the PE curriculum, designed for "physical strengthening."

In 1977 and 1978, the guidelines were further modified, and kendo was redefined as a means of encouraging individual expression rather than technical conformity. For the first time in postwar education, kendo was acknowledged as being more than just a simple sport; it was recognized as a cultural pursuit with the potential for spiritual growth.

This was an important turning point. Although school regulations were becoming less preoccupied with technique and more open to imparting traditional cultural values, the MOE was still wary. The AJKF, however, began to take a more proactive stance in its dissemination strategies, strongly promoting kendo's goals of "character development" (*ningen-keisei*), as outlined in its official teaching guide for children in the community, "Guidelines for Teaching Kendo to Children" (*Yōshōnen kendō shidō yōryō,* 1977).

On the surface, the two organizations seemed to be at odds with each other regarding the degree to which they were advocating the holistic and moral benefits of kendo. Close inspection of the relationship, however, reveals an orchestrated, symbiotic system of kendo promotion. The MOE demonstrated conservative prudence, while the AJKF, as a private organization, was allowed (encouraged even) to be more assertive about the philosophical and cultural value of kendo. The two bodies had what could be described as a marriage of convenience. The AJKF symbolized a bastion of popular nationalism, whereas the MOE represented the state-promoted cultural nationalism. As Brian McVeigh notes, "Non-official or popular cultural nationalism overlaps in some senses with state-promoted cultural nationalism, but it includes more than just aesthetic themes, being concerned with explaining or legitimating behavior by grounding it in the values, social structures, or heritage of a national community."[21] In this sense, the AJKF fed off the MOE by being afforded the task of elaborating on finer details concerning methods and motivations for teaching school kendo, while the MOE in turn relied on the AJKF to enact a veiled cultural policy.

They became ideologically closer when revisions to the "School Course Guidelines" in 1989 officially replaced the term *kakugi* with *budō*. Furthermore, as outlined in the 1993 MOE publication "Kendo Instruction Handbook" (*Kendō shidō no tebiki*), "the term *kakugi* was introduced in the 'School Course Guidelines' after the war as the designation for martial arts education as a field of exercise from 1958. Today, budo is recognized throughout the world as Japan's traditional physical culture. That the Japanese Academy of Budo [Nihon Budō Gakkai] and the Nippon Budokan employ the word *budō* is corroboration of its social and academic acceptability."[22] This semantic reversion followed a proclamation by the government in December 1988 stating that education would henceforth focus on "nurturing people with rich minds who are able to adapt to societal changes as the twenty-first century approaches." This was to be achieved by "deepening international understanding, and cultivating an attitude of respect toward Japanese culture and tradition."[23]

"Traditional" budo were perfect for this agenda, and by the late 1980s it was formally acknowledged that they could fill a role in children's education that other PE activities and sports could not. Thus the stigma attached to the word "budo" had melted away, and it was almost fully returned to its prewar, premilitarist status in schools. The new tone in which the budo disciplines were promoted was not so palpably nationalistic, but it is possible to detect allusions to budo's uniqueness in the world. The following passage from the

MOE's 1993 "Kendo Instruction Handbook" implies that budo can offer students a chance to access their "Japaneseness":

> Today there are many sports being played around the world. These sports encompass the "ways of thinking" and "modes of conduct" of the cultures from whence they arose. For example, the conclusion of a rugby match is declared "no side," meaning that there are no enemies or allies. This represents the "way of thinking" and "conduct" of the English people. Similarly, the way of thinking and conduct of the Japanese is enmeshed in the physical culture of budo. As the traditional physical culture of Japan, budo is valued as an educational subject in our schools. Appreciation of the culture and traditions of our country is important for nurturing Japanese people capable of making their way in the world, keeping up with the pace of internationalization. (p. 2)

What is striking about this particular publication is that, for the first time, the MOE was promoting the same message of character development as the AJKF, using the same terms. Given the cautious approach that the MOE took while tiptoeing around this ideological issue for almost four decades after the war, the following statement of intent signifies kendo's elevated role in Japan's educational institutions: "Budo and sports have many things in common, but differ in the matter of character development [*ningen-keisei*]. . . . Compared to sports, which developed in the West, budo contains a stronger bent for moral cultivation and hard training [*tanren;* to forge body and mind] " (p. 2).

Further amendments made to the guidelines for junior and senior high schools in 1998 and 1999, respectively, specified that the purpose of the school curriculum was to "cultivate the 'zest for life' [*ikiru chikara*] by learning and thinking independently," so that each individual could be "rich in humanity, and strong in body." With regard to PE, it was announced that children would be encouraged to enjoy sports more and continue participating in them throughout their lives. As a form of "unique Japanese culture," budo would nurture the "basic physical strength" necessary to excel in the rigors of daily life and afford students an opportunity to experience and respect the traditions, culture, and forms of etiquette of their country.

In 2006, the Ministry of Education, Culture, Sports, Science and Technology (MEXT; the MOE changed its name to this in 2001) modified the Basic Act on Education for the first time since 1947. The revised act set the stage for making budo compulsory for first- and second-year pupils in all junior high schools beginning in 2012. The principal objectives behind the 2006 revision were to cultivate "a rich and wholesome heart and body through solid moral and physical education" and to enhance cultural

Reverence and fairness	• Correct manners and respect for one's opponent • Abiding by the rules and competing fairly
Cooperation and autonomy	• Creating objectives and practicing accordingly • Cooperating with training partners • Analyzing the reasons for wins and losses
Health and safety	• Refraining from endangering oneself or others • Ensuring that training equipment and environment are safe and clean
Lifelong physical education	• Cultivating the will to do kendo throughout one's lifetime

FIGURE 22. The second "pillar" of kendo education: Attitude (*taido*).

education. "The full development of character and [the] nurturing of citizens, sound in mind and body, who are imbued with the qualities necessary to form a peaceful and democratic state and society" was stated as the aim and principle of education. There were several ways in which this would be achieved, such as through the "attainment of wide-ranging knowledge and culture, cultivation of a rich sensibility and sense of morality, and development of a healthy body," and by "fostering an attitude of respecting [Japanese] traditions and culture, loving the country and region that nurtured them, respecting other countries, and contributing to world peace and the development of the international community."[24]

Motomura Kiyoto, an authority on budo education in schools and a former MOE bureaucrat, maintained that, because budo involved directly attacking one's opponent, an attitude of respect and understanding of traditional conduct was required. Apparatus gymnastics, track and field events, and swimming, on the other hand, were individual sports in which no physical contact was made.

Budo practitioners attack each other in matches and training. Without respect for the opponent, which is expressed through traditional protocols of etiquette (*reihō*), the exercise would be no more than brawling. Motomura explained that *reihō* denotes "self-discipline" and symbolizes the fundamental ideals of traditional conduct, which in their highest form manifest as

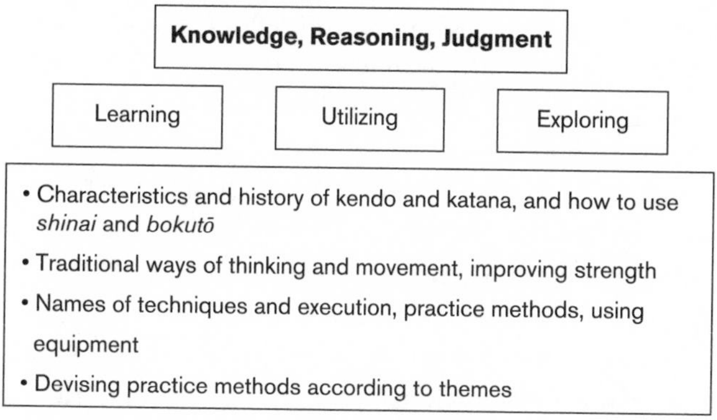

```
┌─────────────────────────────────────────┐
│      Knowledge, Reasoning, Judgment      │
└─────────────────────────────────────────┘

┌──────────────┐  ┌──────────────┐  ┌──────────────┐
│   Learning   │  │   Utilizing  │  │   Exploring  │
└──────────────┘  └──────────────┘  └──────────────┘
```

- Characteristics and history of kendo and katana, and how to use *shinai* and *bokutō*
- Traditional ways of thinking and movement, improving strength
- Names of techniques and execution, practice methods, using equipment
- Devising practice methods according to themes

FIGURE 23. The third "pillar" of kendo education: Knowledge, reasoning, and judgment.

michi, or a "way of life." It is precisely this important aspect of Japanese culture that is imparted to pupils in compulsory budo classes.[25]

The three main objectives of budo education, as outlined in the "School Course Guidelines," are developing "skills," "attitude," and "knowledge, reasoning, and judgment." "Skills" in the case of kendo refers to the basic techniques used for attack and defense. The other two objectives are shown in figures 22 and 23.[26]

The MEXT allocated a significant budget for introducing martial arts education into junior high schools as a compulsory subject, including ¥44.73 billion to build training halls and suitable facilities for classes, ¥4.94 billion to train teachers, ¥3.58 billion for regional sports support, and around ¥600,000 per year for each of the approximately ten thousand junior schools to purchase and maintain equipment. Nevertheless, one cannot help but think that the decision had not been well thought out by the government. Money was allocated for building facilities, but there is still a shortage of qualified instructors today. It is estimated that over 70 percent of schools opted to introduce judo because it does not require expensive equipment, it is technically easier to teach given constraints on time, and the rules are easier to understand. Kendo is taught in around 25 percent of schools, and the remaining 5 percent teach other budo, such as kyudo, karate, sumo, and naginata.

A remarkably underpublicized fact in Japan is the number of deaths caused by judo at schools in the last three decades. An article published in the *Japan Times* on August 26, 2010, stated that "over the twenty-seven-year period between 1983 and 2009, 108 students aged 12 to 17 died as a result of judo accidents in Japanese schools, an average of four a year." This death toll is "more than five times higher than in any other sport. About 65 percent of these fatalities came from brain injuries. This is clear evidence of a dangerous trend in Japanese schools."

Apart from the horrendous deaths of young people, the fact that hardly any teachers have had charges brought against them in connection with the fatalities is astounding. In Japan, there is no law that states that teachers in the public system should not be held responsible for any injury or death involving their charges in club activities or class, but to date none have been convicted as responsible individuals. It is also astonishing that, given the history of budo as an instrument of militarism, there was little opposition to the decision to make budo compulsory in schools, even from the left-wing Japan Teachers Union (JTU). The JTU is famous for its critical stance against the screening of history textbooks by the government, as well as the mandatory singing of "Kimigayo" (the Japanese national anthem) and the raising of the Japanese flag at school ceremonies. Based on their slogan, cir-culated in 1951—"Do not send our students to war again"—they are consid-ered to be at the vanguard of opposing nationalism in schools. Maybe the conspicuous lack of protests to the reintroduction of budo as compulsory education, as it was during the war years, is indicative of the JTU's shrinking membership and weakening influence.

Irrespective of political parallels to prewar and wartime education policy regarding budo, I would have thought that the fact that so many children's deaths at the hands of judo instructors have gone unanswered would have sparked heated debate in the media and other forums regarding the merits and dangers of compulsory budo education. For what-ever reason, however, this did not happen. The policy was passed with surprising ease.

THE UNBEARABLE LIGHTNESS OF PLAYING

The doctrine of kendo as a form of hallowed culture that transcends simple concerns of victory or defeat in competition is ardently defended by most of its adult practitioners. There has always been passionate opposition by many kendo practitioners to the notion that kendo is a sport. The Olympic Games held in Tokyo in 1964 were a significant turning point in the postwar revival of kendo. Kendo was featured as a demonstration sport at the newly built

Nippon Budokan, a specialist martial arts hall erected in Tokyo to serve as the venue for judo's debut as an official Olympic event. Upon the opening of the Budokan, Shōriki Matsutarō (1885–1969), a prominent politician and businessman and the first president of the Nippon Budokan, described its role as:

1. To promote the spirit of budo as the basis for the Japanese national character;
2. To popularize budo among the Japanese people, especially for the purpose of rearing healthy youth; and,
3. To help elevate kendo, judo and other budo to compulsory subjects in the school curriculum.[27]

Judo's inclusion in the Olympics signified a postwar renaissance for the budo arts—and kendo was one of the most popular in terms of domestic practitioners. Kendo's popularity continued to grow after the Olympics, and there was a significant increase in the number of both female and student practitioners. A growing number of schools taught kendo as a PE subject, and extracurricular kendo clubs were booming. Parents urged their children to do kendo because it had become widely recognized as a means of instilling discipline and teaching etiquette. Community and police dojos in the late 1960s and 1970s found it impossible to accommodate the large number of hopeful parents who queued up to register their children in beginner courses.

Most children, however, are inspired by the excitement of competition rather than the discipline forced upon them by zealous instructors and parents. Successful tournament results help students gain entry into prestigious schools or universities on sports scholarships. Although the crème de la crème of kendoists will never become celebrity professional athletes like their peers in baseball or soccer, competitive success can open doors for a career in the police, in schools as a PE teacher, or even in companies with in-house kendo teams. Dojos or schools that perform well in competitions bring considerable prestige to their instructors. Although most instructors preach the "party line" extolling kendo's holistic benefits, they are certainly not averse to teaching their students strategies and ploys to help win matches.

Although the AJKF and the MOE, to varying degrees, stressed the potential of kendo to foster personal development, the reality for young practitioners was—and generally still is—that competing and winning is what counts, and the number of tournaments held throughout the country proliferated to meet the thirst for competition.

The successful dissemination of kendo throughout Japan was a triumph for the AJKF, although the increased popularity was also a liability. For example, there was a growing proclivity among young practitioners to adopt tricks to win matches, which was viewed as a deviation from proper kendo values. Furthermore, to the perpetual dismay of traditionalists, the *shinai* became disassociated from traditional concepts of the Japanese sword and was treated as little more than a piece of sporting equipment used to score points.

To halt the perceived decay of kendo's revered traditional values, the AJKF formulated an official guiding concept to ensure the survival of its integrity. The result, published in 1975, was the "Concept of Kendo," a brief declaration of the basic aim of kendo. An additional supplement called "The Purpose of Practicing Kendo" was added in the hope that teachers and students would consider kendo to be a path to self-cultivation based on the "principles of the sword." The following statements became official in 1975 and have remained the guiding principles of kendo to this day.

The Concept of Kendo

The concept of kendo is to discipline the human character through the application of the principles of the *katana*.

The Purpose of Practicing Kendo

The purpose of practicing kendo is:

To mold the mind and body,

To cultivate a vigorous spirit,

And through correct and rigid training,

To strive for improvement in the art of kendo,

To hold in esteem human courtesy and honor,

To associate with others with sincerity,

And to forever pursue the cultivation of oneself.

This will make one be able:

To love his/her country and society,

To contribute to the development of culture

And to promote peace and prosperity among all peoples.[28]

More recently, in 2003, the AJKF organized a working group to consider the critical issues seen to be jeopardizing the integrity of kendo culture. I was fortunate enough to attend several of these meetings as an observer in 2006. The committee was tasked with "planning the kendo of tomorrow" and proposing policies to protect kendo's intrinsic values. It sought to clarify the "essence of kendo" with respect to the "Concept." It also advised how to facilitate foreign kendo practitioners' "understanding of the connection between kendo and bushido" and deliberated on the "Olympic problem" (discussed below) and other topics, such as the unification of kendo terminology and rank promotion.

With regard to the "Concept," it was assumed that foreign practitioners and younger generations of Japanese had difficulty grasping the profound importance of the "principles of the sword" (*ken-no-rihō*) and "character development" (*ningen-keisei*) to modern kendo.

The "Concept" was created to curb what some considered the degeneration of kendo and its techniques due to sportification; however, there was no proper explanation as to why sportification should be considered detrimental instead of being seen as a legitimate evolution of "correct kendo." The committee came to the consensus that it would not replace the "Concept" with a more unambiguous doctrine, even though the focus on "the principles of the sword" and character development made it challenging to appreciate for the recent generations of kendoka, who were used to doing kendo as a competitive sport and had never even held a real sword. Instead, they decided to supplement the "Concept" with another, more detailed guideline, the "Mindset of Kendo Instruction," which was completed in April 2006.[29] The "Mindset" put forward the following three standards.

The Significance of the Shinai

For the correct transmission and development of kendo, efforts should be made to teach the correct way of handling the *shinai* in accordance with the principles of the sword.

Reihō (Etiquette)

When instructing, emphasis should be placed on etiquette to encourage respect for partners, and nurture people with a dignified and humane character.

Lifelong Kendo

While providing instruction, students should be encouraged to apply the full measure of care to issues of safety and health, and to devote themselves to the development of their character throughout their lives.

The first article addresses the problematic notion that the *shinai* represents a lethal Japanese sword and should therefore be used in accordance with the hazy idea of the "principles of the sword." From the perspective of a modern kendo practitioner, trying to abide by theoretical principles of mortal combat while attempting to score two points to win a match is perplexing, to say the least.

How is one supposed to use the *shinai* as a sword? How should one "cut" with an implement that was designed to strike? What is wrong with relying on athletic dexterity (for example, striking from unorthodox positions and postures) or using feints, blocks, and tricks to defeat an opponent in a match? The double standard applied to the sword and the *shinai* is at the core of the argument over whether kendo should be considered a budo or a sport. Perhaps the dilemma is best summed up by Kagaya Shin'ichi, former standing director of the AJKF, in his report to members regarding the "Mindset":

> Now *shinai*-kendo is prevalent, and the *nihontō*, the antecedent of the *shinai*, is almost nonexistent in people's memory. Valid cuts and thrusts with a live blade are different from those performed with a *shinai*, and it does seem peculiar to call a *shinai* a *nihontō*. Be that as it may, great kendo masters such as Mochida Moriji and Saimura Gorō said wholeheartedly to "use the *shinai* as if it were a sword [*shinken*]" and "not to strike excessively or unnecessarily." This remains an important theme in kendo today. It points to the importance in a kendo bout of "getting the first cut in [*shodachi*]." The battle of the minds and the clash of *ki* before unleashing the strike are what make the face-off so impassioned. The depth of unifying mind, spirit, and technique [*shin-ki-ryoku-itchi*] renders kendo into something that can be practiced over a lifetime and provides the link between fighting with real swords and *shinai*-kendo— reminding us of the inextricable nexus between the *katana* and the *shinai*.[30]

To avoid confusion, the authors of the "Mindset of Kendo Instruction" decided that issuing explanatory notes for each clause was in order. "The Significance of the Shinai" was clarified as follows: "Kendo is a way where one cultivates one's mind (the self) by aiming for *shin-ki-ryoku-itchi* utilising the *shinai*. The 'shinai-sword' should be not only directed at one's opponent but also at the self. Thus, the primary aim of instruction is to encourage the unification of mind, body and *shinai* through training in this discipline."

The "Mindset of Kendo Instruction" remains highly abstract, but this was not unintentional; the authors did not wish to surrender the mysticism of kendo, as this is the very aesthetic that defines its Japanese essence. However, an attempt was made to connect the ideal of the sword with the *shinai* by unpretentiously referring to it as the "*shinai*-sword" (*shinai to iu ken*).

The notion that "the '*shinai*-sword' should not only be directed at the opponent but also at the self" stems from the *setsunin-tō* (death-dealing blade) and *katsunin-ken* (life-giving sword) philosophy of the Yagyū Shinkage-ryū (see chapter 2). Only the life-giving sword, or *ken,* is double-edged, with cutting edges directed toward both the opponent and the wielder. The inference is that, although the swordsman tries to cut his opponent with the outward facing blade, he is simultaneously seeking self-improvement through the ongoing act of self-castigation, represented metaphorically by the inward-facing cutting edge. In this sense, the English translation of the "Concept" is conceptually mistaken in using the term "katana"—a single-edged sword—instead of *ken,* as it is written in Japanese. In any case, such notions are fanciful and irrelevant in the modern kendo athlete's quest to win matches, but this is exactly why the AJKF is trying to salvage and promote these traditional values.

Given the symbolic brutality of striking one's opponent with a "*shinai*-sword," *reihō* (etiquette or respect) is a fundamental aspect of the study of kendo (and indeed of all of the Japanese martial arts). This point is elaborated on in the explanatory notes of the second clause of the "Mindset": "Even in competitive matches, importance is placed on upholding etiquette in kendo. The primary emphasis should thus be placed on instruction in the spirit and forms of *reihō* so that the practitioner can develop a modest attitude to life, and realize the ideal of *kōken-chiai* (the desire to achieve mutual understanding and the betterment of humanity through kendo)." The element of *rei,* and its physical expression, *reihō,* are emphasized at all levels of kendo. One often hears the maxim "beginning with courtesy, and ending with courtesy" (*rei ni hajimari, rei ni owaru*) in the dojo. Ōya Minoru has noted that because ferocious blows are exchanged in the process of learning kendo, it's important for opponents to express gratitude and respect to each other through meticulously prescribed protocols: "They affirm that they are not only opponents trying to defeat each other, but are also cooperating with each other as enthusiasts of the 'Way' of kendo, and their interaction is beneficial to both as they progress." In addition to adhering to prescribed conventions, such as bowing to each other at an angle of fifteen degrees, it is essential that opponents maintain an internal feeling of respect, as it "encourages the practitioner to concentrate and focus, remain calm, and control emotions."[31]

According to the MOE's 1993 kendo instruction manual, the acquisition of good manners has been an important feature of postwar kendo:

In the budo arts of Japan, the ideal of *rei* is different from the patterns of conduct found in other sports. In budo, after rigorous exchanges of attack and defense, even when the psychological excitement has not waned, elation is suppressed and the ceremonies of etiquette performed in an exact manner. Underscoring *rei,* and performing it properly [in form and in mind] is a demonstration of self-control, and shows respect for the opponent. Self-control is integral to self-cultivation. (p. 2)

Furthermore, as *rei* is said to represent the moral standards for maintaining social order, the third article in the "Mindset," which advocates lifelong kendo, explains how the continued study of kendo will enhance the lifestyle of the practitioner and ultimately benefit society at large: "Kendo is a 'way of life' that successive generations can learn together. The prime objective of instructing kendo is to encourage the practitioner to discover and define their way in life through training in the techniques of kendo. Thus, the practitioner will be able to develop a rich outlook on life and be able to put the culture of kendo into use, thereby benefitting from its value in their daily lives through increased social vigor."

Although the "Mindset of Kendo Instruction" is short, its purpose is to implore kendoka not to treat the *shinai* as a sporting implement, like a tennis racket or baseball bat, but to handle it with unconditional respect, as if it were a real sword. By extension, the *shinai* should be viewed as a conduit for cultivating human qualities. While the three articles may seem abstract and impractical, they clearly express the AJKF's intention that kendoka seek a holistic mastery of kendo, in which they compete to score valid points while simultaneously demonstrating beauty in form and attitude, maintaining a sense of urgency, and affording each opponent the utmost respect.

The practitioner should observe strict protocols of etiquette, never performing victory poses, showing displeasure upon defeat, or arguing about referees' decisions. Practitioners are also encouraged to comprehend on a philosophical level that victory or defeat is determined by one's own technical and mental strengths and weaknesses, and that facing an opponent is vital if one is to expunge one's own self of inadequacies. In other words, the kendo match itself should not be the objective, but rather a step in the path to greater spiritual development.

As I relayed in the prologue, although I have been a devoted kendo practitioner for over two decades and truly believe in the potential kendo has for positive personal cultivation, I am enormously wary of the common attitude that one can become a "good person" just by taking up kendo. I also question the general assumption that people with high ranks are morally upright individuals with superior "powers of discernment." Even the dan grades and *shōgō* (teaching titles) in kendo are based on the premise that, by virtue of improving technically, one will mature as a human being.[32] The following are official AJKF explanations of *shōgō* requirements:

> *Renshi* must be accomplished in the principles of kendo, and have distinguished powers of discernment.
>
> *Kyōshi* must be expert in the principles of kendo, and have superior powers of discernment.
>
> *Hanshi* must have mastered the principles of kendo, show maturity in character with extraordinary powers of discernment, and be a person of unimpeachable moral demeanor.

Kendo certainly provides a technical and philosophical framework for physical, psychological, and even moral progression. However, whether or how closely the framework is interpreted and utilized depends entirely on the individual. Narcissistic assumptions about the exceptional capacity of kendo study for self-perfection earn the wrath of some cynical nonpractitioners, who see kendo as somewhat elitist and believe that it is undeservedly treated as special within the education system. The following evaluation of kendo and its practitioners by a Japanese educator belonging to the School Physical Education Research Society is blunt and asserts sentiments rarely expressed in the public domain. Nevertheless, it is pertinent and worthy of reflection.

> The instructors of kendo and [other] budo claimed that they have passed through a uniquely Japanese contemplation of humanity, and that it contains features that are not found in any foreign sport. They place emphasis on the fighting aspects of valid strike and continued alertness and life or death earnestness, which is expressed as "unison of mind, technique and body." They are nationalistic, and while denying the destructive power of the strike and its usefulness in battle, they also refuse to totally endorse its sportification, claiming its value lies in the spiritual self-forging through the interaction of two exponents using swords engaged in mortal combat. Kendo's lack of militaristic application is conversely the impetus to cultivate spiritualistic aspirations, i.e. spiritual pragmatism toward actual battle, [and this is why] there is so much spiritualism and irrationality in budo's competitive form and training.[33]

The aura of samurai-like haughtiness that distinguishes senior kendoists is actually something that less-experienced practitioners seek to embody. Satō

Nariaki, one of today's leading kendo instructors, points out that in order to pass the higher grades in kendo the practitioner must be accomplished in the "technical aspects of attacking or defending" and also be able to demonstrate maturity of character with "panache [*fūkaku*] and a commanding presence [*kigurai*] that comes with a high level of improvement."[34] These qualities are demonstrated through elegance of movement and confidence inside and, ideally, outside of the dojo.

Such a demeanor could easily be interpreted as arrogant, but mature practitioners aspire to attain these aesthetic qualities. Furthermore, the lofty ideals and concepts espoused by the AJKF and kendo practitioners serve a dual function: in addition to providing a spiritual or philosophical objective, they act as a psychological rejoinder to the externally violent nature of kendo. This idea is summed up by Kenneth Sheard, who states: "Devotees of violent sports often feel under pressure to counter the accusation of 'barbarism' and 'cruelty' to which their commitment gives rise and may feel constrained to construct ideological defenses and legitimations in order to make their participation possible, that is to make it possible for them to participate without, or with a minimum of, psychic discomfort, and to provide resources to deflect abolitionist movements."[35]

With these considerations in mind, a commonly contemplated question in Japan is whether kendo should be defined as a "sport." Those who adhere to the metaphysical doctrine of kendo, however, usually do so without being able to define exactly what "sport" is. There are many possibilities. For example, Allen Guttmann asserts that there are seven distinctive characteristics of modern sports: "secularism, equality of opportunity to compete and in the conditions of competition, specialization of roles, rationalization, bureaucratic organization, quantification, the quest for records."[36] Kendo as it is practiced today certainly meets these criteria. If we use Timothy Chandler's definition of sport as a "structured, goal-oriented, competitive, contest-based, ludic, physical activity" in which overseeing bodies "set the rules, goals, and the criteria by which success and failure can be judged"[37] and participants receive both intrinsic and extrinsic rewards, then kendo is undoubtedly a sport.

Furthermore, David Best defined "purposive sports" as ones in which the purpose or goal "can be specified independently of the means of achieving it as long as it conforms to the limits set by the rules or norms." For example, goals in a soccer match or tries in a rugby game are counted as points regardless of the manner in which they are scored, provided no rules are broken. In "aesthetic sports," however, "the aim cannot be specified in isolation from the manner of achieving it."³⁸ In other words, in sports such as ice skating and gymnastics, aesthetic form, and the manner in which an objective is achieved are important considerations in judging victory or defeat. Kendo has elements of both categories, but leans more toward the realm of "aesthetic sport."

Pierre Bourdieu believed that the point of "amateur sport" was "training in courage and manliness, 'forming the character' and inculcating the 'will to win' which is the mark of the true leader, but a will to win within the rules. This is 'fair play', conceived as an aristocratic disposition utterly opposed to the plebeian pursuit of victory at all costs."³⁹ Thus, kendo aligns neatly with the definition of an ethnic Japanese "amateur-aesthetic sport." The question of whether it is a sport or not seems rather pointless, but it is nevertheless a highly debated issue in kendo circles, as can be inferred by the efforts outlined above of the AJKF and the MOE to distinguish traditional budo (including kendo) from Western sports.

Many kendo practitioners think that this debate began with the postwar revitalization of kendo as a "democratic sport." This is far from the truth, however. As mentioned in the previous chapter, the Taishō and early Shōwa periods saw wide-scale condemnation of kendoists whose sole objective was to win matches by any means possible. Similar criticisms were directed at the fencers of Bakumatsu Japan and the *gekiken* meets of the Meiji period. The argument surrounding the difference between budo and sports has always been vibrant, but the main objections are that kendo should never be reduced to a matter of victory or defeat and that it is not about fun or play. Kendo is supposed to be far more serious than that. After all, we do not "play" kendo, we "study" it.

Prominent Shōwa-period kendo master Saimura Gorō offered his thoughts on the difference between kendo and sports in 1941.

With the popularity of sports these days, there are some people who view kendo in the same light. To be sure, given that competitive matches are conducted in accordance with established rules, kendo does appear to have many similarities with sports. However, those who engage in kendo do so to forge themselves along the road to self-perfection. If duty calls, they use their skills to wield a real sword, loyally throwing their bodies into the fray without flinching. In contrast to sports, where participants compete for fun and spectators take pleasure in the spectacle, the purpose of kendo is to travel the righteous path of austere physical and spiritual training [*shugyō*].⁴⁰

The inclusion of judo as an Olympic sport in 1964 was a source of great pride for the Japanese and represented strength of character in the postwar rebuilding process. It also brought the martial arts much-desired worldwide recognition and a feeling of redemption. Nevertheless, martial arts enthusiasts now lament what they consider to be the sacrifice in judo of budo virtues, such as respect, modesty, and general courtesy, for the sake of winning medals. Brian Goodger and John Goodger observed that judo "has become increasingly westernized and oriented towards international competition. The strong competitive ethos, individualism, instrumental views of practice and rational, scientific approaches to training are typical of the wider culture within which judo now flourishes."[41] In Japan, too, the perceived effects of globalization on budo are seen as epitomizing the tainting or diluting of all that is supposed to be good and noble in the martial arts.

The Western influence on budo is undeniable, but the inference that an unwanted invasion of Western ideals is detracting from the purity of budo is rarely considered the responsibility of the federations charged with protecting the cultural integrity of their arts. Instead, blame is apportioned to the unstoppable and undesirable tide of global influences with a simplistic "them versus us" argument. As an extension of this, one of the strange ongoing discussions in the kendo fraternity is the specter of Olympism, even though kendo never has been, and most likely never will be, an Olympic sport.

It is widely believed that if kendo were to be introduced into the Olympics, Japan would lose its position of leadership over the art, as has clearly been the case with judo. As of 2014, the International Judo Federation boasts an enormous membership of around two hundred countries and regions, yet there is not one Japanese representative serving in any official capacity within the federation.

However, the changes to the rules and method of kendo matches that would be needed to meet the IOC's requirements are the most worrying factor. It is believed that the nebulous aesthetic criteria for scoring valid strikes (*yūkō-datotsu*) would have to be rationalized, which would detract from the beauty of the art. The Japanese aesthetic of kendo would be lost forever if it were turned into a purposive sport.

Identifying points scored in kendo is often difficult for both seasoned practitioners and referees. Several years ago, news reached Japan that a splinter group in Korea that was practicing *kumdo* (a Korean variant of kendo) was trying to simplify the refereeing process by developing electrical equipment similar to that used in competitive Western fencing. According to the rules for scoring a point in épée fencing, the target is the whole of the fencer's body, including his clothing and protective equipment, and a touch must be clearly registered by the electronic apparatus to count. In contrast to this relatively clear-cut process, the official FIK *Kendo Shiai and Shinpan Regulations* (2006) stipulate that a valid strike must consist of the following elements: "Article 12: A *yuko-datotsu* is defined as an accurate strike or thrust made onto designated targets (*datotsu-bui*) of the opponent's *kendo-gu*. The strike or thrust must be executed in high spirits with correct posture, using the striking section (*datotsu-bu*) of the *shinai* with the blade on the correct angle (*hasuji*), and followed by *zanshin*" (translation mine). It is not just a matter of whether the *shinai* touches the opponent's body. The rulebook definition of a valid strike involves the stipulated "requirements" listed in Article 12, but there are also other factors to consider. These include adequate strength of the strike (*kyōdo*), "crispness" of the strike's sound (*sae*), correct posture (*shisei*), ample vocalization (*kiai*), appropriate spatial interval between opponents (*maai*), footwork and body movement (*tai-sabaki*), seizing apposite striking opportunities rather than hitting randomly (*kikai*), and correct usage of the hands and grip to get the right amount of resonance in the strike (*tenouchi*).

Even if it looks as though the *shinai* has connected with the target, the technique may not be deemed valid if one or more of the aforementioned criteria are not satisfied. It is no wonder that mistaken referee decisions are a common occurrence in kendo bouts, but woe betide any competitor who expresses disagreement.

In kendo, aesthetic form is judged, not just the point of impact. The entire process of a strike from start to finish is assessed, starting with the application of pressure to create an opening, the selection of an appropriate technique, timing and execution, precision, and continued psychological and physical readiness (*zanshin*) after the strike. To use Bourdieu's words, all of these combined factors symbolize a "whole set of moral 'virtues'—rectitude, straightforwardness, dignity (face to face confrontation as a demand for respect)—and also physical ones—vigor, strength, health."[42] In addition to observing and assessing the accuracy of the physical strike on the target, the referee reads between the lines to make instantaneous decisions regarding the appropriateness of the competitor's physical and spiritual attitude before, during, and after the strike. This entails a "moral judgment" that is as much subjective as it is objective.

An indispensable feature of any Olympic sport is its accessibility to spectators who have never participated in the sport. If kendo were to become an

Olympic sport, the difficulty in judging or understanding what constitutes a point would necessitate far-reaching rule changes, potentially leading to an oversimplification of the scoring process.

The convoluted process of scoring epitomizes the aesthetic principles of kendo. The common consensus in Japan is that the criteria for scoring a point must be retained at all costs, even if this means casual observers are unable to follow match procedure. It would be close to impossible for kendo to become an official Olympic sport in its current form.

The irony is that the Olympic Games themselves have been transformed from an event encouraging sportsmanship and holistic development to a massive economic undertaking in which sponsorship deals and elitism prevail. A glance at the ideals stated in the Olympic Charter suggests that the games' original values are at great odds with the reality today: "Olympism is a philosophy of life, exalting and combining in a balanced whole the qualities of body, will and mind. Blending sport with culture and education, Olympism seeks to create a way of life based on the joy found in effort, the educational value of good example and respect for universal fundamental ethical principles." In fact, Olympic ideals have much in common with the kendo values outlined in the "Concept" and "Mindset" and even more so with the "Philosophy of Budo" that I covered in the introduction.

Even though most kendo enthusiasts in Japan oppose induction into the Olympic family, affiliation with the IOC by joining the General Association of Sports Federations (GAISF, now SportAccord) was supported by smaller kendo federations around the world, especially those in the European Kendo Federation.[43] The reason was simple: affiliation would enhance the standing of kendo as a minority sport, thereby increasing the chance of receiving funding from governments. At the FIK Board of Directors meetings held at the Santa Clara World Kendo Championships in 2000 and the Glasgow World Kendo Championships in 2003, European countries registered their desire to become affiliated with GAISF for this reason.

Belonging to GAISF does not qualify a sport for the Olympics, but it does entail inclusion in the Olympic movement. The affiliated organization is considered to be the official international representative of that sport and is allowed to vie for admission as an Olympic sport if that objective is desirable and viable. The AJKF was initially reluctant to venture down this slippery slope, but it realized that a kendo organization from another country (such as Korea) might seek GAISF membership first if they did not take the initiative. The mere thought of this forced Japan's hand, and in April 2006 the International Kendo Federation became affiliated with GAISF, making it the formally recognized international representative for kendo.

Overall, affiliation has been beneficial for kendo's international profile and prestige. Kendo has featured in both of the prestigious SportAccord Combat Games in Beijing in 2010 and Saint Petersburg in 2013. However, there is also the tedious and costly matter of mandatory anti-doping testing at international events, in accordance with World Anti-Doping Agency regulations. Perhaps naïve in this day and age, kendoka have been, for the most part, blissfully detached from the doping problem in world sports until now. Many still fail to see the relevance of anti-doping in kendo, construing such issues as otiose annoyances concomitant with the course of internationalization.

Guttmann claims that the spread of Japanese martial arts to the West has been accompanied by modernization and "transformation in accordance with Western assumptions about the nature of sports."[44] In the case of kendo, however, modernization and transformation have actually been in accordance with Japanese assumptions or prejudices about the nature of sports. What Guttmann is alluding to is Western "cultural imperialism" with regard to sporting norms and morality; but one could say that a tinge of Japanese cultural imperialism is detectable in how kendo has been promoted in the international community by the AJKF, the FIK, and the Japanese government, who consider it a valuable "gift to the world." This gift supposedly exceeds the capacity of other sports to enhance the lives of practitioners at a spiritual level, and it even contributes to international peace and understanding—as long as it is done the "Japanese way." But as McVeigh professes, "nationalism often hides behind its opposite: 'internationalism' (an ironic form of official as well as popular nationalism)."[45]

As kendo becomes increasingly popular internationally at a highly competitive level, Japanese resolve to maintain a position of suzerainty is becoming firmer. The question of Japan's responsibility and mission to protect the culture of kendo as an instrument of education and something more than a mere sport will be taken up in the final chapter.

CHAPTER 6

Crossing Swords and Borders

THE GLOBAL DIFFUSION OF KENDO

KENDO'S MIGRATION TO THE EAST AND WEST

Westerners were introduced to the wonders of the Oriental martial arts, namely *jūjutsu* (unarmed grappling), during the Meiji period (1868–1912), when Japanese wrestlers, who were small in stature, defeated much bigger opponents in public matches held in music halls throughout Europe. Some Japanese *jūjutsu* exponents even displayed their tricks in circus shows to the amazement of onlookers.

Japanese martial culture gained a cult following in the West, especially after the Russo-Japanese War of 1904–5. It seemed so remarkable that Japan defeated Russia that American president Theodore Roosevelt felt compelled to buy dozens of copies of Nitobe Inazō's book *Bushido* to give to his friends. He even asked Kanō Jigorō to send him a judo instructor—Yamashita Yoshitsugu—who taught him the art in a makeshift dojo in the White House. On the other side of the world, Sarala Devi Ghoshal of India, a prominent advocate for female education, was also impressed and sought to import the Japanese warrior spirit into the country by opening "a martial arts academy in Calcutta, exhorting Bengali youth to learn 'how to use the staff, the fist, the sword, and the gun.'"[1]

The international spread of kendo has ebbed and flowed over the last century, with the biggest wave of popularity occurring in the 1970s and 1980s. The number of international kendo practitioners pales in comparison to the number engaged in the other budo arts, such as judo and karate. Nevertheless, international kendo is expanding, and the International Kendo Federation (FIK) has fifty-seven registered affiliates as of 2015. Kendo is also practiced in numerous unaffiliated countries. The World Kendo Championships (WKC) are held every three years, and the overall level of the non-Japanese competitors continues to improve.

As the ideological renaissance of kendo unfolded in Japan during the 1970s, kendo's popularity around the world steadily increased. Successful international propagation was initially welcomed as signaling redemption for Japan's wartime past. However, it would ultimately drive the owners of kendo culture to deepen their resolve to be evangelistic but simultaneously protective "keepers of the way," and the ongoing process of dissemination is laced with elements of cultural imperialism. The "way" of kendo refers to the religio-mystical dimension of the art, the teaching of which, according to many Japanese kendo authorities, can be authentically grasped only by Japanese. Ironically, this is an aspect of kendo that multitudes of kendo practitioners outside of Japan yearn for.

Most of kendo's international dissemination took place in the postwar period, but it did have a solid following in some regions of the world by the 1920s, at the same time that it became mainstream in Japan. There were three noteworthy trends in kendo's prewar international migration. First, kendo was introduced to Europe on a very small scale by a handful of European Japanophiles who had developed an interest in Japan and its spiritual and sporting culture while they resided there. Second, kendo's passage to North and South America was facilitated by Japanese immigrants who viewed it as a "cultural artifact that connected students, expatriate businessmen, immigrants, and their families to traditional Japanese culture and values."[2] The third migration of significance was to Korea and Taiwan. Forced participation in Korea in particular eventuated in cultural revisionism, as the Koreans created their own version of kendo, called *kumdo,* which they consider to be a part of traditional Korean culture.

Although the impetuses for kendo's establishment in these regions are disparate, an undercurrent of nationalistic tendencies is always associated with it. These tendencies are manifested in the zealous advocacy of individual Japanese kendo enthusiasts at the grassroots level, and exemplified by the efforts of the Japanese government and organizations such as the AJKF to promote and simultaneously protect the culture of kendo. What are the Japanese objectives for conveying kendo to the world? How do major international events such as the WKC affect the perception and direction of kendo's international spread? What ideological constructs are applied to assert and justify the cultural proprietorship of kendo? And finally, is the impetus behind internationalization actually symptomatic of nationalization? These are all important questions when discussing the international dissemination of kendo.

European contact with Japanese swordsmanship began in the late Meiji era. For example, Thomas McClatchie (1852–86) entered the world of Japanese swordsmanship under the tutelage of Sakakibara Kenkichi (1830–94).

> One day, the young brash McClatchie stomped into Sakakibara's training hall, then located where the Ueno City Office is presently found, walked onto the training area without removing his footwear and challenged one and all to a duel. The Japanese were not very impressed with this invasion of their privacy and abuse of their sacred customs and promptly accepted this challenge. McClatchie was soundly defeated and not being totally ignorant of his infringement on Japanese customs and tradition begged forgiveness and for the opportunity to join the school.[3]

Another Englishman, Francis James Norman (1855–1926), was probably the most accomplished Westerner in *kenjutsu* in his day (figure 24). His book *The Fighting Man of Japan* (1905), written about his extended residency in Japan, offers some marvelous insights into Japanese society in the late Meiji period and is also a fascinating firsthand account of the nature of *kenjutsu* at the end of the nineteenth century. As Norman himself suggests, he was probably the first Western exponent of traditional Japanese swordsmanship to make a detailed study of the art: "While acting in that country as an instructor in some of the leading colleges, both military and civilian, the author has had what are, perhaps, unrivalled opportunities for making a thorough and systematic study of the two 'noble sciences' of *kenjutsu* and *jiujitsu*. The author is, so far as he is aware, the first Occidental who has gone at all deeply into these two branches of Japanese education."[4] This observation is also reflected in the comments of another well-known Western martial artist. Englishman Ernest John Harrison, a judo expert who spent twenty years in Japan as a journalist, from 1897 (overlapping with the end of Norman's sojourn) to 1912, praised Norman for his achievements in the art of *kenjutsu*.

> Perhaps the only foreigner who ever took up *kenjutsu* seriously is Mr. F. J. Norman, late of the Indian Army, a cavalry officer, and expert in both rapier and sabre play. Norman was for some years engaged as a teacher at the Etajima Naval College, and while there devoted his attention to the Japanese style to such good purpose that he speedily won an enviable reputation among

FIGURE 24. F.J. Norman standing in his kendo armor alongside his mentor, Mr. Umezawa. (Author's collection)

the Japanese, and engaged in many a hard-fought encounter. Some few other foreigners have practiced, and doubtless do practice *kenjutsu* for the sake of exercise, but I am not aware that any one of them has won distinction in Japanese eyes.[5]

A small number of other Westerners also studied *kenjutsu* during the Meiji period, but Norman's study of Japanese swordsmanship was considerably more in-depth than other foreigners, who showed only passing interest. He not only excelled in the technical aspects of *kenjutsu* but also made astute observations about the spirit in which it was practiced. He states in his introduction that the benefits gleaned from studying *kenjutsu* have "led him to believe that much advantage might accrue to his native country from the introduction of exercises so admirably calculated to improve the physique and also the morale of its youth and manhood."

He compared the Japanese martial arts with the "favorite games of young England"—probably cricket, rugby, and soccer—declaring that these English sports were necessarily restricted to the upper classes because of the expense of equipment, time, and facilities. "Lookers on, it is said, see most of the game; but neither morale nor physique are thereby greatly benefited, and looking on is apt to degenerate into a dull pastime unless relieved by betting." In the case of *kenjutsu* and *jūjutsu*, he maintained, "all can participate, without risk or danger to life, purse, or limb, but with great benefit both to body and spirit."

Given that Norman was such a proponent of *kenjutsu*, one would assume that, after he returned to England in 1905, his enthusiasm for the art would have resulted in the establishment of a group of eager non-Japanese practitioners to match the growing popularity of *jūjutsu* in Britain. This, however, was not to be. The following excerpt from *The Times* (October 19, 1905) drives home the fact that any aspiration to spread kendo in Europe was premature.

> Ken-jitsu, sword play with the Japanese two-handed sword, was illustrated by Mr. Norman and Mr. Miyake to the great amusement of the spectators – for etiquette seems to ordain that the Japanese swordsman should bark like a dog over the attack, and crow like a cock when he gets a blow home. Mr. Norman also tried a bout with Sergeant-Major Betts, who used a single-stick against his sword, with the result that the sergeant-major was metaphorically bisected once or twice and that Mr. Norman got some shrewd blows. But the impression produced was that Ken-jitsu is not really or nearly so important an exercise as Ju-jitsu.

Nevertheless, a little over a decade later, kendo was introduced at the newly formed martial arts club, the London Budokwai. At the inaugural committee meeting of the Budokwai, held on November 19, 1919, the rules of the organization were established, and it was declared that the aim of the society was "to study Budo (ways of Knighthood) inclusive of Judo, Kendo (fencing) and kindred arts." Practice sessions were held daily, but there is no indication of the size of the kendo group, other than that Mr. Nabubuta was the instructor and that practicing members included "Mr. Brinkley," "Mr. Ashida," and "Mr. Matsuyama."[6] *Jūjutsu* was considerably more popular.

Jūjustu, and later Kōdōkan judo, made significant inroads in Britain, France, and Germany during the Taishō (1912–26) and early Shōwa

(1926–89) periods due to their practical application and the fervent efforts of Kanō Jigorō. Kendo seems to have been limited to a tiny group of aficionados and was performed at *jūjutsu* displays mainly for its novelty value.

The Budokwai was probably the first society offering kendo instruction in Europe. Despite kendo's unconventional look, the benefits of studying it were advertised to the public. The following synopsis of a newspaper report is from the Budokwai's minutes and concerns a speech given by career diplomat Hayashi Gonsuke at the annual Budokwai martial arts demonstration, held at the Stadium Club in London on January 7, 1926:

> There was a lot of talk, continued Baron Hayashi, about the alleged "flabbiness" of modern young men. He did not know how much truth there was in what was being said on this subject, but so far as the Budokwai was concerned, it was certainly not true. Their Society was doing good work among young Japanese and young Englishmen by training their minds and bodies to be strong and active. In these difficult times every nation needed a virile youthful generation, and the Budokwai, by teaching its members how to acquire and apply the strength developed in the practice of Judo and Kendo, was assisting Great Britain and Japan in developing sturdy manhood among the rising generation. Their work was being carried out only on a small scale, but he was sure it was good work, and was greatly appreciated by all who knew of it.

Nevertheless, kendo didn't really take root in Europe until after the Second World War. France and Britain were among the first European countries in which kendo developed a modest following as early as the 1950s, but most other countries created national federations only in the 1980s and 1990s, with the first European Kendo Championships being held in 1974. Now kendo is practiced at a relatively high level in countries such as France, Germany, Hungary, and Italy, and national federations have been formed in most of the nations of Europe—although it is still very much a minority sport. The history of kendo in the Americas is more substantial, due primarily to two factors: widespread participation by Japanese immigrants throughout North and South America, and the establishment of Dai-Nippon Butokukai branches in the region in the 1930s.

Japanese immigrants first founded a dojo in Honolulu, in the Kingdom of Hawaii, in 1890. There they demonstrated kendo and other martial arts for King David Kalākaua as early as 1885. The oldest recorded kendo demonstration in the United States, however, took place in March 1905 to commemorate the opening of the football stadium at the University of Washington in Seattle.[7]

According to documents in the Hans Baerwald collection regarding the dissolution of the Dai-Nippon Butokukai in postwar Japan, the only activity outside Japan in which the Butokukai was officially engaged was a mission to Manchuria in 1941 in celebration of the tenth anniversary of the establishment of Manchukuo. Japanese immigrants sometimes invited individual members to travel abroad. For example, on two occasions members went to the West Coast of the United States at the invitation of Nisei (second-generation Japanese immigrants), and one member went to South America in 1939 on a similar invitation.

The documents state that branch societies were formed in Japanese territories, but that they "were never recognized by [the Butokukai's] home society since they disagreed on the strict standards maintained by the Japanese organization."[8] This is not necessarily an accurate account, as the Butokukai branches formed in Taiwan, Korea, Manchuria, and the United States were recorded in the organization's official membership. In any case, membership was almost entirely made up of Japanese nationals and Nikkei—including both Issei (first-generation immigrants) and Nisei.[9] For Nikkei, belonging to societies such as the Butokukai or community dojos enabled them to maintain links with their Japanese heritage. This was a significant factor behind the earlier organization of kendo in the Americas as opposed to in Europe, where the few Japanese communities that did exist were much smaller and fragmented.

Even so, there were various issues that hindered kendo's spread among early Japanese immigrants, including a lack of time and money for recreational activities, a shortage of qualified teachers, and prejudice. According to Joseph Svinth, "Visions of Japanese agricultural workers attacking their overseers with sticks set off waves of Yellow Peril paranoia, and consequently early community leaders often downplayed Japanese martial traditions."[10] This changed in the 1920s, when Nikkei practitioners overcame their early inhibitions and brought high-level professional instructors from Japan to the United States, such as those who came on the abovementioned tours of the West Coast.

The Butokukai subsequently gained a steady throng of members, especially on the West Coast, where the bulk of Japanese immigrants had settled. A Nikkei American by the name of Bill Fukuda recalls his experiences doing kendo before the Second World War in Seattle:

> I took kendo lessons [taught by the Seattle Butokukai]. The dojo was at the Seattle Baptist Church up on First Hill. So I used to walk all the distance once a week. I remember going to *kangeiko* [midwinter training] in winter at

five o'clock in the morning. We used to go to *keiko* [practice] for two weeks, every morning. It was cold! The instructors were all ex-soldiers of Japan. In a way they treated us like they were in a military camp.... They taught us a lot of manners, *reigi-tadashii* [be polite]. Certainly they taught you that there was a pecking order. You know exactly where you are in the pecking order.[11]

With the start of the Pacific War in 1941, leaders of martial arts clubs were suspected of subversive activities and became the target of FBI investigations. Gary Okihiro reports that by 1941 the FBI had created a list of over two thousand Japanese living in the United States; it included people from all walks of life, including martial arts instructors, and grouped them into "A, B, and C categories" based on their level of perceived danger.[12] North American Butokukai membership logs (*Hokubei kendō taikan,* 1939) threatened to be a useful source of information for the FBI, and members hastily burned copies to avoid identification after Pearl Harbor.

Svinth observes that Japanese Americans and Japanese Canadians had different perceptions of kendo during the war. Until the Second World War, the growth of and attitudes toward kendo had been similar in both countries. Although both groups were incarcerated in internment camps during the war, a clear distinction arose with the induction of interned volunteers into the armed forces. Japanese Americans were allowed to volunteer for the United States military from early 1943. Although there was displeasure shown by some interned Japanese Americans, volunteers were encouraged for the most part, and toward the end of the war, anything closely connected to Japanese militarism, such as kendo, was shunned as unpatriotic. The Japanese Canadians, on the other hand, were not permitted to enlist until 1945, and consequently they viewed kendo as a way of protesting the discrimination they had to endure.

South American countries, such as Brazil, which received droves of Japanese immigrants from around the end of the Meiji and Taishō eras, also saw the early establishment of kendo groups. In the case of Brazil, for example, kendo exponents were onboard the ship the *Kasato-Maru* when the first round of Japanese immigrants disembarked in the city of Santos on June 18, 1908. From modest beginnings with a few dedicated fencers, kendo soon took root in the Japanese community there. In 1921, a local newspaper known as the *Gazeta do Povo* related a kendo performance that seemed to cause quite a stir.

"Gêkkeu" [*sic*]—(fencing) was joined by many Japanese. The competitors wore iron masks on their faces and rubber plates on their chests, held sticks in their hands and started beating and hitting each other with no mercy.... This performance was appreciated by the audience, who wanted to take part in it, and a massive brawl erupted "just for fun." ... Many people left with broken hats and others with lumps on their heads, including our photographer, Juvencio Mayer, who left the camera aside to join the drubbing, as if he was Japanese.[13]

In spite of its rambunctious nature, which actually seemed to appeal to the locals, kendo was publicized as a way of promoting morality and therefore, as it was in Japan at the time, as something more serious than a sport. Luiz Kobayashi located a 1935 interview demonstrating how one of the earliest societies dedicated to the promotion of Japanese martial arts in Brazil, the Hakkoku Jukendo Renmei, was an enthusiastic promoter of the Japanese way.

> The main goal of Hakkoku Jukendo Renmei has been from the outset to be a responsible association to promote moral development.... We must avoid at all costs focusing our attention on techniques, thereby forgetting the most important thing, which is the spirit.... To believe that budo is limited to techniques is a blasphemy to the spirit of budo.... If someone is a member of our association, then he or she is expected to have an unassailable integrity of character.... Wins and losses are entirely secondary. Budo is alive only when we live with such spirit in our society, in our jobs and at our homes. Martial arts devoid of this virtuous spirit are nothing but acrobatics and legerdemain. Alas, martial arts reduced to such a state are totally worthless.[14]

But for many, the "spirit of budo" and the cultivation of a virtuous character were not the only attractions; the link that could be maintained with Japan was also of paramount importance. This was, and still is, true of the thousands of Nikkei who study kendo in Japanese diaspora communities located in Canada, Hawaii and the mainland United States, Brazil, and other countries. From the earliest days of Japanese migration, the Issei were interested in Japanese martial arts as an important element of Nisei education in Japaneseness. American historian Eichiro Azuma asserts, "Not only would these traditional 'sports,' such as judo and kendo, keep youths away from undesirable activities, they would steer the boys and girls toward 'exploring the spiritual aspect of Japanese life' in a most practical way."[15]

Of course, there were some notable non-Japanese practitioners who studied kendo in these communities, such as well-known pioneers Gordon Warner (1912–2010; figures 25 and 26) and Benjamin Hazard (1920–2011). They were an extreme minority who maintained an interest in Japanese

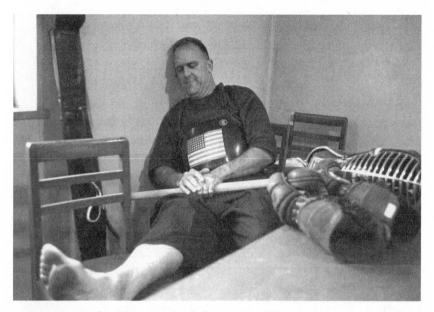

FIGURE 25. Gordon Warner resting before a series of demonstration matches with an American team visiting Japan in November 1956. Most of the American team members were Nikkei, but Warner, who had 3-dan at the time and was over six feet tall, was reported as having put the fear of God into his opponents. This is all the more astounding considering he only had one leg. He was awarded the Navy Cross for extraordinary heroism during action in the Battle of Empress Augusta Bay in November 1943. It was there that he sustained wounds that required the amputation of his left leg. (The Mainichi Newspapers)

martial arts and culture in general, but they were not linked to Japan by blood, which is something Nikkei practitioners took pride in. The connection Nikkei maintained with Japan through the study of kendo can be seen as a form of transnational nationalism, or an expression of pride in their Japanese roots and heritage. The extent of this connection and the consciousness of Japaneseness in recent generations of Nikkei (and those of mixed parentage) is a fascinating subject warranting further investigation. Suffice it to say here that the vast majority of highly ranked kendo practitioners in the Americas are Nikkei.

Although the Koreans took up kendo with a similar passion, their motivations for practicing the art were very different. For the vast Korean kendo population, trying to break the cultural connection with Japan has been an ongoing challenge.

Koreans still remember with resentment the Japanese occupation of their country from 1910 to the end of the Second World War. Assimilation policies

FIGURE 26. Warner (left) taking the *jōdan* stance. He was defeated by his opponent, a Japanese student, by a thrust to the throat and a *kote* strike. (The Mainichi Newspapers)

introduced by the Japanese colonial government were designed to force Koreans to discard their own culture and language in favor of those of Japan. As has been detailed in previous chapters, kendo and other budo arts were made compulsory subjects in schools in Japan in the 1930s and utilized by the government to encourage fighting spirit, instill nationalistic fervor, and nurture pride in Japan's masculine warrior past. The Japanese colonies of Taiwan and Korea were also urged to participate in these activities. Even when the war ended and the Republic of Korea was established, groups of Koreans demonstrated a commitment to kendo that persists to this day, evident in the high level of technical proficiency of Korean kendoka and the large number of enthusiasts in the country.

Taiwan also has a healthy number of kendo practitioners and is considered to be one of the powerhouses of international kendo, although it is not as strong as Korea. The main difference between the two countries lies in their general attitudes toward Japan's colonial intrusion. In Korea, many of the old wounds of the Japanese occupation have still not healed, and, taking an overtly revisionist stance, numerous Koreans refuse to acknowledge that kendo's origins lie in Japan. This is why Korea is the focus of this section rather than Taiwan, as the Japanese believe that the Koreans pose the greatest threat to their proprietorship of kendo. Allen Guttmann points out that "one must expect that the diffusion of sports, like that of any other aspect of culture, will be accompanied by nationalistic resistance to what some will feel to be cultural imperialism."[16] Korea's answer to Japanese cultural imperialism is the claim that *kumdo,* Korean kendo, originated in Korea and not Japan.

Historically speaking, Chinese and Korean influence on the philosophical and intellectual development of Japanese swordsmanship is undeniable. The Chinese and the Koreans had their own styles of swordsmanship within idiosyncratic martial systems, but these had little effect on the way medieval Japanese swordsmanship developed technically. During Korea's Jeongjo era (1776–1800), the military text *Sok Pyungjang Tosul* (Revised illustrated manual of military training and tactics) included sword techniques among the twenty-four martial arts recorded. In addition to Korean forms of swordsmanship, Japanese *kenjutsu* is introduced in illustrations depicting two adepts of the Yagyū Shinkage-ryū. This is evidence that Koreans acknowledged the distinctiveness of Japanese swordsmanship at the time.

Now, however, such texts are often referenced to qualify claims that *kumdo* originated directly from traditional Korean forms of swordsmanship, rather than from Japanese kendo. In recent years, some of the traditional kata explained in historical Korean martial arts texts have been revived and incorporated into the study of *kumdo* as a counterpart to the Nihon Kendo Kata to accentuate this link.

It is interesting to note that, for the most part, the development of modern kendo in Korea followed a path similar to that of Japanese kendo. Training in swordsmanship was introduced into the Korean national military academy and police force in around 1891. Lee Min-ku divides the proliferation of kendo in Korea into the three periods: "educational integration" (1910–19), in which kendo was introduced into schools; "cultural integration" (1919–37), in which kendo became an established form of exercise like other sports; and "militarization" (1937–45), as was the case with "militarized budo" in Japan (see chapter 4).[17]

In recent years, *kumdo* clubs have sprung up in Korean diaspora communities just as kendo clubs have in Nikkei communities. Different groups promote different types of traditional Korean swordsmanship using the generic term *kumdo,* but these are not necessarily related to the type of *kumdo* I am discussing here. I am referring to the *kumdo* that falls under the auspices of the FIK-affiliated Korea Kumdo Association—AJKF's equivalent.

Kumdo and kendo are essentially the same, save for a few superficial differences. Koreans use their native language in *kumdo,* have changed the color of the scoring flags (blue and white as opposed to red and white), and have abandoned the squatting bow (*sonkyo*) and certain other forms of Japanese etiquette that are considered important in Japan. There was also a successful movement, which I will detail below, to use Korean-style *hakama,* which have no *koshi-ita* (the board that sits in the lower back) and are secured with Velcro straps. It was argued that these *hakama* were more practical, but their implementation is viewed as a protest against the Japanese dictation of norms.

Nevertheless, a casual observer would be more likely to notice the similarities between kendo and *kumdo.* Participants train and compete in the same indoor environment, called *dojang* in Korean and dojo in Japanese, using the same techniques and practice methodology. The targets are exactly the same, the same protective equipment is used, and the same criteria for scoring valid points are employed.

In both Japan and Korea, regional and national tournaments are hotly contested at all levels. The two countries value the metaphysical and moral aspects, which include meditation before and after training, ritualized bowing, and prescribed forms of etiquette to express respect. Interaction during training is hierarchically based, and character development is highlighted as an important goal. In fact, *kumdo* and kendo coexist harmoniously in many countries around the world. Apart from differences in terminology and slight variations in style, attitude, and cultural values, most people accept that the sports are, for all intents and purposes, the same.

Perhaps one of the most significant differences between kendo and *kumdo* is the disparity in career opportunities for elite competitors. As I alluded to in the previous chapter, successful competitors in Japan have opportunities to enter high school and then university on scholarship, purely on the basis of their technical skill. The top competitors in the university circuit are often recruited into the police force (typically into riot squad kendo teams), or they may become teachers of physical education or even prison guards. Others stand a good chance of being picked up in the private sector by a company with a strong in-house kendo club. Whatever the case, lifetime employment and job security is virtually assured. In a sense, they become lifelong professional kendoka, albeit as employees of greater organizations.

Elite Korean *kumdo* practitioners, on the other hand, have similar pathways through secondary and tertiary education, but they are not blessed with career options comparable to those of their Japanese peers. There is no guaranteed permanent employment or income beyond one's competitive years. The Korean police force does not have an established *kumdo* section, and although Korea has a formidable company *kumdo* circuit, the recruit's contract expires when he or she is no longer competitive. With no other tangible skills or training applicable to life outside *kumdo,* top practitioners are forced to eke out a living by establishing their own private *dojang* and teaching children, or they have to start from scratch and retrain in a completely different vocation.

Despite these differences, Japan's influence on the form of kendo practiced in Korea cannot be denied. *Kumdo* is essentially Korean-style kendo. However, revisionist Korean authorities continue to assert that *kumdo* arose out of Korean culture and had nothing to do with Japan. To the ire of the Japanese, some even go so far to insist that Japanese kendo has its origins in Korea. The antagonism takes various forms. For example, Korean scholar Na Young-il recounts that in 1977, an official called Lee Ho-am made a proposal to the president of the Korean Kumdo Association regarding the use of Japanese *hakama:* "While advocating arguments for the use of *paji* [Korean trousers] rather than the Japanese pleated culottes [*hakama*] during *gumdo* [*kumdo*] training, he [Lee Ho-am] stated 'in order to respect the creation of "beauty," the ultimate objective of physical education, not the traditional and narrow-minded [view of] Japanese beauty, [we should] aspire to pursue a universal beauty for all humankind,' and went on to say that present-day kendoists sought a form of 'international kendo' not a 'Japanese-centric form.' "[18]

As Guttmann observes with regard to the international diffusion of modern sports, a sport may become so "thoroughly naturalized that the borrowers feel that it is *their* game, an expression of their unique national character, but the transmission of a sport is certainly a complicated matter in which intrinsic ludic properties are jumbled together with extrinsic cultural associations in ways not easy to untangle."[19] This is very much the case with *kumdo* in Korea. Many Koreans believe that the ideals of swordsmanship in Korea predate Japan's at a historical and philosophical level. Although there are most certainly elements of truth to this claim, the modern form of kendo was created in Japan and evolved there. However, this has become a highly emotional point of contention for enthusiasts in both countries as they attempt to claim ownership of the culture. The fact that Korea is extremely competitive at the FIK's World Kendo Championships—and nearly always comes close to defeating Japan in the finals—makes the situation even tenser for both sides, with much at stake in terms of national pride.

Koreans have been vociferous in their criticism of the "hypocrisy" of the internationalization of Japan-centered kendo. For example, Korean scholar and kendo instructor S. Shin published a scathing critique of the twelfth WKC held in Glasgow in 2003. Among his criticisms, he challenges the supposed "impartiality of the referees," 41.5 percent of whom were Japanese, a figure that increases to 58.5 percent if Nikkei (from the United States, Canada, Brazil, and other countries) are included. This could have given Japanese contestants an advantage if they were favored either consciously or subconsciously by Japanese referees. He also laments that, although the Japanese promote kendo as an activity with universal benefits, the fact that they continue to stress the importance of kendo's Japanese cultural traits contradicts this claim and actually impedes the international growth of kendo as a "universal sport."[20] The Koreans are more inclined to promote *kumdo* simply as a competitive sport that aids in character development. "Koreanness" is rarely openly accentuated, unless it is specifically in regard to Japan.

THE COMPLEXITIES OF INTERNATIONAL CONSOLIDATION

The internationalization of kendo has both positive and negative impacts for the Japanese. On the one hand, in order to cast Japan in a better light internationally, it is seen as advantageous at state and popular levels to take the soft power approach by promoting traditional Japanese culture overseas. This, the rhetoric maintains, is the basis of providing the world with a "unique" culture laced with universal concepts to enhance personal cultivation, mutual understanding, and respect, and ultimately to contribute to world peace. On the other hand, somewhat paradoxically, the more Japanese culture is successfully promoted outside Japan, the more paranoia there is inside Japan that it may lose its position of leadership. This is reminiscent of the controversy surrounding the Japanese government's attempts in 2006 to create a certification system for Japanese restaurants abroad. It received widespread international criticism as a "sushi police" system aimed at preventing non-Japanese Asians from profiting from faux Japanese cuisine.

As kendo takes root outside Japan, guidance is increasingly provided by Korean-affiliated experts. This raises concerns that the techniques and spirit of kendo will be tainted by foreign (Korean or other) cultural influences, and that without the benevolent guiding hand of Japan, kendo will become solely competition oriented.

Following the showcasing of kendo as a demonstration sport at the Olympic Games in Tokyo in 1964, the Japan-based International Goodwill Kendo Club held its first international tournament in Taipei in November 1965. This was the first important event in the consolidation of international kendo in the postwar period, even though the world's kendo population was still very small, and the only countries with a significant number of practitioners were Japan, Korea, Taiwan, and some Pan-American countries with sizeable Nikkei communities.

In October 1967, an international friendship tournament sponsored by the AJKF was held at the Nippon Budokan in Tokyo. Representatives from eleven countries attended: the United States, Canada, Brazil, the United Kingdom, West Germany, Switzerland, Australia, South Korea, Taiwan, South Vietnam, and Japan. In addition, Hawaii and Okinawa entered their own teams into the tournament, which was witnessed by the emperor and empress of Japan. At this gathering, participants formally discussed creating the International Kendo Federation.

The international body was inaugurated in April 1970, and to commemorate this event, the first WKC was held in the cities of Tokyo, for the team event, and Osaka, for the individual event (figure 27). The first full affiliates were Australia, Belgium, Brazil, Canada, France, West Germany, the United Kingdom, Korea, Morocco, the Netherlands, the Republic of China, Sweden, Switzerland, the United States, and Japan. Hawaii and Okinawa were also inducted as independent federations at a special meeting.

Kimura Tokutarō was appointed as the first president of the IKF (now referred to as the FIK). At the time, Kimura was also the AJKF's president, and until 2013 the incumbent AJKF president traditionally served concurrently as the president of the FIK.

As of 2015, there are fifty-seven affiliates in the FIK, and a general assembly is convened every three years, just before commencement of the WKC. The board of directors consists of seventeen directors, including the president, four vice presidents, and twelve zone representatives. The balance of officials has been maintained in favor of Japanese voting power since its inception, but this condition could change as the number of affiliates increases.

The growth of kendo internationally has been steady since the international body's launch, but it is difficult to precisely estimate the total worldwide number of practitioners. Currently, it is projected that there are around

FIGURE 27. Ishihara (right) from Japan defeats his Taiwanese opponent in the men's team event with a strike to *men* at the first World
Kendo Championships in Japan, 1970. (Yomiuri Shimbun)

four hundred thousand practitioners in Korea, making it the largest kendo
group outside Japan, which has 1.5 million. France is said to have ten thousand members, and there are around five thousand registered enthusiasts in
the United States. There may be up to five hundred thousand practitioners
outside Japan if unaffiliated countries are included in the count, but kendo
will never be as popular as karate, which has practical applications, and judo,
which is an Olympic sport. The cost of equipment, the shortage of highly
ranked international instructors, and the overall difficulty of learning and
understanding the complicated aesthetic concepts of kendo will keep it in the
minority sport category outside of Japan for years to come.

Although at one level it is generally considered desirable in Japan that
kendo amass a far-reaching international following, the AJKF (which funda-

mentally administers the FIK) is becoming increasingly cautious about how and by whom the art is disseminated. The AJKF is trying to protect the cultural integrity of kendo overseas, which is to say that it is endeavoring to keep kendo as purely Japanese as possible in the face of the perceived corrosive effect of globalization on traditional culture. This has become an urgent issue for Japanese kendoists, especially considering the simmering rivalry with Korea.

For this purpose, the AJKF has been active for several decades in providing foreign kendo enthusiasts with opportunities to learn "Japanese kendo." In 1975, the first Foreign Kendo Leader's Summer Seminar was held in Katsuura City, Chiba Prefecture. It entailed ten days of intensive training under some of Japan's most celebrated instructors. The following year, a second seminar was held at the Gedatsukai headquarters in Kitamoto City, Saitama Prefecture, where it has continued as an annual event ever since.

The AJKF also began sending instructor delegations overseas in 1973, with sponsorship from the Japan Foundation. The AJKF now allocates an annual budget of ¥50 million to sponsor international seminars in which groups of high-level Japanese instructors travel to foreign destinations to pass on their kendo knowledge. This budget has also been used in recent years to publish teaching materials in English, such as *Nippon Kendo Kata Instruction Manual* (2005), *Training Method for Fundamental Kendo Techniques with a Bokuto* (2008), *The Official Guide for Kendo Instruction* (2011), and the *Japanese-English Dictionary of Kendo* (2011). The AJKF has also generously donated thousands of second-hand sets of *bōgu* to countries trying to establish kendo clubs.

It is important to point out that the AJKF is not the only organization that has been actively involved in the promotion of kendo internationally. The Japan International Cooperation Agency is a special public corporation established to assist in economic and social growth and to promote international cooperation through the provision of overseas development assistance. Experts in many fields, including nursing, engineering, and even sports, have been dispatched overseas to assist local groups and agencies. Since its launch in 1974, the agency has sent over sixty specialist kendo volunteers to developing countries to help with technical instruction. The typical term of tenure in this program is two years. The police, in particular the Keishichō (Tokyo Metropolitan Police Department), have also dispatched young instructors overseas for up to six months at a time through private arrangements made with foreign kendo federations.

Perhaps the most significant contributors to the international propagation of kendo are the tens of thousands of individual Japanese who have traveled overseas as immigrants, businessmen, students, and tourists with their kendo armor in tow. Depending on the location, even Japanese visitors with low dan rankings are looked up to in foreign dojos as "couriers of the genuine article" and are usually treated as special guests.

From my observations over nearly three decades, individual Japanese kendoists visiting foreign dojo often see themselves (and are seen) as representatives of kendo and its culture and spirit, and they usually relish the responsibility and opportunity to instruct. A kendo practitioner from Australia commented on a common occurrence in which Japanese kendoists are "put on a pedestal in the dojo simply by virtue of being Japanese. Because they came from Japan, it often seemed to be assumed, their kendo was automatically more authentic and technically developed—sometimes in instances when it actually wasn't."[21] Even low-ranking Japanese kendoka visiting foreign dojos seem to believe that they possess valuable knowledge, and feel a sense of intense pride in being able to convey this to the eager locals. They could be described as taking on the role of cultural evangelist, which fits with the AJKF's design to keep overseas kendo as Japanese as possible.

The stated purpose of the FIK (and hence the international activities of the AJKF) is to popularize kendo globally and increase the number of countries and regions in which kendo is practiced. The promotional activities of the FIK also afford Japanese enthusiasts the opportunity to interact with people from other countries through the medium of kendo as Japanese culture. It is a form of grassroots diplomacy that enhances Japan's reputation in the international arena.

This summation falls neatly in line with Wolf Mendl's assessment of Japan's governmental policies and efforts to introduce Japanese culture to the world: "Their purpose is clearly to promote greater knowledge and sympathetic understanding of Japan and to win friends for the country and thus to extend Japanese influence in the world at large."[22] This is often validated in budo circles by reference to the ideal of "world peace." The subtle implication seems to be that the spirit of budo, as manifested in kendo, is Japan's gift to the world. If all people were to share the same kind of respect and mutual understanding that is invoked through ascetic training in budos, then—somewhat paradoxically, given that the martial arts are forms of combat—there would be no more conflict, and everybody in the world would be able to coexist in harmony.

This interpretation may appear exceedingly idealistic. However, through my experiences as the official interpreter and translator for the Nippon

Budokan, the International Naginata Federation, and the All Japan Kendo Federation, I can attest to the fact that this sentiment is persistent and fundamental to the international propagation of budo. For example, see the "Philosophy of Budo" in the introduction of this book.

To use Brian McVeigh's words, this brand of rhetoric corresponds to a kind of "peace nationalism" which acts as a "counterweight to the strong orthodox (and even ultra-orthodox, Japan-centric) inclinations of certain circles."[23] The contribution that kendo can make in the world by promoting peace and respect is affirmation of a unique kind of Japanese soft power, and this is an aspect of budo culture that is frequently accentuated in governmental and popular cultural propaganda.

Related to this logic, although kendo is perceived by Japanese as a gift from Japan to the world, the AJKF believes that its form and spirit (*seishin*) should not be compromised in any way by foreign influence. The AJKF is averse to using the word *kokusaika* (internationalization) to describe its efforts in spreading kendo. To quote FIK president Takeyasu Yoshimitsu, "The term 'internationalization' applied in economics and society implies adapting to conditions overseas by changing domestic circumstances. From the purview of kendo, we do not consider changing the way kendo is conducted to facilitate international propagation. . . . Our responsibility is to further extend kendo's role as a form of traditional Japanese culture, and to unpretentiously promote the true form of kendo internationally."[24]

The idea of internationalization also implies that the culture of kendo may be adapted to suit the social and cultural milieu in the countries in which it takes root. This is undesirable to the Japanese. However, "international diffusion" (*kokusai fukyū*) is tolerable, so long as it is the diffusion of "correct Japanese kendo." Furthermore, a former AJKF managing director, Takeuchi Jun, stated that kendo must not be spread simply as a competitive sport: "The 'heart' of kendo as a form of Japanese culture—kendo as a way for personal development [*ningen keisei*]—is what we aim to convey to the rest of the world."[25]

Westerners, especially Japanophiles, typically view Japan as mysterious and culturally unfathomable. The ideals of kendo put forth in the "Concept" and "Mindset" (described in the previous chapter), and much of the official and unofficial literature, impart a distinct air of spiritualistic mystique. This is certainly one of the attractions of kendo from the perspective of non-Japanese practitioners, and thus it is one of the ways in which Japan is able to maintain its jurisdiction over kendo internationally.

Commenting on the appeal of the martial arts in the West, Guttmann states that philosophers such as the German Eugen Herrigel, who was "fascinated by Zen in the art of archery, are few compared to the modern missionaries of physical education who venture forth from Europe and North America to convert the world to the gospel of modern sports."[26] This is certainly not the case with kendo; it is the cultural aspects of kendo that are appealing to hordes of non-Japanese practitioners.

Takeuchi cautions that it is dangerous to judge success only on the basis of an increased number of FIK-affiliated countries or the improved technical proficiency seen internationally in recent years. According to Takeuchi, the sporting and technical aspects of kendo are important, but they should not be overrated. In other words, no matter how technically proficient non-Japanese practitioners are becoming, they are not practicing complete (correct) kendo if they do not have an understanding of the highly nebulous spiritual and philosophical traits that are grounded in the ideals of bushido. Although he does not state so explicitly, Takeuchi infers that non-Japanese are at a distinct disadvantage when it comes to comprehending such quintessentially Japanese ideals.

Even though the link between kendo and bushido is tenuous in many respects, Takeuchi is not alone in stressing that the spirit of the samurai needs to be conveyed to the world, and that only through encouraging an understanding of this can meaningful cross-cultural interaction through kendo be achieved. The perceived connection between kendo and bushido is vitally important to the maintenance of Japanese domination over the art. Bushido is widely hailed as representing Japan's loftiest level of morality and ideals. Even if non-Japanese become technically adept in kendo, as many are, the Japanese are the sole guardians of the traditions of bushido.

Furthermore, as Harumi Befu reflects, "discourses are more likely to be successfully adopted if they possess a certain prestige or status, as is the case of norms associated with a powerful class or elite *in that society,* even though the ways of that group may be 'of another world entirely.'"[27] The culture of the samurai is the source of the spiritual mysticism that appeals to many Japanese and non-Japanese practitioners alike; the common contention is that it is owned by the Japanese and can only be imitated by foreigners.

To demonstrate this point, Abe Tetsushi, a respected Japanese scholar of kendo who has taught the art in Hungary for over two decades, relays that, when he practiced in a foreign country for the first time as a student, he "felt intensely the danger that if it was to continue spreading overseas this way, one day foreigners would change the essence of kendo."[28] Although he admits his first impressions were premature, he suggests that there are fundamental differences in the way that Westerners and Japanese approach the study of kendo. He contends that Europeans emphasize the body (*shintai*) in sports and budo, and pay less attention to the spiritual (*kokoro*) side. In other words, to Europeans, "technique" (*gijutsu*) means "body movement" (*shintai no ugoki*); whereas, to Japanese, technique is analogous to body movement combined with "mind movement" (*kokoro no ugoki*).

Abe also suggests that, due to the long spiritual history and evolution of these ideals, people born in the Japanese cultural sphere naturally understand the connection between mind and body as a part of their "genetic makeup." He poses the question, if the Western dualist view of mind and body that was identified by Descartes is applied to kendo, can it really be called Japanese kendo or Japanese culture, or is it merely copying Japanese culture in form only? He suggests that it is very difficult, if not impossible, to fully appreciate kendo from the typical Western Cartesian approach.

Abe's comments and ideas are far from radical. If anything, they typify general attitudes toward the issue in Japan. Solicitous Japanese kendoka feel compelled to demonstrate to the world a model for the sporting side of kendo, but, at the same time, they understand that it is important to enlighten non-Japanese as to the value of kendo as a part of Japanese culture. Such sentiment perfectly demonstrates the almost evangelistic tendencies of Japanese with regard to kendo's propagation overseas.

The improving technical level of world kendo has presented Japan with the possibility that it could someday lose its status as the unchallengable leader of kendo. This has been the case with other budo, such as karate and judo; for decades now, Japanese competitors are frequently defeated in international competitions.

Thus, the gradual improvement of non-Japanese kendo is seen as a threat, chipping away at Japan's hegemony over its own cultural capital. Perhaps in anticipation of the downside of promoting kendo too successfully—the double-edged sword of sharing it with the international community—the common opinion emanating from Japan, which has increased in intensity in recent years, is that while competition is one aspect of kendo, it would be mistaken to apply too much value to competitiveness. Growing in confidence over the years, foreign kendoka are starting to respond in kind with the rhetorical query, With all due respect, is Japan practicing what it preaches?

Sporting nationalism is often seen as an innocent expression of collective identity, but it can have a jingoistic psycho-cultural origin. Japanese team members are held in awe as veritable superstars by non-Japanese competitors who participate at the WKC. Even Korean players revere their Japanese opponents, although their determination to beat them knows no bounds. In the match arena, there is much at stake in terms of patriotic pride and cultural validity for the Japanese and the Koreans. Although preoccupation with winning at all costs runs counter to the kendo way, the match court for the finals of the WKC becomes the Supreme Court that will return a verdict on cultural proprietorship. The reality is that winning is everything at the international competitive level, in spite of the usual hyperbole that kendo is far more than tournament results.

International sporting competitions often arouse great excitement among the spectators and competitors, perhaps because they represent a form of mock battle against an imagined enemy. Michael Billig considers sport to be a facet of banal nationalism when he observed that "international matches seem so much more important than domestic ones: there is an extra thrill of competition, with something indefinable at stake."[29] Despite the importance placed on respecting one's opponent, exercising self-restraint, and fastidiously adhering to protocols of etiquette, international kendo competition is not immune to heated displays of patriotism. There have been several incidents at past WKC involving Japan and Korea in which decorum was brazenly disregarded. For example, at the seventh WKC in Seoul in 1988, soft drink cans were tossed onto the match area from above by disgusted spectators when the Koreans were defeated in the final by the Japanese team. The Japanese players and officials needed protection as they vacated the floor.

At the twelfth WKC, in Glasgow (2003), the Korean manager broke the manager's appeal flag in two out of frustration, and the Korean team was extremely tardy in lining up for the final mutual bow after having been beaten by the Japanese by one point in the final. These incidents may seem trivial compared to antics commonly witnessed in other international sports, but they are taken extremely seriously in kendo. They serve to reinforce Japanese conviction that too much internationalization diminishes the purity of kendo as a vehicle for self-cultivation and nurturing respect. To diminish shows of negative nationalistic emotion in kendo, the FIK decided to cease playing the national anthem and raising the flag of the winner, starting at the 2000 WKC in Santa Clara.

Table 8, which lists WKC medal winners, reveals one glitch—as far as the Japanese are concerned—in the history of the championships so far. Although it has not been uncommon for Japanese players to be beaten by their

TABLE 8 World Kendo Championships results, 1970–2012

Tournament number	Year	Location	Team placings
1	1970	Japan (Tokyo and Osaka)	1st Japan 2nd Chinese Taipei 3rd Brazil, Okinawa
2	1973	United States (Los Angeles and San Francisco)	1st Japan 2nd Canada 3rd USA, Hawaii
3	1976	United Kingdom (Milton Keynes)	1st Japan 2nd Canada 3rd USA, Chinese Taipei
4	1979	Japan (Sapporo)	1st Japan 2nd Korea 3rd USA, Hawaii
5	1982	Brazil (São Paulo)	1st Japan 2nd Brazil 3rd USA, Korea
6	1985	France (Paris)	1st Japan 2nd Brazil 3rd Korea, USA
7	1988	Korea (Seoul)	1st Japan 2nd Korea 3rd Canada, Brazil
8	1991	Canada (Toronto)	1st Japan 2nd Korea 3rd Chinese Taipei, Canada
9	1994	France (Paris)	1st Japan 2nd Korea 3rd Chinese Taipei, Canada
10	1997	Japan (Kyoto)	1st Japan 2nd Korea 3rd Brazil, Chinese Taipei
11	2000	United States (Santa Clara)	1st Japan 2nd Korea 3rd Canada, Brazil
12[a]	2003	United Kingdom (Glasgow)	1st Japan 2nd Korea 3rd USA, Italy
13	2006	Taiwan (Taipei)	1st Korea 2nd USA 3rd Chinese Taipei, Japan

(continued)

TABLE 8 *(continued)*

Tournament number	Year	Location	Team placings
14	2009	Brazil (São Paulo)	1st Japan 2nd USA 3rd Korea, Brazil
15	2012	Italy (Novara)	1st Japan 2nd Korea 3rd Hungary, USA

[a]The first official Women's Championships were held at this meet.

non-Japanese opponents in individual matches, a Japanese player has won the individual competition in every tournament so far, while the Japanese team has also invariably won the coveted men's team event, with one exception. At the thirteenth WKC, held in Taiwan in 2006, the unthinkable happened when Japan was defeated by a supremely confident American team in the semifinals, leading to a final between Korea and the United States. Korea subsequently won the WKC for the first time, although they would undoubtedly have preferred to triumph over Japan in the final as the icing on the cake.

Predictably, the reaction in Japan was one of shock, and the head coach (Kakehashi Masaharu) and captain (Seike Kōichi) officially expressed their apologies to Japan for the "loss of honor," taking the brunt of the responsibility on their own shoulders in the AJKF's monthly newsletter *Kensō* (February 2007). Having already left his post in the AJKF, Takeuchi Jun criticized the federation for forcing this public apology, saying that it was akin to a general making his soldiers apologize for losing a war.

Of course, upsets are not uncommon in the world of sports, or in Japan's domestic kendo competition circuit. Even in the history of sports in Japan, a comparable incident occurred 110 years before the thirteenth WKC, when students of the elite preparatory school in Tokyo, Ichikō, conclusively defeated an American team, the Yokohama Athletic Club, at a game of baseball (29–4) on May 23, 1896. As Guttmann observes, "the 'borrowers' had succeeded in humiliating the game's 'owners,' in a moment of 'sweet satisfaction' in the history of Japanese sports."[30] My comments regarding Japan's defeat in Taiwan were reported in the *Asahi Newspaper* (December 13, 2006): "At least now we can really call the tournament a World Championship." However, it was more than a simple loss in a competition. As the "game's owner," Japan's defeat was a matter of wounded national pride, and it was an epochal moment in kendo's history. Even Japanese kendo authorities reluctantly conceded that, at least technically, non-Japanese kendo practitioners have come a long way.

In a 2003 report titled *About the Future Promotion of International Cultural Exchange,* Japan's Agency for Cultural Affairs acknowledged the necessity to reconsider the belief that the Japanese are the only conveyors of Japanese culture. This seems at odds with the prevailing reluctance to fully accept non-Japanese aptitude in Japanese cultural pursuits. The report was formulated as a result of concerns that young Japanese were neglecting their own traditions, which are recognized even by non-Japanese as being an intimate part of Japan's spiritual and cultural essence. Pointing out that non-Japanese are able to appreciate, and even convey, Japanese culture is intended to encourage Japanese people to reevaluate their own culture and nurture a sense of pride in its values. Nevertheless, the mere fact that the following statement appears in the report is suggestive of the general attitude that non-Japanese are usually not recognized as conveyers of traditional Japanese culture.

> We should assume a posture that culture incubated in Japan is the shared property of people in the wider world. This goes for the tea ceremony, flower arranging and other everyday elements of Japanese culture as well as for judo, karate, aikido and other martial arts, all of which enjoy a large number of admirers and practitioners throughout the world.... It will be necessary to create an environment in which all people who cross Japan's borders to participate in cultural activities are considered to be the bearers of Japanese culture irrespective of their nationality.[31]

The reality is, however, that non-Japanese who excel in a traditional Japanese art are often seen as an anomaly at best, or a potential threat at worst. McVeigh observes that non-Japanese who perform traditional Japanese arts, such as writing haiku or practicing martial arts, are often perceived as being "'out of place,' having transgressed (or trespassed, as the case might be) a highly symbolic, almost sacred, boundary between Japaneseness and non-Japaneseness."[32]

The merits and demerits of the international spread of budo were listed in a 1983 report by the Japanese Budo Association. One of the benefits, according to the report's authors, is that budo can promote mutual understanding and accord between countries. On the other hand, a move away from the traditional spirit of budo, as demonstrated by its commercialization for profit overseas, was slated as an example of the downside of internationalization. In a sense, this protectionist attitude could be considered a manifestation of cultural elitism. Although the stated goal of promoters of Japanese culture is to contribute to "world peace" and facilitate mutual understanding, the reality is that culturally impassable barriers colored by notions of 'Japanese uniqueness' are often placed between Japan and the rest of the world.

Borrowers of any sport are apt to develop their own style to suit their own cultural milieu. Japanese baseball is a case in point. Contrary to the rules of Major League Baseball, tie games are allowed in Japan, a smaller baseball is used, and the strike zone is generally narrower. Also, beginning in its early days, Japanese baseball adopted and has retained many of the traits of budo, with emphasis placed on rigorous drilling in the fundamentals to build physical and mental stamina. Strict adherence to etiquette is also maintained, with players bowing as they enter and leave the grounds, pitchers tipping their caps to show respect, and no harm intended to any batter who gets clobbered by a dead ball. In Japan, baseball is sometimes even referred to as *yakyūdō,* or "the way of baseball."

Similarly, the rules and traditional modus operandi of judo and karate were transformed in their practice abroad and the all-important "budo spirit" was perceived to be attenuated. Witnessing this, authorities have become obsessed with preserving kendo's technical and spiritual veracity and conveying it "correctly." This has resulted in a reluctance to promote competition-oriented kendo overseas, with more emphasis placed on teaching its cultural and ascetic properties through fundamental rather than advanced technical skills.

Nevertheless, Kashiwazaki Katsuhiko and his colleagues argue that, as the number of FIK affiliates increases and more tournaments are conducted overseas, the concept of kendo as an ascetic practice for character development is becoming diluted. Competitive kendo has become the focus, and emphasis is placed on the doctrine that winning is everything. The concept of *ippon* (one point) and how it is interpreted, the standards for the way *yūkō-datotsu* (a valid strike) is judged, the shared understanding and interpretation of terminology, the deportment of players in tournaments, and the manners of spectators, are all serious problems in need of deliberation in order for the Japanese cultural properties that underlie the qualities of kendo to be correctly conveyed internationally.[33]

Obsession with the term *tadashii* ("correct") is a distinguishing feature of kendo literature. In Japan, "correct kendo" refers to technically and aesthetically orthodox kendo with a focus on education in accordance with the principles of the sword, which does not deteriorate into deceitful techniques and strategies for winning matches, as seen in Western sports. "Correct kendo" is, in essence, the upholding of Japaneseness, and arguably it contains the insinuation that, generally, only Japanese can gain an understanding of the true spirit of kendo. Foreigners may become technically proficient, but the heart of kendo is, by implication, a mystical Japanese cultural realm that can be accessed only by Japanese and a minuscule group of select non-Japanese. The latter are lauded for their profound knowledge of Japanese culture and typically have a high degree of fluency in the language. They have to be regarded as "more Japanese than the Japanese" to qualify.

A major problem with this preconception is that a large proportion of Japanese practitioners also demonstrate a propensity to stray from correct kendo for the sake of gaining glory through competition. Ōtsuka Tadayoshi pointed out the inherent dichotomy of what he called "strong kendo" (in which practitioners are technically adept and skilled at winning matches) vis-à-vis officially sanctioned "correct kendo."[34] According to Ōtsuka, "strong kendo" wins matches by whatever means possible, often testing the rules to the limit; whereas "correct kendo," conducted in the spirit of fair play, is scrupulous and stringently adheres to the rules and fundamental protocols, without concern for results. Kendoists in all countries demonstrate a proclivity to perform "strong kendo" in competitions but "correct kendo" in promotion examinations. Being strong through correctness is what kendo practitioners are urged to aspire to, but reality dictates that the majority are caught somewhere between the two extremes, depending on the situation.

Some authorities suggest that the quandary of sport kendo versus correct kendo can only be reconciled by popularizing two types of kendo. The first type would be pure Japanese *kendō* (signified by being written in kanji glyphs), which would uphold the authentic Japanese way based on the principles of the sword. The other would be KENDO—an anglicized word—representing a mixture of Japanese and Western ideals, in which the sporting aspects would be encouraged and Olympic inclusion would be aimed for. The anglicized version would indicate a style of kendo bereft of the finer nuances of tradition contained in the kanji version. This idea is taken from a similar debate regarding traditional judo versus the overtly competitive Olympic judo (*jūdō* compared with JUDO). Many observers lament that even Japanese are showing a tendency to view kendo as a Japanese sport rather than a budo discipline. According to the Japanese Academy of Budo's *Kendō wo shiru jiten* (Encyclopedia of kendo), "If traditional Japanese culture and spirituality (*seishin-sei*) can no longer be evoked in *kendō,* it may just end up as KENDO."[35]

To avoid degeneration and protect the cultural integrity of kendo (that is to say, its Japaneseness), kendo experts in Japan assert that kendo should be propagated as an embodiment of Japanese culture rather than as a competitive sport; otherwise it is not genuine kendo. However, a major cultural barrier for non-Japanese practitioners is their supposed inability to understand the most important aspect of kendo: the complicated process and finer cultural nuances of scoring a valid strike or thrust (*yūkō-datotsu*). According to Abe, because Westerners do not "feel" the *yūkō-datotsu* but need to "rationalize" its components, it is virtually impossible for them to gain a full appreciation of the cultural value of kendo. Therefore, Abe contends, the internationalization of kendo must "focus on 'Japanizing' [*Nihonka*] how foreigners 'feel' kendo."[36]

The common perception in Japan is that it is easier for Westerners to understand kendo as a competitive sport than as Japanese culture. This means, according to Abe's analysis, that by and large Westerners only superficially comprehend kendo as a sport, thereby misunderstanding kendo's deeper essence. The problem he identifies is that people who possess only a shallow understanding of kendo become leaders of local and regional federations and wield a disproportionate amount of influence in the way kendo is governed internationally. Each affiliate in the FIK is theoretically on even footing, so Japan, with over one million members potentially has no more voting power than a country with one hundred members.

The risk to kendo if Japanese hegemony is compromised by a more egalitarian approach to international administration is described by Tanaka Mamoru as a conflict between "*tatami* logic" versus "table logic." The former refers to the traditional Japanese hierarchical way of learning and running organizations by adhering to the teachings and guidance of seniors and teachers. The latter is the Western practice of deciding matters in an open democratic forum. Wary of how rules and conventions in judo have been progressively altered by non-Japanese influence to the sport's ultimate cultural detriment, Tanaka advocates that Japanese step back and reassert the absolute value of the *ippon* (or *yūkō-datotsu*), and promote "educational" kendo over "sports" kendo. To achieve this, "it is vital that '*tatami* logic' controls the 'table' so that budo for the sake of education, based on correct technical principles, can be maintained."[37]

The Japanese government's and the AJKF's cultural policies aimed at controlling the diffusion of kendo culture demonstrate overlapping nationalistic tendencies in the discipline's domestic and international dissemination. According to McVeigh, state cultural policy endorses a proprietary theory of nationalism. So-called proprietary nationalism is the perception that a certain group of people owns certain cultural capital. "The Japanese people, by virtue of being Japanese, own certain items of material culture, artistic expressions, language, and religions. Arguably, such a notion of proprietorship is a form of political mysticism, permitted by a conflation of two different definitions of culture: 'culture as art appreciated by anybody' and 'culture as an exclusive to one group.' "[38]

Kendo is often promoted as a form of culture that can benefit all the people of the world. Nevertheless, many benefactors of kendo strongly desire to preserve it as the exclusive property of the Japanese. Thus, it could be said that the internationalization of kendo actually fuels its nationalization. A cynic may quote Ivan Hall on the matter, as he states that this kind of internationalization "is indeed more a device for continued anxious self-protection than for a fresh outward engagement with the rest of the world."[39]

However, it is important to mention that there are those in Japan, albeit a minority, who see internationalization in a more positive light. They look at it as a way of countering what they decry as dictatorial and contradictory measures enforced by kendo's governing bodies to control the destiny of the discipline in Japan. The late Ōtsuka Tadayoshi, a notable nonconformist in this sense, advocated changing kendo's rules and conventions because of the ambiguous way it is promoted simultaneously as a sport and something greater than a mere sport. He believed that kendo had become a cultural artifact that had not been allowed to keep up with the times. He was not against tradition, but he thought that culture should be constantly revised and that kendo had relied too much on traditional authority, to the detriment of its rational development. In "A Proposal for New Regulations and Organisational Reform in Kendo," he wrote, "Now is the time where modern *kenshi* throughout the world should become the leaders, and become involved in the reformation of kendo."[40]

Japanese kendo authorities were behind the creation of the International Kendo Federation in 1970, and they have continued to demonstrate a paternalistic preoccupation with controlling the way kendo is taught and disseminated overseas. Furthermore, with the growing popularity of kendo and the rising level of technical proficiency seen in other countries, attention has been focused on ensuring the propagation of "correct" kendo. This, it is widely assumed, can be emulated by non-Japanese but never fully comprehended without a deep understanding of Japanese culture and social norms. Thus, even if Japan is occasionally superseded in the competitive arena, the essence of kendo would remain with the Japanese.

There are inconsistencies in the efforts made to internationalize kendo that are difficult to reconcile. Abe Tetsushi's observations epitomize the prevailing patriarchal attitude of Japanese kendoists: "We Japanese should not criticize people doing kendo overseas [for their lack of understanding], but it behooves us to provide a guide so that they do not get mistaken ideas of what kendo is, and are able to gain even a small understanding of kendo's essence."[41]

There are many contradictions in this seemingly placid but culturally nationalistic outlook. Japanese kendoists want to share their culture and genuinely feel that kendo can serve as a vehicle for self-development for all people, but the authoritarian insistence on regulating kendo betrays their paranoid fear of losing control of their own culture. Although grudgingly aware that kendo is being adapted to suit different cultural milieus in foreign countries, many Japanese take solace in the idea that true, "correct" kendo, based on centuries of historical development, can only ever be the cultural domain of Japan. This explains the rationale and the doggedness displayed for promoting kendo overseas as "culture" rather than as a "sport."

Outside influences are unquestionably powerful forces that are further nationalizing Japanese resolve to safeguard kendo as hallowed culture. In this sense, the internationalization of kendo is inextricably linked with its nationalization. In the final analysis, as many kendo experts in Japan admit, the international propagation of kendo does at least have a silver lining in that it provides Japanese with a strong incentive to reflect on the state of the art in Japan.

EPILOGUE

Samurai culture still evokes mostly positive images for Japanese, representing an ideal that embodies strength, stoic resolve, loyalty, valor, honor, and compassion. Shelves in Japanese bookshops are packed with all manner of books seeking to right the social, economic, or cultural woes of contemporary Japan using the tenets of bushido. Following the Tōhoku earthquake and tsunami of 2011, pundits in Japan and around the world applauded the calm demeanor, selflessness, and forbearance shown by the victims of the tragedy. Their remarkable carriage in the face of such adversity was acclaimed as epitomizing the "spirit of bushido." Similarly, any Japanese male who performs well in the international arena of sport—or any other field of note—is proudly referred to as a "samurai."

Likewise, appraisals of traditional budo—the physical embodiment of bushido—are almost always favorable, and the budo arts have a massive following in Japan and around the world. Just as Italian provides the common terminology for music, and English is the language of many sports, Japanese dominates the parlance of martial arts. Budo can surely be regarded as Japan's most successful cultural export. It is studied in earnest by tens of millions of enthusiasts in every country and region of the globe. Although a minority budo compared to the phenomenal international popularity of karate and judo, kendo is considered by many in Japan to represent the closest connection to the "soul of the samurai" and hence the inimitable "Japanese spirit."

My motivation for writing this book was not to pass judgment on whether such notions are true or not, but rather to help readers understand how they have come to be so widely accepted. My discourse is an analysis of the historical evolution of Japanese swordsmanship, its "bushido-esque" elements, and its association with perceptions of Japanese cultural identity. Kendo in its current form is the result of an ongoing process of "invented tradition" that began many centuries before the modern era.

Scholars these days would chide me for stating the obvious. After all, isn't all tradition invented? I absolutely concur. There is nothing extraordinary about the claim that kendo is invented tradition. However, my incentive was not to establish the validity of this argument. Rather, it was to peel away the various cultural and historical layers of Japanese swordsmanship to determine the mechanisms and forces that allowed it to survive and thrive through so many epochal events and in different political and cultural milieus, ending up as a pertinent and richly symbolic mind-body pursuit in the twenty-first century.

In his afterword to *Mirror of Modernity: Invented Traditions of Modern Japan,* Dipesh Chakrabarty submits that there are two ways of viewing tradition: "nostalgic" and "epiphanic." The former view is "located in an experience of loss and calls for a politics of recovery and recuperation, and for political agency adequate to that task." The epiphanic view, on the other hand, sees tradition as something that has always existed but has remained hidden from view "except to a poetic, now realist gaze, as some vision of eternity itself."[1] As a final note to this seminal work, Chakrabarty recommends that future discourse take into consideration the following questions: "What is the history of the embedded subject? . . . How does it connect to the history of state formation? . . . What are the moments where one history exceeds the other?"[2] I hope that my book successfully explores these judicious reflections, as they were at the forefront of my mind as I was writing it.

I started by looking at the "history of the embedded subject" and reassessing the practical usage of the sword and its place in medieval warrior culture. Although effective in close-quarter skirmishes and for self-protection in the course of daily life, swords were secondary weapons on medieval battlefields, employed mainly for the gruesome task of removing heads from fallen foes to be used as trophies.

In spite of the sword's auxiliary role in the samurai's armament, arcane martial art schools of swordsmanship materialized around the fifteenth century and had a profound effect on the development of Japan's martial culture. Progenitors of the prototypical *ryūha* aestheticized and systemized techniques of combat and combined them with occult teachings. They conveyed their artistry to disciples through kata, in a format similar to other artistic and theatrical pursuits, such as Noh. The art of the sword was derived from battlefield training, and, although the modus operandi for martial artistry and soldiery was different, there was a measure of overlap in the psychological posture required; both strived toward achieving transcendence over concerns of life and death.

Practical applications aside, given that the sword has featured in Japan's ancient mythology and is even included as one of the three sacred treasures that make up the imperial regalia, the religio-symbolic importance that has been attached to the weapon since antiquity is indisputable. From the earliest days of Japan, the sword was emblematic of political legitimacy, strength, righteousness, and morality and was viewed as an object of intense spiritual power and beauty.

Considered in this light, and bearing in mind that greater reverence is afforded to the aesthetic exquisiteness of the sword than to any other weapon, it is hardly surprising that the sword was perceived as representing purity and was believed to be able to exorcise evil in one swift stroke. Thus, the sword is eulogized as characterizing the very "soul" of the samurai—and by modern extension, the Japanese people.

The samurai fetish for swords gained prominence during the Great Peace of the Tokugawa era. With no more wars to fight, warriors were denied opportunities to demonstrate heroism. However, irrespective of the peace, samurai were required to maintain military readiness in accordance with their occupational status. Martial schools specialized and multiplied as the memory of war faded. *Kenjutsu* was one of the arts that made up the so-called *bugei-jūhappan*—or eighteen military skills—that warriors, depending on rank, were required to learn, including archery (*kyūjutsu*), horsemanship (*bajutsu*), grappling arts (*jūjutsu*), gunmanship (*hōjutsu*), and spearmanship (*sōjutsu*). Specialist *kenjutsu* schools, however, far outnumbered those of other modes of combat art, with as many as seven hundred *ryūha* in existence by the nineteenth century.

With the "taming" of the warrior class, the martial arts went through a "civilizing process," evolving into "ways" to train body and mind through regimes of ascetic training. Asceticism had always been a feature of *ryūha*, but the era of peace drove a shift toward more pacific objectives, and training became a means of reaching a heightened state of spiritual awareness. Far removed from the reality of war, the flamboyant kata of the schools of Tokugawa *kenjutsu* were panned for being impractical. By the eighteenth century, *kenjutsu* was sardonically referred to as *kahō-kenpō*, or "flowery swordsmanship," due to the spread of kata forms that had never been tested in combat, underpinned by exceedingly esoteric doctrines.

To address the decline in the practicality and perceived value of *kenjutsu,* a full-contact sparring method using bamboo swords and protective equipment was implemented by some schools. Warriors could fence with each other in bouts without fear of being injured or injuring their partner. This progressive style of *kenjutsu* was the forerunner to the modern sport of kendo, and the equipment developed then has remained nearly unchanged. Swordsmanship became a competitive, yet spiritual, sport and flourished in the various provincial domains as well as in the metropolis of Edo (present-day Tokyo), where commercial martial art academies opened their doors to samurai and commoners alike. Talented fencers could hope for employment as instructors in private fencing academies or domain schools, and the best became celebrities in Tokugawa society.

The academies also became meeting places where warriors from different domains could assemble and discuss politics. This became more pronounced in the mid-nineteenth century, when the so-called men of high purpose traveled the country engaging in fencing bouts as they networked with like-minded activists to hatch antigovernment plots. It was they who provided the driving force for massive social and political change in Japan. This is where we start to see how kendo connects with the history of state formation.

In the second half of the nineteenth century, Japan realized it needed guns, cannons, and a new conscript army if it was to compete with the rest of the world. The era abounded with catch phrases such as *wakon-yōsai* (Japanese spirit, Western technology) and *fukoku-kyōhei* (rich nation, strong army) as the authorities strove to indoctrinate the masses with a national identity, arm the nation, and match the civil society and colonial power of the West.

Kenjutsu temporarily fell into obscurity after the 1868 restoration of imperial governance because of its supposed lack of practical application in the modern theater of war. Nevertheless, it was revived before long, with its objectives refocused to suit Japan's forward-looking ambitions. Never completely suppressed, the images of the heroic Japanese warrior and swordsmanship had simply lain dormant, waiting for an opportunity to burgeon in Japan's rapidly modernizing society.

Interest in *kenjutsu* among the general public was piqued by Sakakibara Kenkichi's pay-to-see exhibitions. The Popular Rights Movement also provided an opportunity for more commoners to experience the thrill of the fight, and the police and newly formed armed forces prescribed *kenjutsu* training to keep their men sharp.

Kenjutsu reached a major milestone in its nationalization in 1913, at the end of the Meiji period, when it was adopted into the school curriculum. A central player in this transformation was the Dai-Nippon Butokukai. Its formation in 1895 coincided with a significant rise in nationalistic sentiment after Japan's victory in the Sino-Japanese war of 1894–95. Ideals of the martial spirit (*shōbu*) and patriotism peaked, and revamped notions of Japan's glorious samurai history and culture were popularized and credited as being behind the phenomenal successes Japan was enjoying.

Kenjutsu and other martial arts struck an increasingly emotional chord with advocates of popular nationalism, gaining particular momentum in the Taishō period (1912–26). As a result of Western influence, physical education became an integral part of the education system, and sports became all the rage. Kendo was more widely practiced, especially by students who enjoyed the thrill of competing.

In the militaristic 1930s and 1940s, however, the culture of swordsmanship was exploited by the state as a medium for inculcating Japanese youth with nationalistic fervor. Kendo education became increasingly combative, as nationalistic educational policies took precedence. Because of their association with ultranationalism and militarism, kendo and the other martial arts were subjected to a blanket ban following Japan's defeat in the Second World War.

The Ministry of Education and the newly created All Japan Kendo Federation worked in tandem in the postwar period to rehabilitate kendo's image, exorcising it of its undesirable militaristic elements and bringing it back to mainstream culture as a "modern democratic sport." In the early 1950s, it was accepted as a form of physical education. Match and refereeing procedures were rewritten, and the number of practitioners grew steadily as kendo was incrementally reestablished in schools and the community.

Following the 1964 Olympic Games in Tokyo, in which judo debuted as an official event, the popularity of kendo reached new heights. Tournaments became more frequent and competitive, and practitioners began to focus on learning tricks to win matches. This "victory at all costs" mentality flew in the face of "correct kendo." In 1975, the AJKF formulated two official statements—the "Concept of Kendo" and the "Purpose of Practicing Kendo"—to reaffirm the inherent holistic values of kendo and promote them as an integral part of Japanese culture. The resulting definition of kendo as a vehicle for personal cultivation, which could be achieved by observing the "principles of the sword," was designed to revitalize kendo's waning spirituality. It was also intended to assert kendo's uniqueness and, by implication, its superiority to Western sports. This remains the guiding principle for kendo today.

Thus, to address the last consideration suggested by Chakrabarty—the moments where one history exceeds the other—my investigation established how swordsmanship endured as a mainstay of samurai education during the Tokugawa period and how it was advanced as a vehicle for statist and popular nationalism from the Meiji period through the 1940s. I showed how kendo became a symbolic and discursive medium representing a cultural ethos of "Japaneseness" in the prewar days and an icon of national identity in the cultural nationalism of the postwar period. Kendo is perceived as one of the most representative forms of traditional Japanese culture, and I examined Japan's current predicament as it uneasily faces the possibility of losing its status as the sovereign nation of kendo—that is to say, the exclusive owner and conductor of kendo culture.

The government continues to play an important role in the propagation of kendo ideals by prescribing educational objectives. As of 2012, all Japanese children in their first and second year of junior high school are required to learn budo in PE. This "physical education," however, is meant not only to strengthen bodies but also to inculcate modes of traditional conduct in pupils.

To quote Chakrabarty again, "The past is embodied through a long process of training the senses." It is the culmination of a "long and heterogeneous history of the cultural training of the senses, of making connections with our glands and muscles and neuronal networks."[3] As an extension of this idea, and as a final consideration, I am reminded of a rather tenuous genre of popular theories and discussions about Japanese "uniqueness" called Nihonjinron. Befu maintains that the ideology behind Nihonjinron not only describes the constructed Japanese worldview but also "prescribes what is normatively right and therefore how one should conduct oneself."[4] This serves a dual purpose of propagating the idea of "Japaneseness" in Japan and satisfying the need for Japanese to define themselves and their culture vis-à-vis the rest of the world. And, of course, it helps convince the rest of the world that Japan is indeed unique. Does the fact that kendo has been groomed for this role over the last century make it analogous to a kind of "psychosomatic Nihonjinron"?

I often find myself wondering where exactly I, a longtime expat New Zealander in Japan, fit into this scheme. I am not Japanese, but I have been a committed practitioner and promoter of kendo for nearly thirty years. This culture is surely more a part of me than it is a part of a Japanese person who may have picked up a *shinai* a few times in PE class. I would think my glands and muscles and neuronal networks are completely imbued with the essence of kendo by now!

I asked an elderly Japanese kendoka—*hanshi* 8-dan Inoue Yoshihiko, whom I consider to be one of the greatest, most inspirational kendo masters of the postwar era—"What *is* 'correct' kendo, and to whom does it really belong?" He replied, "Kendo is universal wisdom that teaches us the supreme value of life through knowing the techniques of death. Kendo is always 'correct.' There is no such thing as incorrect kendo, just incorrect practitioners. It has always been that way from time immemorial. It isn't a matter of race, age, gender, or class. It's just a matter of intent." This reaffirmed to me that it is the universality of a tradition rather than its uniqueness that makes it truly valuable to the human experience.

Writing this book was a convoluted way of getting my own thoughts in order—reassessing why I had embarked on this kendo journey in the first place and why I persist in trekking down this intangible, eternal path to self-perfection. It has been a sublimely therapeutic exercise, and it has also alerted me to many other aspects of kendo—and budo in general—that could feed the intellectual appetites of scholars in many different fields. Apart from giving me peace of mind as I take stock of my own kendo experiences, I hope that, if anything, this book inspires more researchers to dig into the rich annals of budo culture. There is so much waiting to be found.

NOTES

INTRODUCTION

1. This definition of kendo was prepared for a pamphlet distributed at the first SportAccord Combat Games, held in Beijing in 2010.

2. The nine federations are the All Japan Judo Federation, All Japan Kendo Federation, All Nippon Kyudo Federation, Japan Sumo Federation, Japan Karatedo Federation, Aikikai Foundation, Shorinji Kempo Federation, All Japan Naginata Federation, and All Japan Jukendo Federation.

3. *Daily Yomiuri,* August 3, 2012.

4. The "Philosophy of Budo" was established October 10, 2008, by the Japanese Budo Association and is available on the Nippon Budokan's website, at www .nipponbudokan.or.jp/shinkoujigyou/rinen_eng.html.

5. Louka and Cook, "Memories of the Great Masters," 28.

6. Koizumi, "Judo and the Olympic Games," 7.

7. Bennett, *Budo,* 210.

8. Ibid., 214.

9. Yamada, "Myth of Zen," 1–30.

10. Befu, *Anthropological Introduction,* 50.

11. Chamberlain, *Invention of a New Religion,* 6.

12. Levinger and Lytle, "Myth and Mobilisation," 175–94.

13. McVeigh, *Nationalisms of Japan,* 201.

1. THE ART OF KILLING

1. For example, see Asakawa, *Documents of Iriki.*

2. Sansom, *History of Japan,* 234.

3. Farris, *Heavenly Warriors,* 367.

4. Friday, *Samurai,* 8.

5. Ibid., 44.

6. Motoki, *Bushi no seiritsu*, 1.

7. The term *bushidō* first appeared in *Kōyō-gunkan*. This treatise, which concerns the life and times of Takeda Shingen and his son Katsuyori and the eventual demise of the Takeda house, is a treasure trove of information about the Sengoku warrior ethos.

8. See Watsuji, *Kenshin no dōtoku to sono dentō*.

9. Friday, *Samurai*, 112.

10. Ikegami, *Taming of the Samurai*, 139.

11. Shimokawa, *Kendō no hattatsu*, 96.

12. Suzuki, *Katana to kubi-tori*, 80.

13. Imamura, "Budōshi gaisetsu," 8–10; Tominaga, *Kendō gohyakunen-shi*, 47–53; Nakabayashi, "Kendō shi," 38–39; Hurst, *Armed Martial Arts of Japan*, 38–41.

14. Suzuki, *Teppō to nihonjin*, 163–83.

15. Suzuki, *Katana to kubi-tori*, 96.

16. For a detailed analysis of the historical religious significance of swords in Japan, refer to Sakai, *Ideology of the Sword*.

17. It is worth mentioning that the custom of rewarding a meritorious deed with a sword remained a common practice in the Tokugawa period. Nothing was valued more than a sword with the signature of the shogun engraved on the tang. Also, a subordinate could present his superior with a fine sword in order to gain his ear. In sum, swords were a coveted form of currency in warrior circles.

18. Friday, "Off the Warpath," 255.

19. Kakei, *Chūsei buke-kakun no kenkyū*, 32.

20. Yoshida, *Buke no kakun*, 83.

21. Ibid., 52.

22. Ibid., 60.

23. Ibid., 48. *Mato* was mounted archery shooting at fixed targets. In *kasagake*, mounted archers galloped down a causeway while releasing hollow whistling *kaburaya* arrows at suspended sedge targets or hats. *Inu ou mono* was a pitiless training method in which a large circular area was roped off with a smaller circle inside. Warriors galloped around the outer ring on their horses and fired their arrows at moving targets—hapless dogs placed in the inner circle.

24. Anshin, *Warrior Culture of Japan*, 43.

25. Friday, "Off the Warpath," 256.

26. Futaki, *Kassen no butai-ura*, 94.

27. McCullough, *Tale of the Heike*, 153.

28. *Yabusame* is still popular as a tourist experience in Kyoto and Kamakura. It involves a mounted archer who releases arrows at three stationary targets or boards while riding a straight course at a full gallop.

29. Friday, "Off the Warpath," 256.

30. Sasamori, *Ittō-ryū gokui*, 632.

31. Friday, *Legacies of the Sword*, 59.

32. Geertz, *Interpretation of Cultures*, 90.

33. Haskel, *Sword of Zen*, 27.

34. The Kashima Shrine is situated in Ibaraki Prefecture, and the deity worshipped there is Takemikazuchi-no-Mikoto, who is believed to have descended from heaven to the Japanese islands with Futsunushi-no-Kami, the resident deity of the Katori Shrine in Chiba Prefecture. According to Shinto mythology, the *kami* arrived ahead of Ninigi-no-Mikoto (grandson of the sun goddess Amaterasu Ōmikami) to orchestrate the transfer of the Japanese islands to descendants of Amaterasu Ōmikami. According to legend, Ninigi's great grandson, Jinmu, founded the current ruling imperial dynasty in the year 660 BCE. Both Takemikazuchi-no-Mikoto and Futsunushi-no-Kami are traditionally connected with military prowess, and for many centuries, warriors visited their shrines to pray for protection and inspiration. The shrines are associated with rich warrior traditions, and modern martial artists still visit them to buy amulets. See Sakai, *History of Kendo*, 123.

35. Ōtake, *Katori Shintō-ryū*, 11.

36. Hinatsu, *Honchō bugei shōden*, 40.

37. It is unclear if Kamiizumi was actually one of Ikō's students; it is more likely that he studied under Ikō's son Koshichirō instead. Kamiizumi was approximately ten years older than Koshichirō. Based on the overlap of techniques, it has also been suggested that Kamiizumi was a student of Tsukahara Bokuden and studied Shintō-ryū, and that he may also have learned the techniques of the Nen-ryū. See Uozumi, "Nihon no budō bunka no seiritsu kiban," 107–44.

38. Kamiizumi Ise-no-Kami Hidetsuna is the name found in documents until 1565. In 1566, Hidetsuna is changed to Nobutsuna. Then, in 1569, Kamiizumi took the title Musashi-no-Kami and was henceforth officially known as Kamiizumi Musashi-no-Kami Nobutsuna.

39. Hinatsu, *Honchō bugei shōden*, 61.

40. Ibid.

41. Ibid., 45.

42. Ibid.

43. Ibid., 54.

44. Friday, "Off the Warpath," 256.

45. Rubinger, *Private Academies*, 176.

2. THE ART OF LIVING

1. Ikegami, *Taming of the Samurai*, 31.

2. Elias and Dunning, *Quest for Excitement*, 21.

3. Rogers, *Military Profession*, 13.

4. Fujiki, *Katana-gari*, 147.

5. Howell, "Social Life of Firearms," 65–80.

6. Tominaga, *Kendō gohyakunen-shi*, 163.

7. Haskel, *Sword of Zen*, 1.

8. Ibid., 14.

9. Some historians, especially former students of the preeminent martial art scholar Watanabe Ichirō of the Tokyo University of Education (now University of Tsukuba), refer to the concept of the life-giving sword as *katsunin-ken*. However, the standard reading is *katsujin-ken*.

10. Twenty-two kata are explained in the text, with an additional eight kata referred to as "sure victory" techniques and listed in name only. Munenori also explains the school's "supreme maneuvers," culminating in the highest teaching of *shinmyōken* (divine sword), so called because it aims to subdue the enemy without actually cutting him down. There is also a description of twenty-seven *kiriai* fighting positions, divided into the three categories of *jo, ha,* and *kyū.* These are practiced with a real sword rather than bamboo or wooden practice swords.

11. Yagyū, *Heihō-kadensho,* 101.

12. Ibid., 100.

13. There are a number of different English translations of *Gorin-no-sho* available, of varying reliability. The most widely read is Victor Harris's *A Book of Five Rings* (London: Allison and Busby, 1974). A recent and very reliable version, *The Five Rings: Miyamoto Musashi's Art of Strategy,* was published by David Groff in 2012 (London: Watkins).

14. Miyamoto Musashi, *Book of Five Rings,* 33.

15. Ibid., 32.

16. Friday, "Off the Warpath," 256.

17. Niwa, *Tengu geijutsu-ron,* 313.

18. In the early years of the Tokugawa period there were increasing instances of samurai following their lords in death by committing ritual suicide, either out of a sense of obligation or because it would be seen as cowardly not to. This practice was known as *oibara* or *junshi,* but it was outlawed by the shogunate in 1663. Enforcement of the ban became more stringent toward the end of the seventeenth century.

19. Suzuki, *Zen and Japanese Culture,* 172.

20. Elias, *Civilizing Process,* 375.

21. See Tōdō, *Bu no kanji bun no kanji,* or Sakai, *History of Kendo.*

22. Elias and Dunning, *Quest for Excitement,* 28.

23. This is a precursor to the management of modern budo federations, which earn a substantial proportion of their operational income from promotion examinations. Classical martial art groups today are hardly considered lucrative businesses, but they sometimes demand exorbitant fees from students, especially when conferring licences of proficiency.

24. Rubinger, *Private Academies,* 178.

25. Imamura, *Jūkyū-seiki ni okeru Nihon no taiiku-shi,* 340–343. Imamura made his study by comparing six different historical martial art chronicles published between 1716 and 1812. It was a complicated task. In a number of instances, a single *ryūha* could be known by different names, and, to add to the confusion, different *ryūha* may have used the same name. Therefore, the data he gathered represents an approximation of actual figures. Furthermore, his figures do not include myriad smaller or provincial *ryūha* that were overlooked by the original authors of the works examined.

26. Rogers, *Military Profession*, 155.

27. Ibid., 150.

28. Elias and Dunning, *Quest for Excitement*, 50.

29. Sasamori, *Ittō-ryū gokui*, 635.

30. Ibid., 638.

31. Anshin, *Warrior Culture of Japan*, 99.

32. Many domain schools were established around the end of the eighteenth century, but this varied considerably between the different domains. Compared to commercial private dojos, domain schools were more concerned with education and taught their students to balance the literary and martial arts. See Nakabayashi, *Budō no susume*, 77, and Ōta, "Bakumatsu ni okeru bujutsu-ba no yōso ni kansuru kenkyū," 3.

33. Rogers, *Military Profession*, 165.

34. Nagai, *Kenjutsu shugyō no tabi nikki*, 45–66.

35. Jansen, *Sakamoto Ryoma*, 81.

36. Yamamoto, *Saitama bugei-chō*, 86–92.

37. Elias and Dunning, *Quest for Excitement*, 138.

38. Ibid., 21.

39. Nagai, *Kenjutsu shugyō no tabi nikki*, 44.

40. Jansen, *Sakamoto Ryoma*, 81.

3. THE FALL AND RISE OF SAMURAI CULTURE

Epigraph: Shimoda, *Lost and Found*, 75.

1. McClatchie, "Sword of Japan," 55.

2. Hobsbawm and Ranger, *Invention of Tradition*, 1.

3. Although classical Japanese swordsmanship is generally referred to as *kenjutsu*, other terms were also widely used. *Gekiken* or *gekken* was coined in the mid-Tokugawa period and referred to fencing with *shinai* and protective armor. Depending on the context, *kenjutsu* had that meaning as well, but it also was used to refer to the kata-only schools. The term *kendō*, although not completely unheard of in the Tokugawa period, did not come into common use until the Taishō era. Thus, although *gekiken* was the prevalent term during the historical period covered in this chapter, the documents quoted jump from one appellation to another. In 1919, Nishikubo Hiromichi changed the suffix from *-jutsu* to *-dō* in the martial arts to accentuate the educational qualities of the martial arts as a "way" of life (*dō*) rather than a quest for technical proficiency. Nishikubo was not the only educator to adopt this viewpoint, and a similar stance was taken by others to emphasize mental discipline in rival schools, such as the Tokyo Higher Normal School, which changed the name of its fencing club from *gekiken* to *kendō*. I believe that Kanō Jigorō's ideals underpinned this adaptation, but this is open to speculation. The MOE officially changed its terminology from *gekiken* to *kendō* much later, in 1926. For a detailed analysis of the transition in terminology in education circles at the turn of the century, refer to Kinoshita, "From Kenjutsu to Kendo," 33–48.

4. Webb, *Understanding Bourdieu*, 10.

5. Bourdieu, *Distinction*, 66.

6. Gluck, *Japan's Modern Myths*, 23.

7. Smith, *National Identity*, 16.

8. Jansen, *Sakamoto Ryoma*, 106.

9. Legal privileges for *shizoku* were abolished in 1882, and by 1914 the term was no longer used in family registers (*koseki*).

10. Sonoda, *Shizoku no rekishi shakaigaku-teki kenkyū*, 17.

11. Friday, "Off the Warpath," 227.

12. Andō Naokata, *Kōbusho*, 16.

13. Imamura, *Jūkyū-seiki ni okeru Nihon taiiku no kenkyū*, 145.

14. Sonoda Hidehiro, *Shizoku no rekishi shakaigaku-teki kenkyū*, 11.

15. Smith, *Nationalism*, 20.

16. Rubinger, *Private Academies*, 211.

17. The convention of using red and white has its roots in the Genpei Disturbance (1180–85)—the conflict between the Genji and the Heike clans that culminated in the establishment of the first shogunate. The Genji were identified by red banners and the Heike by white. Budo competitions typically still use red or white to designate sides, and red and white striped screens are used on auspicious occasions.

18. Okada, "Meiji shoki Hitachi-no-Kuni Kasama wo chūshin to shita gekiken kōgyō no jittai," 1–7.

19. Shimoda, *Lost and Found*, 74.

20. Yamashita, *Kenkyū seinan no eki*, 283–300.

21. Yokoyama, *Nihon budō-shi*, 311–12. I suspect that when Kawaji mentioned his fear of losing traditional Japanese fencing to the Western method he was alluding to the introduction of French fencing into the Toyama Military Academy in 1874.

22. Nakamura, *Kendō jiten*, 161–167.

23. Tokyo Metropolitan Police (Keishichō), *Keishichō budō kyūjūnen-shi*, 419.

24. Doak, *Nationalism in Modern Japan*, 194.

25. Yuasa, "Jiyū minken undō to bujutsu ni tsuite—kōsatsu," 2.

26. Garon, *Molding Japanese Minds*, 8.

27. Doak, *Nationalism in Modern Japan*, 195.

28. Befu, *Japan*, 50, 52.

29. Bennett and Uozumi, *History and Spirit of Budō*, 40.

30. Suzuki, "Conflict Between Educators and Hygienists," 1.

31. Gellner, *Selected Philosophical Themes*, 146.

32. Sakatani, "Nurturing the Human Spirit," 493.

33. Baelz, *Awakening Japan*, 73.

34. Takano, *Kendō*, 290.

35. Ozawa, *Bujutsu taisō-ron*, 109–265.

36. Garon, *Molding Japanese Minds*, 8.

37. McVeigh, *Nationalisms of Japan*, 153.

38. Anderson, *Imagined Communities,* 80–128.

39. Gainty, *Martialing the National Body,* 77.

40. Ibid., 20.

41. By coincidence, I worked for Shirayuki (which is owned by the Konishi Shuzuo Corporation and based in Itami, Japan) from 1990–91. The company still maintains a strong tradition of supporting the martial arts of kendo and naginata, which are practiced at the company's Shūbukan dojo. I was employed in the office of the All Japan Naginata Federation, which was, until recently, sponsored by the Konishi Shuzuo Corporation.

42. Dai-Nippon Butokukai, *Butokushi,* 3. This was written in Japanese and English with the intention of informing Westerners about Japan's unique martial culture. "Butokukwai" is an older form of transliteration used for the name of the organization.

43. Ibid.

44. Nakamura, *Kendō jiten,* 117.

45. The five *kenjutsu* masters from various *ryūha* tasked with this responsibility were Negishi Shingorō, Tsuji Shinpei, Naitō Takaharu, Monna Tadashi, and Takano Sasaburō.

46. The first three techniques of the Nippon Kendo Kata practiced today feature the same *kamae* (stances) as its predecessor, the Dai-Nippon Butokukai Kenjutsu Kata: *jōdan* (upper), followed by *chūdan* (middle), and then *gedan* (lower).

47. Nakamura, *Kendō Jiten,* 56.

48. Smith, *National Identity,* 17.

49. Hobsbawm and Ranger, *Invention of Tradition,* 14.

50. McClatchie, "Sword of Japan," 50–56.

51. Fukuchi, *Shizoku to samurai ishiki,* 33.

4. SHARPENING THE EMPIRE'S CLAWS

Epigraph: Sugahara Tōru, "Gakkō kendō ni tsuite."

1. Kikuchi, *Japanese Modernisation,* 77.

2. Morris, *Nationalism,* xvii–xviii.

3. Spinks, "Indoctrination," 62.

4. Sakaue and Ōtsuka, "Senjika ni okeru kendo no hen'yō katei no kenkyū," 160.

5. Supreme Commander for the Allied Powers, Civil Information and Education Section, "Education in the New Japan," vol. 1, 33.

6. Another institution often associated with budo education even today is Kokushikan University in Tokyo. The forerunner to Kokushikan University was a small private school called Kokushikan Gijuku that was established in 1917. It was founded on the ideas of its creator, Shibata Tokujirō: "When the evil of materialism is predominant, it is spiritual civilization that can lead material civilization back to the righteous path. It is our purpose to cultivate true knowledge to serve as the pillar of society by advocating moral civilization and principled education. Not concerned

with mere form, our institution desires to become a dojo for unreservedly imparting knowledge based on action and morality." In 1929, a college was set up with teacher training courses in Japanese and Chinese Classics, judo, and kendo, based on its contemporaries, the Budo Vocational School in Kyoto and the Tokyo Higher Normal School. Kokushikan remains a powerhouse in college kendo to this day, but it was not as prestigious as the other two schools in the prewar period. However, it is notorious for its proclivity for right-wing and ultranationalistic tendencies. See Bennett, *Budō*, 278.

7. Nishikubo Hiromichi was born into a low-ranking samurai family in the Nabeshima domain (the present-day Saga Prefecture). After graduating from the Shihōshōhō Gakkō (later amalgamated with the Law Faculty of Tokyo Imperial University) in 1895, Nishikubo embarked on an illustrious bureaucratic career, with posts in the police and public administration affiliated with the Home Ministry. He served as the governor of Fukushima Prefecture from 1910 to 1913 and as the director (*chōkan*) of Hokkaidō from 1914 to 1915. In 1916, he retired from his position as police superintendent general and was appointed as a member of the House of Peers (Kizokuin). In 1919, he was assigned the position of Dai-Nippon Butokukai vice president and Bujutsu Vocational College principal. He was a particularly large man in terms of physique, and the following unflattering statement appeared in *Time* magazine shortly after he became Tokyo's mayor in 1926: "Recently the citizens of Tokyo chose famed swordsman-fencer Hiromichi Nishikubo as their Mayor. Last week he stepped upon a pair of scales to determine whether his now sedentary life has affected his weight. It has not. Mayor Nishikubo still weighs 238 pounds" (*Time* magazine, January 31, 1927). He studied Mutō-ryū *kenjutsu* under Yamaoka Tesshū and was awarded the highest kendo title of *hanshi* by the Butokukai in 1929.

8. A curious result of the Butokukai's adoption of -*dō* was the confusion it caused in the world of *jūdō*. The term *jūdō* had been used in reference to the style of *jūjutsu* taught at Kanō's Kōdōkan, but after the switch in terminology the distinction was less obvious. Needless to say, the relationship between Kanō and the Butokukai was strained, even though he was a key figure in the establishment of Butokukai *jūjutsu* protocols and kata in the early years.

9. Morris-Suzuki, "Invention and Reinvention," 766.

10. Mitchell, *Political Bribery in Japan*, 44.

11. Siniawer, *Ruffians*, 113.

12. Supreme Commander for the Allied Powers, Civil Information and Education Section, Education Division, "Education in the New Japan," vol. 1, 37.

13. Nakamura, *Kendō jiten*, 249.

14. Sakaue and Ōtsuka, "Senjika ni okeru kendo no hen'yō katei no kenkyū," 160.

15. Irie, *Nippon fashizumu-ka no taiiku shisō*, 35–37.

16. There were Tenran tournaments for other sports as well, but the first judo and kendo tournament was held May 4–5, 1929. In the division for specially selected competitors, Mochida Moriji won the kendo competition and Kurihara Tamio won the judo competition. The second Tenran tournament for budo was held May 4–5,

1934, in honor of the birth of the crown prince. The third tournament took place June 18–20, 1940, in celebration of the two thousand six hundredth anniversary of the founding of Japan.

17. Abe, Kiyohara, and Nakajima, "Fascism," 23–24.

18. Hongō, "Seishin rikkoku to butoku no tanren," 183.

19. Although kendo was recognized as a regular subject in middle schools and normal schools only in 1911, it had been practiced in educational institutions at the tertiary level as an extracurricular activity and optional subject for some years already. In fact, an intercollegiate federation (Tōkyō Gakusei Rengō Kendōkai) was formed as early as 1906. Many of the great postwar kendo masters have their roots in the student kendo world. In Kansai, Kyoto Imperial University was instrumental in holding national college tournaments for kendo, hosting its first in 1913. A national body, the All Japan Students' Kendo Federation, was inaugurated in 1928, with an initial thirty-two affiliated universities and colleges. This increased to ninety by 1940. With the formation of the federation, students engaged in numerous national and regional tournaments at all levels. Students also made trips, referred to as *musha-shugyō,* to Korea and Manchuria. See All Japan Kendo Federation, *Zen-Nihon kendō renmei gojūnen-shi,* 165.

20. There are many accounts from the Shōwa era that boast about the efficacy of the sword. The following description by career army officer and prolific writer Sakurai Tadayoshi is chilling:

Upon investigating the corpses of Chinese soldiers in the Manchurian Incident, there were many that had been cut in the head. This is telling of our soldiers charging over the enemy huddled in trenches to cut them. It seems clear that they attacked with purpose to score *ippon* on the head target in kendo. Due to the style of uniform worn by the Chinese soldiers it was inevitable that they were cut from the neck up, but I also saw a body that had been dispatched with a fantastic diagonal cut [*kesa-giri*] from the left shoulder down to the right hip. I was impressed with the quality of the cut. Probably, the executor had a fine sword in hand. There is no escaping an enemy with skill and a sword. Chinese soldiers are afraid of the *nihontō.* They do not think much of pistols, but when a *nihontō* is lifted overhead, it seems that their testicles ride up inside their bodies. They believe that they will be reborn as a dog if they get dispatched by a sword, so they despise the weapon. But that cannot be helped. I think that it is best to cut quickly and not be predisposed to a specific target. Not just *o-men* [head], *o-kote* [wrists], *o-dō* [torso], or *o-tsuki* [throat], but the butt or the legs are also legitimate targets. *Kenjutsu* that aims for any target is also the order of the day. In real battle, there is no such thing as *o-men* or *o-kote.* There is no reason to not cut any target that is open. (Sakurai, "Teki wo kiru hanashi," 132)

21. The military interest in swordsmanship led to an increased demand for mass-produced military swords (*guntō*), and various forging innovations made the blades more resilient and battle-effective. For example, a magazine advertisement for the Shōheikan Gunsō Company on page 116 of the October-December 1940 issue of *Katana to kendō* states that its *guntō* will not bend as easily as other blades due to a new forging process in which heat is retained for longer in the blade. They also boast

that it does not cut the hand if touched accidentally and that, "being silent, it is perfect for night operations"—presumably because it did not rattle in the sheath, meaning that the enemy could be dispatched with a silent cut.

22. Kendō Kyōiku Kenkyūkai, *Chūgakkō kendō kaisetsu*, 258.

23. Ibid., 254.

24. Kendō Shingikai Jimusho, "Kendō shingikai ni tsuite," 57–64.

25. Hiranuma, "Kokka no kōbō to kokumin no tanren," 7.

26. Watanabe, "Jikyoku to kendo," 17.

27. Satō Ukichi graduated from the Tokyo Higher Normal School in 1919 and then worked as an assistant to his mentor, Takano Sasaburō. Satō was an influential figure in the 1930s and was central in devising the 1936 syllabus for teaching kendo in schools. He eventually became a full professor at his alma mater in 1940 and also taught at various educational institutions, including Tokyo Gakugei University and Chukyo University. After the war he received the kendo title of *hanshi* and was promoted to the rank of 9-dan.

28. Sakaue and Ōtsuka, "Senjika ni okeru kendo no henyō katei no kenkyū," 159.

29. Nakamura, *Shiryō*, 195–97. For an in-depth examination of the historical significance of *kamidana* and their mandatory introduction into school training halls, see Nakamura, "Budō-jō to kamidana (1)," 35–51, and Nakamura, "Budō-jō to kamidana (2)," 1–17.

30. Sakaue and Ōtsuka, "Senjika ni okeru kendo no hen'yō katei no kenkyū," 160.

31. Supreme Commander for the Allied Powers, Civil Information and Education Section, Education Division, "Education in the New Japan," vol. 1," 35.

32. Watanabe, "Jikyoku to kendo," 17.

33. Sugahara, "Gakkō kendō ni tsuite," 99.

34. Home Ministry (Naimushō), "Budō shinkō no konpon hōsaku ikan," 72.

35. Nakayama, "Budō no seishin," 11.

36. Kendō Shingikai Jimusho, "Kendō shingikai ni tsuite," 60.

37. Spinks, "Indoctrination," 62.

38. Watari, "Nihon seishin to budō," 7.

39. Abe, "Kokumin gakkō to budō," 117.

40. Nakayama, "Budō no seishin," 12, 13.

41. Hurst, *Armed Martial Arts*, 165.

42. "Budō Nihon wo kengen," 130.

43. Takayama, "Budō kaikaku shoken," 31–34.

44. Nakamura, "Gakkō kendo ni tsuite," 89.

45. Ishida, "Kokumin gakkō tairenka budō (kendo) ni tsuite," 132.

46. The Shiseiakai was a group of dedicated, young kendo enthusiasts that was launched in December 1940. The president was Kimura Tokutarō (1886–1982), who would later become the president of the All Japan Kendo Federation. Many Shiseiakai members became officials in the AJKF in the postwar period. In the group's publication, *Shisei*, Kimura writes of his concern over the growing militarism polluting kendo and how "kendo techniques must be studied together with the

kendo heart." See AJKF, *Zen-Nihon kendō renmei gojūnen-shi,* 156. Kimura was the president of the Butokukai's Kendo Division when Japan lost the war. The Greater Japan Kendo Society (Dai-Nippon Kendōkai), established in March 1943, was another group formed by kendo enthusiasts, and the All Japan Students' Kendo Federation was absorbed into it. Takano Sasaburō and Kimura Tokutarō were appointed as vice presidents. The society was at odds with the Butokukai in matters of administration, and it ceased to exist after Japan's defeat.

47. Dai-Nippon Butokukai, "Zaidan hōjin dai-Nippon butokukai," 77.

48. Baerwald, "Information on the Dai Nippon Butoku Kai," BAE-41, nos. 2–10.

49. Nakamura, *Kendō jiten,* 261.

50. Harasono, *Kendō no fukkatsu,* 52.

51. Some considered this to be a ludicrous idea. Sakakida Yaeko, a pioneer in the development of modern naginata, was among them. She was called to a meeting of officials at the MOE regarding her plans for creating a unified style of the martial art to teach to girls across the country. The following excerpt is from an interview with Sakakida published in the *Kendō Nihon Monthly* (June and July), 1982:

> There was a fellow named Onitsuka from the armed forces, a colonel I think. He said, "What's the story with naginata these days. Wouldn't it be better to train in how to use a bamboo spear?" I just about burst when I heard him say that! I felt the blood surging through my veins, and snapped back at this Colonel Onitsuka, "I beg your pardon!" I interjected. I heard afterwards that I even thumped the desk and had a frightful scowl on my face. "Are you saying that we should make naginata and spear training the same?! I will have you know that naginata is supported by the MOE as a form of education for girls, and is not meant to be taught as a way to kill people! If it gets to the stage where naginata has to go to war, then Japan is already beyond help!"

52. The Jigen-ryū was called the "secret sword of Satsuma" because of the remote region where it was located. It developed from the Taisha-ryū, which was an offshoot of the Shintō-ryū and the Shinkage-ryū. Students of the school entered a frenzied state as they hacked furiously at bundled tree branches or wooden poles "3000 times in the morning and 8000 strikes at night." See Bennett, *Budō,* 96.

53. SCAPIN stands for "SCAP Index." SCAP is used in reference to the Supreme Command Allied Powers, which included GHQ (General Headquarters) in Tokyo and related administrative agencies, and also to the Supreme Commander, General Douglas MacArthur.

54. Supreme Commander for the Allied Powers, *Political Reorientation of Japan,* vol. 2, 479–82.

55. Baerwald, Memo for the Chief of Staff, "Dissolution of the Dai Nippon Butokukai," August 13, 1946. Quoted in Baerwald, "History of the Purge," 3.

56. Baerwald, "Report Regarding the Procedure for the Liquidation of the Dai-Nippon Butoku Kai," BAE-36, nos. 2–5.

57. Baerwald, "Information on the Dai Nippon Butoku Kai," BAE-41 nos. 2–10.

58. Supreme Commander for the Allied Powers, *Political Reorientation of Japan*, vol. 2, 553.

59. Baerwald, "Dai Nippon Butokukai and the Purge," 3.

60. Beauchamp and Vardaman, *Japanese Education*, 99.

5. KENDO AND SPORTS

1. Hazard, "An Overview of Kendo," 5.

2. Baerwald, "Report Regarding the Procedure for the Liquidation of the Dai-Nippon Butoku Kai," BAE-36, nos. 2–5.

3. Baerwald, "General meeting of the Directors, Secretaries and Instructors of Butoku Kai, concerning dissolution of the Society." BAE-37, nos. 2–6.

4. Baerwald, "General meeting of the Directors, Secretaries and Instructors of Butoku Kai, concerning dissolution of the Society." BAE-37, nos. 2–7.

5. Neufeld, "Memo to Mr. M. T. Orr."

6. US National Archives, Records Group 331.

7. All Japan Kendo Federation, *Kendō no rekishi*, 216.

8. There were comparatively few gymnasiums in the postwar era, and groups wishing to hold competitions often had little choice but to conduct matches outdoors.

9. The Kokumin Taiiku Taikai, or National Sports Meet, is commonly referred to as Kokutai. It began in 1946 as one of the representative comprehensive amateur sports events in Japan for manifold sporting disciplines. It is jointly sponsored by the Japan Amateur Sports Association, MEXT, and the local government of the prefecture chosen to host the year's meet.

10. Sasamori, "Letter to C. I. E. of G. H. Q., March 29, 1950," requesting the inclusion of *shinai-kyōgi* in the National Sports Meet, accessed January 5, 2009, http://ejmas.com/jcs/jcsart_svinth_1202.htm.

11. Nakamura, *Shiryō*, 206.

12. Ibid., 207.

13. Kimura Tokutarō was a graduate of Tokyo Imperial University's Law Department. He started kendo at the university's club and became a registered lawyer after graduating in 1911. Even after graduation he remained heavily involved with student kendo and was eventually appointed president of the Kendo Division of the Dai-Nippon Butokukai in 1942 and vice president of the Dai-Nippon Kendōkai, which was formed in 1943. After the war, he held several influential posts in government, including Minister of Law in the Shidehara and Yoshida Cabinets. He became the first president of the All Japan Kendo Federation when it was established in 1952 and remained in this position until 1972. In this capacity he was at the forefront of kendo's development in the postwar period. Incidentally, all AJKF presidents so far (as of 2015) have been graduates of Tokyo University's kendo club.

14. Another modification was the revamping of the rank system, in particular *shōgō* and dan grades. Initially, it was decided in 1953 that the prewar system of *shodan*

to 5-dan, followed by the *shōgō* titles of *renshi, kyōshi,* and *hanshi* would be continued. It underwent a significant change in 1957 when the AJKF decided to adopt the 10-dan structure utilized in judo. This was possibly due to dissatisfaction in the police department, where both judo and kendo were widely practiced; there was a perception of seniority based on who held higher dan grades, and this was skewed because of the grading differences between the two budo. The question remained of what to do with *shōgō.* This matter was deliberated at length, resulting in the concurrent adoption of both *shōgō* titles and dan ranks, with clarified definitions of what each represented. *Shōgō* were defined as denoting "character, technical mastery, knowledge, and efforts made to promote the Way of kendo." *Dan* ranks, on the other hand, represented "technical skill level." *Renshi* was attainable after passing the grade of 6-dan, *kyōshi* after 7-dan, and *hanshi* after 8-dan. See AJKF, *Zen-Nihon kendō renmei gojūnen-shi,* 19.

15. Takahashi, *Taiikuka kyōiku-gaku nyūmon,* 31.

16. Kindai Nihon Kyōiku Seido Shiryō Hensankai, *Kindai nihon kyōiku seido shiryō,* vol. 27, 554–57. Emphasis added.

17. Monbushō, *Gakkō kendō no shidō tebiki,* 2–4.

18. All Japan Kendo Federation, *Gakkō kendō no shidō,* 6–18

19. The Japan Amateur Sports Association (Nihon Taiiku Kyōkai) is the national body governing the regulation, promotion, and funding of amateur sports in Japan. It was originally founded in 1911 in preparation for Japan's first participation in the Olympics. Its first chairman was Kanō Jigorō.

20. Morris, *Nationalism,* 40.

21. McVeigh, *Nationalisms of Japan,* 19.

22. Monbushō, *Kendō shidō no tebiki,* 1.

23. Ministry of Education, Culture, Sports, Science and Technology (MEXT), "Gakushū shidō yōryō kaitei no keii."

24. MEXT, www.mext.go.jp/b_menu/kihon/data/07080117.htm, accessed June 20, 2011.

25. Motomura, "'Dentō ya bunka' wa 'budō' de dō uketomeru no ka," 5.

26. All Japan Kendo Federation, *Chūgakkō budō no hisshūka wo fumaeta kendō jugyō no tenkai,* 6.

27. Bennett, *Budō,* 72.

28. The committee members who formulated the "Concept" and "Purpose" were Chairman Matsumoto Toshio, Horiguchi Kiyoshi, Ogawa Chūtarō, Tamari Yoshiaki, Nakano Yasoji, Yuno Masanori, Ōshima Isao, Inoue Masataka, Ogawa Masayuki, Hiromitsu Hidekuni, and Kasahara Toshiaki.

29. The English version of "The Mindset of Kendo Instruction" (*Kendo shidō no kokoro-gamae*), which I translated, was published by the AJKF on March 14, 2007. The text is accessible at www.kendo-fik.org/english-page/english-page2/concept-of-Kendo.htm.

30. Kagaya, "Chōki kōsō kikaku kaigi hōkoku," 20.

31. Ōya, "Instruction of Kendo," 184.

32. According to the definition offered in the AJKF's *Japanese-English Dictionary of Kendo, shōgō* is "a title which indicates one's level of achievement as a kendoist.

In kendo, there are three levels of *shōgō: renshi, kyōshi,* and *hanshi.* These titles are awarded to persons who have been sixth dan, seventh dan, or eighth dan, respectively, for the requisite number of years and who satisfy the given qualification standards. Dan indicate one's technical level (mental elements included), while *shōgō* signify in addition to technical proficiency, the level of one's leadership and judgment as a kendoist. The title *hanshi* is conferred on persons at the absolute highest level of authority as kendoists." See AJKF, *Japanese-English Dictionary of Kendo,* 91.

33. Gakkō Taiiku Kenkyū Dōshikai, *Kokumin undō bunka no sōzō,* 100.

34. Bennett, "Hanshi Says," 8.

35. Sheard, "Aspects of Boxing," 31–57.

36. Guttmann and Thompson, "From Ritual to Record," 115–55.

37. Chandler, *Sport,* 191.

38. Best, *Philosophy and Human Movement,* 104.

39. Bourdieu, *Distinction,* 290.

40. Saimura, "Kendō shugyō no mokuteki," 47.

41. Goodger and Goodger, "Post-War British Judo," 43.

42. Bourdieu, "Sport and Social Class," 298.

43. GAISF, founded in 1967, groups together international sports federations and various associations with the aims of defending worldwide sport, keeping representative bodies informed, and cooperating and coordinating their activities. GAISF, along with other IOC-affiliated groups, such as the Association of Summer Olympic International Federations (ASOIF), the Association of International Winter Sports Federations (AIWF), and the Association of IOC Recognized International Sports Federations (ARISF), look out for the interests of their affiliated sports federations. When the International Kendo Federation successfully affiliated with GAISF, they were forced to accept the acronym FIK because the International Korfball Federation had already laid claim to IKF.

44. Guttmann, "Diffusion of Sports," 125–37.

45. McVeigh, *Nationalisms of Japan,* 20.

6. CROSSING SWORDS AND BORDERS

1. Marks, "Rise of Nationalism," 623.

2. Svinth and Green, *Martial Arts,* 149.

3. Abel, "McClatchie."

4. Norman, *Fighting Man of Japan,* xxv. For a detailed account of F. J. Norman's life, refer to Bennett, "The FJ Norman Saga," 6–15.

5. Harrison, *Fighting Spirit of Japan,* 103.

6. Bowen, "London Budokwai Minutes."

7. Momii, *Cyclopedia,* 7.

8. Baerwald, "Information on the Dai Nippon Butoku Kai," BAE-41 nos. 2–10.

9. "Nikkei" is the generic term for people with Japanese heritage who reside overseas. The terms "Issei," "Nisei," and "Sansei" refer to first, second, and third generations of Nikkei, respectively.

10. Svinth and Green, *Martial Arts,* 149.

11. Takezawa, *Breaking the Silence,* 68.

12. Okihiro, *Whispered Silences,* 160.

13. Kobayashi, "Kendo in Brazil," 27.

14. Ibid.

15. Azuma, *Between Two Empires,* 251.

16. Guttmann, "Diffusion of Sports," 125–37.

17. Lee, "Kendō ni okeru 'ippon' no gainen," 32.

18. Na, "Budō in South Korean Society," 183.

19. Guttmann, "Diffusion of Sports," 344.

20. Shin, "Kendō no sekai-ka, fuhen-ka imada tōshi," 156–157.

21. Jackson, "Unlocking Japan," 43.

22. Mendl, *Japan's Asia Policy,* 133.

23. McVeigh, *Nationalisms of Japan,* 210.

24. All Japan Kendo Federation, *Zen-Nihon kendō renmei gojūnen-shi,* 54.

25. Ibid., 108.

26. Guttmann, "Diffusion of Sports," 353.

27. Befu, *Japan,* 52.

28. Abe, *Nippon kendō,* 79.

29. Billig, *Banal Nationalism,* 125.

30. Guttmann, "Diffusion of Sports," 346.

31. Agency for Cultural Affairs, "About the Future Promotion of International Exchange," 10.

32. McVeigh, *Nationalisms of Japan,* 191.

33. Kashiwazaki, "Various Problems in Modern Budō," 9.

34. Ōtsuka, *Nihon kendō no shisō,* 211.

35. Japanese Academy of Budo, *Kendō wo shiru jiten,* 175.

36. Abe, *Nippon kendō,* 103.

37. Tanaka, *Budō,* 98–101.

38. McVeigh, *Nationalisms of Japan,* 19, 165.

39. Hall, *Cartels of the Mind,* 173.

40. Ōtsuka, "Proposal," 18.

41. Abe, *Nippon kendō,* 104.

EPILOGUE

1. Vlastos, *Mirror of Modernity,* 287–89.

2. Ibid., 296.

3. Ibid., 299.

4. Befu, *Cultural Nationalism in East Asia,* 126.

BIBLIOGRAPHY

Abe Ikuo, Kiyohara Yasuharu, and Nakajima Ken. "Fascism, sport and society in Japan." *International Journal of the History of Sport* 9, no. 1 (1992): 1–28.

Abel, Laszlo. "Thomas Russell Hillier McClatchie (1852–1886)." *Aikido Journal*. Accessed November 4, 2011. www.aikidojournal.com/article?articleID=710.

Abe Mamoru. "Kokumin gakkō to budō" (National People's Schools and *budō*). *Katana to kendō* 9 (January–February 1941): 110–17.

Abe Tetsushi. "Ōshū kara mita kendo no kokusaika" (The internationalization of kendo seen from Europe). *Kendo Nippon* (November 2003): 52–58.

Abe Tetsushi, Kataoka Noboru, Meguro Masao, Kamemoto Ryūtarō, and Andō Masayasu. *Nippon kendō, sekai e* (Japanese kendo, to the world). Tokyo: Ski Journal, 2007.

Agency for Cultural Affairs. "About the Future Promotion of International Exchange." www.bunka.go.jp/english/pdf/gattaiban.pdf, accessed January 2012.

All Japan Judo Federation. *Zen-Nihon jūdō renmei 50-nenshi 1949–1999* (Fifty-year history of the AJJF). Tokyo: All Japan Judo Federation, 2000.

All Japan Kendo Federation. *Chūgakkō budō no hisshūka wo fumaeta kendō jugyō no tenkai* (Developing kendo classes for compulsory budo education in junior high schools). Tokyo: All Japan Kendo Federation, 2009.

———. *Gakkō kendō no shidō: shidō no tebiki kaisetsu* (School kendo instruction: an explanation of the instruction guidebook). Tokyo: Shin Kendōsha, 1953.

———. *Japanese-English Dictionary of Kendo*. 2006. Rev. ed., translated by Alexander Bennett. Tokyo: All Japan Kendo Federation, 2011.

———. *Kendō no rekishi* (The history of kendo). Tokyo: All Japan Kendo Federation, 2003.

———. *Kensō* (monthly newsletter of the AJKF). Tokyo: All Japan Kendo Federation.

———. *The Official Guide for Kendo Instruction*. Translated by Alexander Bennett. Tokyo: All Japan Kendo Federation, 2011.

———. *Suzuka-ke bunsho kaisetsu 1–4* (Explanation of the Suzuka house documents). Tokyo: All Japan Kendo Federation, 2003.

———. *Zen-Nihon kendō renmei gojūnen-shi* (Fifty-year history of the AJKF). Tokyo: All Japan Kendo Federation, 2003.

Anderson, Benedict. *Imagined Communities: Reflections on the Origin and Spread of Nationalism.* 1983. Rev. ed., Pasig City: Anvil, 2003.

Andō Naokata, ed. *Kōbusho (Tōkyō-shi shigai-hen)* (History of Tokyo City). Tokyo: Jukai Shorin, 1988.

Anshin, Anatoliy. "The Intangible Warrior Culture of Japan: Bodily Practices, Mental Attitudes, and Values of the Two-sworded Men from the Fifteenth to the Twenty-first Centuries." PhD diss., University of New South Wales, 2009.

Arai Katsuhiro, Imanishi Hajime, Inada Masahiro, Matsuoka Kiichi, Sugiyama Hiroshi, and Tsurumaki Takao. *Jiyū minken to kindai shakai* (Popular rights and modern society). Tokyo: Yoshikawa Kōbunkan, 2004.

Asakawa, Kan'ichi. *The Documents of Iriki, Illustrative of the Development of the Feudal Institutions of Japan.* New Haven, CT: Yale University Press, 1929.

Azuma, Eiichiro. *Between Two Empires: Race, History, and Transnationalism in Japanese America.* Oxford: Oxford University Press, 2005.

———. "The Politics of Transnational History Making: Japanese Immigrants on the Western 'Frontier,' 1927–1941." *Journal of American History* 89, no. 4 (2003): 1401–30.

Baelz, Toku, ed. *Awakening Japan: The Diary of a German Doctor: Erwin Baelz.* Bloomington: Indiana University Press, 1974.

Baerwald, Hans H. "The Dai Nippon Butokukai and the Purge." Unpublished paper presented at the Luce Foundation Seminar on Japan, February 1982. BAE-103. Hans H. Baerwald Papers. National Diet Library of Japan.

———. "General meeting of the Directors, Secretaries and Instructors of Butoku Kai, concerning dissolution of the Society." October 30, 1946. BAE-37, nos. 2–7. Hans H. Baerwald Papers. National Diet Library of Japan.

———. Hans H. Baerwald Papers (BAE 1–205). National Diet Library of Japan.

———. "History of the Purge." April 1, 1948. BAE-101. Hans H. Baerwald Papers, National Diet Library of Japan.

———. "Information on the Dai Nippon Butoku Kai." November 26, 1946. BAE-41, nos. 2–10. Hans H. Baerwald Papers, National Diet Library of Japan.

———. "Report Regarding the Procedure for the Liquidation of the Dai-Nippon Butoku Kai." BAE-36, nos. 2–5. Hans H. Baerwald Papers, National Diet Library of Japan.

Beauchamp, Edward R., and James M. Vardaman, eds. *Japanese Education since 1945: A Documentary Study.* London: M. E. Sharpe, 1994.

Befu, Harumi. *Japan: An Anthropological Introduction.* Tokyo: C. E. Tuttle, 1981.

———. "Nationalism and *Nihonjinron.*" In *Cultural Nationalism in East Asia: Representation and Identity,* edited by Harumi Befu, 107–35. Berkeley: Institute of East Asian Studies, University of California, 1993.

Bennett, Alexander, ed. *Budō: The Martial Ways of Japan.* Tokyo: Nippon Budokan, 2010.

———, ed. *Budo Perspectives.* Auckland: Kendo World Publications, 2005.

———. "The FJ Norman Saga—The Final Chapter?" *Kendo World* 3, no. 3 (2006): 8–15.

———, trans. "Hanshi Says: 8 Important Points for Shinsa—Professor Satō Nariaki." *Kendo World* 5, no. 3 (2011): 8.

———. "Kendo or Kumdo: The Internationalization of Kendo and the Olympic Problem." In *Budo Perspectives,* edited by Alexander Bennett, 329–53. Auckland: Kendo World Publications, 2005.

———, ed. *Kendo World.* 6 vols. Auckland, Chiba: Kendo World Publications/ Bunkasha International, 2001–12.

Bennett, Alexander, and Uozumi Takashi, eds. *The History and Spirit of Budō.* Chiba, Japan: International Budo University, 2010.

Bennett, Alexander, and Yamada Shōji, eds. *Nihon no kyōiku ni budō wo: 21-seiki ni shin-gi-tai wo kitaeru* (Bringing *budō* into Japanese education: forging mind, technique and body in the twenty-first century). Tokyo: Meiji Tosho, 2005.

Bernstein, Gail Lee. *Recreating Japanese Women, 1600–1945.* Berkeley: University of California Press, 1991.

Best, David. *Philosophy and Human Movement.* London: Allen and Unwin, 1978.

Billig, Michael. *Banal Nationalism.* London: Sage, 1995.

Blackwood, Thomas. "Bushido Baseball? Three 'Fathers' and the Invention of a Tradition." *Social Science Japan Journal* 11, no. 2 (2008): 223–40.

Bourdieu, Pierre. *Distinction: A Social Critique of the Judgement of Taste.* Translated by Richard Nice. Cambridge, MA: Harvard University Press, 1984.

———. "Sport and Social Class." Reprinted in *Sport: Critical Concepts in Sociology,* vol. 3, edited by Eric Dunning and Dominic Malcolm, 286–303. London: Routledge, 2003.

Bowen, Richard, comp. "London Budokwai Minutes." Richard Bowen Collection. University of Bath Archives.

Breaden, Jeremy, *Stacey Steele, and Carolyn S.* Stevens, *eds. Internationalising Japan: Discourse and Practice.* London: Routledge, 2014.

Brown, Philip C. *Central Authority and Local Autonomy in the Formation of Early Modern Japan: The Case of Kaga Domain.* Stanford: Stanford University Press, 1993.

Brown, Roger H. "Yasuoka Masahiro's 'New Discourse on Bushido Philosophy': Cultivating Samurai Spirit and Men of Character for Imperial Japan." *Social Science Japan Journal* 16, no. 1 (2013): 107–29.

"Budō Nihon wo kengen: Shinkō iinkai no hōsaku" (Opinions on budo Japan: The direction of the Deliberation Council). *Katana to kendō* 7 (July–September 1940): 130.

Chamberlain, Basil Hall. *The Invention of a New Religion.* London: Watts and Co., 1912.

Chandler, Timothy, John Lindsay, Mike Cronin, and Wray Vamplew. *Sport and Physical Education: The Key Concepts.* London: Routledge, 2002.

Clark, John. "Japanese Modernisation and Mingei Theory: Cultural Nationalism and Oriental Orientalism." *Journal of Design History* 18, no. 3 (2005): 309–11.

Conlan, Thomas. *Weapons and Fighting Techniques of the Samurai Warrior, 1200–1877*. London: Amber Books, 2008.

Cynarski, Wojciech J. "Social Stratification in Japanese and Some Other Martial Arts: A Comparison and Discussion of Changes." *Physical Culture and Sport. Studies and Research* 59, no. 1 (2013): 49–59.

Dai-Nippon Butokukai. *Butoku.* Vol. 10, *Dai-Nippon butokukai kenkyū shiryō shūsei* (Collection of research documents for the Dai-Nippon Butokukai), edited by Nakamura Tamio. Tokyo: Shimazu Shobō, 2010.

———. *Butokushi.* Vols. 1.1–4.12, June 1906–December 1909. Reprint, Tokyo: Yushōdō Shuppan, 1985.

———. "Zaida-hōjin Dai-Nippon Butokukai" (The government foundation Dai-Nippon Butokukai). 1942. Reprinted in *Shiryō: Kindai kendō-shi,* edited by Nakamura Tamio. Tokyo: Shimazu Shobō, 1985.

Dixon, Boyd, Laura Gilda, and Lon Bulgrin. "The Archaeology of World War II Japanese Stragglers on the Island of Guam and the Bushido Code." *Asian Perspectives* 51, no. 1 (2012): 110–27.

Doak, Kevin. "Culture, Ethnicity, and the State in Early Twentieth-Century Japan." In *Japan's Competing Modernities: Issues in Culture and Democracy, 1900–1930,* edited by Sharon A. Minichiello, 192–98. University of Hawai'i Press, 1998.

———. *A History of Nationalism in Modern Japan: Placing the People.* Boston: Brill, 2007.

———. "What Is a Nation and Who Belongs? National Narratives and the Ethnic Imagination in Twentieth-Century Japan." *American Historical Review* 102, no. 2 (April 1997): 283–309.

Dower, John W. *Embracing Defeat: Japan in the Wake of World War II.* New York: W. W. Norton, 1999.

Draeger, Donn. *Classical Budo.* New York: Weatherhill, 1973.

———. *Classical Bujutsu.* New York: Weatherhill, 1973.

———. *Modern Bujutsu and Budo.* New York: Weatherhill, 1974.

Dunning, Eric, and Dominic Malcolm, eds. *Sport: Critical Concepts in Sociology.* 4 vols. London: Routledge, 2003.

Dunning, Eric, Dominic Malcolm, and Ivan Waddington, eds. *Sport Histories: Figurational Studies in the Development of Modern Sport.* London: Routledge, 2004.

Duus, Peter, and Daniel Okimoto. "Fascism and the History of Pre-War Japan: The Failure of a Concept." *Journal of Asian Studies* 39, no. 1 (November 1979): 65–76.

Elias, Norbert. *The Civilizing Process.* New York: Pantheon Books, 1982.

Elias, Norbert, and Anderic Dunning. *The Quest for Excitement: Sport and Leisure in the Civilizing Process.* Oxford: B. Blackwell, 1986.

Enamoto Shōji. "Kōbusho no kenkyū" (A study of the Kōbusho). *Research Journal of Budo* 8, no. 2 (1975).

Farris, William W. *Heavenly Warriors: The Evolution of Japan's Military, 500–1300.* Cambridge, MA: Council on East Asian Studies, Harvard University, 1992.

Friday, Karl. *Hired Swords.* Stanford: Stanford University Press, 1992.

————. *Legacies of the Sword: The Kashima-Shinryu and Samurai Martial Culture.* Honolulu: University of Hawai'i Press, 1997.

————. "Off the Warpath: Military Science & Budō in the Evolution of Ryūha Bugei." In *Budo Perspectives,* edited by Alexander Bennett, 249–65. Auckland: Kendo World Publications, 2005.

————. *Samurai, Warfare and the State in Early Medieval Japan.* New York: Routledge, 2004.

Frühstück, Sabine, and Anne Walthall. *Recreating Japanese Men.* Berkeley: University of California Press, 2011.

Fuji Naomoto. *Buke jidai no shakai to seishin* (The spirit and society in the age of the warrior houses). Osaka: Sōgensha, 1967.

Fujiki Hisashi. *Katana-gari: buki wo fūin shita minshū* (Sword hunt: the people who concealed their weapons). Tokyo: Iwanami Shoten, 2005.

Fukuchi Shigetaka. *Shizoku to samurai ishiki* (*Shizoku* and samurai consciousness). Tokyo: Shunjusha, 1956.

Fukutake Tadashi. *The Japanese Social Structure: Its Evolution in the Modern Century.* Translated by Ronald Dore. Tokyo: University of Tokyo Press, 1982.

Futaki Ken'ichi. *Chūsei buke girei no kenkyū* (A study of medieval warrior ceremony). Tokyo: Yoshikawa Kōbunkan, 1985.

————. *Kassen no butai-ura* (Behind the scenes of battle). Tokyo: Shinjinbutsu Ōraisha, 1979.

Gainty, Denis. *Martial Arts and the Body Politic in Meiji Japan.* Abingdon, Oxon: Routledge, 2013.

————. "Martialing the National Body: Structure, Agency, and the Dai Nippon Butokukai in Modern Japan." PhD diss., University of Pennsylvania, 2007.

Gakkō Kendō Kenkyūkai. *Gakkō kendo no shidō: shidō no tebiki kaisetsu* (School kendo instruction: an explanation of the instruction guidebook). Tokyo: Shūbunsha, 1958.

Gakkō Taiiku Kenkyū Dōshikai, ed. *Kokumin undō bunka no sōzō* (Creating national sport culture). Tokyo: Taishūkan Shoten, 1989.

Garon, Sheldon. *Molding Japanese Minds.* Princeton, NJ: Princeton University Press, 1997.

Geertz, Clifford. *The Interpretation of Cultures: Selected Essays.* London: Fontana, 1992.

Gellner, Ernest. *Selected Philosophical Themes.* London: Routledge, 2003.

Gendai Nihon Kyōiku Seido Shiryō Henshū Iinkai. *Gendai Nihon kyōiku seido shiryō* (Contemporary Japan education system records). 63 vols. Tokyo: Tōkyō Hōrei Shuppan, 1984–96.

Gilbert, Howard. "Wrestling with Foreign Yokozuna." In *Japanese Cultural Nationalism: At Home and in the Pacific,* edited by Roy Starrs, 279–89. Folkestone, Kent: Global Oriental, 2004.

Gladney, Dru C., ed. *Making Majorities: Constituting the Nation in Japan, Korea, China, Malaysia, Fiji, Turkey, and the United States.* Stanford: Stanford University Press, 1998.

Gluck, Carol. *Japan's Modern Myths*. Princeton, NJ: Princeton University Press, 1985.

Goodger, Brian, and John Goodger. "Organization and Cultural Change in Post-War British Judo." *International Review of Sport Sociology* 15, no. 1 (1980): 21–48.

Green, Thomas A., and J. Svinth, eds. *Martial Arts in the Modern World*. Westport, CT: Praeger, 2003.

Guttmann, Allen. "The Diffusion of Sports and the Problem of Cultural Imperialism." In *The Sports Process: A Comparative and Developmental Approach*, edited by E. Dunning, J. Maguire, and R. Pearton, 125–37. Champaign, IL: Human Kinetics Publishers, 1993.

Guttmann, Allen, and Lee Thompson. *Japanese Sports: A History*. Honolulu: University of Hawai'i Press, 2001.

———. "From Ritual to Record." In *From Ritual to Record: The Nature of Modern Sport*, 115–55. New York: Columbia University Press, 1978.

Hall, David A. *Encyclopedia of Japanese Martial Arts*. New York: Kodansha USA, 2012.

Hall, Ivan P. *Cartels of the Mind: Japan's Intellectual Closed Shop*. New York: W. W. Norton, 1998.

Hall, John W. *Government and Local Power in Japan, 500 to 1700: A Study Based on Bizen Province*. Princeton, NJ: Princeton University Press, 1980.

Hall, John W., and Jeffrey P. Mass, eds. *Medieval Japan: Essays in Institutional History*. New Haven, CT: Yale University Press, 1974.

Harasono Mitsunori. *Kendō no fukkatsu* (Kendo's revival). Tokyo: Shobō Takahara, 1972.

Harrison, Ernest J. *The Fighting Spirit of Japan*. London: T. Fisher Unwin, 1913.

Hasegawa Noboru. *Hakuto to jiyū minken undō* (Gamblers and the Popular Rights Movement). Tokyo: Chūō Kōronsha, 1977.

Haskel, Peter. *Sword of Zen: Master Takuan and His Writings on Immovable Wisdom and the Sword of Taie*. Honolulu: Hawai'i University Press, 2013.

Hayakawa Junsaburō, ed. *Bujutsu sōsho* (Various writings on the martial arts). 1915. Reprint, Tokyo: Hachiman Shoten, 2003.

Hayashiya Tatsusaburō. *Kodai chūsei geijutsu-ron* (Theory of ancient and medieval art). Tokyo: Iwanami Shoten, 1973.

Hazard, Benjamin. "An Overview of Kendo, 1945–2000." *AUSKF Newsletter* 5 (June 30, 2002): 5.

Henshall, Kenneth. *A History of Japan: From Stone Age to Super Power*. Hampshire: Palgrave MacMillan, 2004.

Herrigel, Eugen. *Zen in the Art of Archery*. New York: Pantheon, 1953.

Hiranuma Ryōzō. "Kokka no kōbō to kokumin no tanren" (Defense of the state and training the people). *Katana to kendō* 3 (November–December 1939): 6–9.

Hobsbawm, E., and T. Ranger, eds. *The Invention of Tradition*. Cambridge: Cambridge University Press, 1992.

Home Ministry (Naimushō). "Budō shinkō no konpon hōsaku ikan" (Basic policy for the promotion of budo). *Naimu kōsei jihō* 5, no. 8 (July 1940). Reprint: Tokyo: Bunsei Shoin, 1998.

Hongō Fusatarō. "Seishin rikkoku to butoku no tanren" (Founding the nation's spirit and forging martial virtue). 1930. Reprinted in *Shiryō: kindai kendo-shi*, edited by Nakamura Tamio. Tokyo: Shimazu Shobō, 1985.

Howell, David. "The Social Life of Firearms in Tokugawa Japan." *Japanese Studies* 20, no. 1 (2009): 65–80.

Hughson, John, David Inglis, and Marcus Free. *The Uses of Sport: A Critical Study.* London: Routledge, 2005.

Hurst, G. Cameron. *Armed Martial Arts of Japan: Swordsmanship and Archery.* New Haven, CT: Yale University Press, 1998.

———. "Death, Honor, and Loyalty: The *Bushido* Ideal." *Philosophy East and West* 40, no. 4 (1990): 511–27.

Iida, Yumiko. *Rethinking Identity in Modern Japan: Nationalism as Aesthetics.* London: Routledge, 2002.

Ikegami, Eiko. *The Taming of the Samurai: Honorific Individualism and the Making of Modern Japan.* Cambridge, MA: Harvard University Press, 1995.

Imamura Yoshio. "Budō-shi gaisetsu" (Outline of *budō* history). *Nihon budō taikei* 10 (1982): 5–28.

———. *Jūkyū-seiki ni okeru Nihon taiiku no kenkyū* (A study of Japanese physical education in the nineteenth century). Tokyo: Fumidō Shoten, 1967.

———, ed. *Kindai kendō meichō taikei* (Compendium of modern kendo classics). 14 vols. Kyoto: Dōhō Shuppan, 1985–86.

———. *Nihon budō taikei* (Compendium of Japanese *budō*). 10 vols. Kyoto: Dōhō Shuppan, 1982.

Inoue Kazuo. *Gakkō taiiku seido-shi* (The history of the school physical education system). Tokyo: Taishūkan Shoten, 1970.

Inoue Shun. *Budō no tanjō* (The birth of budo). Tokyo: Yoshikawa Kōbunkan, 2004.

International Kendo Federation. *The Regulations of Kendo Shiai: The Subsidiary Rules of Kendo Shiai and Shinpan.* 1997. Rev. ed., Tokyo: International Kendo Federation, 2006.

Irie Katsumi. *Nippon fashizumu-ka no taiiku shisō* (Ideals of physical education under Japanese fascism). Tokyo: Fumidō Shuppan, 1986.

Ishida Ichirō. "Kokumin gakkō tairenka budō (kendo) ni tsuite" (Kendo classes in National People's schools). *Katana to kendō* 9 (January–February, 1941): 130–32.

Ishigaki Yasuzō. *Jikishin Kage-ryū gokui denkai* (Elucidating the secret teachings of the Jikishin Kage-ryū). Tokyo: Shimazu Shobō, 2001.

Ishii Ryōsuke, ed. *Tokugawa kinrei-kō* (An exploration of Tokugawa prohibitory decrees). 11 vols. Tokyo: Sōbunsha, 1959.

Ishii Susumu. *Kamakura bakufu* (The Kamakura warrior government). Tokyo: Chūō Kōronsha, 1965.

Ishioka Hisao. *Nihon no kobujutsu* (Classical Japanese martial arts). Tokyo: Shinjinbutsu Ōraisha, 1980.

Issai Chozan. *See* Niwa Jūrōzaemon Tadaaki.

Ivy, Marilyn. *Discourses of the Vanishing: Modernity, Phantasm, Japan.* Chicago: University of Chicago Press, 1995.

Jackson, Lockie. "Unlocking Japan." *Kendo World* 6, no. 1 (2011): 43.

Jansen, Marius B., ed. *Sakamoto Ryoma and the Meiji Restoration.* New York: Columbia University Press, 1994.

———. *Warrior Rule in Japan.* Cambridge: Cambridge University Press, 1995.

Japanese Academy of Budo, Kendo Section, ed. *Kendō wo shiru jiten* (Encyclopedia of *kendō*). Tokyo: Tōkyōdō Shuppan, 2009.

Japanese Budo Association. "Gendai budo report." Archived materials of Budō Charter Creation Committee. Tokyo: Nippon Budokan, 1983.

Kagaya Shin'ichi. "Chōki kōsō kikaku kaigi hōkoku (1–4)" (Reports of the long-term planning committee). *Kensō* (December 2006–March 2007), Tokyo: All Japan Kendo Federation.

Kakei Yasuhiko. *Chūsei buke-kakun no kenkyū* (Studies of medieval military house codes). Tokyo: Kazama Shobō, 1967.

Karasulas, Antony. "Zaimokuza Reconsidered: The Forensic Evidence, and Classical Japanese Swordsmanship." *World Archaeology* 36, no. 4 (2004): 507–18.

Kashiwazaki Katsuhiko, Matsuo Makinori, Kimura Yasuko, Yamada Toshihiko, Uozumi Takashi, Tatsugi Yukitoshi, Alexander Bennett. "Gendai budō no shomondai: budō no kokusaika ni tomonau mondai 3" (Various Problems in Modern Budō—The Internationalization of Budō III). *Budō Sports Science Research,* no. 15 (2010): 1–27.

Katana to kendō. 15 vols. (1939–1942). Reprint, Tokyo: Yūzankaku, 1990.

Katō, Jun'ichi. "Current Circumstances in the Korean Kumdo Association." *Kendo World* 5, no. 3 (2010): 79–82.

Kendō Kyōiku Kenkyūkai. *Chūgakkō kendō kaisetsu* (Explanation of kendo in middle schools). In *Kindai kendō meichō taikei* 11, edited by Imamura Yoshio. Kyoto: Dōhō Shuppan, 1985–86.

Kendō Shingikai Jimusho. "Kendō shingikai ni tsuite: zenkoku kendōka shoshi ni tsugu" (About the Kendo Deliberation Council: A call to kendoists throughout the nation). 1940. Reprinted in *Shiryō: kindai kendō-shi,* edited by Nakamura Tamio. Tokyo: Shimazu Shobō, 1985.

Kikuchi, Yuko. *Japanese Modernisation and Mingei Theory: Cultural Nationalism and Oriental Orientalism.* London: Routledge, 2004.

Kindai Budō Kenkyū-kai, ed. *Budō no ayumi 90-nen* (Budo's path over 90 years). Tokyo: Shōkō Zaimu Kenkyūkai, 1961.

Kindai Nihon Kyōiku Seido Shiryō Hensankai. *Kindai Nihon kyōiku seido shiryō* (Modern Japanese education system records). 35 vols. Tokyo: Kōdansha, 1956–59.

Kinoshita Hideaki. "Dai-Nippon Butokukai: Sono sen-kindaisei to kindaisei" (The Dai-Nippon Butokukai: its pre-modern and modern characteristics). *Taiiku no kagaku* (The science of physical education) 15, no. 11 (1965): 640–45.

———. "Historical study of the process of change from Kenjutsu to Kendo." *Taiiku-gaku kenkyū* (Research Journal of Physical Education) 51 (2006): 33–48.

Kobayashi Kazutake, and Noritake Yūichi, eds. *Chūsei sensō-ron no genzai* (The current state of theories on medieval warfare). Tokyo: Aoki Shoten, 2004.

Kobayashi, Luiz. "A Brief Overview of Pre-WWII Kendo in Brazil." *Kendo World* 5, no. 2 (2010): 26–28.

Koizumi, Gunji. "Judo and the Olympic Games." *Budokwai Quarterly Bulletin* 3 no. 1 (April 1947): 7–8.

Kondō Hitoshi. *Buke-kakun no kenkyū* (Research into warrior house codes). Tokyo: Meguro Shoin, 1962.

Kondō Yoshikazu. *Yumiya to tōken: chūsei kassen no jitsuzō* (Bows, arrows and swords: medieval warfare). Tokyo: Yoshikawa Kōbunkan, 1997.

Konishi Yasuhiro. *Kendō to shinai-kyōgi* (Kendo and *shinai-kyōgi*). Tokyo: Kawazu Shoten, 1952.

Lee, Min-ku. "Kendō ni okeru 'ippon' no gainen: Nikkan kendō bunka hikaku-ron" (The concept of "*ippon*" in kendo: A comparison of Japanese and Korean kendo culture). Unpublished master's thesis, International Budo University, 2009.

Levinger, Matthew, and Paula Lytle. "Myth and Mobilisation: The Triadic Structure of Nationalistic Rhetoric." *Nations and Nationalism* 7, no. 2 (2001): 175–94.

Lincicome, M. "Nationalism, Imperialism, and the International Education Movement in Early Twentieth-Century Japan." *Journal of Asian Studies* 58, no. 2 (1999): 338–60.

Louka, André, and Harry Cook. "Memories of the Great Masters: Minoru Mochizuki." *Dragon Times* 13 (1998): 25–28.

Maguire, Joseph A., and Masayoshi Nakayama. *Japan, Sport and Society: Tradition and Change in a Globalizing World*. London: Routledge, 2006.

Marks, Steven G. " 'Bravo, Brave Tiger of the East!' the Russo-Japanese War and the Rise of Nationalism in British Egypt and India." In *The Russo-Japanese War in Global Perspective: World War Zero*, edited by John W. Steinberg, 609–27. Leiden: Brill, 2005.

Mass, Jeffrey P. *The Kamakura Bakufu: A Study in Documents*. Stanford: Stanford University Press, 1976.

Matsumoto David, Takeuchi Masayuki, and Takeuchi Sachiko. "Jūdō ni okeru riidaashippu to kagaku no juyosei- karaa jūdō-gi no mondai" (The need for leadership and science in judo: The problem of color in judo-gi). *Research Journal of Budo* 29 (1997): 44–63.

McClatchie, Thomas. "The Sword of Japan: Its History and Traditions." *Transactions of the Asiatic Society of Japan* 7 (1884): 50–56.

McCullough, Helen Craig, trans. *The Tale of the Heike*. Stanford: Stanford University Press, 1988.

McGuigan, Jim. *Rethinking Cultural Policy*. Berkshire: Open University Press, 2004.

McVeigh, Brian. *Nationalisms of Japan: Managing and Mystifying Identity*. Lanham: Rowman and Littlefield, 2004.

Mendl, Wolf. *Japan's Asia Policy: Regional Security and Global Interests*. London: Routledge, 1995.

Minamoto Ryōen. *Kata*. Tokyo: Sōbunsha, 1989.

Minichiello, Sharon, ed. *Japan's Competing Modernities: Issues in Culture and Democracy, 1900–1930*. Honolulu: University of Hawai'i Press, 1988.

Ministry of Education, Culture, Sports, Science and Technology. "Gakushū shidō yōryō kaitei no keii" (History of changes made to the School Course Guidelines). www.mext.go.jp/b_menu/shingi/chukyo/chukyo3/011/siryo/04070801/005 .htm, accessed November 2011.

Mitchell, Richard H. *Political Bribery in Japan*. Honolulu: University of Hawai'i Press, 1996.

Miyamoto Musashi. *A Book of Five Rings*. Translated by Victor Harris. London: Allison and Busby, 1974.

———. *The Five Rings: Miyamoto Musashi's Art of Strategy*. Translated by David Groff. London: Watkins, 2012.

Molony, Barbara, and Kathleen S. Uno. *Gendering Modern Japanese History*. Cambridge, MA: Harvard University Asia Center, 2005.

Momii, Ikken. *Cyclopedia of the Japanese Kendō Societies in North America, pre-1939*. 1939. Reprint, Tokyo: Bunzei Shoin, 2001.

Monbushō. *Gakkō kendō no shidō tebiki* (Instruction guidebook for school kendo). Tokyo: Tōyōkan Shuppansha, 1953.

———. *Gakkō ni okeru kendō shidō no tebiki* (Instruction guidebook for kendo in schools). Tokyo: Kyōiku Tosho, 1966.

———. *Kendō shidō no tebiki* (Instruction guidebook for kendo). Tokyo: Ōkurashō Insatsu-kyoku, 1993.

———. *Shōgakkō budō kaisetsu* (An explanation of primary school budo). Tokyo: Monbu-Daijin Kanbō Taiiku-ka, 1939.

Morris, Ivan. *Nationalism and the Right Wing in Japan: A Study of Post-war Trends*. London: Oxford University Press, 1960.

Morris-Suzuki, Tessa. "The Invention and Reinvention of 'Japanese Culture.'" *The Journal of Asian Studies* 54, no. 3 (1995): 759–80.

Motoki Yasuo. *Bushi no seiritsu* (The conception of *bushi*). Tokyo: Yoshikawa Kōbunkan, 1994.

Motomura Kiyoto. "'Dentō ya bunka' wa 'budō' de dō uketomeru no ka" (How to catch tradition and culture in budo). *Taiikuka kyōiku* (Physical education) (May 2008).

Murata Naoki. *Jūdō no kokusaika: Sono rekishi to kadai* (The internationalization of judo: its history and issues). Tokyo: Nippon Budokan, 2011.

Na, Young-il. "Confusion in the Concept of Budō in South Korean Society." In *Budo Perspectives,* edited by Alexander Bennett, 171–84. Auckland: Kendo World Publications, 2005.

Nagai Yoshio. *Kenjutsu shugyō no tabi nikki: Saga han hagakure bushi no shokoku kaireki nichi roku wo yomu* (A travel journal of an itinerant swordsman from the Saga domain). Tokyo: Asashi Shinbun, 2013.

Najita, Tetsuo. *Japan: The Intellectual Foundations of Modern Japanese Politics*. Chicago: University of Chicago Press, 1980.

Nakabayashi Shinji. *Budō no susume* (An exhortation of *budō*). Tokyo: Shimazu Shobō, 1994.

———. "Kendō shi," in vol. 10 of *Nihon budō taikei* (Compendium of Japanese *budō*), edited by Imamura Yoshio. Kyoto: Dōhō Shuppan, 1982.

———. "Nihon kobudō ni okeru shintai-ron" (Mind-body theory in Japan's classical martial arts). *Risō* 604 (September 1983): 106–15.

Nakamura Tamio, ed. "Budō-jō to kamidana (1)" (The budo exercise hall and the Shinto altar, part 1), *Fukushima daigaku kyōiku gakubu ronshū* 39 (1986): 35–51.

———. "Budō-jō to kamidana (2)" (The budo exercise hall and the Shinto altar, part 2), *Fukushima daigaku kyōiku gakubu ronshū* 40 (1987): 1–17.

———, ed. *Dai-Nippon butokukai kenkyū shiryō shūsei* (Collection of research documents for the Dai-Nippon Butokukai). 10 vols. Tokyo: Shimazu Shobō, 2010.

———. *Kendō jiten: Gijutsu to bunka no rekishi* (Kendo dictionary: The history of its techniques and culture). Tokyo: Shimazu Shobō, 1994.

———, ed. *Kindai kendō-sho senshū* (Selection of modern kendo books). 11 vols. Tokyo: Hon-no-Tomosha, 2003.

———, ed. *Shiryō: Kindai kendō-shi* (Records of modern kendo). Tokyo: Shimazu Shobō, 1985.

Nakayama Hakudō. "Budō no seishin" (The spirit of budo). *Katana to kendō* 2 (August–October, 1939): 11–14.

———. "Gakkō kendō ni tsuite" (Regarding school kendo). *Katana to kendō* 8 (October–December, 1940): 89.

Neufeld, William. "Memo to Mr. M. T. Orr, Chief, Education Division, 18 August 1948," in *Documentation Regarding the Budo Ban in Japan, 1945–1950.* http://ejmas.com/jcs/jcsart_svinth_1202.htm.

Nippon Budokan, ed. *Report of the 22nd International Seminar of Budo Culture.* Tokyo: Nippon Budokan, 2010.

Nishiyama Matsunosuke, Watanabe Ichirō, and Gunji Masakatsu. *Kinsei geidō-ron* (Theories of early modern artistic ways). Tokyo: Iwanami Shoten, 1972.

Niwa Jūrōzaemon Tadaaki [Issai Chozan]. "Tengu geijutsu-ron." In *Bujutsu sōsho* (Various writings on the martial arts), edited by Hayakawa Junsaburō, 313–42. 1915. Reprint, Tokyo: Hachiman Shoten, 2003.

Nolte, Sharon. "Individualism in Taisho Japan." *The Journal of Asian Studies* 43, no. 4 (1994): 667–84.

Norman, Francis James. *The Fighting Man of Japan: The Training and Exercises of the Samurai.* London: Archibald Constable, 1905.

Oda, Yoshiko, and Kondō Yoshitaka, "The Challenge for the International Expansion of Japanese KENDO." *Journal of the Philosophy of Sport and Physical Education* 34, no. 2 (2012): 125–40.

Ohnuki-Tierney, Emiko. *Kamikaze, Cherry Blossoms, and Nationalisms: The Militarization of Aesthetics in Japanese History.* Chicago: University of Chicago Press, 2002.

Okada Kazuo. "Meiji shoki Hitachi-no-kuni kasama wo chūshin to shita gekken kōgyō no jittai" (The actual condition of Japanese fencing exhibitions in the

Kasama Clan of Hitachi Province in the early Meiji era). *Research Journal of Budo* 23, no. 1 (1990): 1–7.

Okihiro, Gary Y. *Whispered Silences: Japanese Americans and World War II.* Seattle: University of Washington Press, 1996.

Ōta Masayasu. "Bakumatsu ni okeru bujutsu-ba no yōso ni kansuru kenkyū" (Research into aspects of martial art training venues in the Bakumatsu era). *Research Journal of Budo* 35 (2002): 3.

Ōtake, Risuke. *Katori Shintō-ryū: Warrior Tradition.* Berkeley Heights, NJ: Koryu Books, 2007.

Ōtsuka Tadayoshi. *Nihon kendō no rekishi* (The history of Japanese kendo). Tokyo: Madosha, 1995.

———. *Nihon kendō no shisō* (The ideals of Japanese kendo). Tokyo: Madosha, 1995.

———. "A Proposal for New Regulations and Organisational Reform in Kendo— An Attempt to Make Kendo More Comprehensible for the World." *Kendo World* 5, no. 4 (2010): 77–84.

Ōya, Minoru. "Central Issues in the Instruction of Kendo: with Focus on the Inter-connectedness of Waza and Mind." In *Budo Perspectives,* edited by Alexander Bennett, 203–19. Auckland: Kendo World Publications, 2005.

Ozawa Aijirō. *Kōkoku kendō-shi* (Kendo history of the empire). 1944. Reprint, Tokyo: Taiiku and Sports Shuppansha, 2002.

Ozawa Unosuke. "Bujutsu taisō-ron" (Theory of martial art calisthenics). In *Kindai kendō-sho senshū* (Collection of modern kendo classics), vol. 4, *Bujutsu taisō,* edited by Nakamura Tamio. Tokyo: Hon-no-Tomosha, 2003.

Parsons, Talcott. *Societies: Evolutionary and Comparative Perspectives.* Englewood Cliffs, NJ: Prentice-Hall, 1966.

Perrin, Noel. *Giving Up the Gun: Japan's Reversion to the Sword 1543–1879.* Boston: D. R. Godine, 1979.

Ravina, Mark J. "The Apocryphal Suicide of Saigō Takamori: Samurai, Seppuku, and the Politics of Legend." *The Journal of Asian Studies* 69, no. 3 (2010): 691–721.

Reischauer, Edwin O. *Japan, Past and Present.* Tokyo: C. E. Tuttle, 1964.

Reischauer, Robert Karl, and Jean Reischauer. *Early Japanese History, c. 40 B.C.- A.D. 1167.* Princeton, NJ: Princeton University Press, 1937.

Roberts, L. *Performing the Great Peace: Political Space and Open Secrets in Tokugawa Japan.* Honolulu: University of Hawai'i Press, 2012.

Roden, Donald. "Baseball and the Quest for National Dignity in Meiji Japan." *The American Historical Review* 85, no. 3 (1980): 511–34.

Rogers, John M. "Arts of War in Times of Peace: Swordsmanship in *Honchō bugei shōden,* Chapter 5," *Monumenta Nipponica* 45, no. 4 (Winter, 1990): 413–47.

———. "The Development of the Military Profession in Tokugawa Japan." Unpublished PhD thesis, Harvard University, 1998.

Rubinger, Richard. *Private Academies of the Tokugawa Period.* Princeton, NJ: Princeton University Press, 1982.

Sagara Tōru, ed. *Kōyō-gunkan, Gorin-no-sho, Hagakure.* Tokyo: Chikuma Shobō, 1969.

Saimura Gorō. "Kendō shugyō no mokuteki" (The purpose of kendo training). *Katana to kendō* 9 (January–February 1941): 46–49.

Sakai Kenji, ed. *Kōyō-gunkan taisei* (The complete *Kōyō-gunkan*). 7 vols. Tokyo: Namiko Shoin, 1994.

Sakai, T. *A Bilingual Guide to the History of Kendo.* Translated by Alexander Bennett. Tokyo: Ski Journal Publishing, 2010.

———. *Ideology of the Sword: A Spiritual History of Japanese Culture.* Tokyo: Nippon Budokan, 2014.

Sakatani Shiroshi. "On Nurturing the Human Spirit" (part 2). Translated by William Reynolds Braisted. *Meiroku zasshi* 41 (February 1876): 503–7.

Sakaue Yasuhiro, and Ōtsuka Tadayoshi. "Senjika ni okeru kendō no hen'yō katei no kenkyū (sono 1)—shiai no kitei to gijutsu no henka no bunseki" (Research into the process of change in wartime *kendō* part 1: Analysis of changes in match rules and techniques). *The Research Journal of Budo 21*, no. 2 (1988): 159–60.

Sakurai Tadayoshi. "Teki wo kiru hanashi" (Talk of cutting the enemy). *Katana to kendō* 11 (July–September 1941): 11–16.

Sansom, George. *A History of Japan to 1334.* Stanford: Stanford University Press, 1958.

Sasamori Junzō. *Ittō-ryū gokui* (Higher teachings of the Ittō-ryū). Tokyo: Taiiku to Sports-sha, 1986.

———. "Letter to C. I. E. of G. H. Q., March 29, 1950," in *Documentation Regarding the Budo Ban in Japan, 1945–1950.* http://ejmas.com/jcs/jcsart_svinth_1202.htm.

Sasamori Junzō and Gordon Warner. *This Is Kendo: The Art of Japanese Fencing.* Rutland, VT: Tuttle, 1964.

Satō Ukichi. *Kendō.* Vol. 21 of *Nihon taiiku sōsho.* Tokyo: Meguro Shoten, 1928.

Schmidt, Richard J. "KENDO: The Martial Way of Japanese Fencing." *Journal of Physical Education, Recreation and Dance* 53, no. 4 (1982): 31–32.

Sheard, Kenneth G. "Aspects of Boxing in the 'Civilizing Process.'" *International Review for the Sociology of Sport* 32, no. 1 (1997): 31–57.

Shimoda, Hiraku. *Lost and Found: Recovering Regional Identity in Imperial Japan.* Cambridge, MA: Harvard University Asia Center, 2014.

Shimokawa Washio. *Kendō no hattatsu* (The development of kendo). 1925. Reprint, Tokyo: Taiiku and Sports Shuppansha, 2002.

Shin Seongho. "Kendō no sekai-ka, fuhen-ka imada tōshi" (Kendo is still not a world or universal sport). *Gekkan Budō* 444 (November 2003): 172–74.

Shinjinbutsu Ōraisha, ed. *Hiden! bugei ryūha ryūso-roku* (Secret teachings: A record of martial art school headmasters). Tokyo: Shinjinbutsu Ōraisha, 1993.

Shogimen, Takashi. "'Another' Patriotism in Early Shōwa Japan (1930–1945)." *Journal of the History of Ideas* 71, no. 1 (2009): 139–60.

Shōji Munemitsu. *Kendō Hyakunen* (*Kendō* century). Tokyo: Jiji Tsūshinsha, 1966.

Siniawer, Eiko Maruko. *Ruffians, Yakuza, Nationalists: The Violent Politics of Modern Japan, 1860–1960.* Ithaca: Cornell University Press, 2008.

Smith, Anthony D. *National Identity.* London: Penguin, 1991.

———. *Nationalism: Theory, Ideology, History.* Cambridge: Polity, 2001.

So, Doshin. *What is Shorinji Kempo?* Tokyo: Japan Publications, 1973.

Sonoda Hidehiro. "The Decline of the Japanese Warrior Class, 1840–1880." *Nichibunken Japan Review,* no. 1 (1990): 73–111.

Sonoda Hidehiro, Hirota Teruyuki, and Hamana Atsushi. *Shizoku no rekishi shakaigaku-teki kenkyū: bushi no kindai* (Social historical study of *shizoku:* The modern era for *bushi*). Nagoya: Nagoya University Press, 1995.

Spinks, Charles N. "Indoctrination and Re-Education of Japan's Youth," *Pacific Affairs* 17, no. 1 (March 1944): 56–70.

Starrs, Roy, ed. *Japanese Cultural Nationalism: At Home and in the Pacific.* Folkestone, Kent: Global Oriental, 2004.

Steenstrup, Carl. "The Imagawa Letter: A Muromachi Warrior's Code of Conduct Which Became a Tokugawa Schoolbook," *Monumenta Nipponica* 28, no. 3 (1973): 295–316.

Steinberg, John W., and David Wolff, eds. *The Russo-Japanese War in Global Perspective: World War Zero.* Leiden: Brill, 2005.

Sugahara Tōru. "Gakkō kendō ni tsuite" (About school kendo). *Katana to kendō* 1 (May-July 1939): 97–100.

Supreme Commander for the Allied Powers, Civil Information and Education Section. *Education in the New Japan.* 2 vols. Tokyo: General Headquarters, Supreme Commander for the Allied Powers Civil Information and Education Section, Education Division, 1948.

Supreme Commander for the Allied Powers, Government Section. *Political Reorientation of Japan: September 1945 to September 1948.* 2 vols. 1949. Reprint, Grosse Pointe, MI: Scholarly Press, 1968.

Suzuki, Daisetz. *Zen and Japanese Culture.* Princeton, NJ: Princeton University Press, 1970.

Suzuki Kunihiro. *Nihon chūsei no shisen sekai to shinzoku* (The world of private wars and family in medieval Japan). Tokyo: Yoshikawa Kōbunkan, 2003.

Suzuki Masaya. *Katana to kubi-tori* (Swords and head-taking). Tokyo: Heibonsha, 2000.

———. *Teppō to nihonjin: "Teppō shinwa" ga kakushite kita koto* (Guns and the Japanese: What the "myth of guns" has concealed). Tokyo: Yōsensha, 1997.

Suzuki Toshio. "Conflict Between Educators and Hygienists: The Advisory Committee of School Health and the Introduction of Martial Arts to Regular Curriculum." *Hokkaidō daigaku kyōiku gakubu kiyō* (The Annual Reports on Educational Science) 54 (1990): 1–12.

Takahashi Takeo, Okade Yoshinori, Iwata Yasushi, and Tomozoe Hidenori. *Taiikuka kyōiku-gaku nyūmon* (Introduction to Sport Pedagogy). Tokyo: Taishūkan, 2010.

Takano Sasaburō. *Kendō.* 1915. Reprint, Tokyo: Shimazu Shobō, 1982.

Takayama Masayoshi. "Budō kaikaku shoken" (Opinions on budo development). *Katana to kendō* 5 (April-May 1940): 28–39.

Takezawa, Yasuko. *Breaking the Silence: Redress and Japanese American Ethnicity.* Ithaca: Cornell University Press, 1995.

Tanaka Mamoru. *Budō: Kako, genzai, mirai* (Budō: Past, present, future). Tokyo: Nippon Budokan, 2005.

Tōdō Akiyasu. *Bu no kanji bun no kanji: Sono kigen kara shisō e* (The kanji for *bu* and *bun:* From the origins to the evolution of thought). Tokyo: Tokuma Shoten, 1977.

Tokyo City, ed. *Tōkyō-shi shikō (Shigai-hen #55)* (Historical documents of Tokyo City). Kyoto: Rinsen Shoten, 1973.

Tokyo Metropolitan Police Department (Keishichō), ed. *Keishichō budō kyūjūnen-shi* (Ninety-year history of Tokyo Metropolitan Police Department *budō*). Tokyo: Keishichō Keimu-bu Kyōyō-ka, 1965.

Tominaga Kengo. *Kendō gohyakunen-shi* (Kendo's five-hundred year history). 1972. Reprint, Tokyo: Shimazu Shobō, 1996.

Tomozoe, Hidenori, and Tetsuya Wada. "Implication of the Learning Theory of Edo Era Martial Arts to a New Ethical Paradigm of Sports." *Japanese Journal of Sport Education Studies* 13, no. 1 (1993): 45–54.

Toyama Shigeki, and Satō Shigerō. *Jiyūtō-shi* (History of the Liberal Party). Vol. 2. Tokyo: Iwanami Shoten, 1957.

Udagawa Takehisa. *Shinsetsu teppō denrai* (The true story of the transmission of firearms). Tokyo: Heibonsha, 2006.

Uozumi Takashi, Tatsugi Yukitoshi, and Ōboki Teruo. "Nihon no budō bunka no seiritsu kiban: Shinkage-ryū to Ittō-ryū kenjutsu no kenkyū wo tsūjite" (The foundations of Japanese budo culture seen through studies of Shinkage-ryu and Itto-ryu swordsmanship). *Budō-sports kagaku kenkyūjo nenpō,* no. 17 (2011): 107–44.

US National Archives, College Park, Maryland. Records Group 331. Date unknown.

Vlastos, Stephen, ed. *Mirror of Modernity: Invented Traditions of Modern Japan.* Berkeley: University of California Press, 1998.

Wargo, Mark A., Charles L. Spirrison, B. Michael Thorne, and Tracy B. Henley. "Personality Characteristics of Martial Artists." *Social Behavior and Personality: An International Journal* 35, no. 3 (2007): 99–408.

Watanabe Ichirō. *Bakumatsu kantō kenjutsu eimei-roku no kenkyū* (Research into famous Bakumatsu *kenjutsu* exponents in Kantō). Tokyo: Watanabe Shoten, 1967.

———, ed. *Kindai budō-shi kenkyū shiryō* (Modern budo history research sources). 9 vols. Tsukuba: Tsukuba Daigaku Taiiku Kagaku-kei, 1981–88.

———. *Shiryō: Meiji budō-shi* (Documents of Meiji budo history). Tokyo: Shinjin-butsu Ōraisha, 1971.

Watanabe Sakae. "Jikyoku to kendō" (Kendo in the present situation). *Katana to kendō* 2 (August–October 1939): 15–19.

Watari Shōzaburō. "Nihon seishin to budō" (The Japanese spirit and budo). *Katana to kendō* 4 (January–March 1940): 6–14.

Watatani Kiyoshi. *Nihon kengō 100-sen* (A selection of 100 Japanese swordsmen). Tokyo: Akita Shoten, 1971.

Watsuji Tetsurō. *Kenshin no dōtoku to sono dentō* (The moral of selfless dedication and its tradition). Self-published, 1940. doi:10.11501/2532454.

———. *Nihon Rinri Shisō-shi* (The history of Japanese ethics and thought). 2 vols. Tokyo: Iwanami Shoten, 1952.

Webb, Jen, Tony Schirato, and Geoff Danaher. *Understanding Bourdieu.* London: Allen and Unwin, 2002.

Yagyū Munenori. *Heihō-kadensho,* in vol. 1 of *Nihon budō taikei* (Compendium of Japanese *budō*), edited by Imamura Yoshio. Kyoto: Dōhō Shuppan, 1982.

Yamada, Shōji. "The Myth of Zen in the Art of Archery." *Japanese Journal of Religious Studies* 28, nos. 1–2 (2001): 1–30.

Yamada Tadachika and Watatani Kiyoshi. *Bugei ryūha daijiten* (Encyclopedia of martial art schools). 1963. Rev. ed., Tokyo: Tokyo Copy Shuppan-bu, 1978.

Yamamoto Kunio. *Saitama bugei-chō* (Martial arts in Saitama). Saitama: Saitama Shuppankai, 1981.

Yamamura, Kozo. "The Decline of the Ritsuryō System: Hypotheses on Economic and Institutional Change." *Journal of Japanese Studies* 1, no. 1 (1974): 3–37.

Yamashita Ikuo. *Kenkyū seinan no eki* (Satsuma Rebellion research). Tokyo: Sanichi Shobō, 1977.

Yokoyama Kendō. *Nihon budō-shi* (The history of Japanese budo). Tokyo: Shimazu Shobō, 1991.

Yoshida Yutaka. *Buke no kakun* (Military house codes). Tokyo: Tokuma Shobō, 1972.

Yoshino, Kosaku. "Culturalism, Racialism, and Internationalism in the Discourse on Japanese Identity." In *Making Majorities: Constituting the Nation in Japan, Korea, China, Malaysia, Fiji, Turkey, and the United States,* edited by Dru C. Gladney, 13–30. Stanford: Stanford University Press, 1998.

———. *Cultural Nationalism in Contemporary Japan: A Sociological Enquiry.* London: Routledge, 1995.

Yuasa Akira. *Budō densho wo yomu* (Reading martial art texts). Tokyo: Nippon Budokan, 2001.

———. "Jiyū minken undō to bujutsu ni tsuite—kōsatsu" (A study on the relation between liberty and the people's rights movement and martial arts in the Meiji era). *Research Journal of Budo* 32, no. 2 (1999): 1–13.

Zen-Nihon Shinai Kyōgi Renmei. *Shinai-kyōgi: kitei no kaisetsu to kihon* (*Shinai-kyōgi:* An explanation of the rules and the basics). Tokyo: Myōgi Shuppan, 1951.

INDEX

kyōdo (adequate strength of strike), xxx, 197
Kyō Hachi-ryū (Eight Schools of Kyoto), 48
Kyoraika (Zeami), 39
Kyō-ryū, 48
Kyōshin Meichi-ryū, 77, 80, 103
Kyoto, 37, 48, 91, 116
kyudo (way of the bow), 5, 16–18, 19, 145; Allied Occupation of Japan and, 156, 157; focus on culture and spirituality, 6; girls' study of, xxxiii, 134; postwar reinstatement of, 170; *shahō-hassetsu* method, 17
kyūjutsu (traditional archery), 17, 71, 93, 114, 233

Lee Ho-am, 213
Lee Min-ku, 211
leg strikes, 83
Lian Chen, 13
liberalism, 128, 131
Ling, Per Henrik, 114
lower-body protector (*tare*), xxv, *xxvi*

MacArthur, Gen. Douglas A., 155, 156, 249n53
Makimura Masanao, 108
Manchuria, 13, 131, 206
Manchurian Incident (1931), 133, 148, 247n20
manga, 55
Maniwa Nen-ryū, 51, 74, 81
Marishiten (Buddhist deity), 50
martial arts, Chinese and Korean, 13, 44, 211
martial arts, Japanese. *See* budo (Japanese martial arts)
Martial Arts and the Body Politic in Meiji Japan (Gainty), 23
Martial Virtue Festival, 118
Marume Kurandosuke, 51, 53
Marxism, 128, 129
Masakado-ryū, 48
masculinity, 60, 210
masks, protective (*men*), xxv, xxvi, *xxvi,* 74
Mass, Jeffrey, 27
mato (mounted target-shooting archery), 39, 240n23

Matsumoto Bizen-no-Kami, 48, 51, 52, 54
Matsumoto Toshio, 251n28
McClatchie, Thomas, 86, 99, 121–22, 202
McVeigh, Brian, 22, 182, 199, 219, 225, 229
Meiji, Emperor, 91, 104
Meiji period (1868–1912), 1, 9, 23, 85, 127, 195; archery in, 17; creation of national identity in, 24; education system of, 108, 110; fencing in, 83; Japanese emigration to Brazil in, 207; Japanese nationalism of, 21, 236; *jūjutsu* demonstrations in Europe, 200; *kenjutsu* and national spiritual culture in, 86–87; military culture of Japan in, 15; reinvention of *kenjutsu* in, 96–115, 121; resurgence of *kenjutsu* in mid-Meiji, 87–88; warrior hegemony dismantled in, 86–96; Western contact with budo during, 203
Meiji Shrine Citizen's Training Tournament (Meiji Jingū Kokumin Rensei Taikai), 138
Meiji Shrine Sports Tournament (Meiji Jingū Taikai), 130, 138
Meirokusha, 110
meitō (sword of special significance), 36
men (head) strikes, 1, 83, *216*; concerns over brain injuries, 112–13; fatal cuts in war, 247n20; in jukendo, 16; militarized budo techniques, 153; sequence of, *xxxi*
Mendl, Wolf, 218
Mibu Motonaga, 117
"Middle School Kendo Description" (*Chūgakō kendō kaisetsu*), 134
Mikami Genryū, 49
Minamoto (Genji), house of, 29, 244n17
Minamoto Yoritomo, 27, 29
mind-body dualism, Western/Cartesian, 221
Ministry of Education (MOE), Japanese, 8, 10, 126, 138, 187, 235; AJKF and reinstatement of kendo, 173–184; Allied Occupation of Japan and, 158, 160, 163; budo instruction guidelines of, 141–42; *bujutsu* in schools and, 108, 109, 110, 125; Dai-Nippon Butokukai and, 119–120, 158; on etiquette (*rei*), 191–92; evolution of term *kendō* and, 243n3; Kendo Deliberation Council and, 135; naginata and,

setsunin-tō (the death-dealing blade), 62, 63, 191
shagekidō (way of marksmanship), 147, 156
Shaolin Monastery (China), 13, 14, 15
Sheard, Kenneth, 194
shiai (matches), xxix, xxxi–xxxii, 128
Shibata Kokki, 109
Shibata Tokujirō, 245n6
Shiba Yoshimasa, 38, 39
shidō. *See* bushido (way of the warrior)
Shigakkan dojo, 80
shikake-waza (attacking techniques), xxx
Shimazu Hisamitsu, 91
Shimokawa Ushio, 34
Shinagawa Yajirō, 80
shinai (bamboo swords), *xxvii*, 1, 16, 75, 132, 142; correct handling of, 189; description of, xxvii; etiquette rituals and, 120; fencing with, *76*; *fukuro-shinai*, 53, 167; introduction of, 73; leather sheaths (*fukuro-shinai*), 74; *nihontō* (Japanese sword) in relation to, 190; training with, xxix; valid strikes (*yūkō-datotsu*) with, 197
shinai (bamboo swords), length of, 83, 85, 98, 103, 104; postwar reinstatement of kendo and, 173; in *shinai-kyōgi*, 167; in wartime militarized kendo, 148–49, 151, 161
shinai-kyōgi (Westernized version of kendo), 25, 166–171, *168*, 176, 179–180, *179*
Shintō Munen-ryū, 51, 77, 103, 104; Meiji Restoration and, 89; Renpeikan dojo, 80, 81
Shindō Musō-ryū, 51
Shingyōtō-ryū, 51, 77
Shin Kage-ryū, 51
Shinkage-ryū (New shadow school), 48, 50, 53, 249n52; historic lineage of, 51; kata of, 62, 242n10
shinmyō-ken (divinely inspired sword), 47
Shinpūren Rebellion, 96
Shin Shin Tōitsu Aikido, 12
Shinto, 8, 9, 11, 45; altars in martial arts halls, 137; *kami* in mythology of, 241n34; syncretic religious culture of Japan and, 46

Shintō-ryū (Bokuden-ryū), 47, 48, 55, 64, 241n37; historic lineage of, 51; Jigen-ryū and, 249n52
Shioda Gōzō, 12
Shirai Tōru Yoshinori, 67–68
Shirayuki (sake brand), 116, 245n41
Shiseikai, 147, 171, 248n46
shishi ("men of high purpose"), 89, 91, 96, 106
shizoku (former samurai), 92, 95–96, 100, 244n9; in Boshin Civil War, 101; Diet members, 115; Hara's renunciation of status as, 129; *kessha* nationalist groups and, 106; opposition to popularization of martial arts, 107
Shōdōkan, 4, 12
shōgō (teaching titles), xxxiii, 193, 251–52n32
Shōriki Matsutarō, 187
shorinji kempo, 5, 6, 13–15
Shorinji Kempo Foundation, 239n2 (Intro)
Shōwa period (1926–89), early, 124, 128, 132, 136, 137, 204–5
shugyō (ascetic training), 45
Shūtokukan, 19
Siffleet, Leonard George, 162
Siniawer, Eiko Maruko, 129
Sino-Japanese War (1894–95), 115, 116, 235
Sino-Japanese War, Second (1937–45), 131, 135, 139
Smith, Anthony, 88, 95, 121
Sō Dōshin (Nakano Michiomi), 13–14
sōjutsu (spearmanship), 13, 15, 71, 73, 83; *bugei-jūhappan* (eighteen military skills) and, 233; at Kōbusho, 93
sōke (head of tradition), 2
Sok Pyungjang Tosul (Revised illustrated manual of military training and tactics), 211
sonkyo (squatting bow), 120, 121, 212
sonnō-jōi ("Revere the emperor, expel the barbarians"), 89, 91
Sonobe Hideo, 19
Sonoda Hidehiro, 92
Sō Shigetō, 13
South America, 201, 205, 206, 207–8
Sō Yūki, 14
sparring, free-practice (*randori*), 6
Spinks, Charles Nelson, 124, 141